The Lennon Companion

Twenty-five Years of Comment

Elizabeth Thomson, born in London in 1957, read music at Liverpool University. She edited *Conclusions on the Wall: New Essays on Bob Dylan* and has contributed to various publications, including *Woman's Journal*, *Melody Maker*, *History of Rock*, *The Listener*, *The Times* and *Books and Bookmen*. She has broadcast on radio, both in Britain and abroad, and is currently a staff writer for *Publishing News*.

David Gutman, born in London in 1957, studied history at St John's College, Cambridge, and librarianship at North London Polytechnic. He has written for *Brio* and *Books and Bookmen*, contributed various record sleeve notes, and appeared on radio. He is the author of an illustrated biography of Prokofiev.

The Lennon Companion

Twenty-five Years of Comment

Edited by

ELIZABETH THOMSON AND DAVID GUTMAN

DA CAPO PRESS
A Member of the Perseus Books Group

For our parents

Cataloging-in-Publication data for this book is available from the Library of
Congress.

First Da Capo Press edition 2004
ISBN 0–306–81270–3

Published by Da Capo Press
A Member of the Perseus Books Group
http://www.dacapopress.com

This Da Capo Press edition of *The Lennon Companion* is an unabridged
republication of the edition first published in 1987. It is reprinted by
arrangement with Elizabeth Thomson and David Gutman.

Da Capo Press books are available at special discounts for bulk purchases in
the U.S. by corporations, institutions, and other organizations. For more
information, please contact the Special Markets Department at the Perseus
Books Group, 11 Cambridge Center, Cambridge, MA 02142, or call (800) 255-
1514 or (617) 252-5298, or e-mail specialmarkets@perseusbooks.com.

Contents

4. Mind Games

5. I'm Stepping Out

6. Carry That Weight

7. Tomorrow Never Knows

8. *Remember*

Editors' Note

This book, first published in 1987, has been out of print for a while. We are grateful to our present publisher for suggesting that it might be revived. As with our similar collections on Bob Dylan and David Bowie, our aim has been to present 'classic' material of enduring interest. Our take on Lennon has not changed and we have not wanted to revamp *The Lennon Companion* so as to make it appear falsely contemporary. That said, we have updated the bibliography and discography, and a substantial afterword contextualizes recent developments, looking back with older, if not necessarily wiser, eyes—and ears. A full forty years on from The Beatles' conquest of America, Lennon's legacy resonates still. 'When you get to the top, there is nowhere to go but down', wrote poet Philip Larkin some twenty years ago, 'but The Beatles could not get down. There they remain, unreachable, frozen, fabulous'. Lennon most of all.

ET and DG
London, April 2003

Acknowledgements

We are grateful for the help and enthusiasm of all those who contributed to *The Lennon Companion*; particular thanks are due to Lukas Foss, Pauline Kael, Peter Schickele, Pauline Sutcliffe and John Tavener. Picture research was undertaken by Mike Evans and the Editors.

In addition, we would like to thank a number of others who were prepared to share their ideas: Alenka Barber-Kersovan, David Bedford, William Bolcom and Joan Morris, Peter Gabriel, Albert Goldman, Christopher Marshall and Alexander Plunket Greene.

We are indebted to the following institutions for their assistance in tracking down an extraordinary range of materials: Cambridge University Library, Camden Libraries, the House of Commons Library and the National Sound Archive.

Thanks also to David Harman, Sue Harris, Richard Lester, John Peacock, Tom Schultheiss, Michael Stewart, Jonathan Warner, family, friends and colleagues. And, of course, to Alyn Shipton, Jannet King and all at Macmillan.

Copyright permissions

Introduction

In March 1987, after lengthy negotiations and with much fanfare, EMI began to release The Beatles' *oeuvre* on Compact Disc. The restoration discloses the vibrant colours and broad brush strokes of some familiar old masters. But the gain in immediacy brings a loss of remembered perfection. The ambient glow of nostalgia no longer conceals the squeaky drum pedal, the poorly executed guitar riff, the not quite pure vocal harmonies.

The re-release brought The Beatles once more into the charts. Baby-boomers with families and saloon cars rushed to purchase shiny, over-priced reminders of a lost youth. The lovable Mop Tops were back, for ever this time, preserved in aluminium aspic. Four young men, eminently ordinary, from a dirty provincial city that had seen better days. If they could make it, wasn't there hope for us all? 'England was an aristocracy gone to seed, exhausted by war and responsibility, and very nearly tired of life.' So wrote Jan Morris in August 1966. 'It was the Angry Young Men of the Fifties who shocked the old body into self-awareness: The Beatles and their friends . . . put her into mini-skirts.'[1]

For a brief but intense era, now irretrievably past, The Beatles and their peers did represent a vigorous new start, and the kaleidoscope of images endures: the student revolution, the storming of barricades, social liberalisation, the summer of '67, sex, flowers, idealism, a certain universality. Always rock music orchestrates the themes. 'Do we really need all this to sustain us When We're 64?' asked Leonard Bernstein, Beatlefan, in 1979. 'Well, today I am almost 64, and three bars of "A day in the life" still sustain me, rejuvenate me, inflame my senses and sensibilities. [Daughter] Nina, who was two way back then in '64, is now 17; and only last week we took out that thick, wretched Beatles volume of ill-printed sheet music and reminisced at the piano. We wept, we jumped with the joy of recognition ("She's a woman")—just the two of us, for hours ("Ticket to ride", "A hard day's night", "I saw her standing there") . . . That was last week. The Beatles are no more. But this week I am still jumping, weeping, remembering a good epoch, a golden decade, a fine time, a fine time . . .'[2]

And yet for Nina and *her* generation this is scarcely the whole (or even the relevant bit) of the story. We need something more than a yearning for that 'fine time', something more than astute corporate marketing to account for the obstinate durability of the Beatle phenomenon in the late 1980s. For those who missed out on the frenzy of Beatlemania, the questions remain.

The standard British rock biography wraps a poster round a press release and calls itself a book and there have been hundreds of books about The Beatles as a band and John Lennon as its avatar. Some lacquer the legend. Others knock it. Few could be considered serious works. Arguably, it was Hunter Davies who launched the genre: his authorised biography of the mid-Sixties had the advantages and disadvantages of full cooperation from and extensive vetting by The Beatles' extended family. *Shout!* (1981) was Philip Norman's appreciably better than average showbiz biography. 1983 brought *The Love You Make*, a would-be revelatory account by former confidant Peter Brown with Steven Gaines. As for Lennon himself, Anthony Fawcett's *John Lennon: One Day at a Time* (1976) provided a sympathetic insider's look at the onset of Ono. Cynthia Lennon recalled *her* years with John in *A Twist of Lennon* (1978), a simple unaffected memoir. The usually reliable Ray Connolly rushed out a biography in the weeks following the murder. And 1984 saw the emergence of Ray Coleman's massive, two-volume, 700-page study of Lennon, 'the cocky rocker' with the 'softie's heart'. Long, certainly—but *definitive*? Dr Albert Goldman's heavyweight biography should at least present a sceptical alternative.

It hardly needs saying that Lennon was no ordinary rock 'n' roller. He fancied himself as 'the literary Beatle', as artist and campaigner for social justice. Inevitably uneven but always stimulating, his work helped fracture barriers between art and entertainment, demanding new critical approaches to the study of popular culture in society: 'The unprecedented response to Lennon's death should not be mistaken for just another well-orchestrated media event,' cautioned *Radical History Review*.

> The widespread mourning and depression came out of the recognition of his role in a generation's shared past. The easy cynicism we often fall into must not become the tool for our understanding John Lennon or the

'legacy' of our own formative experience. We should recognise what Lennon represented in our history and that, in the uneasy formation of our culture and politics, he helped define and compose some of what we are now and what we hope to create.[3]

Blake Morrison disagreed.

Many people . . . were tempted to believe that The Beatles in some way acted, spoke and sang on their behalf. The truth seems to be that the group stood for very little at all, merely clarified the options. Sexual freedom, experimentation with drugs, political commitment, transcendental religion, counter-cultural activity of all kinds: their songs simultaneously incited us to try these things, and warned that we'd in the end be disappointed, as they had been. The ambivalence was the appeal.[4]

The Lennon Companion takes a fresh, and we hope objective, approach. The editors have no axe to grind and no lurid hypothesis to sustain. Our aim is simply to present the best of 25 years of comment and commentary engendered by the man and his music. It is up to the reader to make an individual assessment. The raw material is assembled here. Something of the kind has been tried before, at any rate in the United States. In 1968, the Cowles Education Corporation published *The Beatles Book*, a necessarily interim collection of 14 articles, mostly overawed by *Sgt Pepper*. In the wake of Lennon's murder, the editors of *Rolling Stone* put together more than 30 deferential essays, interviews and personal recollections to delineate the story of a relationship—*The Ballad of John and Yoko* (1982). Charles P. Neises edited *The Beatles Reader* for the Pierian Press in 1984. He too concentrated on American source material. *The Lennon Companion* is not only the first anthology to originate from Britain, but the first to deal with John Lennon's career in its entirety.

That said, a substantial portion of the text inevitably relates to Lennon's output as a Beatle. At the time of *his* Lennon interview, conducted in New York in December 1970,[5] even Dr Goldman had no inkling that he might become Lennon's biographer: his interest was in the *group product*. As was half the world's: 'At that time it appeared that Lennon was in the middle of the journey of this life and that it would be many years until his work was done. In fact, he had written and recorded already everything upon which his fame rests. The rest was anticlimax as regards the artist, though far from that as regards the man.'[6]

Ten years later, a macabre kind of pop fetishism had taken over. First the market was primed for a spate of myopic paperback tributes, sentimental and spiteful by turns. Film director Richard Lester: 'After John Lennon's death and the proliferation and pollution of all the

tributes, articles and factions about his life and work, I determined not
to make any contribution myself . . .'[7]

But more than that, the 'assassination' served to warp our
perspective on even the quite recent past. Today, Lennon is canonised
'Saint of this parish, the American-speaking world . . .' (Julie
Burchill).[8] And the new martyr has his Soviet bloc adherents too.
Perhaps the trend is not wholly inexplicable. The deification of this
particular Beatle began after all with Brian Epstein himself,[9] and the
perceptive and balanced early commentary of Gloria Steinem,
Maureen Cleave and others was rightly Lennon leaning.

Here is Tony Palmer, stating *his* case in 1967:

> And in our adulation, what we have . . . singularly failed to realise is
> that The Beatles are not one person but four, and not four equal persons,
> but one giant, his side-kick and two midgets. Ringo, it is said, continues
> to bang away happily, although rumour has it that he no longer plays the
> more complicated tracks such as those on 'Strawberry Fields'—a rumour
> which recording manager George Martin hotly denies. Harrison is lost,
> all lost, in his Indian fog. He has none of the articulate mysticism of his
> teacher, Ravi Shankar, but appears content with a vague Oriental haze
> and the left-overs of latter-day Buddhist sayings—'life flows on within
> you and without you'. His one song on the [*Sgt Pepper*] record was left
> alone by the others, and they in turn seem to have ignored him.
> McCartney still whistles tinkly little tunes which please the Mums and
> Hayley Mills. Unable to write down a single note of music, a moderate
> performer on keyboard instruments, a lyricist of dubious sentimentality,
> McCartney drifts through the new Beatles' world, warily. That world
> lives in the mind of Lennon . . .[10]

In 1987, the distorting lens is that much more firmly fixed. Or as
Peter Gabriel put it in a letter: 'Although I was and am a big Lennon fan
I feel the canonisation of this particular hero of mine has overlooked
the formative roles of the other Beatles, particularly Paul and George,
and I am a little concerned that your project may give the gloss and
blessings of the arts establishment to a one-sided memory.'[11] Lloyd
Rose says as much in her opening piece: 'McCartney . . . has spent
much of the past five years weathering criticism for being neither
brilliant nor dead . . .'[12] It is not our intention to bury him here.

Instead, within a broadly chronological framework, we have sought
first to focus the argument on pertinent aspects of Lennon—man,
musician, figurehead, catalyst, icon. That the writing be stimulating on
its own account, retaining its vitality and impact, was our second and
sometimes overriding principle. We have opted in the main for
contributors on the periphery or outside the world of pop. Some of our
articles entertain; others instruct so that, from time to time, enthusiasm
takes a back seat to clear-headed analysis. Some are gut reactions by

contemporary critics of the 1960s and 1970s, others pointed re-evaluations by writers of the 1980s. Nearly 60 pieces are included, the majority reproduced in their entirety. Where cuts have been made, it is never in order to maintain a particular line, nor to excise an unfavourable remark. Rather we have trimmed the all-too-familiar biographical detail (necessarily a feature of earlier items) since The Beatles' story scarcely needs retelling and straight biography is not anyway a function of this *Companion*. Lloyd Rose's interpretive biographical review is perhaps an exception, while Pauline Sutcliffe, working from first-hand knowledge, offers an entirely novel perspective on Beatle relationships. Writing extracted from a larger context—like diary entries or Parliamentary debate—has been edited to maintain relevance and topicality. We have not sought to rescue John Lennon's own occasional 'journalism' from *Merseybeat* or *The New York Times*: that's an idea for another book.[13] Nor is every album dissected, every news item exhaustively recalled. (With the insatiable enthusiast in mind, Carol D. Terry's *Here, There and Everywhere: The First International Beatles Bibliography* (1985)—for International read mid-Atlantic!—exhumes 8,000 citations.) As well as commissioning a number of essays on significant aspects of Lennon's life and art, we have made a point of reviving pieces to which the passing years have accorded almost mythic status—texts often quoted in part, never seen complete.

William Mann's comments are a good case in point. They are nearly all here, including the celebrated discussion from 1963 of The Beatles' 'pandiatonic clusters'. Mann was in fact the first to treat the group as a musical entity rather than just another teenage fad. And all this in the staid old *Times*, a decade before Wilfrid Mellers' *Twilight of the Gods* (1973), a post-Leavisite musicological squib that still strikes sparks but at times seems to value style above accuracy. As early as *Caliban Reborn* (1968), Mellers had provided an interesting analysis of the traditional English element in Beatles' music, perceiving ideas and fragments of musical vocabulary more redolent of Orlando Gibbons and Giles Farnaby than Buddy Holly and the blues. Could it have been the tension between the 'literate' and 'illiterate' elements in the work of these quasi-folk artists that accounts for the resonance in simple songs of deeper currents, innocent and ageless? The Professor (retd) is represented here by two later studies of Lennon's solo output.

By the end of 1966, The Beatles were already a long way musically from the songs of which Mann first wrote so presciently. Joshua Rifkin, the protean American musician best known for his scholarly work on Bach and his determined advocacy of Scott Joplin, first demonstrated an affection for Beatles music in 1965 with *The Baroque Beatles Book* LP

(Elektra EKS-7306). He tackled Beatles musicology on the eve of *Sgt Pepper*, but his findings are published here for the first time. Through detailed, step-by-step analysis, he shows how inventive and complex were many Lennon–McCartney compositions. His discussion of the intricate evolution of, for example, 'Strawberry Fields' provides much musical food for thought. How obvious, yet how subtle, is the song's development!

Writing in 1968, from the rather different standpoint of a British musicologist cold-shouldering the post-tonal posturings of Stockhausen and Co., Deryck Cooke makes an equally compelling case, though his particular laurels go to a McCartney song, 'Yesterday'. By discussing elements of melody, harmony, phrase-structure, and relating them to the lyrics, he gives a powerful glimpse of the unique character of the song. Another 'conservative', Pulitzer Prize-winning composer Ned Rorem, has written enthusiastically of The Beatles' arrival, citing it as 'one of the healthiest events in music since 1950'. In 1987, he retracts 'not a word' of his essay, though he feels strongly that 'the quality of pop music in the intervening two decades has been very thin indeed'.[14]

The paeans come also from the modernists. Italy's Luciano Berio expounds on the 1960s rock scene, its antecedents and implications. The impetus for the piece is clearly mid-period Beatles. *New York Times* music critic John Rockwell's self-confessed 'pontification about the whole Beatles phenomenon'[15] is a much more recent entry, prompted by the release in 1982 of the remastered audiophile LP collection in the United States. Not included here are the structuralist pyrotechnics of John Beatty's 'Eleanor Rigby: structure in the arts'[16] in which the Lennon–McCartney song is used to present 'an approach . . . for developing methodologies for the analysis of the structures through which art forms communicate'.[17] We learn that 'the waiting done by Eleanor Rigby by the window is sedentary, and not the agitated type of waiting done by someone like Elektra in Richard Strauss's opera of the same name'.[18] Nor is there space for David R. Reck's 'Beatles Orientalis: influences from Asia in a popular song tradition',[19] a less contentious but seemingly interminable treatise.

From the groves of academe, the submissions of Terence J. O'Grady and Eric Tamm represent just the tiniest tip of a looming iceberg. In the post-*Pepper* era, many students made a thesis out of a hobby. And professors with a taste for popular culture do sometimes like to turn their intellectual guns on the tunes they hear at student parties. Unfortunately, little of this attention adds much to our general appreciation of the music. The high-flown theorists are apt to forget that popular music is there to be enjoyed, and the analysts are up against a perennial problem of rock music criticism: the absence of classical music's 'full score'. Lennon and The Beatles committed their works to tape, not paper, and because empirically created yet definitive studio effects cannot be replicated in print, sheet music reduces them to sterile basics. Illumination of a text is what conventional musical analysis is, or should be, all about—the task for which its obsessive terminology has evolved. The lack of a score, the impossibility of reinterpretation—these stymie the academicians of pop.

O'Grady's original full-length, doctoral study, 'The music of The Beatles from 1962 to *Sgt Pepper's Lonely Hearts Club Band*' lays out its terms of reference with care. His field is 'style analysis'—the comparison of different composers' use of similar musical elements in their work—and he gives an elegant and informative run-down on The Beatles' early influences. All very laudable. Unfortunately, what follows is largely descriptive, with a tendency to lapse into rudimentary harmonic analysis (strings of roman numerals to the rest of us) at the slightest hint of fresh insight. In Steven Clark Porter's painstaking and exhaustive thesis of 1979, O'Grady's neat synopsis of pre-Beatle pop becomes an extended trudge through 70 years of popular music practice. Porter leaves a fraction over half his dissertation to tell us something about 'Rhythm and harmony in the music of The Beatles'. Which he does, in what Joshua Rifkin would describe as a 'heady blend of Schenker, Schoenberg and logical positivism'.[20] William Dale Cockrell (who supplied *The New Grove* Beatle entry) has what should be an attractive brief for his MMus, 'The Beatles' *Sgt Pepper's Lonely Hearts Club Band* and *Abbey Road* Side Two: Unification within the rock recording'. He avoids O'Grady's protracted chord progressions, but separates textual from musical analysis, concluding helplessly that 'the ultimate importance of these two recordings lies in their abilities to synthesize disparate musical philosophies into a whole, and to take this unity and make its vehicle of expression the recording.'[21] Anyone interested in following up such academic leads will find appropriate references in the bibliography at the end of this book.

While we make no apologies for weighting our collection towards Lennon's musical achievement, The Beatles' involvement in film was clearly a crucial element in their success: their celluloid personae were established in countries where the group themselves could never have played. The reviews here are appropriately international in scope and a new piece by Neil Sinyard explores the role of Private Gripweed in Lennon's subsequent political activity. John's part in Yoko's idiosyncratic film projects seems to us of less interest, although in more general terms her artistic attitudes had an influence which should not be underestimated.

Often portrayed as the woman who broke up The Beatles, the indifferent artist who saw fame by association as her one route to immortality, Ono did not need Lennon to launch her own career. As John Jones shows, she was a familiar presence on the New York avant-garde circuit, a cult figure even before her first meeting with Lennon in 1966. Perhaps the humour of her work, with its satiric disdain for the official arts establishment, appealed to Lennon the unruly art student. Mike Evans places the teenage John in the unfamiliar context of the Liverpool arts scene, showing how Lennon's fascination with the surreal in art suffused his literary endeavours. These were always controversial, John Wain and Tom Wolfe taking seriously the Joycean parallels in Lennon's jottings while the House of Commons berated the *illiterate* Lennon. Only Michael Wood, writing in the late 1960s, offers a more balanced assessment; he prefers to dwell on the lingering resonances of a Liverpool childhood.

As Lennon grew away from his roots, to affluent Manhattan via bourgeois Weybridge, he gave freer rein to a gamut of progressive sentiments. When in 1966 he proclaimed The Beatles 'more popular than Jesus now' and his disciples 'thick and ordinary', he intended no more than a statement of fact, without pejorative overtones. Lennon, of course, was always the most explicitly political of The Beatles, so his brief flirtation with the New Left was unsurprising and more than a way of 'struggling with being rich'—the problem for every socially aware rock star. Paul Hodson brings *that* story up to date. For some, Lennon's political posturings of the early 1970s were just that. Julie Burchill: 'his politics were strictly of the splash-it-all-over school; something he did to make him smell better and feel stage centre in the world's drama'.[22] A key text is the lengthy interview he and Yoko gave to *Red Mole*; like so many of our pieces it is only superficially familiar. In America, a terminally paranoid Nixon Administration saw even the most Utopian politicking as a threat. The Lennons had to go and Jon Wiener shows how the FBI determined to get rid of them.

Their campaigning and the Executive reaction to it forced some re-evaluation in the Eastern bloc. When Western pop music first made an impact on the USSR in the late Sixties, the bureaucratic response was not to ban it outright but to create an acceptable home-grown alternative: 'official' pop groups playing 'honest' Soviet songs. In Russia, The Beatles have always been the most idolised of Western musicians, despite meagre press coverage in the early years. 'The Beatles are the classics for our musicians,' a reverential Kolya Vasin told *The Observer* in 1985. 'They are our teachers. All Russian pop started with them.'[23] In Yugoslavia, Beatles' records were actually issued, albeit not until 1967, and by 1968 the group themselves had been shown twice on television. Alenka Barber-Kersovan has explained how 'young people were forced to build up their behavioural patterns according to the possibilities available.' Beatlemania came late, but with the same compulsion.

> One could not ignore the phenomenon, unless one wanted to be isolated. Passive adoration and endless discussions on the subject of The Beatles were followed by the will to imitate. Not only the controversial length of the hair, the black pullovers and the roll-neck shirts, but also the general attitude and the music itself became subjects of imitation. Possession of a guitar doubled individual prestige value, which multiplied if one played in a band. It became very important to know some members of a band at least, or even better to help a little bit around the stage. If none of this was possible, it helped a lot if you pretended; this was because members of a band enjoyed a special social status, demonstrated in public by even longer hair, even more colourful gear and so on. All this, of course, had consequences. For the band Kameleoni, for instance . . . everyone knew their names, likes and dislikes in the same way they knew about The Beatles. The first domestic stars were born.[24]

By December 1980, the official Communist line on these puppets of capitalism had softened. At the top, Lennon's murder provided a welcome metaphor for the decline of Western civilisation. Among ordinary people there was genuine regret, a sense of loss, and demonstrations in Moscow and Prague, where 'Give peace a chance' remains a potent anthem for the musical dissidents of Jazz Section.

In the West the torrent of Lennoniana continues. We've chosen to feature some of the more touching personal obituaries and reminiscences from the days following Lennon's death. Three serious composers working within their own genre conventions pay fresh tribute to the extraordinary impact of John Lennon and The Beatles.

'Biography will neither account for The Beatles nor explain our need for them . . . What it does not show is why The Beatles' music was so much more profoundly interesting than it need have been—and why a notoriously cloth-eared public for once got it right.' (Russell Davies)[25] Until now, the weight of tabloid journalism has tended to swamp perceptive discussion. *The Lennon Companion* seeks to redress the balance, drawing on a variety of critical languages to present an intelligent and accessible form of popular cultural commentary.

Elizabeth Thomson and David Gutman
London, April 1987

Notes

1. Jan Morris, 'The monarchs of the Beatle empire', *Saturday Evening Post* (27 August 1966) p. 26

2. Leonard Bernstein, 'Introduction' to *The Beatles* by Geoffrey Stokes (New York: Rolling Stone Press, 1980)

3. Jeanie Attie and Josh Brown, 'John Lennon', *Radical History Review*, 24 (Fall 1980) p. 190

4. Blake Morrison, 'The sound of the Sixties', *Times Literary Supplement* (15 May 1981) p. 548

5. Albert Goldman, 'Future past—an interview with John Lennon', *Charlie* (June 1971) pp. 24–7 and (July 1971) pp. 27–8, 58

6. Albert Goldman, letter to the editors, 28 October 1986

7. Richard Lester, letter to the editors, 4 June 1986

8. Julie Burchill, in 'Frontlines', *Time Out* (14 November 1985) p. 11

9. *see* Brian Epstein, *A Cellarful of Noise* (London: Souvenir Press, 1964)

10. Tony Palmer, 'Tomorrow and tomorrow', *London Magazine* (September 1967) pp. 75–6

11. Peter Gabriel, letter to the editors, 29 August 1986

12. Lloyd Rose, 'Long gone John: Lennon and the revelations', *Boston Phoenix* (10 December 1985) p. 1

13. Some of these occasional pieces were collected in *Skywriting by Word of Mouth* (London: Pan, 1986)

14. Ned Rorem, letter to the editors, 4 May 1986

15. John Rockwell, letter to the editors, 20 June 1986

16. John Beatty, 'Eleanor Rigby: structure in the arts', *Centerpoint*, IV/2 (1980) pp. 14–35

17. ibid, p. 14

18. ibid, p. 35

19. David R. Reck, 'Beatles Orientalis: influences from Asia in a popular song tradition', *Asian Music*, XVI/1 (1985) pp. 83–131

20. Joshua Rifkin, 'On the music of The Beatles', *see* pp. 113–26

21. William Dale Cockrell, 'The Beatles' *Sgt Pepper's Lonely Hearts Club Band* and *Abbey Road* Side Two: Unification within the rock recording', diss. U of Illinois (1973) p. 169

22. Julie Burchill, op. cit., p. 13

23. Kolya Vasin, in 'Back in the USSR', *The Observer* (4 August 1985) supplement p. 15

24. Alenka Barber-Kersovan, 'Tradition and acculturation as polarities of Slovenian popular music' in *Popular Music Perspectives: Papers from the First International Conference on Popular Music Research, Amsterdam, June 1981* (Göteborg & Exeter: IASPM, 1982) pp. 181–2

25. Russell Davies, 'Life with Aunt Mimi', *The Observer* (8 July 1984) p. 21

Listening to The Beatles' records again from the long corridor of middle age, the spell is gone. The songs are still delightful, but the thrill surrounding them has vanished as imperceptibly as youth itself. Each lyric conjures automatically The Beatles sound. Each sound recalls the definitive phrasing The Beatles gave to their words. Their three-minute epiphanies were, for many, how time was measured and history recalled in the 1960s. Were The Beatles the Schuberts and Bachs of contemporary music? Such lavish comparisons were made, but they hardly seem to matter. Then, as now, the songs renovated life with their articulate energy. Familiarity has robbed the music of its astonishment, but the songs still have the power to tap ancient longings. 'Once there was a way to get back homewards,' Paul's sweet voice intones, with a sense of loss that hits hard in adulthood. The sound of a hard-driving Beatles song, heard as you are inspecting the crows' feet and the other crenulations of age in the bathroom mirror, can get you moving, mouthing the magic of an earlier time to banish the fear of death. 'Yeah, yeah, yeah.' Once again, the old and good times roll. The Beatles' music makes joy; and that joy, once felt, is never easily forgotten.

John Lahr from 'The Beatles', *New Republic*,
2 December 1981

ONE

Only a Northern Song

LLOYD ROSE

Long gone John: Lennon and the revelations

Boston Phoenix, 10 December 1985

In the window of a pharmacy on Columbus Avenue near 72nd Street in
Manhattan sits a black-and-white photograph of John Lennon taken by
Annie Leibovitz. He's wearing a black leather jacket and sitting, one
knee up, in the window of one of his apartments at the Dakota. The
picture is crowned with a hand-lettered sign that reads, 'Let us not
forget our beloved JOHN LENNON. His message of Peace and Love
will live Forever.'

This is Lennon the legend, the rock-and-roll saint. It's not the
Lennon Paul McCartney talked about to Hunter Davies four years ago
in an interview reprinted in Davies's just-released revised edition of
his 1968 *The Beatles*. McCartney, who has spent much of the past five
years weathering criticism for being neither brilliant nor dead, told
Davies in a moment of bitterness that Lennon was 'a manoeuvring
swine.' 'Now since his death he's become Martin Luther Lennon. . . .
He wasn't some sort of holy saint.' The newspapers have gleefully
played this up: Paul McCartney, pop's Mr Muzak, slurring out of envy
the slain genius. Yet it's McCartney's Lennon, not the sentimentalists'
liberal, who stares out of another Leibovitz photograph, this one on
the cover of Ray Coleman's *Lennon*, the first book [sic] devoted to John
alone rather than to all four Beatles. Fixing the camera with his small
hard eyes, he looks grim and unsettlingly dangerous—snake thin and
snake mean.

Coleman's and Davies's books are the most recent in a series of
generally terrible biographies and memoirs of Lennon that have been
published since his murder, five years ago. Everyone, it seems—ex-
wife, ex-mistress, ex-best-friend, ex-tarot-card-reader—has been

heard from. The authors all assure us that Lennon was a great songwriter and a great guy before going on to record so many examples of his pettiness, cowardice and cruelty that McCartney's comments begin to sound not just understated but almost protective.

With all their dirt-dishing, not one of these books adds to our understanding of Lennon. There are new details to be sure—the kinds of drugs he took; specific examples of his physical violence—but anyone reading between the lines of Davies's original edition of *The Beatles* could have guessed at almost every new revelation. Expurgated as it was, that book revealed that Lennon beat his first wife, Cynthia, quoted him talking freely about drugs, and described his withdrawn, daydreaming anomie in his house at Weybridge, England, in the late Sixties. That he was tormented and furious had been obvious for a long time—it was partly what made him the 'thinking man's Beatle' and allowed him, a suburban boy, to adopt without challenge the title of 'working-class hero'. It had also been obvious that mixed in with the anger and the pain were not only wit, brains, and talent, but a peculiar innocence, egotistical yet genuine, that led him time and again—with the 'We're more popular than Jesus' remark, the nude *Two Virgins* cover, the Amsterdam Bed-In for Peace—to make a well-meaning public fool of himself. It would seem to be the job of a biographer to give the reader some understanding of how these extremes were combined in him—under what circumstances they were integrated enough for him to function in a world so fame-distorted that it made Wonderland look like Des Moines, and when and why they tore him apart and sent him into drug addiction or out on violent binges. It was the unique fusion of innocence and viciousness in Lennon that kept him from being just another superstar jerk. He was a dervish of moods, impulses and beliefs, all of them circling the eye of his personal storm: the conviction, as Utopian as the vision of any of his political songs, that there was a measure of peace for him somewhere if he could only figure out a way to it. Of all the people who have written on Lennon, only two have shown any imaginative grasp of him: Philip Norman, whose gentlemanly but shrewd *Shout!* remains the best book written on The Beatles, gives a gritty sense of Lennon's loneliness; and Albert Goldman, warming up for a full-length biography to come, does a few hot, hip licks on his music in his collection of pop-culture essays, *Freakshow*.

But mostly the chroniclers of his life and times drag out the same old facts and lay them lifeless on the page. The traditional account of his family traumas, for example, hardly varies from one telling to another. His father deserted his mother when she was pregnant; his mother found another man and left John to be brought up by his adoring, childless aunt, Mimi Smith, and her husband, George. His mother visited him more and more often as he became a teenager, and they formed a close, warm bond. Then, when he was 17, she was killed in a car accident and he never got over it. Twelve years later, he ended *John Lennon/Plastic Ono Band* by singing in a voice so electronically altered and remote that it sounded as if it were coming from some echo chamber of the damned: 'My mummy's dead; I can't get it through my head, though it's been so many years. My mummy's dead.'

The father Lennon knew was George Smith, the dairyman who provided him with a comfortable lower-middle-class home. Smith taught him to read, bought him his first mouth organ, spoiled him behind the strict Mimi's back. He died when Lennon was 14. He rates a couple of references in Hunter Davies's biography, is mentioned on five pages in *Shout!*, and appears on 22 of Coleman's 640 pages. He's the forgotten man in Lennon's life, yet his influence on the fatherless boy must have been enormous.

Philip Norman astutely begins *Shout!* with an account of Mimi Smith's running to the hospital through the streets of Liverpool in the middle of a bombing raid in order to hold her sister's newborn son in her arms: 'I couldn't stop thinking, "It's a boy, it's a boy. He's the one I've waited for".' 'The minute I saw John, that was it,' she told Davies; 'I was lost forever.' Cynthia Lennon lived with Mimi twice, once before her marriage to John and once after; both times were strained. 'Two women loving the same man inevitably leads to jealousy somewhere along the line,' she commented with placid understatement in her memoir *A Twist of Lennon*. It's possible that Uncle George was shunted off to the side while Mimi lavished all her affection on her nephew, that Lennon's childhood experience of the traditional family drama amounted to his winning his substitute mother away from his substitute father—not necessarily a good thing, as another working-class hero, D. H. Lawrence, could have told him.

Whatever the exact nature of its disturbances, his childhood apparently put him on a permanent pendulum, swinging between fury and an acute, neurotic sensitivity. He implied many times in interviews that his life was one nerve-burning pulse of emotional pain after another. Even allowing for self-aggrandisement and self-pity, it's hard not to believe him. As early as *Rubber Soul*, his songs have a flat yet acidic quality, as if he were impacted with anger and depression. 'Was she told when she was young that pain would lead to pleasure?' he sings on 'Girl', ending with, 'Will she still believe it when he's dead?' 'In my life' is melancholy; 'Run for your life' frankly aggressive—'I'd rather see you dead, little girl, than to be with another man.' He wrote his first 'confessional' song, 'I'm a loser' (imagine the complacent

McCartney singing those words) as early as 1965, and for the next 15 years his songs, with the exception of a few love ballads, went their unhappy way: dulled and lost, as with 'Strawberry Fields forever', 'Nowhere man', and 'I'm so tired' (with its three-o'clock-in-the-morning cry, 'I'd give you everything I've got for a little peace of mind'); sharp-edged and wounding, as with 'Happiness is a warm gun' and 'Cold turkey'; desperate, as with 'Help!' and 'Don't let me down'; or wistfully buoyant with dreams of escape, as with 'Lucy in the sky with diamonds' or 'Across the universe'. Occasionally he shifted tone in mid-song, as in 'She said she said', in which he slides from an 'affectless' opening to the poignant, hopeless 'When I was a boy, everything was right.' His longing for the innocence of his childhood shows up at times in other places, such as these lines from a poem he wrote in his teens: 'I remember a time when/Belly buttons were knee high/When only shitting was/Dirty and everything else/ Clean and beautiful.'

According to Coleman, when Lennon was eight or nine, he wandered into Mimi Smith's kitchen and told her he had just seen God. When she asked what He had been doing, Lennon replied, 'Oh, just sitting by the fire.' This early religious fantasy, with its mystical overtones, was a precursor to some very peculiar adolescent experiences. In the *Playboy* interview with David Sheff that he gave just before his death, Lennon goes on at some length about his hypersensitive consciousness during his childhood and adolescence: 'Surrealism to me is reality. Psychedelic vision is reality to me and always was. When I looked at myself in the mirror at twelve, thirteen . . . I used to, literally, trance out into alpha. . . . I would find myself seeing these hallucinatory images of my face changing, becoming cosmic and complete. I would start trancing out and the eyes would get bigger and the room would vanish.'

What on earth was going on with him? Was he wandering around his aunt's suburban villa and through the halls of Quarry Bank Grammar having—depending on your prejudices—either hallucinations or mystical experiences? Even if these episodes were rarer than he implies, it's clear he took at least a couple of journeys to a state of mind not even on most people's maps. Did he later drink and take drugs to escape this condition, or, having lost it, to try to get it back? Or could he drift into it at will and return carrying 'Strawberry Fields forever' or 'I am the walrus'—exquisite examples of his consciousness-bypass style of songwriting.

He certainly seems to have been familiar with and dependent on his unconscious to a very strong degree. Apparently songs often just 'came' to him and, unlike the meticulous McCartney, he never much tidied them up once they were there—he didn't *tamper* with them. It's as if they had washed up on the beach of his mind, beautiful, many-whorled shells, complete in themselves. He speaks to Sheff of writing 'Across the universe' and 'Nowhere man' as if he were '*possessed*; like a *psychic* or a *medium*.'

According to The Beatles' producer, George Martin, 'The lyrics would lead and develop John's songs.' There's no way of knowing whether this was the case in his post-Beatles period, when his lyrics were very simple and pared down. But in the late Sixties, even when he was not being deliberately obscure, his best lyrics were a semi-poetic jumble of images and incomplete thoughts, often as arresting and private as the 'word salad' mutterings of a schizophrenic. His songs are startling and evocative precisely because they don't reveal but suggest. There's a shattered, broken-mirror quality to much of his work, and the flying shards stick in the listener's mind and find reflections there. A lot of this was a product of drugs, of course, but a lot of it seems to have been Lennon's natural way of writing. His verse and stories in his collection, *In His Own Write*, exhibit the same scattered quirkiness and are riddled with puns ('poisonous snacks such as the deadly cobbler and the apply python') and odd bits of whimsy (the unseen lady whose singing enchants the poet turns out to be 'a tiny little tiny pig').

'John's concept of music is very interesting,' Martin told Davies. 'I was once playing Ravel's *Daphnis and Chloé* to him. He said he couldn't follow it because the melodic lines were too long. He said he looked upon writing music as doing little bits which you then join up.' This 'joining up' between Lennon and McCartney produced some amazing results—most notably the ashy, apocalyptic 'A day in the life', the result of their merging two songs—the ones each happened to be working on at the time. In Lennon's case this lack of musical sophistication and his refusal, or inability, to become more sophisticated account for the bite and distinction of his songs. Through the years they retained a 'found object' quality, the sense of being put together from bits and pieces of things he had stumbled on and liked: newspaper stories ('I read the news today, oh boy'), circus posters, ads. His unwillingness to do much work on them in the studio, which he often regretted afterward, blaming McCartney or Martin for not having given him enough attention, was probably based in part on a fear that he couldn't do much better (a constant worry of someone with little conscious control over what he produces). But it may also have come from an instinctive understanding that the slapdash, the incomplete, the fragmented were his native stylistic elements. He achieved naturally, in its most powerful, primitive form, what the

Surrealists espoused as the highest state of artistic consciousness: the drawing up of the unsullied waters of the unconscious. 'Language and song is to me', he said to Marshall McLuhan in an interview, 'just like trying to describe a dream.'

This fluid interchange with his unconscious coupled with his sensitivity to the social currents of his time—a sensitivity so acute he often seemed to be forecasting what he was only reflecting—account in large part for the relationship he had with his generation. He was, to use a phrase popular at the time 'plugged in' to the irrational elements in both himself and society—in giving form to one he gave form to the other. It was this, apparent in how he lived his life as well as his music, that made him a star.

He hated his stardom, but he also needed it. He defined himself by it to the extent that he found nothing foolish in returning his MBE 'in protest against Britain's involvement in the Nigeria–Biafra thing, against our support of America in Viet Nam, and against "Cold turkey" slipping down the charts.' In his first heady period away from The Beatles, he tried, with Yoko Ono's encouragement, to turn his fame into a power for social change—staging the Bed-In for Peace, supporting various radical causes, and sending out musical messages like 'Give peace a chance' (this preaching impulse was nothing new; it went back at least as far as 'All you need is love').

It was during this period that he told Coleman he and Yoko Ono would like to be remembered 'if possible, just as John and Yoko who created world peace for ever [*sic*].' He also grew his hair and beard long, dressed in all white, and got chummy with Jesus, addressing him in 'The ballad of John and Yoko' in a spirit of martyred fellowship: 'Christ, you know it ain't easy / You know how hard it can be / The way things are going / They're gonna crucify me.' On an acid trip with his boyhood friend Pete Shotton, he decided he *was* Christ come again and summoned the other Beatles to let them in on the secret. They took it in their stride.

Much of this Christ identification, with its implications of limitless power and meaningful suffering, may simply have been an extreme reaction to his discovery that to be the hero and representative of a generation was to be trapped into fulfilling that generation's expectations. He developed a sceptical, bitter appreciation of the coffin-narrow confines of his fame. In one interview he explained that he was never 'cuddly', that he was always 'just Lennon'. But 'just Lennon'—the peacenik, the druggie, the loudmouth, the lover and then the husband of Yoko Ono, the man Peter Brown refers to in *The Love You Make* as 'the Lenny Bruce of rock and roll'—wasn't what the public wanted. It wanted John the Beatle. (There is some indication that his murder was the final punishment for not being what his fans expected him to be. Both Peter Brown in *The Love You Make* and Jon Wiener in *Come Together* report that Mark David Chapman made his decision to murder Lennon after reading an *Esquire* cover story by Laurence Shames that denounced Lennon for letting his admirers down by becoming a showbiz millionaire.)

A cop who broke up one of his drunken Los Angeles revels asked in awe, once he realised whom he was holding a shotgun on, 'Do you think The Beatles will ever get back together?' Under the circumstances Lennon answered diplomatically, 'You never know.' But usually the question drove him crazy. 'That is *over*, man,' he told Sheff. 'It's just irrelevant, *absolutely irrelevant*.' He had been saying the same thing again and again for 10 years, since *John Lennon/Plastic Ono Band* in 1970. In 'God' he sang, 'I don't believe in Beatles', and went on, 'The dream is over / What can I say? / The dream is over / Yesterday / I was the dreamweaver / But now I'm reborn / I was the walrus / But now I'm John / And so dear friends / You just have to carry on / The dream is over.'

In their uninspired triteness more than their direct statement, these lyrics make clear that he was indeed no longer the dreamweaver. Nor, though he was a mega-celebrity whose appearance on stage could pack a house, was he a powerful cultural influence. He wasn't picking up the current of his times anymore; there was no voltage in his songs.

This artistic decline has been attributed to his no longer having McCartney to compete with and bounce ideas off. It also had a great deal to do with something many of his admirers have trouble admitting: he really did make Yoko Ono not just his wife but his new partner. He had always needed a partner and supporter—Shotton in his boyhood, Cynthia Lennon and his close friend Stu Sutcliffe in art college, McCartney in his Beatles period. Shotton notes this curious weakness in his book, *John Lennon: In My Life*, and both Brown and Davies depict Lennon as being lost after The Beatles stopped touring. Lennon himself, with his usual frankness, mentioned in several interviews his fear of going off on his own. Throughout his life he charged restlessly from one idea or person to another, picking up and then discarding friends, lovers, gurus, therapists, charlatans, drugs, political stances, until finally, in Yoko Ono, he found, in his own words, 'The One'. His nickname for her was 'Mother'.

With her he produced three albums of avant-garde doodles, political anthems ('Give peace a chance', 'Power to the people'), bad agitprop (the album *Some Time in New York City*, for which they co-authored many of the songs), pale imitations of his earlier dream visions ('#9 dream'), and a series of pallid love songs. 'Imagine', his most enduring post-Beatles hit, was his 'Yesterday'—gentle and pretty. Its lyrics represent a rich celebrity's soft-minded Utopia (as a cynical listener wrote to *Rolling Stone*, 'Imagine John Lennon with no possessions'). He defended Yoko's contribution to his growth as an artist, no doubt in large part because she continually urged him to 'be himself'. This may have been damaging advice since, despite his strong personality, Lennon appears to have been uncertain to a crippling extent of just what his self was.

Shortly before he shut himself away in the Dakota for five silent years, he released an album in which he regressed all the way back to his roots, *John Lennon/Rock and Roll*. The album fails for a number of reasons—it's poorly produced; Lennon isn't in good voice; it's spiritless—but the worst thing about it is the way Lennon time-trips back to the period before The Beatles. *Rock and Roll* isn't so much a tribute to the music that inspired him as it is a denial of what he himself produced. It's hard to listen to it without the sinking feeling that he really believed 'Be-bop-a-lula' was greater than anything he'd ever written and that it was a relief to him, rather than a shaming frustration, to admit that fact.

Lennon did make one great album after he left The Beatles, *John Lennon/Plastic Ono Band*. Clumsy, raw, and embarrassing, it carries his music into the stoniest of territories, where there is no spring of either melodic beauty or lyrical magic. Here there is no water, only rock. *Plastic Ono Band* is an album without grace and without the culture-expressing breadth of Lennon's work with The Beatles. But it has the unguarded, jotted-down immediacy of a diary. Lennon's primitivism has never served him better. If the songs had been embellished at all with self-conscious 'artistry', the album would have come out as self-pitying muck. Instead it's all jagged edges and bloody surfaces. In his renunciation of everything beautiful or crowd-pleasing, Lennon prefigures the defiant posture of punk.

His voice, too, from our vantage point 15 years later, sounds eerily modern—his atonality and restricted emotional expressiveness are forerunners of the new wave singing style. He had one of the great rock-and-roll voices, but he hated it. '*Do* something with my voice!' he'd beg George Martin. 'Smother it with tomato ketchup or something.' He may have feared comparison with McCartney's commercially acceptable tenor, and certainly by traditional standards his voice was mediocre: inflexible, nasal, and without much richness or range. And whether he was singing out of anger or pain or dreamy, tender longing, he always sounded slightly flattened out emotionally, as if his voice couldn't carry all he felt. Alienation was built into his singing style. Whenever he tried for let-it-all-hang-out power, he never quite made it. On his most famous screamer, 'Twist and shout', he sounds strained almost to the strangling point. He couldn't relax into pain and make it seem depthless. He sang an urgent, constricted blues, a white man's blues. He sang *angst*.

On *Plastic Ono Band*, he uses a delay that puts his voice at one remove from the listener, and at times his vocals take second place to the instrumentation (the piano on 'Mother' keeps pounding right over him). Yet this distancing, and the way it buffers the raw emotions of the songs, seems right—he sounds as if he were imprisoned in his work. The flat lyrics—'Mother, you had me but I never had you / I wanted you but you didn't want me / So I got to tell you / Goodbye goodbye' or 'Love is you / You and me / Love is knowing / We can be'—actually work for him. Their banality, the uninspired melodies, and the sound-wall of the delay are like a barrier that he, moaning and raging, can never break through. In 'Working class hero' his voice isn't distorted, but he sings in a beaten-out, exhausted style, taking a despairing fall on the line 'When you can't really function you're so full of fear.' *Plastic Ono Band* is often referred to as the 'primal scream album', as if Lennon sang his way to a therapeutic catharsis. But there's no release: he ends as he began, singing of his mother's death. It's an album of defeat.

He was dead 10 years later, having never, in the autobiographical albums that followed *Plastic Ono Band*, done anything of comparable interest. What he did produce in those years, as he had earlier, was interviews. He was a great talker—witty, quick, lyrically caustic; he could sing an interview like a song. Here he is on his Uncle George's death in Davies's book: 'Mimi was crying over the carrots. She used to take in students at the time. They were sitting around, trying to look sad, but knowing they weren't going to get a proper meal and Mimi would be suffering for months.' There's a novelist's eye in this, and also a certain deadpan fury. His response when told of Elvis Presley's death is just as tough: 'The difference between The Beatles and Elvis is that with Elvis the king died and the manager lived and with The Beatles the manager died and we lived.' He could be off-the-wall and self-deprecating, too; discussing with Sheff his and Yoko's problems conceiving a child, he explained, 'The prognosis was "She's too old and you've abused yourself too much. You blew your jism by abusing your sperm as a rock 'n' roll patriot".' It hardly matters that he was 'on' in these interviews, playing the media game, hiding behind a show of candour; he still had a force and reality none of the writing about him conveys. Along with his songs, these fragments of conversation are his autobiography. Just as you're getting fed up with reading about his silliness or meanness, his own words spark up off the page—savvy, funny, rueful—and you understand why people fell for him. 'He was a terrible guy, actually,' a Liverpool Art Institute acquaintance told Coleman, 'but I liked him.'

MIKE EVANS

The arty Teddy Boy

It was during the late 1950s, while still a grammar-school boy in North Wales, that I began to get involved with the artistic bohemia of Liverpool 8. At that point, I knew the 'full time' painters better than the students from the College of Art, although I was acquainted with Lennon's flatmate Rod Murray and, in passing, the bunch of boisterous cronies he hung round with, though none of them by name. I do remember my art teacher at school, a genial character called David Kinmont, referring to the new breed of art student emerging at the time as 'nothing better than arty Teddy boys'. Twenty-five years later, while helping with my research for the *Art of The Beatles* exhibition subsequently staged at Liverpool's Walker Art Gallery, Peter Blake recalled a similarly hard-nosed crowd of students from Liverpool who graduated to London's Royal College of Art in the early 1960s. He called them 'the Liverpool toughies'.

John Lennon, regardless of his ability—or lack of it—in visual art, was an archetype: the product of a clash of cultures that first occurred in the English grammar schools, and more specifically art colleges, and manifested itself generally in the popular culture of the 1960s.

England has been, and still is, the most class-conscious of countries. Ironically the 'levelling' of society by post-war egalitarianism only served to throw traditional class differentials into sharper focus, and to introduce new ones. The 1944 Education Act had two direct effects on matters of class as far as the generation of 'war babies' was concerned. The entry-by-merit established in the 11+ exam for the traditional grammar schools meant that working-class children for the first time entered the mainstream of higher education in large numbers. However, the class-by-birth barriers this helped to erode were replaced by a new set of status values governed by intellectual ability.

Almost regardless of their background, children from the working and lower middle classes were categorised at 11 into the achievers and the no-hopers, those with career potential and those doomed, like their fathers, to the life of industrial and rural labour. (Another anomaly in the system was that the upper classes never had the rigidity of this academic apartheid forced upon them, fee-paying education being untouched by the changes in the State sector.)

So strong were the identity pressures associated with 'grammar' or 'secondary' education that, by the mid-1950s, when John Lennon was in his teens, the lines were fairly clearly drawn in terms of the new youth culture which was springing up all round. Grammar school culture tended to be 'posh'—even more so if the background was solidly working class. They were the 'swots', the kids more likely, in the mid-1950s, to have cottoned on to jazz. The Goons were the schoolyard cult *par excellence*; folk music and skiffle abounded; CND found its largest following. By the end of the decade, along with university fodder, the grammar schools had produced (with the help of Fleet Street) the beatniks.

Secondary schools, on the other hand, represented the mainstream proletarian teenager, who for reasons more economic than artistic now also had a cultural identity: an identity which was non-academic, non-literary, essentially anti-art, and centred on the style and music surrounding rock 'n' roll.

The institutions of further education—universities, teacher-training colleges, art schools—were open to the grammar-school educated offspring of the masses. But whereas most establishments had specific academic criteria for entry, the art schools had a much looser system of recruitment. In the case of John Lennon, with his paucity of academic achievement, this was just as well. Despite being intellectually able, he resented and rejected the disciplines involved in passing exams, ending up with no O-levels at all—not even in English and Art, the two subjects where his teachers admitted he showed a real talent. Throughout school, especially during the last two years, he was branded a troublemaker, the classroom joker, more interested in his embryo skiffle group and his ad hoc cartoon-sheet, *The Daily Howl*, which featured his own graphic caricatures of the teaching staff. As if in desperation to find a role for the wayward Lennon, the headmaster at Quarry Bank suggested he use the cartoons he was producing so prolifically as the basis for a portfolio to seek entry into Liverpool College of Art. It was possible to join the basic Intermediate course at a local art school on the merits of artwork alone. The door was now open to 'non-academic' students who happened to show some artistic ability, the broad spectrum of would-be artists.

Since post-war National Service imposed conscription on all males at the age of 18, further education had been a catch-all for bright kids who wanted to avoid the call up; most students were simply exempt. Even after conscription was abolished in the mid-1950s, college continued to attract not only the career-minded, but those still anxious to avoid a 'real job' for a year or two. What the art schools offered to those of an artistic inclination was the chance to avoid adult responsibility, and the opportunity to indulge in both the technical disciplines and the Bohemian lifestyle of the art student. For many people, the latter was indeed a greater attraction than the former.

Out of these tensions, disparate cultural pressures and influences, came a new kind of rebel. Not, on the one hand, the acceptably unconventional student, the duffle-coated radical conforming to the stereotype of the pipe-smoking jazz fan, his roots in the Angry Young Men of earlier in the decade, John Osborne's Jimmy Porter personified. And certainly not mere miscreant youth, which is all the Teds added up to in most cases: essentially conservative in their chauvinism and with limited aspirations—a revolt in style inexorably linked to a music (that of early Elvis, Buddy Holly, Little Richard) which was already just a memory on provincial jukeboxes by the closing years of the 1950s. What hit the art schools at precisely this time was a potent hybrid of these models of the teenage malcontent. From the social melting pot of the grammar schools came a mixed bag of cultural references: kids from terraced back streets more interested in pulp comics than Picasso; suburban romantics hung up on the new American Beat writers; and everywhere the all-pervasive influence of rock 'n' roll and the English skiffle craze that went with it. The result was a species of which the 17-year-old John Lennon was both typical and one of the first—the art-student-as-Teddy-boy.

With his greased-back hair, narrow-as-permissible trousers and 'slim jim' ties, Lennon already looked 'a bit of a Ted' at Quarry Bank, and he stuck out like a sore thumb at Art College. Fellow student Helen Anderson recalls, 'I liked John, we all thought he was great fun, but I never fancied him. He was greasy, a bit of a Ted, and he always smelled of chips.' Chip-shop diet notwithstanding, just a couple of years after Lennon's entry into Liverpool College of Art in 1957, the style had established itself; hence Blake's reference to the 'Liverpool toughies' who left the College a couple of years after John. Students suddenly appeared on post-graduate courses in London, at the RCA and the Slade, revelling in their working-class (i.e. regional) accents, swaggering round like macho motorbikers, swearing a lot, getting into the occasional fight, terrifying some of the tutors, mesmerising most of the girls. But when he burst on to the Intermediate course at Liverpool back in '57, Lennon's gritty style and coarse manner was almost unique. Almost, but not quite.

There was one other quasi-Ted among the students, a year ahead of John, who, if only for reasons of image, Lennon would inevitably have been drawn to: Stuart Sutcliffe. As it emerged, after their introduction through graphics student and amateur journalist Bill Harry, Stuart's sense of style went much deeper than just his dress, although in 1957 that in itself certainly set him apart from his fellow students. Almost as soon as he had left Prescot Grammar School, during the summer vacation prior to his first term at Liverpool in the autumn of '56, Sutcliffe began to adapt his schoolboy 'sticky out' hair (as everyone described it) and 'swotty' glasses to look reminiscent of his recently deceased hero James Dean. By the time the young John Lennon entered the course a year later, Sutcliffe already struck a highly individual pose, with his tight drainpipe trousers, sandals, combed-back quiff and sunglasses. None of these diverse elements were, in themselves, particularly alien to art-student fashion of course, but their combination by Stuart made for a striking image that soon became the talk of the College.

But it was Sutcliffe's *concern* with style, his attitude to the visual, that sparked in John an enthusiasm that he recognised somewhere in himself. They spent hours talking, Stuart enthusing about his painter heroes (he was considered the bright new talent among College painters), about James Dean, about life in general; John raving about his rock 'n' roll ambitions with a manic sense of humour that came out in gobbledegook word-play and pungent wit.

Stuart was basically intellectual rather than intuitive, John the reverse. In this respect he was more 'arty' than Lennon, who very consciously wore the mantle of the anti-intellectual Teddy boy. But both rubbed off on each other. John admired, albeit tacitly, Stuart's ability, his self-discipline and knowledge. Sutcliffe, on the other hand, saw in Lennon the primitive, the intuitive artist he could never be although in many ways his progress to totally abstract painting could be seen as a way of achieving the 'natural' and unrepresentational quality of music. Stuart articulated things in this way, analysed them. If John hadn't known him better, he would quickly have dismissed him as an arty pseud. Conversely, Lennon felt that if you wanted to paint in a certain way, play music in a certain way, you did it—without wasting time talking about it. It was an attitude that was to permeate much of what he did for the rest of his life.

Sutcliffe loved rock 'n' roll, and in John's natural dynamism he perceived the romantic vision of the rock 'n' roll musician, a vision rooted in the *image* as much as in any personal ambition actually to

17

play. So when eventually John offered him a place with his skiffle-group-turned-rock-combo, he was in without hesitation.

Once Johnny and the Moondogs started gigging with Stuart Sutcliffe on bass guitar, he and John Lennon agreed that the first thing they needed was some sort of on-stage image. Although John revelled in his Ted image around the beard-and-sandals corridors of the art school, neither he nor Stuart wanted the group to ape the appearance of all the other Liverpool rock 'n' roll outfits, real-life Teddy boys to a man. Not for them the mohair and lamé of pop circa '59. Right from the start they adopted a 'cooler' look. While the haircuts were definitely based on teenage America, the clothes constituted a darker, subtler look than those of other groups of the time: black polo-neck sweaters, dark blue jeans and white sneakers.

This trend in the early visual impact of The Beatles was confirmed and developed when the group made the first of several visits to the German fleshpots of Hamburg. There, The Beatles were taken up by a group of local art students. Prominent among these new camp-followers were photographer Jurgen Vollmer, artist and musician Klaus Voorman, and his girlfriend, another photography student, Astrid Kirchherr.

After parting with Voorman—who nevertheless remained part of this avant-garde fan club—Astrid, as Stuart's girlfriend, had a significant influence on the subsequent visual development of the (then) Silver Beatles. The group had already adopted a 'black' look, and this probably helped attract the German entourage in the first place. They were the local *exis*—self-styled existentialists—whose own uniform across Western Europe made much use of black sweaters, black stockings, white make-up. And leather. Soon Astrid, through Stuart, had the group in black leather jackets and trousers, winkle-picker shoes and black T-shirts. A look that reflected exactly what John had always dreamed of.

Then, as if once again to throw in a contradiction, the leather-clad greasy rockers from Liverpool—first Stuart, then George, John and Paul—had their hair cut, long at the side but flat on top. A bit like Anthony Perkins, Marlon Brando, certainly not like rock 'n' rollers—in fact, just like art students. After Brian Epstein 'smartened up' his boys (against Lennon's immediate instincts), the 'mop top' remained. It became even more pronounced—and the key to the Fab Four's image worldwide.

Lennon later confessed that, right through the three mad years that constituted Beatlemania on the road, inside the tight-buttoned, round-collared Pierre Cardin suits there was a Liverpool Ted struggling to get out: '. . . as soon as we made it, we made it, but the edges were knocked off. Brian puts us in suits and all that and we made it very, very big. But we sold out. . . .' (Jann Wenner, *Lennon Remembers*). As their fame progressed, so the image became further distanced—anticipating young fashion generally—from the twin '50s traditions of Teddy boys and beatniks.

The 'arty Teddy boy' syndrome wasn't just about style, but the *attitude* that produced that style. Even at the height of flower power, which in *Sgt Pepper* combined The Beatles' most ludicrous image with their creative peak as recording artists, the ambitious flights of musical and lyrical fantasy were anchored by a solid bedrock of simple rock 'n' roll. In the great pop tradition, no track on *Pepper* except for 'A day in the life' ran longer than a regular commercial single.

Unlike the beatniks, the art students, the so-called intellectuals of late 1950s teenagehood, the Teds were unashamedly anti-intellectual and therefore anti-art. Lennon embraced this stance with gusto as he regaled phonies in the art-school pub, Ye Cracke. He declared more than once that 'avant-garde is French for bullshit'. Yet, in a way that would have been equally pretentious to a genuine Ted, he was intrigued by the nonsense humour of Edward Lear and The Goons, and subsequent notions (introduced in the main by Sutcliffe rather than by his tutors) of Surrealism and Dada—the latter itself being deliberately 'anti-art' in its contempt for formal values and bourgeois pretensions.

These ideas about art neatly coincided with, and helped justify and rationalise, his own gut instinct, which was always in favour of inspiration rather than technique as a prime criterion for creative activity. All through his career—from his art student days when he ignored 'real' painting in favour of off-the-cuff cartoons, and championed Stuart as a bass player because he had the right 'attitude', to his 'stream of consciousness' Surrealism and eventual promotion of Yoko Ono's seemingly minimal musical talents—Lennon's inclination was to let intuition and inspiration rule; the rest would follow. With the partnership of the more workmanlike McCartney and the inbuilt discipline of writing for a working group, follow it usually did. Without such constraints, Lennon's solo work, while frequently brilliant, included a proportion that was at best unmemorable, at worst incomprehensible—an accusation that could rarely be levelled at the music of The Beatles.

The audacious nature of elements of 1960s culture—poets 'performing' their work accompanied by painters and pop groups, hallucinogenic lyrics in the Top Ten, pop art itself—was in part a result

19

of the class mix, the grammar school input into the corridors of pop-culture power. Along with Bailey, Quant, Hockney and the rest, Lennon and The Beatles personified that culture.

Right up to his death, particularly in the years when the pressures of superstardom fell away and he could concentrate on domestic priorities and work at a natural (leisurely) pace, Lennon more and more voiced an affection for the places and lifestyle of his youth. It was a lifestyle in suburbia, treelined and peaceful, where even looking a bit of a Ted was rebellion in itself, and art students were the oddballs in *everyone's* eyes.

Out of these constraints and contradictions the most famous Working Class Hero of them all emerged—king of the Liverpool toughies, Doctor Winston O'Boogie, the ultimate arty Teddy boy.

PAULINE SUTCLIFFE

Isolation: Sutcliffe, Epstein, Lennon and loss*

Stuart Sutcliffe, Brian Epstein and John Lennon. All three were connected to The Beatles phenomenon. All were eldest or only sons. All died prematurely, leaving behind them not only bereft admirers but grieving family. Above all, the three mothers, adoptive and otherwise.[1]

These mothers were exposed to their own grief and that of their son's family, partners and children—as well as that of the public. Both Brian and John and to a lesser extent Stuart have become immortalised, even idealised, by the public, and possibly by their mothers. Although Mrs Sutcliffe's son died of natural causes, there was sufficient doubt for the media to describe the death as 'mysterious', with much hunting around for the 'real' explanation. Mrs Epstein had to cope with the public revelation of her son's lifestyle and the ambiguous circumstances of his death. Mrs Smith was not allowed such

---

* This article is taken from a longer paper which presents a psychoanalytical discussion of grief and mourning in the context of family systems.

uncertainty: her son was gunned down outside his home in the most dramatic and universally public way.

Of The Beatles, John Lennon was the first member the Sutcliffe family met. Initially, they were somewhat surprised at this choice of friend as he was quite unlike Stuart: a rough sort of chap, not easy to befriend and lacking in certain social niceties. However, it soon became clear that his mother was as concerned as Stuart's to know what sort of fellow her son was mixing with. In many ways, this maternal interest could be regarded as perfectly normal.

Stuart's joining the band highlighted a number of maternal similarities, suggesting that John, too, was from a family with some characteristics of enmeshment. Despite seldom meeting, both mothers ensured that a ready flow of communication passed between them, expressing mutual concerns about their sons' involvement with pop music. They were equally complimentary to one another about their sons, indicating their approval of the friendship. Equally, they acknowledged surprise that two such different personalities as Stuart and John should become friends. Mrs Smith was particularly impressed by Stuart's manners and gentleness and Mrs Sutcliffe had by now transformed John's toughness and lack of social graces into all manner of positive characteristics. Throughout, both mothers maintained this position of uncritical acceptance of their son's friend. This perhaps protected each of them from acknowledging any loss of their son to the friendship.

Beyond their mothers' mutuality, Stuart and John had other elements of similarity in their respective family systems. Both had absent fathers, either through loss or work patterns. Both families functioned on a peripheral male or one-parent family model. As a way of avoiding their feeling of loss, both mothers appear to have filled this power vacuum by elevating their 'only' son into the space.

Perhaps it is significant that John addressed Mrs Smith by her Christian name, Mimi. This may have been a way of defining their relationship, an indication to the young John that his natural mother's place had not been filled by his Aunt. But it could also have introduced confusion as to the nature of their relationship, blurring the generational boundary. It is possible, therefore, that John was regarded by Mimi sometimes as a peer, sometimes as a child. Indeed a quote from *Shout!* appears to exemplify this muddle:

> Even by transatlantic telephone, Mimi and John could have memorable rows. There was one, over the bungalow's repainting, which ended with Mimi shouting 'Damn you, Lennon!' and slamming the receiver down. A moment later the telephone rang again. John's voice came anxiously

from the distant hemisphere. 'You're not still cross with me Mimi, are you?'[2]

Unlike Stuart, John had no siblings and so had no obvious reference point to serve as a reminder of life in a sibling group. This could have left him feeling high and dry and, ultimately, angry and rebellious (needing to reject such adult responsibility) or very protected, safe and secure. Stuart, on the other hand, because of the temporary nature of his elevation and the checks and balances provided by the other siblings, probably experienced the conflict of not quite knowing his place. This could account in part for his respectful and grown-up manner but also his deep attraction to John's rebellious qualities. Not to mention the statement he was making by joining a pop group.

As each Beatle friendship developed, a similar pattern of over-involvement continued between Stuart and John's mothers, each now able to express to the other reservations about the musical venture and occasional criticism of the other members of the group, but never about their sons. Both went occasionally to see them play and to survey the scene for any undesirable elements.

The Sutcliffe siblings (of whom I was one) were also instructed to view the scene and report back. Indeed, by now Stuart was so well established as a parental figure that he could with impunity take his youngest sibling with him to gigs. He always ensured that she did not mix with anyone by posting her in a safe place where she could watch the performance but not be seen nor tempted to stray. He could not, despite his efforts, protect her from feeling excited by the dangers she perceived, symbolised by the police vans and dogs waiting outside the venues to quell the warring mobs. He had learned well the art of conveying confusion to others by the ease with which he moved along the continuum from over-protective to permissive. In considering John's later years leading up to his death, one could identify similarly learned artistry from the school of enmeshment: not leaving home for five years to raise his new baby, thus providing an enclosed and over-involved cross-generational diad (father and child) while his wife went out into the world—perhaps replicating for him an old family pattern of the peripheral 'father', in this case, Yoko.

Any evidence of enmeshed features existing in Brian Epstein's family system can only be extrapolated from mostly third-hand information and his mother's reported reaction to his death and her continued state of ill-health (though the loss of both a husband and a son in such a short space of time could well be too much for any mother to bear).

Brian was the eldest of two sons and if they were in any way true to their Jewish culture, the family system would, by tradition, be characterised by matriarchy. In *Shout!*, Philip Norman describes Brian's close identification with his mother, the '. . . love of refinement, and a feeling for style manifest even as a toddler. He would stand in his mother's bedroom while she got ready to go out, and gravely confer with her about which dress she should wear.'[3] Perhaps evidence of over-involvement and even rumblings of a cross-generational diad? Also, too, an insight into the nature of the relationship between Brian and Stuart whom he perceived as refined and cultured.

In August 1966, on the flight home from San Francisco after The Beatles' last concert, Brian was heard to say repeatedly, 'What am I going to do now? Shall I go back to school and learn something new?' According to Norman, Brian had '. . . lived for them (The Beatles) and through them, with an intensity granted to a few born under his unlucky star. He had loved them, not shamefully, not furtively, but with an idealism which millions found to share. That love was as . . . the parent for his children . . .'[4]

Shortly after his father's death, Brian's mother stayed with him for 10 days in London. During her stay, 'Queenie (Mrs Epstein) would wake him each morning, drawing his bedroom curtains as she used to when he was small, and they would have breakfast together in his room.'[5] Both these adults had sustained a recent and very major loss and yet it would appear that Mrs Epstein, by maintaining her old pattern of parental concern for her son's well-being and with Brian's apparent acquiescence, enabled both of them to avoid their individual expressions of grief.

Both extracts from *Shout!* suggest that Brian, like Stuart and John, moved with ease (and no doubt confusion) across the generational boundary—one moment mother's peer or parental protector, the next moment (even though chronologically an adult) mother's child. With Stuart and John, Brian all too easily inverted his hierarchical role of manager and related as their child.

According to Salvador Minuchin, who introduced the concept of Structural Family Therapy, unresolved mourning is always present in enmeshed family systems, either as a cause or an effect. If correct, my speculation that all three men were raised in family systems that would fall towards the enmeshed end of Minuchin's continuum of family functioning would support my further speculation that all three mothers did not or have not resolved their losses.

In order to have resolved their losses, these mothers would have needed therapeutic help. By the time this became fairly readily available in Britain, Mrs Sutcliffe, Mrs Epstein and Auntie Mimi's identities as 'mother of the late Stuart, Brian or John' may have become too entrenched. The 'gains' of this subordinate identity (i.e. as X's or Y's mother) may have interfered with a wish to be otherwise. The mothers' own possible history of enmeshment may have left them without a sense that they had a choice. Because they remained their families' symptom bearers, they enabled other family members to remain symptom free. These mothers perhaps offered their loss of a primary identity as women as their sacrifice to ensure that, paradoxically, they protected themselves and their families from losing their sons through their prolonged (morbid) expression of grief and loss. The wider systems (i.e. the media) unwittingly ensure that this status quo is maintained by their frequent requests of these women to remain in their roles as 'grieving mothers', requiring them to recall all too familiar anecdotes about their lost sons. Too often, when listening or reading their reminiscences, one notices their heightened sense of recollection, more often recounted in the form of a dialogue as if it happened yesterday. Perhaps it is too much to expect these women not to want to be remembered, for example, as John Lennon's Auntie Mimi—what an identity!

Notes

1.   For the purposes of this article I will regard John Lennon's Auntie Mimi as his 'mother'—not least because she nurtured him as a primary parent, as a 'mother' would from infancy. For the same reason I will refer to Uncle George as if he were John's father.

I have highlighted the mother–son relationship because of its primacy and for the way in which each family depended on this cross-generational diad for its sense of well-being.

2.   Philip Norman, *Shout! The true story of The Beatles* (London: Elm Tree Books, 1981) p. 397

3.   ibid., p. 117

4.   ibid., pp. 277–8

5.   ibid., p. 295

TWO

Ticket to Ride

What songs The Beatles sang . . .*

The Times, 27 December 1963

The outstanding English composers of 1963 must seem to have been John Lennon and Paul McCartney, the talented young musicians from Liverpool whose songs have been sweeping the country since last Christmas, whether performed by their own group, The Beatles, or by the numerous other teams of English troubadours that they also supply with songs.

I am not concerned here with the social phenomenon of Beatlemania, which finds expression in handbags, balloons and other articles bearing the likenesses of the loved ones, or in the hysterical screaming of young girls whenever the Beatle Quartet performs in public, but with the musical phenomenon. For several decades, in fact since the decline of the music-hall, England has taken her popular songs from the United States, either directly or by mimicry. But the songs of Lennon and McCartney are distinctly indigenous in character, the most imaginative and inventive examples of a style that has been developing on Merseyside during the past few years. And there is a nice, rather flattering irony in the news that The Beatles have now become prime favourites in America too.

The strength of character in pop songs seems, and quite understandably, to be determined usually by the number of composers involved; when three or four people are required to make the original tunesmith's work publicly presentable, it is unlikely to retain much individuality or to wear very well. The virtue of The Beatles' repertory is that, apparently, they do it themselves; three of the four are composers, they are versatile instrumentalists, and when they do borrow a song from another repertory, their treatment is idiosyncratic—as when Paul McCartney sings 'Till there was you' from

---

* This article was printed unsigned but has since been attributed to William Mann.

The Music Man, a cool, easy, tasteful version of this ballad, quite without artificial sentimentality.

Their noisy items are the ones that arouse teenagers' excitement. Glutinous crooning is generally out of fashion these days, and even a song about 'Misery' sounds fundamentally quite cheerful; the slow, sad song about 'This boy', which figures prominently in Beatle programmes, is expressively unusual for its lugubrious music, but harmonically it is one of their most intriguing, with its chains of pandiatonic clusters, and the sentiment is acceptable because voiced cleanly and crisply. But harmonic interest is typical of their quicker songs too, and one gets the impression that they think simultaneously of harmony and melody, so firmly are the major tonic sevenths and ninths built into their tunes, and the flat-submediant key-switches, so natural is the Aeolian cadence at the end of 'Not a second time' (the chord progression which ends Mahler's *Song of the Earth*).

Those submediant switches from C major into A-flat major, and to a lesser extent mediant ones (e.g. the octave ascent in the famous 'I want to hold your hand') are a trademark of Lennon–McCartney songs—they do not figure much in other pop repertories, or in The Beatles' arrangements of borrowed material—and show signs of becoming a mannerism. The other trademark of their compositions is a firm and purposeful bass line with a musical life of its own; how Lennon and McCartney divide their creative responsibilities I have yet to discover, but it is perhaps significant that Paul is the bass guitarist of the group. It may also be significant that George Harrison's song 'Don't bother me' is harmonically a good deal more primitive, though it is nicely enough presented.

I suppose it is the sheer loudness of the music that appeals to Beatle admirers (there is something to be heard even through the squeals), and many parents must have cursed the electric guitar's amplification this Christmas—how fresh and euphonious the ordinary guitars sound in The Beatles' version of 'Till there was you'—but parents who are still managing to survive the decibels and, after copious repetition over several months, still deriving some musical pleasure from the overhearing, do so because there is a good deal of variety—oh, so welcome in pop music—about what they sing.

The autocratic but not by any means ungrammatical attitude to tonality (closer to, say, Peter Maxwell Davies's carols in *O Magnum Mysterium* than to Gershwin or Loewe or even Lionel Bart); the exhilarating and often quasi-instrumental vocal duetting, sometimes in scat or in falsetto, behind the melodic line; the melismas with altered vowels ('I saw her yesterday-ee-ay') which have not quite become mannered, and the discreet, sometimes subtle, varieties of instrumentation—a suspicion of piano or organ, a few bars of mouth-organ obbligato, an excursion on the claves or maraccas; the translation of African blues or American Western idioms (in 'Baby, it's you', the Magyar 8/8 metre too) into tough, sensitive Merseyside.

These are some of the qualities that make one wonder with interest what The Beatles, and particularly Lennon and McCartney, will do next, and if America will spoil them or hold on to them, and if their next record will wear as well as the others. They have brought a distinctive and exhilarating flavour into a genre of music that was in danger of ceasing to be music at all.

RICHARD F. SHEPARD

Stokowski talks of something called Beatles

The New York Times, 15 February 1964

In between the majestic rock of Beethoven's Fifth and the melodic roll of Stravinsky's *Firebird*, Leopold Stokowski conducted a dialogue on The Beatles yesterday with teenagers at Carnegie Hall.

From all five boroughs, 2,700 junior high school students and teachers flocked into the hall for each of two concerts, the last of 12 presented by the American Symphony Orchestra in association with the Board of Education under the sponsorship of the Samuel Rubin Foundation.

The youngsters were noisy, but not unruly, as the maestro took time out from the classics—which the audience listened to quietly and applauded enthusiastically—and started his discussion.

'A few nights ago in this hall on this stage'—laughing and some stillborn shrieks—'You know what I'm going to say'—more laughing, loud applause—'Four young men with long hair played, but it was not long hair music. Where did they come from?'

'England,' came a thunderous reply.

'Mars,' shouted a dissident nonconformist.

As the ushers scurried under Mr Stokowski's direction to children he pointed out in the audience, the noise grew, although it did not get out of hand.

'You see,' he continued, 'there are many kinds of music. How many like classical?' A fair but not staggering show of hands. 'How many like rock 'n' roll?' A forest of hands and a rustle of noise. 'I see; 2,600,' Mr Stokowski said.

'There are those who like only popular or only classical,' he said. 'I am one who likes both.'

Mr Stokowski observed that although he had not seen The Beatles a friend had told him that the youngsters made so much noise that The Beatles couldn't be heard.

'Why do you like that music when you make so much noise that you can't hear it?' he asked.

'Because they're so great,' said a dark-haired girl into a microphone.

'If you can't hear them, why are they so great?' the conductor persisted.

'Because they're cuties,' a red-haired girl volunteered. Another girl waved a Beatle banner and another brought out a portrait of The Beatles in a magazine.

'Look what America's coming to, man,' muttered a boy, shaking his head sadly.

'Because they're cute—that's the answer every time,' a teacher said.

In his dressing room after the concert, Mr Stokowski spoke with youngsters from Junior High School 259 in Bay Ridge, Brooklyn.

'You teenagers, I will give you a good idea,' he told them. 'Whatever you enjoy doing, do it. Goodbye.'

Z. Grabkowska, one of the Mazowsze Polish dance troupe who attended the concert to learn about American children, told Mr Stokowski that there was no music like Mozart or Bach.

Mr Stokowski does not resent The Beatles as a musical phenomenon, even sight unseen, although he plans to watch the act on television tomorrow.

'They give the teenagers something that thrills them, a vision,' he said. 'The boys and girls of this age are young men and women looking for something in life that can't always be found, a *joie de vivre*.

'I like anything that makes for self-expression. Life is changing all the time. We are all looking for the vision of ecstasy, of life. I am too.'

GLORIA STEINEM

Beatle with a future

Cosmopolitan, December 1964

In Britain, The Beatles outdraw Queen Elizabeth. In America, they attract bigger crowds than the President and Elizabeth Taylor combined. All over Europe and even in Hong Kong, teenagers turn out in droves whether or not they understand the lyrics. The Beatles have become, quite literally, the single biggest attraction in the world.

Show business experts disagree on the sociology or psychology or simple merchandising behind this success, but they agree on one thing: like every craze from the hula-hoop to the ancient Celts' habit of painting themselves blue, it must come to an end, and probably an abrupt one. At ages 21 to 24, they don't seem to have thought about the problem much, but under pressure of constant questions from reporters, they have come up with a few clues. George Harrison, the youngest Beatle and the only one who shows any interest in the business side of their career, might produce records for other pop music stars. Paul McCartney—at 22, the Beatle with the best looks and on-stage personality—is likely to continue a show business career as a solo. Ringo Starr (born Richard Starkey), the oldest of the four and the prototype of a non-verbal pop musician, hasn't voiced a preference for anything but a future of playing the drums and tossing his eyebrow-length hair. Only John Lennon, 24 and the one married Beatle, has shown signs of a talent outside the hothouse world of musical fadism and teenage worship: he has written a book titled *In His Own Write*—a slender, whimsical collection of anecdotes, poems and Thurber-like drawings—that is in its seventh printing here.

. . . The difficulty of getting to The Beatles at all (one London columnist claimed he had had less trouble interviewing De Gaulle) plus Lennon's extreme reluctance to talk to strangers (he cares, explained Epstein, 'not a fig or a damn or a button for anyone save a tight, close-guarded clique of less than a dozen') have kept him a mystery. Yet he continues to be spoken of as 'the Beatle who will last', 'the intellectual one' and 'a popular hero who, like Sinatra, gained fame through teenage adulation, but can keep it through talent'.

Will he last?

There is no sure answer, but an observation of the odd world The Beatles inhabit, a few hours with that 'close-guarded clique' and some words from Mr Lennon himself offer a few clues.

By the end of their recent, 32-day American tour, The Beatles had given concerts in 24 cities, grossed a record $2 million, spent two days relaxing on their first American ranch, flown back to New York via carefully guarded chartered plane ('like,' as one reporter put it, 'a troop movement in wartime or a shipment of gold to Fort Knox'), been spirited by helicopter and car into Manhattan's Paramount Theatre, and were getting ready for their last chore before returning to London: a half-hour performance as the climax of a show benefiting United Cerebral Palsy and Retarded Infants Services, Inc.

Tickets were expensive . . . but the theatre was sold out and screaming, non-ticket-holding fans had forced police to set up barricades near the Paramount at nine o'clock in the morning.

Those fans—the thousands of weeping, screeching girls—surrounded the theatre completely, and wading through them was a process so slow that it was possible to interview a few on the way. Most of them seemed to be lank-haired, single-minded, under 16 and carrying homemade placards ('I Love You, Ringo', 'If You Can't Marry Me, George Please Just *Look* at Me'), record jackets to be autographed or photographs of their favourite. (Feather Schwartz, ex-secretary of The Beatles fan club of America, discovered that the average Beatle fan is 13 to 17 years old, of middle-class background, white, Christian, a B-minus student, weighs 105 to 140 pounds, owns a transistor radio with an earplug attachment and has Beatle photographs plastered all over her room.) One girl paused in her effort to climb over a five-foot-high police barricade to tell me that she was 'crazy wild about John' because he was 'utterly fab'. Another said she was 'passionately in love with Ringo', and had saved $25 dollars of her allowance to get there from Pennsylvania. Tears were streaming down her face; she had yelled herself hoarse at passing taxis, unaware that her beloved had entered the Paramount secretly, two hours before. Would she go out with Ringo if he asked her? Would she like to marry him? She looked startled. 'I don't think so,' she said. 'I hardly know him.'

When I finally reached a harried policeman, he was turning away a pretty blonde with a letter of accreditation from a high school newspaper in New Jersey. He turned away my press credentials with the same: 'We got orders, lady. No press,' and shoved me back into the crowd. A girl with braces on her teeth and a life-size picture of John pinned to her chest was sympathetic. 'They turned away a guy who said he was from *The New York Times*,' she said soothingly, 'and boy was *he* mad.'

Forty-five minutes and several pleadings later, a policeman let me in the stage door ('OK lady, I guess you're too persistent to be a nut') and warned me I was on my own. That left only five flights of stairs, six policemen and three private guards between me and Bess Coleman, the representative of The Beatles' New York office who was very apologetic ('I told all the policemen I saw to let you through but there are *so many*') and assured me that my interview with John Lennon was set.

Miss Coleman ushered me into a room where I was to wait and left me with its assorted occupants: a blonde girl with her hair in purple plastic curlers, four men with black suits and briefcases, a young man in corduroy pants and Beatle-length hair and a pretty matron in a cocktail dress. I walked to the window and looked down. A roar like the distant sound of an Army–Navy football game came up from the crowd five storeys below. 'You better not stand there, honey,' the blonde girl said kindly. 'They go crazy when they see somebody, *anybody*. The police told us to stay away from the windows.' The pretty matron introduced herself as a writer for a national women's magazine. She had been on most of the month-long tour, she said, but had not yet been able to interview one of The Beatles: if I got to see John, might she sit in and listen? I told her she was welcome to come if it turned out to be a public interview, but that I hoped to talk with him privately. The Beatle-haired young man—identified by the matron as Neil Aspinall, The Beatles' road manager—broke his consultation with the men in black suits and smiled. 'Well, then,' he said with a Liverpudlian lilt, 'we're very optimistic now, aren't we?'

In the hall, while looking for reassurance and Miss Coleman, I discovered two more roomsful of waiting people, glimpsed Ed Sullivan disappearing into a third, answered a ringing pay phone ('Please tell Paul McCartney that he doesn't know me but I'm very pretty and I'll be in the first booth at the Astor drugstore after the show') and was given a paper cup filled with The Beatles' favourite drink, an equal-parts combination of warm Coca-Cola and Scotch. The Beatles, Miss Coleman assured me, were much too exhausted to see anyone before the show; would I mind waiting until afterward? She introduced me to a reed-thin, shirt-sleeved young man named Derek Taylor—head of publicity and public relations for The Beatles—sat us down in the room, now deserted by everyone but the matron, and asked Taylor to turn the other way while she changed her dress.

Eyes to the wall, Taylor explained that they were all exhausted from the long tour of one-night stands and sleeping only on the chartered plane ('In Kansas City, we stayed in a hotel; the next day the manager was offered $750 for one of The Beatles' sheets'), and that the two-day ranch vacation ('The Beatles rode and fished and stayed up all night playing poker') hadn't helped much. Though the ranch was 13,000 acres in the middle of Missouri and 'surrounded only by the tiniest hamlets', local disc jockeys had learned of The Beatles' presence. By midnight of the first day, all roads to the ranch were jammed and carloads of teenagers had arrived from St Louis. And, though Neil Aspinall had learned by experience how to move The Beatles ('The plane stops at the end of the runway; we use special cars and drivers to bash up to hotel and theatre entrances, sometimes we use tunnels . . . There's really no precedent for this sort of thing'), Ringo had had his shirt torn off, and Brian Epstein was once nearly pushed in front of an oncoming train.

. . . It was time for The Beatles' performance. Everyone crowded into the hall, looking expectantly at the room in which The Beatles had been 'incommunicado' and 'resting', the same room into which I had seen Ed Sullivan disappear. Paul McCartney came out first, looking soft-faced and vulnerable as a choirboy. George Harrison and Ringo Starr followed animated and laughing. John Lennon moved quickly behind them, but his face was stoic and aloof behind his dark glasses (the face that inspired a London journalist to write, 'It has the fear-neither-God-nor-man quality of a Renaissance painter's aristocrat'). Behind Lennon came three chic young girls, two brunettes and a blonde, in their late teens or early twenties. McCartney jerked his head toward them as he got in the elevator and told some of his staff members to 'look after the birds now, won't ya'.

I turned to Derek Taylor, about to comment that—what with Ed Sullivan and these three—The Beatles hadn't been so incommunicado after all, but Taylor was already looking harassed and apologetic. 'Look,' he said. 'You've got to be patient with them. If you just come to the party they're having afterwards at the hotel, I'm sure John will talk to you.' We were challenged by a policeman but Taylor showed a lapel pass and we got to the elevator. 'You'll be more sure of getting to The Beatles,' he said helpfully, 'if you stick with the birds.'

The Beatles' entourage crowded together in the wings, and I talked to the birds. Were they working for The Beatles or interviewing them? No, they were just friends. 'We met The Beatles at a press conference in Philadelphia,' said the pretty blonde, 'that's where we're from.' Two of them wore wool suits with short culotte skirts. They all looked as if they had stepped from the pages of a teenage fashion magazine, and one carried a comb and hairbrush which she used frequently and passed around to the others. 'Well, two of us had met them,' corrected the friendly blonde, 'and this time we brought along a friend.'

Out in the dark, crowded theatre, we stood by the apron of the stage and watched the show: sobs, shouts and piercing screams ('I'm over here, Ringo. *Please!*') drowned out all but an occasional drumbeat. Girls were hanging precariously from the two large balconies and standing on the arms of their chairs. Behind me, a woman held her six-year-old on her shoulders and four girls with linked arms were jumping up and down in time to the music and crying.

Taylor stood next to me and tapped my arm just before each chorus of screams reached a crescendo. 'You can always tell,' he explained calmly. 'It happens just after one of them tosses his hair or lifts his guitar.' What about the strange, firecracker bursts of light? Was that part of the lighting effect? 'No,' he smiled. 'It's the flashes from everyone taking pictures.' Three overweight, poorly dressed girls were sobbing and calling out as they pressed against us, and a fourth girl with an exceedingly large nose was waving a banner that said, 'Georgie, You Are My Dream'. 'Sometimes,' said Taylor, 'when we pick a few girls to come in and get autographs, we pick pretty ones like those.' He nodded at the birds who were watching the stage with secret smiles. 'But I usually try to pick the ones with braces on their teeth and acne. Meeting a Beatle helps. And they can impress their friends.'

Ringo tossed his hair, and a fresh wave of screams went up. Paul smiled and looked endearing. John lifted his guitar, setting off more screams, but he sang without smiling ('That's because,' fellow Liverpudlian Neil Aspinall had once explained to a reporter, 'he's giving you his soul when he sings.'). The crush was so great that our arms were pinned to our sides, but a path suddenly cleared as if by magic, and the slim, elegant figure of Brian Epstein—the 30-year-old mastermind behind The Beatles' success—strode to the end of it, leaving a lingering trail of shaving scent. The girl with the banner had been pushed out of the way. 'I don't *like* Englishmen,' she said, and resumed her screaming. The three birds, who never screamed, looked at her with curiosity. One began idly to brush her hair with her eyes glued to the stage. 'How do you like The Beatles?' the blonde shouted into my ear. 'Fine,' I said. 'Just fine.'

The Beatles were leaving for London early the next morning. That, plus the fact that several Manhattan hotels had turned them down, brought them to the Riviera Motor Inn at Kennedy Airport. The rooms were small, barely big enough for a bureau, twin beds and a television set but they had commandeered a whole floor and there were policemen guarding the halls. Our room was jammed with carts of Scotch and Coca-Cola, trays of sandwiches and two photographers, the young ladies from Philadelphia, a tall girl who had followed The Beatles from San Francisco, several journalists who had been on the Beatle tour, a pretty airline stewardess in a very lowcut dress who was acting as hostess, and, occasionally, Neil Aspinall and Derek Taylor. Two of The Beatles were in other rooms, but Ringo Starr and Lennon were in the one adjoining us with the door locked. It was opened only to admit Aspinall, Taylor, one or two other selected young men and liquor.

At three o'clock, I had still not seen a Beatle, but I had spent two hours interviewing the entourage, who told me some facts of Lennon's life. . . . Everyone agreed on one thing: Lennon was certainly the most talented in diverse ways, and therefore the most likely to succeed creatively even after the Beatle craze was over. As Epstein had written in his autobiography, 'Had there been no Beatles and no Epstein participation, John would have emerged from the mass of population as a man to reckon with.' 'He's untutored,' said Taylor, 'but he's a natural writer. He loves the sound of words. He's an original.'

The door to the next room opened and Taylor, who seemed to remember everybody else's problems in spite of his own exhaustion ('I'm worried about him,' confided the matron, 'he's slept hardly at all for five days'), ushered me in and introduced me. It was 4 a.m. and the small group—Lennon, Ringo, American folk singer Bob Dylan, Dylan's manager, the tall girl from San Francisco, photographer Bob Freeman who designed the titles of The Beatles' movies and Lennon's book, and an unidentified, bearded journalist—were in the combined grip of fatigue and a crisis involving Brian Epstein. Taylor, it seemed, had told The Beatles that Epstein had refused to let the three birds ride in his limousine, and Epstein was furious at Taylor.

Lennon received me calmly ('Oh, I know about that article') and went on giving desultory advice to Taylor on the care and handling of Epstein. ('He's all right, but he doesn't understand people having a few laughs, not even me laughs with me wife.') The conversation dwindled into silence. Would Lennon come with me for an interview? 'Oh, well now, I don't have anything to say. My friends and those other articles will tell you all.' The voice was musical, but the face behind the sunglasses was impervious.

Wouldn't he like to set the record straight, to check the information I already had? 'No, I don't think so.' Silence. The tall girl leaned over to Lennon and told him that his skin was looking mottled again. 'I know,' he said and looked embarrassed. 'It's nerves.'

The phone rang several times and no one answered. I picked it up. A Princess Mary somebody-or-other was calling from a phone booth. Could she please speak to a Beatle? I asked Lennon if he would like to speak to the Princess. 'No,' he said. I hung up.

Taylor came back from a conference with Aspinall about whether or not he should leave his post as publicity chief and go back to being a newspaperman ('The Beatles are fine,' said Taylor, 'but their life is unbearable') and asked Lennon if there wasn't something he could do about Paul who had barricaded his door and gone to bed without saying goodbye to his friend from Philly. 'She's rather upset,' Taylor explained. 'After all, Paul did make a big thing of her and now he won't even say goodbye.' 'Look,' Lennon said patiently, 'Paul is Paul and nothing's going to change him.' Ringo, in a purple silk shirt with white polka dots, shifted his weight mournfully. 'Always worrying about people,' he said.

The phone rang again. The Princess, now at her home phone and reduced to saying that she was a friend of The Animals, hoped very much she could speak with The Beatles and invite them to an island hotel. 'No,' said Lennon, 'hang up.' 'Don't answer the phone,' counselled the bearded journalist. 'You can't answer all the calls around here, you'd go crazy.'

Wouldn't Lennon answer any interview questions at all? 'I don't think so,' he said and addressed the journalist. 'You ought to get out of your hotel room, see a little more of our country, beautiful monuments and all that. See the Statue of Liberace.' It was a good imitation of an interview, and we all laughed. 'Statue of Liberace is good,' said Bob Freeman. 'Is that the first time you've used that?'

At that point, Lennon was staring into his drink. Ringo observed meditatively that he didn't see why policemen had to stand right in front of the door, and that in one hotel, the police had stolen souvenirs from their rooms. More silence. It was 5 a.m.

I told Lennon that I understood how tired he must be of answering questions, and began to say goodbye. He looked surprised. Aspinall came back, explaining comfortingly to Taylor that Brian Epstein had once slapped him, but that was just one of the manager's moods that had to be understood. . . . 'Listen,' said Freeman kindly, nodding toward me, 'she's all right. She's a friend of friends.' The effect on Lennon was as magical as an OK from the Mafia. He smiled for the first time, and told me not to leave. 'But she's the press,' Ringo muttered sceptically. 'You see,' said Taylor reasonably, 'they've been exploited so much that it's hard for them to trust anyone.'

Would Lennon like to write another book?

'I would, but you can't plan it. I just put things down and stuff them in my pockets until I have enough.'

Had he been influenced by the authors he was compared to?

'I mean to read Joyce but I never have. I got a laugh from all those intellectuals saying I was like him. I've read some Thurber stories though. And *Alice in Wonderland*.'

We checked a few biographical details and discussed their second movie, which they plan to begin in February. ('I wouldn't write the script for it. I wouldn't know how.') He now lives just outside London with his wife and infant son. He owns a Rolls-Royce. (How does it feel?

'Great!') He likes America and doesn't like New Zealand. He loves the Crazy Gang kind of comedy, and he adores Peter Sellers. (It's true that he improvised some of the first film's dialogue, including the interchange between an Old School Britisher and a Beatle. Britisher: 'I fought the war for your sort.' Beatle: 'And aren't you sorry now.') He has no plans to retire while the money is coming in, unless the life should become unbearable. What about reports that, since the Establishment has accepted them, British teenagers have gone on to other groups? 'That's all the same. We'll just be us.' He is enthusiastic about rival groups, The Rolling Stones and The Animals. How much money has he made? 'A lot.' Has success changed him? 'Yes, it's made me richer.' Does he aspire to change socially? 'No, I'm from Liverpool.'

Would he like to be a writer?

'I don't know. I guess so. I write what I think of, when I think of it.'

Was he surprised by his good reviews?

'Yes, I love those hellishly intellectual things they say, but I'd keep on writing whether they said them or not.'

What will he do when there are no more Beatles?

'That's the question everybody asks us, but I'll tell you this. I know this thing can't last. I'm saving the money. And I've got a lot of things I want to do.'

I thanked Taylor who, having made the decision to quit the life of The Beatles and become a newspaperman again, looked relieved and, for the first time, cheerful.

I thanked Lennon, who looked worried, and said, 'I hope you're as true as you seem.'

I said goodbye to the three birds who still sat in the adjoining room. Two were stretched out on the bed and a third was applying eye shadow. ('Women,' Lennon had once told a reporter, 'should be obscene and not heard.') They smiled their Mona Lisa smiles.

A fat policeman, yawning and red-eyed, said goodbye to me.

Outside it was dawn, but four girls were sitting patiently on the curbstone. Had I seen The Beatles, had I touched them? I said yes. A girl in an outgrown raincoat stretched out a Beatle photograph. 'Here,' she said, 'Sign this for me.'

PAUL JOHNSON

The menace of Beatlism

New Statesman, 28 February 1964

Mr William Deedes[1] is an Old Harrovian, a member of the cabinet and the minister in charge of the government's information services. Mr Deedes, it will be remembered, was one of those five ministers who interviewed Mr Profumo on that fateful night and were convinced by him that he had not slept with Miss Keeler. Now any public relations man, even a grand one who sits in the cabinet, can use a touch of credulity; but even so I remember thinking at the time: 'If Deedes can believe that, he'll believe anything.' And indeed he does! Listen to him on the subject of The Beatles:

> They herald a cultural movement among the young which may become part of the history of our time . . . For those with eyes to see it, something important and heartening is happening here. The young are rejecting some of the sloppy standards of their elders, by which far too much of our output has been governed in recent years . . . they have discerned dimly that in a world of automation, declining craftsmanship and increased leisure, something of this kind is essential to restore the human instinct to excel at something and the human faculty of discrimination.

Incredible as it may seem, this was not an elaborate attempt at whimsy, but a serious address, delivered to a meeting of the City of London Young Conservatives, and heard in respectful silence. Not a voice was raised to point out that the Emperor wasn't wearing a stitch. The Beatles phenomenon, in fact, illustrates one of my favourite maxims: that if something becomes big enough and popular enough—and especially commercially profitable enough—solemn men will not be lacking to invest it with virtues. So long as The Beatles were just another successful showbiz team the pillars of society could afford to ignore them, beyond bestowing the indulgent accolade of a slot in the Royal Variety Performance. But then came the shock announcement that they were earning £6,250,000 a year—and, almost simultaneously, they got the stamp of approval from America.

This was quite a different matter: at once they became not only part of the export trade but an electorally valuable property. Sir Alec Home promptly claimed credit for them, and was as promptly accused by Mr Wilson of political clothes-stealing. Conservative candidates have been officially advised to mention them whenever possible in their speeches. The Queen expressed concern about the length of Ringo's hair. Young diplomats at our Washington embassy fought for their autographs. A reporter described them as 'superb ambassadors for Britain'. It is true that the Bishop of Woolwich has not yet asked them to participate in one of his services, but the invitation cannot be long delayed. And, while waiting for the definitive analysis of their cultural significance by Messrs Raymond Williams and Richard Hoggart we have Mr Deedes' contribution on behalf of the cabinet.

Of course, our society has long been brainwashed in preparation for this apotheosis of inanity. For more than two decades now, more and more intellectuals have turned their backs on their trade and begun to worship at the shrine of 'pop culture'. Nowadays, if you confess that you don't know the difference between Dizzy Gillespie and Fats Waller (and, what is more, don't care) you are liable to be accused of being a fascist.

To buttress their intellectual self-esteem, these treasonable clerks have evolved an elaborate cultural mythology about jazz, which purports to distinguish between various periods, tendencies and schools. The subject has been smeared with a respectable veneer of academic scholarship, so that now you can overhear grown men, who have been expensively educated, engage in heated argument on the respective techniques of Charlie Parker and Duke Ellington. You can see writers of distinction, whose grey hairs testify to years spent in the cultural vineyard, squatting on the bare boards of malodorous caverns, while through the haze of smoke, sweat and cheap cosmetics comes the monotonous braying of savage instruments.

One might, I suppose, attribute such intellectual treachery to the fact that, in jazz circles, morals are easy, sex is cheap and there is a permissive attitude to the horrors of narcotics. Men are, alas, sometimes willing to debauch their intellects for such rewards. But I doubt if this is the real reason. The growing public approval of anti-culture is itself, I think, a reflection of the new cult of youth. Bewildered by a rapidly changing society, excessively fearful of becoming out of date, our leaders are increasingly turning to young people as guides and mentors—or, to vary the metaphor, as geiger-counters to guard them against the perils of mental obsolescence. If youth likes jazz, then it must be good, and clever men must rationalise this preference in intellectually respectable language. Indeed, whatever youth likes must be good: the supreme crime, in politics and culture alike, is not to be 'with it'. Even the most unlikely mascots of the Establishment are now drifting with the current: Mr Henry Brooke,[2] for instance, finds himself appointing to the latest Home Office committee the indispensable teenager, who has, what is more, the additional merit of being a delinquent.

Before I am denounced as a reactionary fuddy-duddy, let us pause an instant and see exactly what we mean by this 'youth'. Both TV channels now run weekly programmes in which popular records are played to teenagers and judged. While the music is performed, the cameras linger savagely over the faces of the audience. What a bottomless chasm of vacuity they reveal! The huge faces, bloated with cheap confectionery and smeared with chain-store makeup, the open, sagging mouths and glazed eyes, the hands mindlessly drumming in time to the music, the broken stiletto heels, the shoddy, stereotyped, 'with-it' clothes: here apparently, is a collective portrait of a generation enslaved by a commercial machine. Leaving a TV studio recently, I stumbled into the exodus from one of these sessions. How pathetic and listless they seemed: young girls, hardly any more than 16, dressed as adults and already lined up as fodder for exploitation. Their eyes came to life only when one of their grotesque idols—scarcely older than they—made a brief appearance, before a man in a camel-hair coat hustled him into a car. Behind this image of 'youth', there are, evidently, some shrewd older folk at work.

And what of the 'culture' which is served up to these pitiable victims? According to Mr Deedes, 'the aim of The Beatles and their rivals is first class of its kind. Failure to attain it is spotted and criticised ruthlessly by their many highly-discriminating critics.' I wonder if Mr Deedes has ever taken the trouble to listen to any of this music? On the Saturday TV shows, the merits of the new records are discussed by panels of 'experts', many of whom seem barely more literate or articulate than the moronic ranks facing them. They are asked to judge each record a 'hit' or a 'miss', but seem incapable of explaining why they have reached their verdict. Occasionally one of the 'experts' betrays some slight acquaintance with the elementals of music and makes what is awesomely described as a 'technical' point: but when such merit is identified in a record, this is usually found to be a reason for its certain commercial failure.

In any case, merit has nothing to do with it. The teenager comes not to hear but to participate in a ritual, a collective grovelling to gods who are themselves blind and empty. 'Throughout the performance,' wrote one observer, 'it was impossible to hear anything above the squealing except the beat of Ringo's drums.' Here, indeed, is 'a new cultural movement': music which not only cannot be heard but does not *need* to be heard. As such I have no doubt that it is, in truth, 'first class of its kind'.

If The Beatles and their like were in fact what the youth of Britain wanted, one might well despair. I refuse to believe it—and so I think will any other intelligent person who casts his or her mind back far enough. What were we doing at 16? I remember the drudgery of Greek prose and the calculus, but I can also remember reading the whole of Shakespeare and Marlowe, writing poems and plays and stories. It is a marvellous age, an age of intense mental energy and discovery. Almost every week one found a fresh idol—Milton, Wagner, Debussy, Matisse, El Greco, Proust—some, indeed, to be subsequently toppled from the pantheon, but all springing from the mainstream of European culture. At 16, I and my friends heard our first performance of Beethoven's Ninth Symphony; I can remember the excitement even today. We would not have wasted 30 seconds of our precious time on The Beatles and their ilk.

Are teenagers different today? Of course not. Those who flock round The Beatles, who scream themselves into hysteria, whose vacant faces flicker over the TV screen, are the least fortunate of their generation, the dull, the idle, the failures: their existence, in such large numbers, far from being a cause for ministerial congratulation, is a fearful indictment of our education system, which in 10 years of schooling can scarcely raise them to literacy. What Mr Deedes fails to perceive is that the core of the teenage group—the boys and girls who will be the real leaders and creators of society tomorrow—never go near a pop concert. They are, to put it simply, too busy. They are educating themselves. They are in the process of inheriting the culture which, despite Beatlism or any other mass-produced mental opiate, will continue to shape our civilisation. To use Mr Deedes' own phrase, though not in the sense he meant it, they are indeed 'rejecting some of the sloppy standards of their elders'. Of course, if many of these elders in responsible positions surrender to the Gadarene Complex and seek to elevate the worst things in our society into the best, their task will be made more difficult. But I believe that, despite the antics of cabinet ministers with election nerves, they will succeed.

BEN PERRICK

Lennon's literary lunch

I have to confess that I feel somewhat out of place as a contributor to this volume. I am in no way qualified to assess John Lennon's talents as a musician, or to comment on the complications and contradictions of his life. I have merely to tell the story of the Foyles Literary Luncheon held in Lennon's honour to celebrate the publication of *In His Own Write*.

The suggestion for the luncheon came to Christina Foyle from G. Wren Howard, the chairman of Jonathan Cape, the book's publisher. It was held at the Dorchester Hotel on 18 April 1964. Osbert Lancaster, the cartoonist, agreed to take the chair and the top table guests included Yehudi Menuhin, Mary Quant, Alma Cogan, Dora Bryan, Wilfrid Bramble, Lionel Bart, Arthur Askey, Cicely Courtneidge, Giles, Harry Secombe, Victor Silvester, Colin Wilson and Helen Shapiro. John's fellow Beatles were invited but did not attend.

On the Sunday prior to the lunch, Cape had a small launch party in their Bloomsbury offices and I attended with my daughter, a great Beatles fan. We had a long conversation with John and we both found him immensely charming. He asked me about the forthcoming luncheon and I told him that there would be about 600 guests and that everyone was looking forward to seeing him. He appeared quite happy at the prospect of making a short speech, although he claimed that he couldn't imagine what he would say. I assured him that, although large, Foyles luncheons were always pleasantly informal and that he had no cause for worry; he appeared to be well satisfied. I was much impressed by his gentleness and modesty.

The day before the lunch I had a telephone call from Brian Epstein. 'About this luncheon for John Lennon,' he said. 'I have to let you know that he'll not be speaking.' Mr Epstein added that, if we wished, he would fill the gap and speak about John and The Beatles. I reported this to Christina Foyle and although we were both taken aback, we assumed that what Epstein meant was that John didn't feel up to making a *long* speech. We felt quite confident that he would say a few words.

That evening, I was dining with Robert Pitman, the book critic and columnist, and his wife, Pat. Pat knew Lennon and when I mentioned Brian Epstein's phone call she said: 'John Lennon is a very determined young man and if he says he will not speak, you can be sure that nothing will make him change his mind.' She proved to be right.

On the day of the lunch, John arrived at the Dorchester in a most affable mood. He thanked Christina Foyle for hosting the function and all seemed well. He made no mention of not wishing to speak but during the meal he confided to the chairman that he did feel nervous. Sir Osbert made his introductory speech as planned. He said: 'At John Lennon's request, I must pay a tribute to his Beatles colleagues. I have only, alas, seen them through the medium of the television screen. In the Royal Variety Show they shone out like a good deed in a naughty world. They have re-established something pretty rare—something that has the same measure of success as the old English music-hall; an accord between the stage and the audience. They represent, however different their methods may be, the genuine strength of English entertainment far more successfully than rows of ladies and gentlemen tramping about with bustles and false whiskers. Therefore, it gives me great pleasure to propose the toast of one of The Beatles today—the one who has produced his first book. I find his book enormously provocative. Its message comes through straight and clear.' John Lennon then half-rose from his chair, murmured 'Thank you and bless you' to the audience and sat down again. There was some slight feeling of bewilderment but the toastmaster quickly called upon Brian Epstein to speak.

It said a great deal for John Lennon's charm and charisma that he fully retained his audience's affection. As they later queued for him to sign copies of his book, they showed little sign of disappointment and John himself seemed perfectly content.

In later years, when Lennon had established himself as a confident and competent public speaker, eager and willing to express his views on most of the world's problems, it was difficult to explain his reticence at the Foyles luncheon. But I have known many celebrities before and since that time who have experienced enormous nervousness at the prospect of speaking in public and I can well appreciate John Lennon's qualms.

I never met John Lennon again but in those years when his whole appearance and personality seemed to be transformed, I always recalled that fresh-faced young man at the Jonathan Cape launch party. That's the John Lennon I like to remember.

TOM WOLFE

A highbrow under all that hair?

Book Week, 3 May 1964

First off, about 100 years ago, there was Artemus Ward, the American genius-savage, who opened his first lecture in London by pursing his lips upcountry Maine-style and twiddling his thumbs until the audience began stomping on the floor and hooting, whereupon he eyed them all and said, 'If the awjince has ceased interruptin', I will corntinoo my discourse'. That went over so well, they had him writing dialect American for *Punch* until the day he died in the West End of tuberculosis and fatigue.

Next came Joaquin Miller, the Wild West poet, America's first professional Bohemian, who went through the receiving lines of Mayfair with his beard down to his sternum and his riding chaps flying shaggy with goat hair from his hip sockets to his boots. He was hailed as a primitive Prometheus of the New World.

Then came Mark Twain, guying his linen vests and playing naive like a fox, and so on and so on until Brendan Behan, the Irishman, who was invited to almost all the parties even long after he had demolished half of them like a Samson with flailing elbows and roaring-drunk Irish songs.

And today, Loud Allmarshy, as James Joyce used to say, yonder in the parlou⸱ stands another one, another genius-savage—John Lennon, one of the four rock-and-roll performers, The Beatles.

As Lennon tells it, he started writing these stories, poems, fables, playlets, parodies, and doing drawings to go with them, at night after the shows, in the dressing rooms, when the shrieks of The Beatles' lanuginous epopts were still warm and the cords of the electric bass and two electric guitars had barely been unplugged. Barely had the manuscript been delivered to the British publisher, Jonathan Cape, before the London–New York literary grapevine had it that underneath the layer of ciliation that had descended over Lennon's forehead like the ice age was nestled the brain of a man who wrote like Edward Lear, Lewis Carroll and Joyce, or at least like Joyce wrote in *Finnegans Wake*, and who drew like a cross between James Thurber and Paul Klee. The critics agreed. The London *Times Literary Supplement* said of the book, 'It is worth the attention of anyone who fears for the impoverishment of the English language and the British imagination.'

Literary London, from parlour to arty mews—has been one great wide open door for noble primitives, even though London literati still live in the mental atmosphere of the 19th-century aristocracy, in the world of the universities, nutty sherry, curly Shelley hair, parlour floor libraries with trestle ladders, and mandarin wit. The enthusiasm for genius-savages has been in part a guilty sympathy for the proles and primitives and in part a romantic awe of raw vitality. Nevertheless, the case of John Lennon is exceptional. He is one of the few Englishmen whom English literati have hailed as a genius of the lower crust. He comes out of the very vortex of something intellectuals all over the West have begun to turn to as a new fashion in artistic taste: namely, mass culture, which has been the material, in painting, for the genre known as 'pop art'. The pop artists sit on the floor wearing Levis and Zorrie sandals in the same old calcimined lofts painting pictures of comic strips, tail fins, motel archways, tuxedo ads, housing development floor plans. But Lennon steps right out of mass culture, the 'Beatlemania', without benefit of a middle man, we are assured, and becomes the artist himself, writing stories such as this one about a marijuana (Indian hemp) party:

> Dressed in my teenold brown sweaty I easily micked with crown at Neville Club a seemy hole. Soon all but soon people accoustic me saying such thing as
> 'Where the charge man?' All of a southern I notice boils and girks sitting in hubbered lumps smoking Hernia taking Odeon and going very high. Somewhere 4ft high but he had Indian Hump which he grew in his sleep. Puffing and globbering they drugged theyselves rampling or dancing with wild abdomen, stubbing in wild postumes amongst themselves.
> They seemed olivier to the world about them. One girk was revealing them all over the place to rounds of bread and applause. Shocked and mazed I pulled on my rubber stamp heady for the door.
> 'Do you kindly mind stop shoveing,' a brough voice said.
> 'Who think you are?' I retired smiling wanly.
> 'I'm in charge,' said the brough but heavy voice.
> 'How high the moon?' cried another, and the band began to play.
> A coloured man danced by eating a banana, or somebody.
> I drudged over hopping to be noticed. He iced me warily saying 'French or Foe'.
> 'Foe' I cried taking him into jeapardy.

This is nonsense writing, but one has only to review the literature of nonsense to see how well Lennon has brought it off. While some of his homonyms are gratuitous word play, many others have not only double meanings but a double edge.

His inspiration in verse seems to be Lewis Carroll. Carroll wrote,

> Twas brillig, and the slithy toves
>   Did gyre and gimble in the wabe:
> All mimsy were the borogroves
>   And the mome raths outgrabe.

Lennon writes,

> Thorg hilly grove and burly ive,
> Big daleys grass and tree
> We clobber ever gallup
> Deaf Ted, Danoota, and me.

But Lennon adds an anarchic cynicism that, for better or worse, goes beyond Carroll's kind of jabberwocky:

With faithful frog beside us,
Big mighty club are we
The battle scab and frisky dyke
Deaf Ted, Danoota, and me.

He seems to take the general format for his stories, fables, playlets, poems and drawings from a British humorist named Spike Milligan. But the underlying bitterness of much of what Lennon writes about marriage and family life, for example, as well as his Joycean excursions into language fantasies, are something else altogether.

The intimations of Joyce—the mimicry of prayers, liturgies, manuals and grammars, the mad homonyms, especially biting ones such as 'Loud' for 'Lord', which both use—are what have most intrigued literati here and in England.

. . . Lennon is today, of course, a rich man, and his book will make him still richer. The initial printing in England, 50,000 copies, was sold the first day. Simon and Schuster has a first printing, reportedly, of 90,000 in the US.

These figures, of course, mean almost nothing other than that here is a book by a Beatle. The time to watch will be next time around. Nonsense humour is a bit of an easy crutch, even for James Joyce. John Lennon's real test will come when he turns loose his wild inventiveness and bitter slant upon a heavier literary form.

Lennon's near-literacy

from: The Automation Debate, House of Commons (19 June 1964)

At 12.48 pm **Mr Charles Curran** (Conservative, Uxbridge) rose to move,

That this House, recognising the social consequences that follow when automation increases production by using a smaller labour force and when people below a minimum standard of ability and education may consequently find it hard to obtain employment, calls on Her Majesty's Government to state their policy for improving still further the educational facilities provided for less gifted children who may otherwise be excluded from an automated labour market.

. . . I do not want to see—none of us does—a large mass of people in this country with great difficulties in communication. It is very undesirable politically to have an electorate with a sizeable part of it outside the reach of any arguments except the crudest and most simplified assertions. It seems to me to be socially necessary, as well as necessary in terms of economics, that we should do a great deal more than we are doing in some parts of the country to provide for children in secondary modern schools a kind of education which is not basically vocational, not basically practical, but is—I will not run away from the word—academic.

Let me try to convey to the House one of the consequences of not providing this kind of education for the kind of children about whom we are talking. I want to quote an expert whose name is famous not only here, but throughout the world. He is perhaps almost the most celebrated living Englishman. His name is John Lennon and he is one of The Beatles. I have never seen or heard The Beatles, but I have been very interested indeed to read a book by John Lennon, published in America and, I believe, in this country. It is called *In His Own Write*.

The book contains a number of poems and fairy stories written by Lennon. These tell a great deal about the education he received in Liverpool. He explains that he was born there in 1940 and attended various schools, where he could not pass examinations. I would like to quote one of the poems. It is one that the Ministry of Education and Science might well distribute to every member of its staff concerned with the kind of children we are discussing. It is called 'Deaf Ted, Danoota, and me'.

I will quote three verses from it:

'Never shall we partly stray,
Fast stirrup all we three
Fight the battle mighty sword
Deaf Ted, Danoota, and me.

Thorg Billy grows and Burnley ten,
And Aston Villa three
We clobber ever gallup
Deaf Ted, Danoota, and me.

So if you hear a wondrous sight,
Am blutter or at sea,
Remember whom the mighty say
Deaf Ted, Danoota, and me.'

I quote that poem not because of its literary merit, but because one can see from it, as from other poems and stories in the book, two things about John Lennon: he has a feeling for words and story telling and he is in a state of pathetic near-literacy. He seems to have picked up bits of

Tennyson, Browning and Robert Louis Stevenson while listening with one ear to the football results on the wireless.

The book suggests to me a boy who, on the evidence of these writings, should have been given an education which would have enabled him to develop the literary talent that he appears to have. I do not know whether my Honourable Friend the Joint Under-Secretary of State can tell us anything about what kind of school this Beatle went to. The volume from which I have quoted strikes me as singularly pathetic and touching.

The boy appears to be a sort of throwback to H. G. Wells's 'Mr Polly', who was brought up in much the same fashion and who was also a boy with a love for and ability with words which he was unable to get developed in school so that, when he was grown up, he talked about 'Sesquipedarian verbijooce'. 'Mr Polly' went to school nearly 100 years ago, but it seems that the kind of education that made him talk like that was still being supplied in Liverpool when John Lennon was at school in the 1950s. I would like my Honourable Friend to tell us what the secondary modern schools of Liverpool are like now. What sort of education is being provided for that sort of boy at present? . . .

At 1.32 pm **Mr Norman Miscampbell** (Conservative, Blackpool, North) rose to speak.

We have had a very interesting opening to this debate, a stimulating new view about automation. I should like to follow some of the views which have been thrown out this morning by my Honourable Friend the Member for Uxbridge (Mr Curran).

. . . I was interested in my Honourable Friend's mention of The Beatles. It is unfair to say that Lennon of The Beatles was not well educated. I cannot say which, but three of the four went to grammar school and as a group are highly intelligent, highly articulate and highly engaging.

I think that we would draw the wrong conclusions if we thought that the success which they are having came from anything other than great skill. They provide an outlet for many people who find it difficult to integrate themselves into society when they move into adolescence. The Beatles, and groups like them, are giving such people an outlet, and are taking up the slack which ought to have been provided by a deeper education.

Liverpool was my home town. The arrival of the various groups there has had a remarkable effect. As those who practised in the courts in Liverpool in the early part of the 1950s know, deep-seated crime, which was becoming all too prevalent, has to a large extent disappeared. The crime rate is still high there, as it is everywhere else, but the gangs which were causing such trouble have largely disappeared. I agree, of course, that it may be rather facile to assume that the groups who go out at night and play this music have occupied all who might otherwise be ill-occupied, but undoubtedly they do fulfil a greatly felt need among many young people. That is a digression, but it is true that we have to educate, and educate in a different way. Education, though it will change and help, is only part of our problem.

ANDREW SARRIS

A Hard Day's Night

Village Voice, 27 August 1964

A Hard Day's Night is a particularly pleasant surprise in a year so full of unexpectedly unpleasant surprises. I have no idea who is the most responsible—director Richard Lester or screenwriter Alun Owen or the Messrs John Lennon, Paul McCartney, George Harrison, and Ringo Starr, better known collectively as The Beatles. Perhaps it was all a happy accident, and the lightning of inspiration will never strike again in the same spot. The fact remains that *A Hard Day's Night* has turned out to be the *Citizen Kane* of jukebox musicals, the brilliant crystallisation of such diverse cultural particles as the pop movie, rock 'n' roll, *cinéma vérité*, the *nouvelle vague*, free cinema, the affectedly hand-held camera, frenzied cutting, the cult of the sexless sub-adolescent, the semi-documentary, and studied spontaneity. So help me, I resisted The Beatles as long as I could. As a cab driver acquaintance observed, 'So what's new about The Beatles? Didn't you ever hear of Ish Kabibble?' Alas, I had. I kept looking for openings to put down The Beatles. Some of their sly crows' humour at the expense of a Colonel Blimp character in a train compartment is a bit too deliberate. 'I fought the war for people like you,' sez he. 'Bet you're sorry you won,' sez they. Old Osborne ooze, sez I. But just previously, the fruitiest looking of the four predators had looked up enticingly at the bug-eyed Blimp and whimpered 'Give us a kiss.' Depravity of such honest frankness is worth a hundred pseudo-literary exercises like *Becket*.

Stylistically, *A Hard Day's Night* is everything Tony Richardson's version of *Tom Jones* tried to be and wasn't. Thematically, it is everything Peter Brook's version of *Lord of the Flies* tried to be and wasn't. Fielding's satiric gusto is coupled here with Golding's primordial evil, and the strain hardly shows. I could have done with a bit less of a false sabre-toothed, rattling wreck of an old man tagged with sickeningly repetitious irony as a 'clean' old man. The pop movie mannerisms of the inane running joke about one of the boys' managers being sensitively shorter than the other might have been dispensed with at no great loss.

The foregoing are trifling reservations, however, about a movie that works on every level for every kind of audience. The open-field helicopter-shot sequence of The Beatles on a spree is one of the most exhilarating expressions of high spirits I have seen on the screen. The razor-slashing wit of the dialogue must be heard to be believed and appreciated. One as horribly addicted to alliteration as this otherwise sensible scribe can hardly resist a line like 'Ringo's drums loom large in his legend.'

I must say I enjoyed even the music enormously, possibly because I have not yet been traumatised by transistors into open rebellion against the 'top 40' and such. (I just heard 'Hello, Dolly' for the first time the other day, and the lyrics had been changed to 'Hello, Lyndon'.) Nevertheless I think there is a tendency to underrate rock 'n' roll because the lyrics look so silly in cold print. I would make two points here. First, it is unfair to compare R&R with Gershwin, Rodgers, Porter, Kern, *et al.*, as if all pre-R&R music from Tin Pan Alley was an uninterrupted flow of melodiousness. This is the familiar fallacy of nostalgia. I remember too much brassy noise from the big-band era to be stricken by the incursions of R&R. I like the songs The Beatles sing despite the banality of the lyrics, but the words in R&R only mask the poundingly ritualistic meaning of the beat. It is in the beat that the passion and togetherness is most movingly expressed, and it is the beat that the kids in the audience pick up with their shrieks as they drown out the words they have already heard a thousand times. To watch The Beatles in action with their constituents is to watch the kind of direct theatre that went out with Aristophanes, or perhaps even the Australian bushman. There is an empathy there that a million Lincoln Center Repertory companies cannot duplicate. Towards the end of *A Hard Day's Night* I began to understand the mystique of The Beatles. Lester's crane shot facing the audience from behind The Beatles established the emotional unity of the performers and their audience. It is a beautifully Bazinian deep-focus shot of hysteria to a slow beat punctuated by the kind of zoom shots I have always deplored in theory but must now admire in practice. Let's face it. My critical theories and preconceptions are all shook up, and I am profoundly grateful to The Beatles for such a pleasurable softening of hardening aesthetic arteries.

As to what The Beatles 'mean', I hesitate to speculate. The trouble with sociological analysis is that it is unconcerned with aesthetic values. *A Hard Day's Night* could have been a complete stinker of a movie and still be reasonably 'meaningful'. I like The Beatles in this moment in film history not merely because they mean something but rather because they express effectively a great many aspects of modernity that have converged inspiredly in their personalities. When I speak affectionately of their depravity, I am not commenting on their private lives, about which I know less than nothing. The wedding ring on Ringo's finger startles a great many people as a subtle Pirandellian switch from a character like Dopey of the Seven Dwarfs to a performer who chooses to project an ambiguous identity. It hardly matters. When we are 14 we learn to our dismay that all celebrities are depraved and that the he-man actor we so admired would rather date a mongoose than a girl. Then at 15 we learn that all humanity is depraved in one way or another and Albert Schweitzer gets his kicks by not squashing flies. Then at 16 we realise that it doesn't matter how depraved we all are; all that matters is the mask we put on our depravity, the image we choose to project to the world once we have lost our innocence irrevocably. There is too much of a tendency to tear away the masks in order to probe for the truth beneath. But why stop with the masks? Why not tear away the flesh as well and gaze upon the grinning skeletons lurking in all of us?

Consequently, what interests me about The Beatles is not what they are but what they choose to express. Their Ish Kabibble hairdos, for example, serve two functions. They become unique as a group and interchangeable as individuals. Except for Ringo, the favourite of the fans, the other three Beatles tend to get lost in the shuffle. And yet each is a distinctly personable individual behind their collective façade of androgynous selflessness—a façade appropriate, incidentally, to the undifferentiated sexuality of their sub-adolescent fans. The Beatles are not merely objects, however. A frequent refrain of their middle-aged admirers is that The Beatles don't take themselves too seriously. They take themselves seriously enough, all right; it is their middle-aged admirers and detractors they don't take too seriously. The Beatles are a sly bunch of anti-Establishment anarchists, but they are too slick to tip their hand to the authorities. People who have watched them handle their fans and the press tell me that they make Sinatra and his clan look like a bunch of rubes at a county fair. Of course, they have been shrewdly promoted, and a great deal of the hysteria surrounding them has been rigged with classic fakery and exaggeration. They may not be worth a paragraph in six months, but right now their entertaining message seems to be that everyone is 'people', Beatles and squealing sub-adolescents as much as Negroes and women and so-called senior citizens, and that however much alike 'people' may look in a group or a mass or a stereotype, there is in each soul a unique and irreducible individuality.

The MBE controversy: reflected in the pages of The Times

15 June 1965: MBE returned to Queen

A former RAF squadron-leader, Mr Paul Pearson, has posted his MBE back to the Queen as a protest against The Beatles and Ena Sharples getting awards in the Birthday Honours List.

Mr Pearson, who was awarded his medal for commanding air-sea rescue operations in the Channel, said at his home at Haywards Heath, Sussex, early today: 'I feel that when people like The Beatles are given the MBE the whole thing becomes debased and cheapened. I am making this gesture in the hope that the Queen's position in this situation can be reinforced so that she can resist and control her Ministers.'

16 June 1965: In defence of The Beatles' honour

Liverpool MPs last night tabled a motion in the Commons defending the award of the MBE to The Beatles. Two more men, however, said they were returning their honours in protest and a coastguard was considering returning his.

Mr Lester Pearson, Prime Minister of Canada, who arrived in London yesterday for the Commonwealth Prime Ministers' conference, said he was 'hanging on' to his OBE.

The MPs' motion states:

'Recognising the great good and happiness that The Beatles have brought to millions throughout the world and furthermore being the first entertainment group that has captured the American market and brought in its wake great commercial advantage in dollar earnings to this country, this House strongly appreciates the action of Her Majesty awarding The Beatles the MBE.'

Mr Eric Heffer, London member for Walton, who tabled the motion, said last night: 'I think that those people who have returned their MBEs in protest against the award to The Beatles are being plain silly and rather snobbish. Whilst there may still be outmoded awards or recognitions, the fact is that nowadays honours are being given on a much wider and more democratic scale than before.'

The signatories to the motion—all Labour MPs—include Mr James Dunn (Kirkdale), Mr Eric Ogden (West Derby), Mr W. H. Alldritt (Scotland), Mr R. Crawshaw (Toxteth), Mr Edmund Dell (Birkenhead), and Mr W. Molloy (Ealing North).

For service

Sir,—What is the point of serving a country that awards MBEs to a group of young pop singers?
Yours faithfully,
K. S. Nash
Pembroke Road, Ruislip, Middx.

17 June 1965: Two to one against The Beatles

The Prime Minister has received many letters from people who felt impelled to comment on the award of the MBE to The Beatles. The letters are said to be numbered 'in scores rather than hundreds', and for every one in favour of the award two are against.

Some of the letters are from fan clubs supporting other pop groups. They complain about the omission of their own favourites from the Honours List. Only one of the MBE decorations which individuals have said they will return in protest against the award to The Beatles has yet been received at 10 Downing Street.

Yesterday more Labour MPs signed the motion which Mr Heffer, Labour member for Walton, Liverpool, has tabled in the Commons defending the award to The Beatles.

A retired Army officer, Colonel F. W. Wagg, of Old Park Avenue, Dover, said last night that as a further protest against the award to The Beatles he was resigning from the Labour Party and cancelling a £12,000 bequest he was making to the party in his will. He has already returned nine war medals and three foreign decorations to the Queen.

'I have nothing against The Beatles personally. But I do object to this kind of award. In my opinion an order of public utility—as opposed to an order of chivalry—should be instituted for this type of case', he said.

The Mayor of Poole, Councillor L. Drudge, who was made MBE two years ago for his services to war pensioners and disabled ex-Servicemen, has asked Mr H. O. Murton, Conservative member for Poole, to raise The Beatles' award in Parliament. He hoped that 'strong representations' would be made to ensure that there would never again be such a belittling of the award.

Two of his brothers are also MBEs. He added: 'One of them won it for combating three enemy planes at a height of 20,000ft, in 1917. Giving it to The Beatles is an insult to all of us.'

Mr C. Adlington, a company director, of Rutland Court, Hove, Sussex, said yesterday that he would join the protest against honouring The Beatles by sending back the BEM he was awarded for 'gallant and distinguished service' in a tank battle in Italy in 1945.

18 June 1965: Honours

Sir,—The answer to the question raised by your correspondent in today's issue of *The Times* under the heading 'For service' would appear to be fully answered by the motion tabled by the Liverpool MPs.

As for those who have seen fit to return their decorations, 'methinks they do protest too much'. They have indirectly drawn attention to themselves and the services they rendered, which were in other times and other circumstances. Comparisons in such a field are unlikely to be particularly profitable.

The Beatles have clearly done a great service within the Commonwealth, particularly for those of their own generation, and in my view thoroughly deserve to be admitted to the ranks of the Order [*sic*] of the British Empire.
Yours faithfully,
H. Murray
Cornwall Gardens, SW7

Ignore Talent?

Sir,—What *would* be the point of serving a country that tried to ignore the talent, vivacity, and even the dollar-earning capacity of its young?
Yours faithfully,
R. I. L. Guthrie
Cambridge House, Camberwell Road, SE5

Associations

Sir,—The Beatles should now return their MBEs because they do not wish to be associated with petty snobbery.
Yours faithfully,
P. J. Collingwood
The Leys School, Cambridge

19 June 1965: Honours

Sir,—May I list a few of the reasons why many people think national recognition of The Beatles quite appropriate?

1. They are significant earners of foreign exchange.

2. They have, to quote Mr Heath when he was President of the Board of Trade, 'saved the British corduroy industry'.

3. They have helped to correct the foreign vision of Britain as a country entirely populated by middle-aged conservatives of all sorts—e.g., stock-brokers, wild-cat strikers, Beefeaters and Pembrokeshire coracle fishermen.

4. They are representative of a movement which has raised 'pop' music to a degree of sophistication and sheer musical interest never before attained.

5. They have started a fashion of music-making among the young in the street and have made it smarter to tote a guitar than a cosh.

6. They have given much pleasure to all age groups in all sections of the population.
Yours faithfully,
Charles de Hoghton
Blomfield Road, W9

Main Object

Sir,—It is a poor compliment (Mr Nash's letter 'For service') to the host of people who serve their country in a voluntary capacity to suggest that their main object is to appear in the Honours list. It just isn't true.
Yours faithfully,
M. R. Strover
Lodge Hill Road, Farnham, Surrey

22 June 1965: Author returns his military medal

Port Moresby, June 21—Mr Richard Pape, an official of the New

Guinea Government, is returning his Military Medal to the Queen as a protest against the award of the MBE to The Beatles. 'The Beatles' MBE reeks of mawkish, bizarre effrontery of our wartime endeavours', he said today.

Mr Pape, author of *Boldness Be My Friend*, is a publications officer with the Department of Information in Port Moresby.

More protest over The Beatles

Montreal, June 21—Dr Gaetan Jarry, a former lieutenant-commander in the Royal Canadian Navy, today sent a telegram to the Defence Minister, Mr Paul Hellyer, renouncing his MBE. 'For the next war do not count on me—use the Beatles or the Beatniks', he said.

NOËL COWARD

The Diaries

Wednesday 23 June 1965

I have finished the rewriting of *A Song at Twilight*, and I really do think I have improved it enormously. The weather has slightly improved. The Swiss social world continues to revolve sluggishly but quite agreeably. I dined with the Chevreau d'Antraigues and visited the Queen of Spain after dinner. The poor old girl is not well and shows signs of breaking up.

I have had to deliver a lecture to Nicky. He must concentrate on learning about me and my life and works, even if it means the dreaded necessity of reading the printed word occasionally. He is a dear boy and everyone likes him, but he *is* 35 and not 22.

There has been another high-flown debate in the House of Lords about suggested (idiotic) amendments to the Homosexual Bill, in the course of which Lord Montgomery announced that homosexuality between men was the most abominable and bestial act that any human being could commit! It, in his mind, apparently compares unfavourably with disembowelling, torturing, gas chambers and brutal murder. It is inconceivable that a man of his eminence and achievements could make such a statement. The poor old sod must be gaga.

The Beatles have all four been awarded MBEs, which has caused a considerable outcry. Furious war heroes are sending back their bravely won medals by the bushel. It is, of course, a tactless and major blunder on the part of the Prime Minister, and also I don't think the Queen should have agreed. Some other decoration should have been selected to reward them for their talentless but considerable contributions to the Exchequer.

Sunday 4 July 1965

Today Audrey [Hepburn] and Mel [Ferrer, her then husband] came to lunch. She enchanting as ever and he really extremely nice. I got back on Thursday after an interlude in Rome in time to dine with Adrianne and Dorothy Hammerstein [Oscar's widow], whom I love. Rome was fascinating and fraught with drama. The temperature all the time hovered between 88° and 98°. Princess Torlonia's wedding was beautiful to look at but too many *paperazzi* flashing cameras all through even the most serious parts of the ceremony. I went with Kay Thompson and Merle Oberon. I then changed into a dinner jacket and went to the *Grand Recepsione* which was *inferno* owing to there being no air-conditioning. It looked beautiful, however, and was crowded with Maria Pias and Maria Gabriellas.

On the Sunday night, I went to see The Beatles. I had never seen them in the flesh before. The noise was deafening throughout and I couldn't hear a word they sang or a note they played, just one long, ear-splitting din. Apparently they were not a success. The notices were bad the next day. I went backstage to see them and was met by Brian Epstein, who told me they had gone back to the hotel and would I go there. So off I went and, after being received by Brian Epstein and Wendy Hanson [Beatles' publicist] and given a drink, I was told that The Beatles refused to see me because that ass David Lewin [*Daily Mail* columnist] had quoted me saying unflattering things about them months ago. I thought this graceless in the extreme, but decided to play it with firmness and dignity. I asked Wendy to go and fetch one of them and she finally reappeared with Paul McCartney and I explained gently but firmly that one did *not* pay much attention to the statements of newspaper reporters. The poor boy was quite amiable and I sent messages of congratulation to his colleagues, although the message I would have liked to send them was that they were bad-mannered little shits. In any case, it is still impossible to judge from their public performance whether they have talent or not. They were professional, had a certain guileless charm, and stayed on mercifully for not too long.

I was truly horrified and shocked by the audience. It was like a mass masturbation orgy, although apparently mild compared with what it usually is. The whole thing is to me an unpleasant phenomenon. Mob hysteria when commercially promoted, or in whatever way promoted, always sickens me. To realise that the majority of the modern adolescent world goes ritualistically mad over those four innocuous, rather silly-looking young men is a disturbing thought. Perhaps we are whirling more swiftly into extinction than we know. Personally I should have liked to take some of those squealing young maniacs and cracked their heads together. I am all for audiences going mad with enthusiasm after a performance, but *not* incessantly *during* the performance so that there ceases to be a performance.

KENNETH TYNAN

Help!

from: *Tynan Right and Left* (1967)

THIS this THIS this THIS is the kind of THING (from outer SPACE?) you can expect from *Help!*, the new (and BAM!! it's new or never) film directed by focus-pulling, prize-winning, gag-spawning, zoom-loving Richard ('The KNACK') Lester, shot (POWWW!) in Eastmancolour but influenced by Observercolour and suggesting whole libraries of colourmags sprung BOING! to instant obsolescent life, complete with COOL gaudy consumer-tailored featurettes (one Lester missed: 'Tread Softly: The Dream-World of Wall-To-Wall Carpeting') and genuine only-connecting ADS (another Lester missed: 'Why not fly to the Aleutians in your custom-built Hammond Organ?'), not to mention FOUR EXPENSIVE TWO-DIMENSIONAL OBJECTS—namely John Lennon, the snickering heavyweight punster; surly, bejewelled Ringo Starr; George Harrison, the 12-string narcissist; and Paul McCartney, the boy next fibre-glass-electric-eye-operated door (under that wig he's really—GASP!—Anne Rutherford)—who are flung about (URGGHH!), battered (SPLAT!!) and flattened (KER-PLUNK!!!) in a comic-strip chase through tourist-enticing London, the whiter-than-white Austrian Alps and selected sunsoaked Bahamas, pursued by Oriental goodness-gracious villains (' "It's a Sellers' market," quips writer Charles Wood') and guaranteed mad scientists, all plotting to slice (EEK!) a magic ring from surly Ringo's bejewelled finger, while off-beat Lester movie garners harvest of heady hosannas ('LOFTY GROSSES LOOM FOR MOPHEADS' LATEST—Flicker's Total Sexlessness Augurs Wham Family Fare') from notoriously hard-to-please CRITICS (ECCHH!!) in American trade press. . . .

In other words, *Help!* is a brilliant, unboring but ferociously ephemeral movie. Richard Lester's direction is a high-speed compendium of many lessons learned from Blake Edwards, Frank Tashlin, Goon comedy, fashion photography and MGM cartoons. The Beatles themselves are not natural actors, nor are they exuberant extroverts; their mode is dry and laconic, as befits the flat and sceptical Liverpool accent. Realising this, Lester leaves it to his cameraman (David Watkin) to create the exuberance, confining The Beatles to deadpan comments and never asking them to react to events with anything approaching emotion. He capitalises on their wary, guarded detachment. 'There's something been in this soup,' says John, having calmly removed from the plate a season ticket and a pair of spectacles.

The script (by Marc Behm and Charles Wood) is chopped into fragments; hundreds of half-heard gags zip by, of which we are given time to laugh at about two dozen. The best-sustained sequence is the one where Ringo is trapped by an escaped tiger that can be tamed only by a full choral rendering of Beethoven's Ninth. The musical items are superbly shot, and the title song is the most haunting Beatle composition to date.

To sum up *Help!* I must go to Coleridge, who said that whereas a scientist investigates a thing for the sheer pleasure of knowing, the non-scientist only wants to find out whether it will 'furnish him with food, or shelter, or weapons, or tools, or ornaments, or *play-withs'*. *Help!* is a shiny forgettable toy; an ideal play-with.

JOHN WAIN

In the echo chamber

New Republic, 7 August 1965

'Jack the Nipple' said Womlbs puffing deeply on his wife, 'is not only a vicious murderer but a sex meany of the lowest orgy.' Then my

steamed collic relit his pig and walkered to the windy of his famous flat in
Bugger St in London where it all happened. I pondled on his statemouth
for a mormon then turding sharply I said 'But how do you know
Womlbs?'

That fragment of Joyce pastiche is the work of John Lennon, Esq.,
MBE, known wherever human beings walk the earth as the Writing
Beatle. I didn't, as it happens, read his first book, *In His Own Write*, and
I don't think I'll bother now, but this new one is worth a glance, if only
because it will be read and absorbed by virtually the whole generation
of adolescents in Britain and a good many in America too.

The first thing any literate person will notice on reading through Mr
Lennon's book is that it all comes out of one source, namely the later
work of James Joyce. Not only the determination to communicate
almost exclusively in puns, but the equally determined smutty,
blasphemous and subversive tone, are Joycean. *Finnegans Wake* and
the nighttown scene in *Ulysses* are now available by proxy to thousands
of minds which would normally be prevented from coming anywhere
near them; prevented, that is, by a sheer social brick wall, for the
printed book simply does not enter into the out-of-school life of a
subspecies of the modern adolescent. Anything that does not reach
him by TV, radio, film, or the pages of a few popular newspapers, does
not reach him, period. It takes a Beatle to crash this barrier, since The
Beatles are a law unto themselves and will be followed anywhere they
choose to go. Hence the huge, but rapidly dwindling, piles of this book
in every English bookshop.

That is fact number one. By crashing the barrier normally erected
against the book, Mr Lennon has, at one stroke, put the young
non-reader in touch with a central strand in the literary tradition of the
last 30 years in every English-speaking country. For *Finnegans Wake*,
once considered impossibly withdrawn, solipsistic and obscure, has in
fact become one of the most universally accepted books of the 20th
century. Not many people read it, in the usual sense of sitting down
with it and going from beginning to end; but virtually everyone who
reads at all has read bits here and there, and most literary people have
given assent to its main proposition, namely that language is
potentially, and ought to be actually, multidimensional. Joyce, who
never had good sight and therefore lived mainly in the blind man's
world of aural and tactile experiences, approached language through
his ears and hands rather than through his eyes. This tendency is
already very evident in *Ulysses*:

'Bloom ate liv as said before. Clean here at least. That chap in the
Burton, gummy with gristle. No-one here: Goulding and I. Clean tables,

61

flowers, mitres of napkins. Pat to and fro, bald Pat. Nothing to do. Best value in Dub.

'Piano again. Cowley it is. Way he sits in to it, like one together, mutual understanding. Tiresome shapers scraping fiddles, eye on the bowend, sawing the 'cello, remind you of toothache. Her high long snore. Night we were in the box. Trombone under blowing like a grampus, between the acts, other brass chap unscrewing, emptying spittle. Conductor's legs too, bagstrousers, jiggedy jiggedy. Do right to hide them.

'Jiggedy jingle jaunty jaunty.'

The language, here, still remains close to the 'normal', mainly cognitive use; but already we can discern that the participation to which this writing invites us is as much physical as intellectual: the tongue, lips, throat muscles, are involved as they are in eating; when Mr Lennon writes, 'Father Cradock turns round slowly from the book he is eating and explains that it is just a face she is going through', or says that someone has a 'sliced Aberdeen-Martin accent', he might be talking about language as Joyce used it.

With *Finnegans Wake* Joyce moved the pun in to the centre and made it the main instrument of his writing. Why did he need to do this, and why have we all so unresistingly followed him? Some of Joyce's reasons may have been to do with his lofty and uncompromising literary programme; he wanted to present human life as an indivisible simultaneity and to banish the idea of linear time, so that the last sentence of *Finnegans Wake* comes back to the first, and the language is given an extra dimension to convey that sense of density, that refusal to isolate experiences and take them one at a time. Joyce was, of course, influenced by Giambattista Vico, whose view of history as not linear but contrapuntal has become more widely known partly because of the attention focused on him by Joyce. Language, which stores the experience of a people in forms that are in constant daily use, seemed to Joyce a living demonstration of the truth of Vico's thesis. Another reason is that Joyce, as an Irishman, felt the inevitable resentment at having to use the language of England, and as a connoisseur and scholar of languages he took delight in making his own instrument of communication.

There were, doubtless, other reasons, but let us take these two for the present. Joyce's distrust of linear conceptions of time would certainly be shared (consciously or unconsciously) by more people today than in his own lifetime. A narrative, unilinear view of experience, which underlay the work of both novelist and historian in the 18th and 19th centuries, is an abstraction. It results from standing back and reasoning about experience, sorting out its thick, knotty textures into manageable threads. There is nowadays a general reluctance to stand back and ratiocinate, and this is why the traditionally written novel is in such trouble; it has so lost conviction that even the people who write it aren't convinced, and feel (wrongly, in my opinion) that they must inject increasing doses of propaganda to give it the appearance of vitality; as for the traditional historian, he has disappeared altogether. Professor Marshall McLuhan has found wide acceptance for his view, expressed in *The Gutenberg Galaxy*, that the invention of movable type moved the sensibility of Western man on to a unilinear plane, and that the consequences were felt in every area of life.

'Everyone is familiar', McLuhan writes, 'with the phrase, "the voices of silence." It is the traditional word for sculpture. And if an entire year of any college programme were spent in understanding that phrase, the world might soon have an adequate supply of competent minds. As the Gutenberg typography filled the world the human voice closed down. People began to read silently and passively as consumers. Architecture and sculpture dried up too. In literature only people from backward oral areas had any resonance to inject into the language—the Yeatses, the Synges, the Joyces, Faulkners, and Dylan Thomases.'

Though McLuhan tries to maintain strict impartiality between the brawling media, the tone of disapproval is marked here. The human voice 'closed down', it sounds very much as if the inhabitants of 'backward' areas—Ireland, Wales, the American South—come into the story like the US Cavalry in a Western. They beat back the marauding forces until the railroads can be built and the channels of communication opened. And now that the Gutenberg era is past, we can all recover the 'human voice'. We can enter the echo chamber with J. M. Synge, Dylan Thomas and The Beatles.

All this may seem a grotesquely long detour to explain why one young man writes a little book in Joycean punning language. But large-scale cultural shifts are not confined to major artists and sensitive critics. The reasons why Mr Lennon imitates Joyce are, in the end, the same reasons that made Pasternak break with traditional form in writing *Dr Zhivago*. The life-history of Yuri Zhivago is told in a manner as far removed as possible from the old linear narrative form which progressed from one event to the next against a tidily arranged 'background'. Quite apart from the fact that the story itself lurches from one coincidence to another, there is no separable 'foreground' or 'background'. Everything that happens—the death of a man, an idea occurring to a philosopher or a line of verse to a poet, a storm, the birth of a child, an outbreak of street fighting, an evening party at which people make speeches—seems to occur on the same level of significance and at the same closeness to the camera-eye. The effect is electrifying simply because it reveals how false the idiom of the novel, with its tidiness and predictability, had become. Not that Pasternak necessarily has to use revolutionary techniques to convey this. Some of his techniques are revivals of older ones; for example, the Dickensian way of giving human characteristics to inanimate things so as to enroll them as characters. At one point, Yuri says to Lara, 'Mother Russia is on the move, she can't stand still, she's restless and she can't find rest, she's talking and she can't stop. And it isn't as if only people were talking. Stars and trees meet and converse, flowers talk philosophy at night, stone houses hold meetings.' It would be a mistake to dismiss this as a literary man's fancifulness. At a time of great upheaval, nothing remains unaltered: landscape, objects, plants, even the weather, partake of the change inasmuch as they strike the perceiving eye in a different way. Joyce would have understood perfectly how it is that stone houses one has known all one's life suddenly begin, at such times, to 'hold meetings'. Their grouping takes on significance, and they suddenly appear to have a relationship with one another. Modern cinema techniques have exploited this awareness to the point of cliché, but in the novel its use is still unexpected. (The French *nouveau roman* has tried to obliterate the conventional distinction between foreground and background, but in so clumsy and unimaginative a way as to obfuscate the whole subject and put the clock back ten years.)

John Lennon (yes, him again) has, in an interview, denied any knowledge of James Joyce, at any rate when he began using the punning method. This does not surprise me; in fact, it is what I would have expected. The language of *Finnegans Wake* liberated many things in the 20th-century consciousness that needed to be liberated. Almost at once the method was taken over by the literary intelligentsia for lighter purposes—one recalls, for instance, Edmund Wilson's brilliant fable of the 'three limperary cripples' in *Notebooks of Night*; from there, it widened to a generally more tactile and multidimensional use of language. The vogue of Lallans among Scotch poets, for instance, was largely the product of a wish to exploit the semantic gap between Scots words and the English words they suggested, and thus obtain a multidimensional effect. By refusing to stick to one region or one period of history, but culling their vocabulary from any source—Highland, Lowland, medieval, modern, formal, colloquial—the Lallans poets hoped to gain the freedom to move in any direction, to provide Scots English with a richness it had never in fact possessed at any one time. (Whether they achieved this object in any poem one could point to, I must leave to better qualified judges to decide.) Only one thing is clear, over the whole spectrum: the formal, controlled use of language that resulted from the 19th century's drive towards logic, systematisation and the shading out of ambiguities, has been decisively rejected.

This universal literary movement has now, finally, broken the levees and overflowed into the territory where literature cannot follow. *Finnegans Wake* is now merged, in the sensibility of the age, with the TV scripts and the ads. After an exposure to Lennon, the present-day adolescent will be able to take Joyce in comic-strip form. And this is another major tendency of the present time. The 1960s are witnessing a gigantic scrambling of cultural levels. Whereas even 20 years ago there was a culture for the few that was recognisably apart from the culture of the many, we have now reached a point where popular and non-popular forms have flowed together in a huge morass, whether fertile or poisonous remains to be seen. James Joyce, who considered himself a man of the people, a life-long socialist and iconoclast, also knew that as an artist he was aristocratic. But in the world that has produced pop-art, cool jazz, goon humour, Kama Sutra sculpture welded out of junk, the Brecht vogue and The Beatles' MBE, no one cares to say any longer where one category ends and another begins. It has finally happened. The offensive launched 50 years ago by the first wave of 'modern' artists has succeeded beyond anyone's wildest dreams.

In this world, any statement can be made interesting by putting it into the appropriate idiom, as a can of Campbell's soup takes on significance inside a picture-frame. So we can imagine Mr Lennon's youthful readers hanging entranced on his words as he tells them:

> Azue orl gnome, Harrassed Wilsod won the General Erection, with a very small marjorie over the Torchies. Thus pudding the Laboring Partly back into powell after a large abcess. This he could not have done withoutspan the barking of thee Trade Onions . . .

Like a pop artist or anyone else who communicates largely through style, he need have nothing personal to communicate. The language is doing the talking, delightedly revealing its own potentialities to a youthful mass audience which has, so far, responded to nothing in written form. Mr Lennon, coasting downhill with this huge gravitational pull, need provide nothing in the way of content except his automatic youthful irreverence. If, one day, he should decide to try to communicate something, we shall see whether he has any gifts apart from the ability to thumb a lift from the *Zeitgeist*. At the moment, there's no means of telling.

Notes

1. Born 1913. Conservative MP for Ashford, Kent, 1950–74; Editor *Daily Telegraph*, 1974–86

2. Born 1903. Conservative MP for Hampstead, 1950–66; Home Secretary, 1962–4

Courtesy of Express Newspapers plc

Working drawing for *Yellow Submarine* (*courtesy TVC Ltd.*)

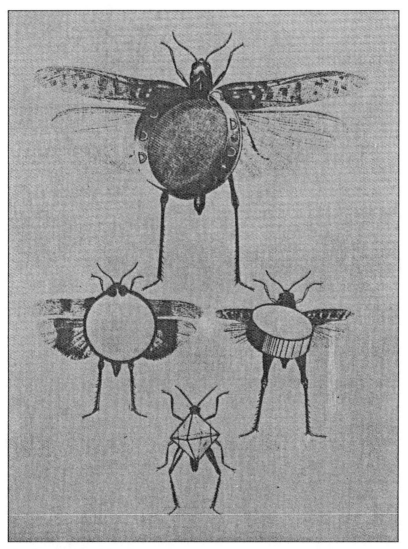

Beatles 1969 by Max Ernst an

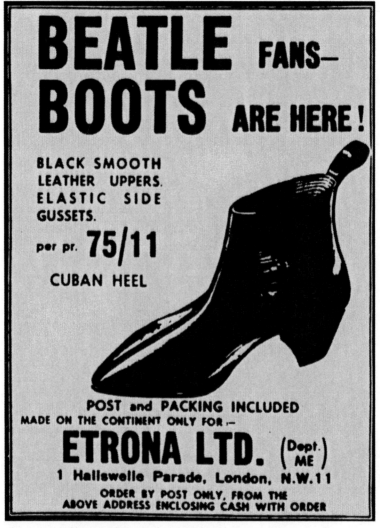

(courtesy Bill Harry/Merseybeat Archive)

THREE

Getting Better

TERENCE J. O'GRADY

Rubber Soul and the social dance tradition

from *Ethnomusicology* xxiii/1 (January 1979)

By the end of 1965, The Beatles had established themselves as successful hit-makers in both an up-tempo pop-rock style and a moderate or slow tempo ballad style. The first of these had been influenced by various precursors—Buddy Holly, the Everly Brothers, Chuck Berry, and a number of black Motown singers—but had coalesced by 1964 into an original combination of inventive melodic and harmonic gestures and compelling, if occasionally simplistic, lyrics. Their ballad style had drawn from the standard Fifties' white ballad style of Holly and others as well as the more tension-filled black idiom, while demonstrating glimpses of a sophisticated adult commercial style.

The British version of the *Help!* album (released in August, 1965) showed a further development of the pop-rock style, along with the finest example of the adult commercial style to date—McCartney's 'Yesterday'. Nevertheless, it was The Beatles' next opus, *Rubber Soul*, that conclusively demonstrated their ability to transcend the conventions of the popular music of the period.

For Wilfrid Mellers, the title, *Rubber Soul*, 'hints at greater flexibilities of irony and compassion',[1] and this interpretation does account for the consistently thoughtful and serious nature of most of the lyrics for the songs on both the British and American albums. Certainly the use of the word 'soul' has no specifically musical implication insofar as any reference to the popular black rhythm and blues of the period is intended. In terms of the influence of black music, probably no Beatle album has as little 'soul' as this one.

But while the title appears to have little musical significance, the

69

album itself demonstrates a very distinctive musical personality. . . . While not all its songs are remarkable or even unconventional in respect of musical style or lyrics, there is no question that the album as a whole represents a new departure in The Beatles' music: it demands a redefinition of much of its material in a context unrelated to the traditional social dance function previously considered inseparable from rock and roll. Whereas earlier Beatle experimentation had generally been concerned with innovations of harmony, melody, and—to a lesser degree—instrumentation or arrangement, in *Rubber Soul* The Beatles moved to deny the very social and functional origins of rock and roll and demanded that their music be experienced exclusively through the aural process. This is not to suggest that The Beatles' music on *Rubber Soul* cannot be, or has not been, danced to, but rather to assert that the music is no longer primarily concerned with expediting the dance.

Furthermore, the majority of the songs contained on the album are unified in their demonstration of a new approach to rock and roll—an approach that focuses on musical detail and conceptual originality rather than on the massive, ear-catching sound gestures of the earlier pop-rock songs. This disregard for the traditional requirements of simplicity and dance potential was manifest in a few earlier Beatle recordings, but no previous album was so consistent in its denial of commercial conventions. This disregard may, paradoxically, have been made feasible only by the absolute guarantee of commercial success for any Beatle venture in 1965, and the relatively generous amount of studio recording time justified thereby.

A second specifically musical attribute shared by several songs on *Rubber Soul* involves the incorporation of country-western or folk elements. Both were, of course, contained in earlier Beatle songs, if only as modifiers of the pop-rock tradition, not as a main component or stylistic feature. This new departure is particularly evident in Lennon's songs. Folk and particularly rockabilly elements had been demonstrated in some earlier examples—the 1964 'You've got to hide your love away' and 'I'm a loser'—but their function was decorative in a style that remained fundamentally pop-rock. Such Lennon songs as 'Norwegian wood' and 'In my life' are unprecedented—conceptually folk-like. And since Lennon's compositions for *Rubber Soul* cannot be said to be particularly remarkable or innovative from a melodic, harmonic or rhythmic standpoint (less so, in fact, than the contributions by McCartney and Harrison), it is for their conceptual novelty that they are most significant.

It was not The Beatles' intention to produce folk or country music *per se*; rather to reconcile it with pop-rock in order to produce a new hybrid form. The country and folk styles are used simply as a source for melodic-harmonic material and sound ideas that had not been drained of their originality by over-exposure on the popular market.

American folk-rock, as exemplified by The Byrds, opted for a more aggressive rock feel, with a solid, eminently danceable beat. Compared to this, The Beatles' understated style on *Rubber Soul* was, with its subtle instrumental backings and demure stylistic borrowings, tantamount to a return to purity.

The Beatles soon proved themselves equal to other conquests. And yet it is doubtful that any of these surpasses the subtle triumph of *Rubber Soul*.

MAUREEN CLEAVE

How does a Beatle live? John Lennon lives like this

Evening Standard, 4 March 1966

It was this time three years ago that The Beatles first grew famous. Ever since then, observers have anxiously tried to gauge whether their fame was on the wax or on the wane; they foretold the fall of the old Beatles, they searched diligently for the new Beatles (which was as pointless as looking for the new Big Ben).

At last they have given up; The Beatles' fame is beyond question. It has nothing to do with whether they are rude or polite, married or unmarried, 25 or 45; whether they appear on *Top of the Pops* or do not appear on *Top of the Pops*. They are well above any position even a Rolling Stone might jostle for. They are famous in the way the Queen is famous. When John Lennon's Rolls-Royce, with its black wheels and its black windows, goes past, people say: 'It's the Queen,' or 'It's The Beatles.' With her they share the security of a stable life at the top. They all tick over in the public esteem—she in Buckingham Palace, they in the Weybridge–Esher area. Only Paul remains in London.

The Weybridge community consists of the three married Beatles; they live there among the wooded hills and the stockbrokers. They have not worked since Christmas and their existence is secluded and curiously timeless. 'What day is it?' John Lennon asks with interest when you ring up with news from outside. The fans are still at the gates but The Beatles see only each other. They are better friends than ever before.

Ringo and his wife, Maureen, may drop in on John and Cyn; John may drop in on Ringo; George and Pattie may drop in on John and Cyn and they might all go round to Ringo's, by car of course. Outdoors is for holidays.

They watch films, they play rowdy games of Buccaneer; they watch television till it goes off, often playing records at the same time. They while away the small hours of the morning making mad tapes. Bedtimes and mealtimes have no meaning as such. 'We've never had time before to do anything but just be Beatles,' John Lennon said.

He is much the same as he was before. He still peers down his nose, arrogant as an eagle, although contact lenses have righted the short sight that originally caused the expression. He looks more like Henry VIII than ever now that his face has filled out—he is just as imperious, just as unpredictable, indolent, disorganised, childish, vague, charming and quick-witted. He is still easy-going, still tough as hell. 'You never asked after Fred Lennon,' he said, disappointed. (Fred is his father; he emerged after they got famous.) 'He was here a few weeks ago. It was only the second time in my life I'd seen him—I showed him the door.' He went on cheerfully: 'I wasn't having *him* in the house.'

His enthusiasm is undiminished and he insists on its being shared. George has put him on to this Indian music. 'You're not listening, are you?' he shouts after 20 minutes of the record. 'It's amazing this—so cool. Don't the Indians appear cool to you? Are you listening? This music is thousands of years old; it makes me laugh, the British going over there and telling them what to do. Quite amazing.' And he switched on the television set.

Experience has sown few seeds of doubt in him: not that his mind is closed, but it's closed round whatever he believes at the time. 'Christianity will go,' he said. 'It will vanish and shrink. I needn't argue about that; I'm right and I will be proved right. We're more popular than Jesus now; I don't know which will go first—rock 'n' roll or Christianity. Jesus was all right but his disciples were thick and ordinary. It's them twisting it that ruins it for me.' He is reading extensively about religion.

He shops in lightning swoops on Asprey's these days and there is some fine wine in his cellar, but he is still quite unselfconscious. He is far too lazy to keep up appearances, even if he had worked out what the appearances should be—which he has not.

He is now 25. He lives in a large, heavily panelled, heavily carpeted, mock Tudor house set on a hill with his wife Cynthia and his son Julian. There is a cat called after his aunt Mimi, and a purple dining room. Julian is three; he may be sent to the Lycée in London. 'Seems the only place for him in his position,' said his father, surveying him dispassionately. 'I feel sorry for him, though. I couldn't stand ugly people even when I was five. Lots of the ugly ones are foreign, aren't they?'

We did a speedy tour of the house, Julian panting along behind, clutching a large porcelain Siamese cat. John swept past the objects in which he had lost interest: 'That's Sidney' (a suit of armour); 'That's a hobby I had for a week' (a room full of model racing cars); 'Cyn won't let me get rid of that' (a fruit machine). In the sitting room are eight little green boxes with winking red lights; he bought them as Christmas presents but never got round to giving them away. They wink for a year; one imagines him sitting there till next Christmas, surrounded by the little winking boxes.

He paused over objects he still fancies; a huge altar crucifix of a Roman Catholic nature with IHS on it; a pair of crutches, a present from George; an enormous Bible he bought in Chester; his gorilla suit.

'I thought I might need a gorilla suit,' he said; he seemed sad about it. 'I've only worn it twice. I thought I might pop it on in the summer and drive round in the Ferrari. We were all going to get them and drive round in them but I was the only one who did. I've been thinking about it and if I didn't wear the head it would make an amazing fur coat—with legs, you see. I would like a fur coat but I've never run into any.'

One feels that his possessions—to which he adds daily—have got the upper hand; all the tape recorders, the five television sets, the cars, the telephones of which he knows not a single number. The moment he approaches a switch it fuses; six of the winking boxes, guaranteed to last till next Christmas, have gone funny already. His cars—the Rolls, the Mini-Cooper (black wheels, black windows), the Ferrari (being painted black)—puzzle him. Then there's the swimming pool, the trees sloping away beneath it. 'Nothing like what I ordered,' he said resignedly. He wanted the bottom to be a mirror. 'It's an amazing household,' he said. 'None of my gadgets really work except the gorilla suit—that's the only suit that fits me.'

He is very keen on books, will always ask what is good to read. He buys quantities of books and these are kept tidily in a special room. He has Swift, Tennyson, Huxley, Orwell, costly leather-bound editions of Tolstoy, Oscar Wilde. Then there's *Little Women*, all the *William* books from his childhood; and some unexpected volumes such as *Forty-One Years In India*, by Field Marshal Lord Roberts, and *Curiosities of Natural*

History, by Francis T. Buckland. This last—with its chapter headings 'Ear-less Cats', 'Wooden-Legged People,' 'The Immortal Harvey's Mother'—is right up his street.

He approaches reading with a lively interest untempered by too much formal education. 'I've read millions of books,' he said, 'that's why I seem to know things.' He is obsessed by Celts. 'I have decided I am a Celt,' he said. 'I am on Boadicea's side—all those bloody blue-eyed blondes chopping people up. I have an awful feeling wishing I was there—not there with scabs and sores but there through *reading* about it. The books don't give you more than a paragraph about how they *lived*; I have to imagine that.'

He can sleep almost indefinitely, is probably the laziest person in England. '*Physically* lazy,' he said. 'I don't mind writing or reading or watching or speaking, but sex is the only physical thing I can be bothered with any more.' Occasionally he is driven to London in the Rolls by an ex-Welsh guardsman called Anthony; Anthony has a moustache that intrigues him.

The day I visited him he had been invited to lunch in London, about which he was rather excited. 'Do you know how long lunch lasts?' he asked. 'I've never been to lunch before. I went to a Lyons the other day and had egg and chips and a cup of tea. The waiters kept looking and saying: "No, it *isn't* him, it *can't* be him".'

He settled himself into the car and demonstrated the television, the folding bed, the refrigerator, the writing desk, the telephone. He has spent many fruitless hours on that telephone. 'I only once got through to a person,' he said, 'and they were out.'

Anthony had spent the weekend in Wales. John asked if they'd kept a welcome for him in the hillside and Anthony said they had. They discussed the possibility of an extension for the telephone. We had to call at the doctor's because John had a bit of sea urchin in his toe. 'Don't want to be like Dorothy Dandridge,' he said, 'dying of a splinter 50 years later.' He added reassuringly that he had washed the foot in question.

We bowled along in a costly fashion through the countryside. 'Famous and loaded' is how he describes himself now. 'They keep telling me I'm all right for money but then I think I may have spent it all by the time I'm 40 so I keep going. That's why I started selling my cars; then I changed my mind and got them all back and a new one too.

'I want the money just to *be* rich. The only other way of getting it is to be born rich. If you have money, that's power without having to be powerful. I often think that it's all a big conspiracy, that the winners are the Government and people like us who've got the money. That joke about keeping the workers ignorant is still true; that's what they said about the Tories and the landowners and that; then Labour were meant to educate the workers but they don't seem to be doing that any more.'

He has a morbid horror of stupid people: 'Famous and loaded as I am, I still have to meet soft people. It often comes into my mind that I'm not really rich. There are *really* rich people but I don't know where they are.'

He finds being famous quite easy, confirming one's suspicion that The Beatles had been leading up to this all their lives. 'Everybody thinks they *would* have been famous if only they'd had the Latin and that. So when it happens it comes naturally. You remember your old grannie saying soft things like: "You'll make it with that voice."' Not, he added, that he had any old grannies.

He got to the doctor 2¾ hours early and to lunch on time but in the wrong place. He bought a giant compendium of games from Asprey's but having opened it he could not, of course, shut it again. He wondered what else he should buy. He went to Brian Epstein's office. 'Any presents?' he asked eagerly; he observed that there was nothing like getting things free. He tried on the attractive Miss Hanson's spectacles.

The rumour came through that a Beatle had been sighted walking down Oxford Street! He brightened. 'One of the others must be out,' he said, as though speaking of an escaped bear. 'We only let them out one at a time,' said the attractive Miss Hanson firmly.

He said that to live and have a laugh were the things to do; but was that enough for the restless spirit?

'Weybridge,' he said, 'won't do at all. I'm just stopping at it, like a bus stop. Bankers and stockbrokers live there; they can add figures and Weybridge is what they live in and they think it's the end, they really do. I think of it every day—me in my Hansel and Gretel house. I'll take my time; I'll get my *real* house when I know what I want.

'You see, there's something else I'm going to do, something I must do—only I don't know what it is. That's why I go round painting and taping and drawing and writing and that, because it may be one of them. All I know is, this isn't *it* for me.'

Anthony got him and the compendium into the car and drove him home with the television flickering in the soothing darkness while the Londoners outside rushed home from work.

DAVID FROST

John's gospel

Spectator, 12 August 1966

'The Beatles, ladies and gentlemen, The Beatles. . . .' Mr Tommy Trinder announced to a television audience. 'They're going to have Ringo for Pope . . . They are . . . well, they've already had John and Paul. . . .'

It caused a tiny fuss. Mr Trinder must have watched amused this week as Mr John Lennon's somewhat ill-advised decision to take the analogy a stage further—linking The Beatles and Jesus—caused a rather larger furore. Or did it—*really?*

The whole incident has been an interesting little saga of press activity, of delayed effect news-making. From the moment that John Lennon gave a splendidly bravura, splendidly written interview to Maureen Cleave, it has been clear that one paragraph has been lying quietly, insidiously like an unexploded time-bomb, waiting for someone in search of ammunition. The fateful words were finally seized upon by *Datebook*: 'Christianity will go. It will vanish and shrink. I needn't argue about that; I'm right, and I will be proved right. We're more popular than Jesus now; I don't know which will go first—rock 'n' roll or Christianity. Jesus was all right but his disciples were thick and ordinary.'

Even the current explosion may not have been 100 per cent genuine. For the first day or two, the stories coming over the wires from New York were alarmingly general in their first paragraphs—stations were banning Beatle records, organising burning ceremonies, American teenagers were revolting, and so on—but always suspiciously vague when it came to particular examples which seemed to hinge mainly on one Mr Tommy Charles of station WAQY in Birmingham, Alabama— scarcely the barometer of the American nation: Mr Charles, who says he is 36 'but I think like a teenager' or is, in other words, mentally retarded on his own admission by about 21 years.

This is a key problem about all stories in the British press emanating from the United States. A key problem for news editors as well as readers. It is so easy to make a trivial, untypical incident sound as if it were happening all over the American continent, and so difficult to sort out the deeper significance of three paragraphs from Washington.

It was obviously his realisation of this that made Brian Epstein get up from his sick-bed and fly over to New York to find out what on earth was going on. And yet paradoxically, by this very action, he probably gave further life to the story, which now achieved a sort of verification for the first time.

After a series of further accounts, the story reached its denouement when The Beatles' office in London issued a long and extraordinarily detailed apology and denial: 'Quoted and misrepresented entirely out of context, Lennon is deeply interested in religion and was at the time having serious talks with Maureen Cleave . . . concerning religion. What he said and meant was that in the last 50 years the Church in England and therefore Christ had suffered decline in interest. He did not mean to boast about The Beatles' fame. He meant to point out that The Beatles' effect appeared to be a more immediate one upon certainly the younger generation. The article was understood to be exclusive to the London *Evening Standard*. It was not anticipated that it would be displayed out of context and in such a manner as it was in an American teenage magazine.'

An interesting new concept this. All right for the London *Evening Standard*, but not for an American teenage magazine. What if it had been the American *New York Times*? or an English teenage magazine? or the London *Evening News*? And indeed what should one's attitude be to an American teenager reading the London *Evening Standard*? Anyway, the statement concludes: 'In the circumstances John is deeply concerned and regrets that people with deep religious beliefs should have been offended in any way.'

Well . . . what does one make of all that? It is not merely a question of what you think of John Lennon's original statement. You may think it was splendidly refreshing to hear a pop singer speaking his mind, whether you agreed or disagreed with what he was saying. Or you may just have thought that The Beatles were going too far and ought to be stopped by some means or other. That, however, is basically irrelevant.

First and foremost, the recantation is obviously one giant euphemism—it does not really reflect the feelings of John Lennon at the moment he made the original remark. Secondly, as Henry Thody pointed out in the *News of the World*, it does not really reflect the views of The Beatles' fans either here or in New York who all asked Thody 'Who goes to church any more except squares?' and words that were generally to that effect. Thirdly, of course, the statement does not really reflect the true feelings of our two societies—the affronted devout worshipping unanimity it seems to summon up just does not exist in the Western world any more. However, as always happens when a society rightly or wrongly is laying aside the old canons and searching for new ones, the public surface maintenance of the old canons becomes even more important. It has been the same for the past few years with the Roman Catholic Church and their position on birth control. The Beatles' statement has been wrung out of them by society for their failure to adhere to a code which in the main The Beatles themselves have rejected, their fans have rejected, and that self-same society has rejected.

Personally, I did not agree with much of John Lennon's statement but whatever one thinks of it and the code it attacks, should not on principle a civilised society be beyond the point where one paragraph by anyone about anything can produce this sort of hysteria?

And if, gentle reader, the events of the past week have still left you feeling bitterly that the outrageousness of people like Mr Lennon must be stopped at all costs, I would suggest, as an antidote, that you spend the next seven days reading the collected interviews of Cliff Richard.

ROBERT E. DALLOS

Beatles strike serious note in press talk

The New York Times, 23 August 1966

The usually lighthearted Beatles press conference took on a serious tone yesterday as the mop-haired singers fielded questions on the war in Vietnam, bigotry in the United States and the comments by one member of their quartet on Christianity.

The British rock 'n' roll group, which arrived in the city early yesterday, answered the first question at the 25-minute news conference in unison. 'We don't like war, war is wrong,' each said several times in a low, nearly inaudible voice when asked to comment on any aspect of the Vietnamese conflict.

The four performers—Ringo Starr, Paul McCartney, John Lennon and George Harrison—sat at a long table at the second-floor conference in the Warwick Hotel, their New York headquarters. All appeared tired and pale.

As he bit his fingernails, Mr McCartney added that he would be able to express his sentiments on the war more fully in England. 'What we say would not be misinterpreted in England the way it would be here,' Mr McCartney said. 'You can say things like that in England. People listen a bit more. In America, they hold everything you say against you.'

Mr Lennon, whose comment that The Beatles are more popular than Christ has resulted in strong protests in the United States, turned to his partner, saying, 'You'll have to answer for that tomorrow.'

When Mr Lennon was asked why his remark on The Beatles' popularity had stirred such a controversy here, he said, 'there are more people in America so there are more bigots also. You hear more from American bigots.' But so as not to be misunderstood, he quickly added, 'Not everyone in America is bigoted.' Mr Lennon declined to comment further on his comment on Christianity. 'I've already said enough. I'd just go over the same thing again. It's all a lot of rubbish.' They admitted that the comment might have had some effect at the box office, but Mr McCartney added, 'We don't care about those who don't like us because of the statement. We'd rather perform for people who do like us.'

For a moment, it might have seemed that one of The Beatles' press aides was requesting the reporters and photographers present to pay obeisance to the quartet. 'The Beatles are about to enter,' he said, 'and I'd like to ask you people in front to kneel.' After the remark was greeted by an outburst of laughter, the aide quickly added that he just wanted to make sure 'the guys in back can get their pictures.'

They were asked if they would like to perform in the capitals of some Communist nations. 'I don't fancy it,' said Mr Harrison. 'But that's personal. There are lots of other places we haven't been to yet that interest me more.'

Though the conference was mostly serious, there were some light moments. They were also asked about recent rumours that they wear wigs. 'You don't really believe that,' answered Mr McCartney.

A reporter asked if they were not tired of all the 'hocus-pocus' and if they would not rather sit on their 'fat wallets'.

'When we do get tired,' answered Mr McCartney, 'we take fat vacations on our fat wallets.'

Mr Starr, the quietest of the four, was asked that now that his son is almost a year old, 'can you tell us what he'd like for Christmas.'

'I don't know. He doesn't talk yet,' the drummer replied.

When asked if they were disappointed that only nine teenagers were on hand when they arrived at La Guardia Airport a little after 3 yesterday morning in the smallest reception they had had in New York, they all chimed in sarcastically: 'Yeah, we were real brought down by it. . . . We expected millions.'

Meanwhile, at the Americana Hotel, which is on Seventh Avenue between 52nd and 53rd Streets, the police rescued two teenage girls from Staten Island who'd threatened to jump from a narrow ledge on the 22nd floor unless they could see The Beatles. Two husky patrolmen grabbed the pair in mid-afternoon after 30 minutes of coaxing during which a traffic and pedestrian jam developed below.

. . . The Beatles' reception at the Warwick, at 54th Street and the Avenue of the Americas, also was calmer than it had been last August. The police kept teenagers a block away from the hotel. About 400 young fans—mostly girls—stood behind a police barricade on the southwest corner of 53rd Street and the Avenue of the Americas.

'We want Paul, we want Paul,' they chanted.

A police sergeant chanted: 'Why don't you go home, why don't you go home.'

Thirteen-year-old Sondra Albano of Brighton Beach, Brooklyn, came with a set of binoculars to look at The Beatles' window. 'I saw Ringo,' she said. 'He has a beautiful nose.'

The Beatles are scheduled to fly to Los Angeles tomorrow night immediately after their concert at Shea Stadium.

PETER CLAYTON

Revolver

Gramophone, October 1966

While the Ku Klux Klan was busy making the world safe for Christianity by attacking Negroes and burning Beatles records, I received my copy of the new Beatles LP, *Revolver*. I can see what the Klan's on about. The record's full of decadent pernicious stuff like compassion (in 'Eleanor Rigby'), wit (in 'Taxman'), fantasy ('Yellow submarine'), good humour ('Good day sunshine') and originality (most of the 14 tracks).

This really is an astonishing collection, and listening to it you realise that the distance these four odd young men have travelled since that first record of 'Love me do' in 1962 is musically even greater than it is materially. It isn't easy to describe what's here, since much of it involves things which are either new to pop music or which are being properly applied for the first time, and which can't be helpfully compared with anything. In fact, the impression you get is not of any one sound or flavour, but simply of smoking hot newness with plenty of flaws and imperfections, but *fresh*. Two tracks fight for first place in my personal poll—'Eleanor' and 'For no one'. But George Harrison's 'Taxman' and his mini-raga 'Love you to', and the fascinating 'Dr Robert' are close behind. Even 'Yellow submarine' which I'd been just tolerating on the radio, begins to grow on you. If there's anything wrong with the record at all it is that such a diet of newness might give the ordinary pop-picker indigestion.

LEADER COMMENT

Penny Lane for a song

The Times, 1 April 1967

Anyone who knows Liverpool is probably startled by the sudden fame of an ordinary road in the amorphous muddle which is Liverpool 18. It is easy to understand why there should be songs referring to Piccadilly and Leicester Square, to the Strand and Richmond Hill—all, at least superficially, more memorable than Liverpool's Penny Lane.

Yet it is this undistinguished road which has been singled out in song and which, rather than any of the city's unique features, has come to symbolise the fascinating sprawl of Liverpool in the minds of many young people who have never even seen the place. This is one likeable feature of a pleasant song which seems to be entirely in an honourable tradition. To see that some apparently ordinary place is unlike any other and to express for it a nostalgia unmixed with any chauvinistic notions of its superiority is a pleasant but forgotten art. Popular songs are naturally sentimental, but the sentiments of this one are gently affectionate and unexceptionable.

'Penny Lane', indeed, looks back to the days when parochialism was not an attitude to be derided. To the musically unsophisticated, the new ballad is delightful because it seems to be entirely original in concerning itself with such gentle normalities. But its old-fashioned parochialism reminds us of something else. Although we have paid a great deal of attention to its creators' use of 'sophisticated' chords and chord sequences which, in reality, we hear whenever we listen to any modern music, it is possible to see in The Beatles' music a synthesis in which one of the strongest elements has been a powerful and probably instinctive Englishry, hidden from the unobservant by electronic impediment, which goes back through *Hymns Ancient and Modern* to pastoral pentatonic tunes and other revitalised archaisms.

To read popular attitudes into or deduce trends of thought from Britten's next song cycle or Stravinsky's next elliptical epigram would be foolish. It is musicians like The Beatles who express what is going on in the popular mind, and while it may seem that a commonplace suburb is a pleasanter source of inspiration than a psychedelic ecstasy, it may also be that the song is instinctively satisfying a youthful appetite for simplicity, naturalness, and the ordinary which might be a hopeful sign for the future. 'Pop' by its nature lags behind the conscious art which since the 1920s has preferred to avoid emotional inflations, and it may be that their minstrels are at last going to teach the young that small things have their value, that there is a difference between pleasure and rapture everywhere but in love songs, and that the ordinary world is worth attention.

JOHN LAHR

Up Against It

from: 'Introduction' to Joe Orton's *Up Against It—a screenplay for The Beatles*

'Well, the sound and the fury is over', Orton wrote to an American friend in October 1966. 'LOOT and JOE ORTON (as you can see from the reviews) a great success. I feel exhausted. 18 months of struggling to vindicate the honour of my play (my own is beyond vindication) have left me weak at the knees.'

By January 1967, Orton's sense of exhaustion had given way to exhilaration. He had just turned 34. His reputation had been secured. The grind of *Loot*'s rewrites had paid off not only in acclaim but in craft. And Orton knew it. He was riding high and entering the most fecund period of his literary life. His career had acquired a new velocity. By the second week of January, the first draft of his farce masterpiece *What the Butler Saw* was completed and tucked away in the drawer beneath his divan bed to 'mature' for six months. A TV production of *The Good and*

Faithful Servant with Donald Pleasence was in rehearsal. *Entertaining Mr Sloane*, after being scuttled by ITV, was rescheduled. *Loot* had been bought for Broadway. And on January 11, Orton stepped up to the podium at Quaglino's in a large flowered tie and a wide grin to accept the *Evening Standard* Award for the Best Play of the Year.

'I was on the front of the *Evening Standard* receiving the award,' Orton wrote in the diary he'd begun a few weeks earlier and puckishly called *Diary of a Somebody*, 'I'm very happy.' The word 'happy' is so rare in Orton's diaries as to be startling. He distrusted happiness; and in this case, it didn't last long. The TV programme that broadcast the ceremony ran its credits over Orton receiving the award. 'The whole had the effect of the man with the bladder hitting the Emperor on the head as he rode in triumph. Just to take him down a peg and remind him that he wasn't a god.'

But Orton was in a weird state of grace, and even this minor disappointment was quickly forgotten the next day when Orton was contacted to work on a film script for The Beatles. In the aristocracy of success, Orton was learning fast, there were no strangers.

Orton had never written a film script. In 1964, he worked up a 19-page treatment for Lindsay Anderson who wanted to make a modern movie version of *The Bacchae*. The film never got off the ground; and Orton turned his notion into *The Erpingham Camp*. Funny as Orton's treatment was, his arch style didn't seem to suit the camera. 'Not film dialogue, is it?' was Lindsay Anderson's verdict. But since then, Orton's understanding of plot and tone had become more sophisticated. In his rewrites of *Loot* and the first draft of *What the Butler Saw* he worked hard to make his stage pictures as startling as his words. His comedy was becoming more visual. To match The Beatles' high jinks with his own wicked fun was an irresistible challenge. Always the tease, Orton tried to hide his enthusiasm when Walter Shenson called him. Shenson, who had produced *A Hard Day's Night* and *Help!*, wanted Orton to 'punch-up' a dull script The Beatles had already commissioned. Orton recorded the conversation in his diary:

> 'Would you like to see it with a view to working on the film script?' I was very impressed by this, but I put on a nonchalant manner. 'Well, I'm frightfully up to my eyes in it at the moment,' I said. 'I'm writing my third play.' 'I'd certainly love to have you take a look at this draft,' he said. 'I've discussed it with the boys. I mean I mentioned your name to them. They've heard of you. They didn't react too much, I must say. But I think I can persuade them to have you.' By this time I was feeling foolish and not at all nonchalant. 'Yes,' I said. 'Please send the script over and I'll read it.'

Orton read The Beatles' script on January 15, the day he re-read the first draft of *What the Butler Saw* ('Pleased, but still work to be done'). After such hard and inspired writing, he needed a change of pace and The Beatles' script promised to be more a romp than a slog. He was full of fun and ideas. And, besides, the script had possibilities.

> Like the idea. Basically it is that there aren't four young men. Just four aspects of one man. Sounds dreary, but as I thought about it I realised what wonderful opportunities it would give. The end in the present script is the girl advancing on the four to accept a proposal of marriage from one of them (which, the script coyly says, we shall never know). Already have the idea that the end should be a church with four bridegrooms and one bride. THE HOMECOMING in fact, but alibied in such a way that no one could object. Lots of opportunities for sexual ambiguities—a woman's bedroom at night, her husband outside and four men inside. I also would like to incorporate a lot of material from the first novel Kenneth [Halliwell] and I wrote called THE SILVER BUCKET. In it a young girl is expelled from her native village for some unnamed offence. Already see how it could be one boy expelled from some great industrial metropolis by a ceremony of mammoth proportions. Could be funny. As long as I wasn't expected to write a naturalistic script. Rang Walter Shenson . . . Arranged to meet him tomorrow.
>
> Basically The Beatles are getting fed up with the Dick Lester type of direction. They want dialogue to speak. Also they are tired of actors like Leon McKern [*sic*] stealing scenes. Difficult this as I don't think any of The Beatles can act in any accepted sense. As Marilyn Monroe couldn't act. Hope to discuss this problem in detail tomorrow.

Before seeing Shenson, Orton met with his agent Peggy Ramsay. It was nearly three years to the week since she'd summoned him to her office in St Martin's Lane and agreed to represent *Entertaining Mr Sloane*. As Orton was getting up to leave from that first meeting, she'd asked him what he lived on while he wrote. Orton explained that he was on the dole and surviving on £3. 10s. a week. She immediately marshalled her forces and found him a producer within three weeks. Orton's advance on the play had been £100. Now Peggy Ramsay was telling him, 'We'll ask ten thousand. Not a hope of getting it, of course. But we'll allow ourselves to be beaten down.'

. . . Orton was an outsider; and it was precisely his rejection of the bourgeois world which made his laughter dangerous. Nonetheless, he relished infiltrating alien territory. Any association with The Beatles would put him at the hot centre of pop culture. In meeting Shenson, Orton was taking his first steps down the corridors of commercial power. His diary shows how carefully he watched every move.

> I went into a door with a sheet of paper pinned onto it saying 'With the compliments of Walter Shenson (films) Inc.' Inside was a small office. Empty. I looked into a further office. In it was a man about thirty-five, pinkish face, rather a bright, cringing air. 'Are you for Walter?' he said.

'Yes,' I said. 'My name is Joe Orton.' I said this in a bold, confident tone. He squeezed past me in the doorway. 'Walter!' he gave a quick, sharp call. A man appeared in a far doorway. Middle-aged. Short hair going to grey. A bald patch. He started towards me, his hand outstretched. In fact he'd begun the motion of shaking hands before his hand touched mine. 'Come into my office,' he said. 'That's the wrong door.' 'I thought it was a bit crummy,' I said. 'For a film producer.' 'Heh, heh, heh,' laughed Walter Shenson. 'Throw your coat over here, heh, heh, heh.' I put down my coat and he disappeared into another office . . . While he was gone I looked around. It was a big, long room. On the shelf over the fireplace was a cube with the faces of the four Beatles on each side of the cube. I picked it up and opened the lid, inside was a card saying 'Horse shit'. 'Heh, heh, heh,' said Walter Shenson, appearing behind me, 'That's a joke thing some guy sent me from back home. They're quite a thing over there, now, heh, heh, heh.'

We talked for a while about the script. I gave away a few of my ideas. Enough to whet his appetite . . . Over lunch he said that one of the ideas for a new Beatles' film was *The Three Musketeers*. 'Oh, no!' I said. 'That's been done to death.' 'Brigitte Bardot wanted to play Lady de-Winter,' he said. 'She's been done to death as well,' I said. 'Oh, heh, heh, heh, boy!' he said. 'You certainly are quick' . . .

By the end of the day, Orton had a title for his original film script: *Up Against It*, and had written the first two pages. 'Miss Drumgoole and Father Brodie have come to life as interesting characters. Which should delight The Beatles,' he wrote. 'I'm not bothering to write characters for them. I shall just do all my box of tricks—Sloane and Hal on them. After all if I repeat myself in this film it doesn't matter. Nobody who sees the film will have seen *Sloane* or *Loot*.'

The film was a lark, and Orton never invested it with the care or passion he gave his plays. His instructions to Peggy Ramsay on January 25, reflected his insouciance:

'We should ask £15,000,' I said, 'and then if they beat us down, remember no lower than 10,000. After all, whether I do it or not is a matter of indifference to me.' Peggy agreed. 'If they won't pay us 10 they can fuck themselves,' I said. 'Of course, darling,' Peggy said.

Shenson had promised to arrange a meeting between Orton and The Beatles. In his talk Orton heard the first seductive stroke of the movie rubdown, the slap and tickle of famous names and big paydays:

'You'll be hearing either from Brian Epstein or Paul McCartney [Shenson told Orton on January 17]. So don't be surprised if a Beatle rings you up.' 'What an experience,' I said. 'I shall feel as nervous as I would if St Michael, or God was on the line.' 'Oh, there's not any need to be worried, Joe,' Shenson said. 'I can say, from my heart, that the boys are very respectful of talent. I mean, most respectful of anyone they feel has talent. I can really say that, Joe.'

The Call finally came at dinner time a week later on January 23. 'Epstein's adviser rang while I was eating a meal of mashed potatoes, tinned salmon and beetroot', Orton noted wryly.

Orton arrived promptly the next day at Epstein's office to be faced with the screenwriter's first debilitating hazard: waiting. 'After about five minutes or so a youngish man with a hair-style which was way out in 1958, short, college-boy came up and said, ". . . I'm Brian Epstein's personal assistant",' Orton wrote in his diary on January 24.

> It crossed my mind to wonder why the English have never got around to finding a perfectly respectable word for 'boy-friend'. 'I'm afraid there's been a most awful mix-up. And all the boys' appointments have been put back an hour and a half.' I was a bit chilly in my manner after that. 'Do you want me to come back at six?' I said. 'Well, no. Could we make another appointment?' 'What guarantee is there that you won't break that?' I said. 'I think you better find yourself a different writer.' This said with indifferent success, though the effect was startling. He asked me to wait a minute and went away to return with Brian Epstein himself. Somehow I'd expected something like Michael Codron. I'd imagined Epstein to be florid, Jewish, dark-haired and overbearing. Instead I was face to face with a mousey-haired, slight young man. Washed-out in a way. He had a suburban accent. I went into his office, 'Could you meet Paul and me for dinner tonight?' he said. 'We do want to have the pleasure of talking to you.' 'I've a theatre engagement tonight,' I replied, by now sulky and unhelpful. 'Could I send the car to fetch you after the show?' I didn't much relish this flim-flammery, left almost tripping over the carpet and crashing into the secretary who gave a squeal of surprise as I hurtled past her. This I never mention when re-telling the story. I always end on a note of hurt dignity.

Orton's first glimpse of The Beatles' world caught the ludicrous contradiction in these cultural supermen: playing rebel and living posh.

> Arrived in Belgravia at ten minutes to eight . . . I found Chapel Street easily. I didn't want to get there too early so I walked around for a while and came back through a nearby mews. When I got back to the house it was nearly eight o'clock. I rang the bell and an old man entered. He seemed surprised to see me. 'Is this Brian Epstein's house?' I said. 'Yes, sir,' he said, and led the way to the hall. I suddenly realised that the man was the butler. I've never seen one before . . . He took me into a room and said in a loud voice, 'Mr Orton'. Everybody looked up and stood to their feet. I was introduced to one or two people. And Paul McCartney. He was just as the photographs. Only he'd grown a moustache. His hair was shorter too. He was playing the latest Beatles record 'Penny Lane'. I like it very much. Then he played the other side—Strawberry something. I didn't like this as much. We talked intermittently. Before we went out to dinner we agreed to throw out the idea of setting the film in the Thirties. We went down to dinner. The trusted old retainer—looking too much like a butler to be good casting—busied himself in the

corner. 'The only thing I get from the theatre,' Paul M. said, 'is a sore arse.' He said *Loot* was the only play he hadn't wanted to leave before the end. 'I'd've liked a bit more,' he said. We talked of the theatre. I said that compared with the pop-scene the theatre was square. 'The theatre started going down hill when Queen Victoria knighted Henry Irving,' I said. 'Too fucking respectable.' We talked of drugs, of mushrooms which give hallucinations—like LSD. 'The drug not the money,' I said. We talked of tattoos. And after one or two veiled references, marijuana. I said I'd smoked it in Morocco. The atmosphere relaxed a little. Dinner ended and we went upstairs again. We watched a programme on TV; it had phrases in it like 'the in crowd' and 'swinging London'. There was a little scratching at the door. I thought it was the old retainer, but someone got up to open the door and about five very young and pretty boys trouped in. I rather hoped this was the evening's entertainment. It wasn't, though. It was a pop group called The Easybeats. I'd seen them on TV. I liked them very much . . . A French photographer arrived . . . He'd taken a set of new photographs of The Beatles. They wanted one to use on the record sleeve. Excellent photographs. The four Beatles look different in their moustaches. Like anarchists in the early years of the century. After a while . . . I talked to the leading Easybeat. Feeling slightly like an Edwardian masher with a Gaiety girl. And then I came over tired and decided to go home. I had a last word with Paul M. 'Well,' I said, 'I'd like to do the film. There's only one thing we've got to fix up.' 'You mean the bread?' 'Yes.' We smiled and parted. I got a cab home. Told Kenneth about it. Then he got up to make a cup of tea. And we talked a little more. And went to sleep.

While the contract was being negotiated (£5,000 for the first draft with the right to buy the script back if unacceptable to The Beatles), Orton grew a moustache and blithely got to work. 'I shall enjoy writing the film,' he wrote in his diary.

Orton worked fast, aided by the discovery—'inspiration' was his word for it—of an old novel which provided the backbone of the scenario. 'I'd already written the beginning of the script up to where McTurk is thrown out of town,' he wrote on January 29. 'And then I remembered that in the cupboard somewhere was the manuscript of a novel I'd written in 1959 called THE VISION OF GOMBOLD PROVAL [posthumously published as *Head To Toe*]. It had always been my intention some day to rewrite it. I decided to get it down and see if there was anything I could use. I found, to my surprise, that it was excellent. It has great faults as a novel, but as the basis for a film it was more than adequate. So I'm rewriting the whole thing. Miraculously towards the middle of the novel four young men appear.' By February 11, when Orton was summoned to Shenson's office for one final pep talk before the contract was signed, the script was almost completed. Shenson 'was most concerned to impress me that "the boys" shouldn't be made to do anything in the film that would reflect badly on them,'

Orton wrote, getting his first dose of the screen-writer's second debilitating hazard: the commercial compromise. ' "You see," he said, "the kids will all imitate whatever the boys do." I hadn't the heart to tell him that the boys, in my script, have been caught *in flagrante*, become involved in dubious political activity, dressed as women, committed murder, been put in prison and committed adultery. And the script isn't finished yet. I thought it best to say nothing of my plans for The Beatles until he had a chance of reading the script. We parted at five o'clock amicably. With the contract, according to him, as good as signed. And on my part, the film almost written.'

. . . Orton had written *Up Against It* so fast that he asked Peggy Ramsay to wait three weeks before submitting it. She found the script 'splendid', although, as Orton noted in his diary, 'she was worried by the way what she called my "dubious morality" showed through. Especially the killing of the Prime Minister.' The script was sent to Shenson on March 6. 'Peggy feels it will be too much for him,' Orton wrote in his diary. She was right. He called the next day, saying he was 'fascinated' but worried whether it should be four boys or four aspects of one person.

'. . . As you know, Joe, we're all different people. And we have to learn to live with those aspects. I understand that the original idea was to show how a man can live with himself.' Which is pretentious shit. I can't write that, or, what is more important, alter my script to fit that idea. I'd much rather have it about four boys anyway. Shenson is going to speak to Epstein from Los Angeles tonight. He has suggested Antonioni to direct. Rubbish!

By March 29, Orton had still heard nothing from The Beatles. He fixed on Brian Epstein as the culprit: 'An amateur and a fool. He isn't equipped to judge the quality of a script. Probably he will never say "yes" equally hasn't got the courage to say "no". A thoroughly weak, flaccid type.' And then on April 4, *Up Against It* was returned. 'No explanation why. No criticism of the script. And apparently, Brian Epstein has no comment to make either. Fuck them.'

WILLIAM MANN

The Beatles revive hopes of progress in pop music

The Times, 29 May 1967

A few Saturdays ago, on *Juke Box Jury*, Paul Jones let fall a remark about the depressing state of pop music; the programme's compère, David Jacobs, countered, a trace primly, that some people considered the pop scene to be in unusually healthy condition. My sympathies at the time were firmly with Mr Jones. The quantity of nondescript songs then figuring in the hit parade was sad even when one admits that dozens of boring creations have to be sifted, in every field of art always, before something of real quality is discovered. The picture looks much more gay now that The Beatles have produced their new LP, *Sgt Pepper's Lonely Hearts Club Band*. In fact it has not looked so cheerful since their last LP *Revolver*. After listening to *Sgt Pepper*, I have been reflecting on what happened to pop music in the meantime, and some not unhealthy and quite interesting trends do emerge; if they are connected with these two LPs and with the excellent intervening Beatles single, 'Penny Lane' and 'Strawberry Fields', that is hardly to be wondered at.

Pop music in the last few months, as for the last 12 years or more, has been dominated by ballads and beat music, and not all are or have been pot-boilers. There has also been a progressive broadening of interest in genres that could appeal without necessarily dragging pop through the artistic mire: oriental sounds, folk music, creative revivals of pop classics, novelty numbers and in particular vaudeville as a style, creative raids on classical styles and idioms, and looting (not always just vulture-like) of earlier experiments by the most progressive groups. Spurring these varied developments is the recognition that popularity has many faces.

The young teenagers of 1963 who fell like hungry travellers upon the Merseyside Beat are now much older and more sophisticated, and more experienced in adult ways. Pop music still has to cater for them and for the distinctive characteristics they have by now assumed. Mod, rocker, intellectual, rebel, permissive, careerist, all get comfort or inspiration from different music, and The Beatles have held their supremacy because they can dip into all these inkwells with equally eloquent results. There is still a faithful pop following among the generations who cut their teeth on Tommy Steele, Alma Cogan, Vera Lynn, Bing Crosby and George Formby, to go no farther back. And since 1963 a new generation of young people has arrived, demanding (or maybe only enthusiastically accepting) the pop music appropriate to its own age.

One can imagine a new pop group deciding cold-bloodedly to concentrate commercially on appealing to one of these age-groups. The creators of The Monkees do not deny having done so and even virtuoso pop musicians are galled by the success of a group that was brought, Frankenstein-fashion, into being without reference to musical talents. Their songs are carefully modelled on early Beatle style uncreatively but skilfully manipulated. Their first single, 'Last train to Clarksville', flopped in Britain at first but zoomed up the charts as soon as The Monkees began to appear in weekly short films on television (the manner of presentation heavily indebted to *A Hard Day's Night*). Just now The Monkees are idols of the pre-teenage generation and are not quite despised by those approaching O-levels. This has been their year, in the absence of anything more remarkable, and the showmanship involved has to be admired, if not the musical artistry. I suspect that their songs were written by a computer fed with the first two Beatle LPs and *The Oxford Book of Nursery Rhymes*.

It has also been a period of nursery lyrics. The Lennon–McCartney 'Yellow submarine' set the ball rolling and of late we have had no end of songs whose words bring out the delayed adolescence in all of us: The Alan Price Set's 'Simon Smith and his dancing bear', Manfred Mann's 'Ha-ha said the clown', Sandie Shaw's 'Puppet on a string' (which alarmingly, though to the delight of unmusical patriots, won the Eurovision Song Contest), The Hollies' 'Lullaby for Tim', Dave Clark's 'Tabitha Twitchit'. All these encourage separatists in their belief that pop music is strictly for the pre-adolescent—not to mention [David Bowie's] heavy-handedly facetious number about a laughing gnome which was ecstatically plugged for several weeks by the pirate stations but steadfastly remained the flop it deserved to be.

The words of songs are as important as the music: Monteverdi, Schumann, Wolf, Britten have all accepted this belief to their advantage, and pop music has benefited whenever composers have done likewise. The Moon–June syndrome is nowadays frowned on. There were skilful, imaginative lyrics in the 1930s (think of Ira Gershwin and, earlier, of 'St James's Infirmary Blues'). But the importance of the lyric in modern pop songs owes more to Bob Dylan than to anybody. Dylan was part of the protest folksong movement, and though nowadays this is in abeyance and Dylan a sick man slowly on the mend, with only a very pop number about a leopardskin hat to keep his laurels green, his influence on the content of pop lyrics is still strong: think of The Bee Gees' 'New York mining disaster 1941' (music essentially early Beatles), and The Animals' 'When I was young', and Cat Stevens's 'Matthew and Son' of a while back. Social comment is helpful to a pop song, and some of these have deservedly done well in the charts. The sneering lazy Dylan voice, and the folksong ballad type of tune he favours, are still much copied. Folksong is very much a part of pop, as is testified by the success of The Dubliners' 'Seven drunken nights' (a favourite Irish closing-time number) and, on a slightly different wavelength, the Russian-derived 'OK' of Dave Dee, Dozy, Beaky, Mick and Tich.

Folksong as an ingredient of pop is an exhumation of the past (paralleled in straight music by the new popularity among concertgoers of preclassical music, and in art by the resurgence of *Art nouveau*), and in the past 12 months there has been an even more prevalent revival of the 1920s vaudeville number. 'Winchester Cathedral', by the New Vaudeville Band, set it going last September. Since then we have had 'Peek-a-boo' and 'Finchley Central'; and The Kinks, who had already moved into the contemporary satire sphere, have lately jumped into vaudeville with their very likeable 'Waterloo sunset' (part of a place-names cult, connected with 'Penny Lane', perhaps with 'A nightingale sang in Berkeley Square' and even 'Let's all go down the Strand' or 'Basin Street Blues').

The idea of reviving vaudeville is rather artificial, not to say escapist, but it accords with a certain camp trend in fashions and in decorative art. It may be thought by some people no more odd than the revitalised honky-tonk and boogie-woogie of some Rolling Stones numbers in their recent turncoat LP, *Between the Buttons* (which includes one ultra-camp song, 'A strange thing happened to me yesterday'). And there is the rare but often appealing grope back to classical or baroque musical language, as in the Alberti string figuration of The Beatles' 'Eleanor Rigby' (another song with a powerful lyric) and the new, distinctly Bach-derived 'Whiter shade of pale' by Procol Harum (whose name is supposedly Latin, even if it should be 'procul') which has its pop parentage in some Animals numbers and is very beautiful indeed. There is the growing allure of oriental, at present chiefly Indian, music initiated by George Harrison of The Beatles, taken up by The Rolling Stones and nowadays quite common as an accompanying texture (like the revival of the harpsichord a few years ago). From The Beatles also came the current preoccupation with more or less disciplined whorls of electronically manipulated clusters of sound, famous through 'Tomorrow never knows' but audible on all sides, and adopted in concerts by several groups spectacularly as well as audibly. In some records by The Righteous Brothers and The Walker Brothers, and in some of Jimi Hendrix's songs, it is just an all-too generalised effect. But in 'Strawberry Fields', and The Stones' 'Paint it black', it was poetically and precisely applied. The vogue word for this is psychedelic music.

There remain the beat-songs and ballads. Beat music has, by natural evolution, become more varied and occasionally more subtle than it used to be. It is no longer fettered to unchanging two or four in a bar, nor need it be harmonised entirely diatonically in root positions; the bass-line can be vivid, like the words, but usually is not. Most groups are content to put over something enthusiastic and with a big, noisy sound, though The Rolling Stones, The Hollies, The Moody Blues, Manfred Mann, The Who (these last two groups for the moment less actively) have shown, like The Beatles, that beat music can be as diverse as any other sort. Ballads are the despair of forward-looking pop students. Not that they are irredeemable: there are cool ballads, and ballads with a vital pulse, and ballads with distinctive tunes or interesting words. But again and monotonously again, the sticky, sweaty, vacuous ballad reaches to the melting hearts of housewives who prefer the lowest when they hear it, and accordingly it soars to the top like a jetplane made of golden syrup.

There is hope for all these pop genres, and *Sgt Pepper's Lonely Hearts Club Band* provides it in abundance. Two of the tracks are quasi-ballad: 'Fixing a hole' is cool, anti-romantic, harmonically a little like the earlier 'Yesterday' and 'Michelle'; 'She's leaving home' is a slow waltz reminiscent of old musical comedy but with a classically slanted accompaniment for harp and string quartet [*sic*], and with ironical words about a minor domestic tragedy (the texts, which are of consistently lively poetic interest, are printed in full on the back cover). There is a neat vaudeville number 'When I'm sixty-four', which comments pointedly on this old-time vogue and its relevance for modern beat song. George Harrison's 'Within you without you' carries the manner of Indian music farther into pop than ever before though the tune of the song is recognisably mixolydian; there are hints of Indian atmosphere in some of the other songs (which are all by Lennon and McCartney).

Psychedelia can be diagnosed in the fanciful lyric and intriguing asymmetrical music of 'Lucy in the sky', as well as in the sound effects of 'Lovely Rita' (she is a parking meter warden), and the hurricane glissandi of 'A day in the life' which has been banned by the BBC for its ambivalent references to drug-taking—though if anything on the record is going to encourage dope it is surely the 'tangerine trees and marmalade skies' and the 'girl with kaleidoscope eyes' in 'Lucy in the sky' which contains none of these whoosh noises. I greatly enjoy the five-bar phrases of 'Good morning good morning' which is something like a novelty number; and the tidy simplicity and shapely bass-line of

'A little help from my friends', the only track that would have been conceivable in pop songs five years ago.

Any of these songs is more genuinely creative than anything currently to be heard on pop radio stations, but in relationship to what other groups have been doing lately *Sgt Pepper* is chiefly significant as constructive criticism, a sort of pop music master class examining trends and correcting or tidying up inconsistencies and undisciplined work, here and there suggesting a line worth following. The one new exploration is the showband manner of the title-song, its reprise, and its interval song, 'Being for the benefit of Mr Kite'. These three give a certain shape and integrity to the two sides, and if the unity is slightly specious the idea is, I think, new to popsong LPs, which are usually unconnected anthologies, and it is worth pursuing. Sooner or later some group will take the next logical step and produce an LP which is a popsong-cycle, a Tin Pan Alley *Dichterliebe*. Whether or not the remains of Schumann and Heine turn in their graves at this description depends on the artistry of the compiler.

Note

1. Wilfred Mellers: *Twilight of the Gods: the Beatles in Retrospect* (London, 1973) p. 58

FOUR

Mind Games

LUCIANO BERIO

Comments on rock

from: *Nuova Rivista Musicale Italiana*, May/June 1967

. . . It is remarkable that . . . the phenomenon of rock (whose origins can be found in American popular music) needed an English group, The Beatles, in order to burst into full flower. . . .

Rock as it is at present in the USA (above all in California) and in England (above all in The Beatles' records) represents an escape from the restrictions of its stylistic origins, a tribute to the liberating forces of eclecticism. The musical eclecticism which characterises its phenomenology . . . is not a fragmentary and imitative impulse and it has nothing in common with the spent residue of abused and stereotyped forms—which are still identifiable as rock and roll. Rather, it is dictated by an impulse to accept and include—and using rather rudimentary musical means—to integrate the (simplified) idea of a multiplicity of traditions. . . . With the exception of the beat, loud and often unvaried, all its musical characteristics seem sufficiently open to allow for every possible influence and event to be absorbed. . . .

. . . One of its most attractive vocal characteristics is the naturalness, the spontaneity and the multitude of sounds. It's true that, most of the time, the singing is on the level of a scream, but everyone screams in his own fashion without affectation. The words, too, when they are not reduced to verbal ritual, to nonsense, or to instrumental onomatopoeia, are rarely stereotyped and rarely superfluous (although a certain superfluity comes inevitably with the repetitive form of rock songs). The effort sometimes required to understand the words and to grasp their different levels of comprehensibility is analogous to the effort required to disentangle the message of a psychedelic poster. . . . Voices and instruments are very much amplified. . . . Microphones, amplifiers and loudspeakers become not only extensions of the voices and instruments but become instruments themselves, overwhelming at times the original acoustic qualities of the sound source. One of the most seductive aspects of rock vocal style is, in fact, that there is no style. Voices . . . are magnified in all their naturalness and spontaneity, creating the sort of relationship *vis-à-vis* formalised styles of singing that a cinematic close-up bears to a classical portrait.

Similarly, the all-embracing nature of rock is linked to the absence of any preconceived structure. From this tendency to accept the reality of things as they are, in various ways and attitudes, there derives a certain epic quality. . . .

Rock harmonies are based essentially on the major and minor triads, plain and simple, without any interest in the mellifluous and sophisticated harmonies of post-Gershwin cocktail lounges. Often, therefore, rock music abandons the routine of chords I, IV and V, more or less encrusted with sevenths and ninths, in favour of unusual relationships which give an unmistakable Elizabethan flavour. Often too, successive chords with an open character can be distinguished: these chords are, within certain limits, interchangeable and their sequence could be interrupted and started again at any point.

Some pieces take their inspiration from Indian music, either through instrumentation (as shown in the use of tablas, of the sitar, and of the tremolo arm which enables a normal electric guitar to imitate the sound of the sitar) or through the adoption of a certain formal suspension or a particular scale. In 'Love you to', for example, The Beatles develop, on a drone pedal, two melody lines almost impossible to relate to the conventional criteria of tonal harmony. The self-sufficient character of these lines can sometimes produce a sense of peace and pluralism which has little in common with the more conventional examples. The rhythmic structure too displays rather rare characteristics (especially when it is considered that 3,000 people may be dancing to it): bars in 3/4 and 6/8 time alternate with bars in 4/4, speeding up and then slowing down the rhythm; motifs occur in 5, 7, and 11 time, unpredictable in their length. In the rhythmic patterns of the drums, the normal accentuated beats are not forcefully stressed.

Finally, some pieces (and especially the recorded ones) suggest something more than the idea of song, and develop into 'sound drama', made up of fragments of dialogue, of clips, superimpositions of different recordings and electro-acoustic experimentation: the form may be best described as collage. Those pieces by The Rolling Stones, The Four Tops, The Mothers of Invention, The Grateful Dead and above all The Beatles that are particularly dependent upon studio techniques are practically impossible to perform live. These experiments, introduced for the first time by The Beatles, avoid sound effects and tricks: the reference to surrealism is obvious.

When a *rock* group uses other instruments besides the guitar, the drums and the electric organ, it does so without too many compromises: the 'extra' instruments are used as if freshly discovered, as if they come from afar, in a manner which suggests the Utopia of a return to origins. The sound of the trumpet, for example, is always simple and spare, without mutes or special effects, as in a painting by Grandma Moses: its sound is either baroque or Salvation Army.

I am convinced that the 'decadent' sound of trumpets played with mutes would be the signal that the moment for Rock at the Philharmonic has arrived. I sincerely hope that this moment will never come. . . .

NED ROREM

The music of The Beatles

New York Review of Books, 18 January 1968

I never go to classical concerts anymore, and I don't know anyone who does. It's hard still to care whether some virtuoso tonight will perform the 'Moonlight Sonata' a bit better or a bit worse than another virtuoso performed it last night.

I do often attend what used to be called avant-garde recitals, though seldom with delight, and inevitably I look around and wonder: What am I doing here? What am I learning? Where are the poets and painters and even composers who used to flock to these things? Well, perhaps what I'm doing here is a duty, keeping an ear on my profession so as to justify the joys of resentment, to steal an idea or two, or just to show charity toward some friend on the programme. But I learn less and less. Meanwhile the absent artists are home playing records; they are *reacting* again, finally, to something they no longer find at concerts.

Reacting to what? To The Beatles, of course—The Beatles, whose arrival has proved one of the healthiest events in music since 1950, a fact which no one sensitive can fail to perceive to some degree. By healthy I mean alive and inspired—two adjectives long out of use. By music I include not only the general areas of jazz, but those expressions subsumed in the categories of chamber, opera, symphonic: in short, all music. And by sensitive I understand not the cultivated listening ability of elite Music Lovers so much as instinctive judgment. (There *are* still people who exclaim: 'What's a nice musician like you putting us on about The Beatles for?' They are the same who at this late date take theatre more seriously than movies and go to symphony concerts because pop insults their intelligence, unaware that the situation is now precisely reversed.) As to what occurred around 1950, that will be the starting concern of this brief essay, an essay with a primarily musical approach. Most of the literary copy devoted to The Beatles extols the timely daring of the group's lyrics while skirting the essential, the music. Poetry may be the egg from which the nightingale is hatched, though in the last analysis the nightingale must come first.

My 'musical approach' will be that of what once was termed the long-hair composer, somewhat disillusioned, nourished at the conservatory yet exposed all his life (as is any American, of necessity) to jazz. It will not pretend to a total appraisal, only to the fact that I and my colleagues have been happily torn from a long antiseptic nap by the energy of rock, principally as embodied in The Beatles. Naturally I've grown curious about this energy. What are its origins? What need does it fill? Why should The Beatles—who seem to be the best of a good thing, who in fact are far superior to all the other groups who pretend to copy them, most of which are nevertheless American and perpetuating what once was an essentially American thing—why should The Beatles have erupted from *Liverpool*? Could it be true, as Nat Hentoff suggests, that they 'turned millions of American adolescents on to what had been here hurting all the time . . . but the young here never did want it raw so they absorbed it through the British filter'? Do The Beatles hurt indeed? And are they really so new? Does their attraction, be it pain or pleasure, stem from their words—or even from what's called their *sound*—or quite plainly from their tunes? Those are the questions, more or less in order, that I'd like to examine.

Around 1940, after a rather undifferentiated puberty, American music came into its own. Composers burgeoned over the land which, then deprived of foreign fertilizer, began producing an identifiably native fruit. By the War's end we had cultivated a crop worthy of export, for every branch of the musical tree was thriving: symphonies of all shapes were being ground out in dozens; opera concepts were transplanting themselves into midwestern towns; and, for consideration here, vocal soloists were everywhere making themselves heard. On one side were Sinatra, Horne, Holiday, stylists of a high order, gorgeously performing material whose musical value (when not derived from the Twenties of Gershwin or Porter) was nevertheless middling and whose literary content was dim. On the other side were specialised concert singers—Frijsh, Fairbank and Tangeman—who, though vocally dubious, still created a new brand of sound by persuading certain youngish composers to make singable songs based on texts of quality.

By 1950 the export was well under way. But our effervescence soon flattened when we realised that no one abroad cared much. Jazz, of course, had always been an attraction in the Europe that dismissed American 'serious' music as not very serious; Europe, after all, was also reawakening after two numb decades under Hitler's shadow. But that awakening was into the past, namely into the dodecaphonic system which in America had atrophied, and in Germany had been forgotten by the War. This device (no, not a device but a way of thinking, a philosophy) was being revitalised not in the Germany where it had all begun, but in France, of all places! By 1950 Pierre Boulez had single-handedly cleared the path and set the tone that music would follow for the next decade throughout the world. And America took the cue, allowing her new-found individuality to dissolve into what ultimately became the bandwagon of International Academicism.

This turn of events surprised no one more than everyone, namely our most personal and famous composers. The lean melodism conscientiously forged by Aaron Copland, which had become the accepted American Style, was now tossed out by the young. The complicated romantic Teuton soup in which music had wallowed for a century was, in the Twenties, reacted against either by the Spartan purification of a Satie or a Thomson (wherefrom Copland's 'Americanism') or by the laughing iconoclasm of Dada which—though primarily, like Surrealism, a painters' and poets' medium—was musically exemplified in certain works of *Les Six*. Now in the Fifties complex systems were revived, literally with a vengeance by certain of the middle-aged (Elliott Carter, Milton Babbitt, Arthur Berger, etc.) whom fame had bypassed during the Coplandesque Forties, and by the young in general. If Dada randomness was reanimated by John Cage, this time with a straight face, Copland himself now chose to become re-engaged in serial formality, also with a straight face, as though intimidated by those deadly serious composers half his age.

These 'serious' youngsters, in keeping with the times, were understandably more geared to practical concerns of science than to 'superfluous' considerations of Self-Expression. When they wrote for the human voice (which they did less and less) it was treated not as an interpreter of poetry—nor even necessarily of words—but as a mechanism, often electronically revamped. Verse itself was no longer married *to* the music, or even framed *by* the music, but was illustrated *through* the music. And there was little use left for live singers.

Live singers themselves, at least those of formal training, weren't interested anyway. Modern music was too difficult. Besides it had no audience, and neither anymore did the classical song recital so beloved in the already distant years of Teyte and Lehmann. Young singers were lured away from *lieder*, from *la mélodie*, from their own American 'art song', until not one specialist remained. They had all been seduced by the big money and hopeful celebrity of grand opera. Even today the few exceptions are European: Schwarzkopf, Souzay, Fischer-Dieskau. Our accurate Bethany Beardslee certainly makes no money, while her excellent West Coast counterpart, Marni Nixon, now does movie dubbing and musical comedy. But most modern song specialists have awful voices and give vanity concerts for invited guests.

Elsewhere was developing the Progressive, or Cool, jazz of Brubeck and Kenton and Mulligan, a rarefied expression that permitted neither song nor dance. The Hit Parade was defunct, Negro stylists out of jobs and vulgar vocalists of college bands in low esteem. Song was out.

Meanwhile the wall separating so-called classical from so-called jazz was crumbling, as each division sought somehow to join with and rejuvenate the other. Yet the need for 'communication' so widely lamented today seemed to be satisfied less through music—any music—than through other outlets, particularly movies. Movies, in becoming accepted as a fine art, turned out to be the one medium which could depict most articulately the inarticulateness of today, even to intellectuals. Whereas the intellectualisation of music had ironically alienated the intellectual and has not much interest for anyone else. Stravinsky, for example, may be a household word, but in fact little that he composed since 1930, and virtually nothing since 1950, is in the concert repertory anywhere. Stravinsky's recent music is heard exclusively when accompanied by the visuals of Balanchine, when performed biannually by Robert Craft (the presence of the master himself at these performances being the drawing card), or when conducted by the composer on Columbia Records with whom he has an exclusive contract.

I and a handful of songwriting friends (Paul Bowles, Daniel Pinkham, William Flanagan, David Diamond), who began in the Forties, I consider as having come in at the end, as having attempted the irrelevant resuscitation of a creature with sleeping sickness. Most of us have written depressingly few songs lately, and those few emerged less from driving need than from ever rarer commissions extended by die-hard specialists. Since there's little money, publication, recording, performance or even concern for songs, our youthful enthusiasm for that most gently urgent of mediums has, alas, pretty much dampened.

But if the once-thriving Art of Song has lain dormant since the War, indications now show it restirring in all corners of the world—which is not the same world that put it to bed. As a result, when Song really becomes wide awake again (the sleep has been nourishing), its composition and interpretation will be of a quite different order and for a quite different public.

Since big-time vocalists like Leontyne Price are, for economic reasons, no longer principally occupied with miniature forms, and since 'serious' composers like Stockhausen are, for scientific reasons, no longer principally occupied with human utterances (of which singing is the most primitive and hence the most expressive), and since a master like Stravinsky (who anyway was never famed for his solo vocal works) seems only to be heard when seen, the artful tradition of great song has been transferred from elite domains to The Beatles and their offshoots who represent—as any non-specialised intellectual will tell you—the finest communicable music of our time.

This music was already sprouting a decade ago through such innocent male sex symbols as Presley in America and Johnny Halliday in France, both of whom were then caricatured by the English in a movie called *Expresso Bongo*, a precursor of *Privilege*, about a none-too-bright rock singer. These young soloists (still functioning and making lots of money) were the parents of more sophisticated, more *committed*, soloists like Dylan and Donovan, who in turn spawned a horde of masculine offspring including twins (Simon and Garfunkel, the most cultured), quintuplets (Country Joe & The Fish, the most exotic), sextuplets (The Association, the most nostalgic), even septuplets (Mothers of Invention, the most madly satirical). With much less frequency were born female descendants such as Janis Ian or Bobbie Gentry (each of whom has produced one, and only one, good song—and who may be forgotten or immortal by the time this is read) and the trio of Supremes. Unlike their 'grandparents', all these groups, plus some twenty other fairly good ones, write most of their own material, thus combining the traditions of 12th-century troubadours, 16th-century madrigalists and 18th-century musical artisans who were always composer-performers—in short, combining all sung expression (except opera) as it was before the 20th century.

For this expression one must now employ (as I have been doing here) the straightforward word *Song*, as opposed to the misleading *lieder* which applies just to German repertory, or the pretentious *art song* which no longer applies to anything. (The only designation in

English that ever really distinguished 'serious art song' from what used to be named 'pop tune' was 'recital song'.) Now, since pop tunes as once performed by such as Billie Holiday and the big bands during an epoch not merely dormant but dead are heard not only in nightclub and theatre but in recital and concert, and since those tunes are as good as—if not better than—anything 'serious' being composed today, the best cover-all term is simply *Song*. The only sub-categories are Good and Bad. Curiously, it is not through the suave innovations of our sophisticated composers that music is regaining health, but from the old-fashioned lung exercise of gangs of kids.

That the best of these gangs should have come from England is unimportant; they could have come from Arkansas. The Beatles' world is just another part of the undifferentiated International Academicism wherein the question is to be Better rather than Different. It seems to me that their attraction has little to do with (as Hentoff implied) 'what had been here hurting', but on the contrary with enjoyment.

No sooner does Susan Sontag explain that 'the new sensibility takes a rather dim view of pleasure' than we discover her 'new' sensibility growing stale. Her allusion was to a breed of suspiciously articulate composers—suspicious because they spend more time in glib justification than in composition—and who denigrate the *liking* of music, the *bodily* liking of it. Indeed, one doesn't 'like' Boulez, does one? To like is not their consideration; to comprehend is. But surely fun is the very core of The Beatles' musically contagious expression: the Japanese, the Poles (who ignore the poetic subject matter of suicide and bombs) love them as much as their English-speaking fans; and surely that expression, by the very spontaneous timeliness of its nature, is something Sontag must approve of. The Beatles are antidote to the new (read 'old') sensibility, and intellectuals are allowed to admit, without disgrace, that they like this music.

The Beatles are good even though everyone knows they're good, i.e., in spite of those claims of the Under Thirties about their filling a new sociological need like Civil Rights and LSD. Our need for them is neither sociological nor new, but artistic and old, specifically a *renewal*, a renewal of pleasure. All other arts in the past decade have to an extent felt this renewal; but music was not only the last of man's 'useless' expressions to develop historically, it is also the last to evolve within any given generation—even when, as today, a generation endures a maximum of five years (that brief span wherein 'the new sensibility' was caught).

Why are The Beatles superior? It is easy to say that most of their competition (like most everything everywhere) is junk; more important, their betterness is consistent: each of the songs from their last three albums is memorable. The best of these memorable tunes—and the best is a large percentage ('Here, there and everywhere', 'Good day sunshine', 'Michelle', 'Norwegian wood' are already classics)—compare with those by composers from great eras of song: Monteverdi, Schumann, Poulenc.

Good melody—even perfect melody—can be both defined and taught, as indeed can the other three 'dimensions' of music: rhythm, harmony, counterpoint (although rhythm is the only one that can exist alone). Melody may be described thus: a series of notes of varying pitch and length, which evolve into a recognisable musical shape. In the case of a melody (*tune* means the same thing) which is set to words, the musical line will flow in curves relating to the verse that propels it inevitably toward a 'high' point, usually called climax, and thence to the moment of culmination. The *inevitable* element is what makes the melody good—or perfect. But perfection can be sterile, as witness the thousands of thirty-two-bar models turned out yesterday in Tin Pan Alley, or today by, say, Jefferson Airplane. Can we really recall such tunes when divorced from their words?

Superior melody results from the same recipe, with the difference that certain of the ingredients are blessed with the Distortion of Genius. The Beatles' words often go against the music (the crushing poetry that opens 'A day in the life' intoned to the blandest of tunes), even as Martha Graham's music often contradicts her dance (she gyrates hysterically to utter silence, or stands motionless while all hell breaks loose in the pit). Because The Beatles pervert with naturalness they usually build solid structures, whereas their rivals pervert with affectation, aping the gargoyles but not the cathedral.

The unexpected in itself, of course, is no virtue, though all great works seem to contain it. For instance, to cite as examples only the above four songs: 'Here, there and everywhere' would seem at mid-hearing to be no more than a charming college show ballad, but once concluded it has grown immediately memorable. Why? Because of the minute harmonic shift on the words 'wave of her hand', as surprising, yet as satisfyingly *right* as that in a Monteverdi madrigal like 'A un giro sol'. The notation of the hyper-exuberant rhythms in 'Good day sunshine' was as aggravatingly elusive to me as some by Charles Ives, until I realised it was made by *triplets over the bar*; the 'surprise' here was that The Beatles had made so simple a process *sound* so complex to a professional ear, and yet (by a third convolution) be instantly imitable by any amateur 'with a beat'. 'Michelle' changes key on the very second measure (which is also the second word): in itself this is 'allowed'—Poulenc often did it, and certainly he was the most derivative and correct composer who ever lived; the point is that he *chose* to do it on just the second measure, and that the choice worked. Genius doesn't lie in not being derivative, but in making right choices instead of wrong ones. As for 'Norwegian wood', again it is the arch of the tune—a movement growing increasingly disjunct, an inverted pyramid formed by a zigzag—which proves the song unique and memorable, rather than merely original.

The Beatles' superiority, of course, is finally as elusive as Mozart's to Clementi: they spoke skilfully the same tonal language, but only Mozart spoke it with the added magic of genius. Who will define such magic? The public, in realising this superiority, is right, though not, as usual, for the wrong reason—as it was, say, ten years ago with *Lolita*. For while *Lolita* was accepted pretty much as just a naughty novel, The Beatles can legitimately be absorbed by all ages on all levels: one is allowed to dance or smoke or even have a funeral (playwright Joe Orton's in London) while listening to this music. The same public when discussing The Beatles does not do so by relating them to others, but by relating them to aspects of themselves, as though they were the self-contained definition of an entire movement, or as though in their so-brief career they had (which is true), like Picasso or Stravinsky, already passed through and dispensed with several 'periods'. For example, no sooner was the *Sgt Pepper* album released than a quiver of argument was set off as to whether it was inferior to their previous album *Revolver*, or to *Rubber Soul*. The Beatles, so to speak, had sired themselves. But was 'Eleanor Rigby' their mother or daughter? Was 'Michelle' their grandmother or granddaughter? And was the She of 'She's leaving home' perhaps a sister, since she was the most recently born, or a wife?

And what's this one hears about their sound, those psychedelic effects produced from orchestration 'breakthroughs' presumably inspired by Paul McCartney's leanings toward Stockhausen and electronics? Well, as first demonstrated in 'Tomorrow never knows' and 'Strawberry Fields', the sound proves less involved with content than colour, more with glamour than construction. McCartney's composition has not been affected by these 'innovations' which are instrumental tricks glossily surrounding the composition. Nor is any aspect of that composition itself more 'progressive' than the big bands of yore, or the Cool groups of yesterday. The harmony at its boldest, as with the insistent dissonances of 'I want to tell you', is basically Impressionist and never more advanced than the Ravel of *Chansons Madécasses*. The rhythm gets extremely fancy, as in 'Good day sunshine', but nearly always falls within a 4/4 measure simpler than the simplest Bartók of 50 years ago. The melodies, such as 'Fixing a hole' or 'Michelle', are exquisitely etched, but evolve from standard modes—those with the lowered thirds and sevenths of the blues. The counterpoint when strict, as in parts of 'She's leaving home', is no more complex than 'Three blind mice', and when free, as in 'Got to get you into my life', has the freedom of Hindemith—which is really Bach without the problems, meaning without the working out of the solutions presented by the rigours of 18th-century part-writing. (The Supremes, not to mention instrumentalists like Ornette Coleman, go much farther out than The Beatles in this domain.) As for the overall form, the songs of *Sgt Pepper* are mostly less complicated than those of previous albums which, themselves, seldom adventured beyond a basic verse/chorus structure. It is not in innovation that Paul McCartney's originality lies, but in superiority. It remains to be seen how, if ever, he deals with more spacious forms. But of that miniature scene, Song, he is a modern master. As such he is The Beatles' most significant member.

The lyrics, or rather the poems, of John Lennon have been psychoanalysed beyond recognition. They are indeed clever, touching, appropriately timely and (which is most important) well mated with the tunes. Yet without the tunes, are they really all that much better than the words of, say, Cole Porter or Marc Blitzstein? Certainly Blitzstein's music succeeds in spite of the dated commentary of his words, and Porter's songs remain beautiful with no words at all. We are often told (for instance by Korall in *Saturday Review*) that The Beatles 'are shouting about important things', but are these things any more pertinent than 'Strange fruit' yesterday or 'Miss Otis regrets' the day before? Was Peggy Lee's crooning 'Where or when' less psychedelic than 'Lucy in the sky'? And even if they are, could that be what makes The Beatles good? While the film *Privilege* portrays a rock singer so subversive he requires total control, the fact is, as Gene Lees puts it, that 'thus far no rock group, not even the entire rock movement put together, has made a government nervous, as Gilbert and Sullivan did.' Even if, in a pinch, poems can be successfully political, no music can be proved to 'signify' anything, neither protest, nor love, nor even bubbling fountains, nothing. John Lennon's words do indeed not only expose current problems ('A day in the life') but suggest solutions ('Fixing a hole'); and the music—which is presumably set to the verse, not vice versa—works fine. But that music is stronger; and, like the slow and metreless Gregorian Chant which altered the 'meaning' of the rapid and ribald street chanties it stemmed from, Lennon's words do or don't matter according to how they're sung.

With Billie Holiday it was not so much the song as her way with the song; like Piaf she could make mediocrity seem masterful. With The Beatles it's the song itself, not necessarily their way—like Schubert whom even a monster can't destroy. 'Michelle', for example, remains as lovely but becomes more clearly projected when performed by a 'real' singer like Cathy Berberian. Her diction (and the diction of nearly everyone) is better than theirs, at least to non-Cockney [*sic*] ears. Even if the words did not come second, The Beatles oblige you to judge the music first, by virtue of their blurred enunciation.

As for George Harrison's excursions into India, they seem the least persuasive aspect of the more recent Beatle language. Like McCartney with electronics, Harrison seems to have adopted only the frosting; but in pretending to have adopted also the structure, his two big pieces, 'Love you to' and 'Within you without you', end up not hypnotic, merely sprawling. Harrison's orientalism is undoubtedly sincere but sounds as fake as the pentatonicism of Country Joe & The Fish. Debussy, like all his cohorts, was profoundly influenced by the Balinese exhibits at the Paris World's Fair of 1900, which inspired his *Pagodes* and *Lindaraja*. These pieces were as persuasive in the same genre as were the concert works many decades later by Henry Cowell or Harry Partch or even Peggy Glanville-Hicks. But whereas these sophisticated musicians without concern for 'authenticity' translated Eastern sound effects into Western jargons and then spoke those jargons with controlled formality, Harrison still flounders for faithful meaning where it just won't work: good will and 'inspiration' will never provide him with the background—the birthright—which of necessity produced the music he would emulate.

Ringo Starr's projects, when not involved with his comrades, are unknown, though he does seem to be learning to sing with what is quite literally an unutterable charm. Nor have I seen John Lennon's war movie. Thus far, however, when The Beatles are a conjointly creative process (even more than as a performing unit) they are at their most enticing.

Just as today my own composition springs more from pristine necessity than driving inspiration (I compose what I want to hear because no one else is doing it), so I listen—sifting and waiting—only to what I need. What I need now seems less embodied in newness than in nostalgia: how many thrilling experiences do we get per year anyway, after a certain age? Such nostalgia appears most clearly engendered by The Beatles. There isn't much more to say, since structurally they're not interesting to analyse: they've added nothing new, simply brought back excitement. The excitement originates (other than, of course, from their talent) in their absolutely insolent— hence innocent—unification of music's disparate components—that is, in using the most conservative devices of harmony, counterpoint, rhythm, melody, orchestration, and making them blend with an infectious freshness. (Parenthetically, their latest, 'I am the walrus', seems a bit worrisome, more contrived, less 'inspired' than anything hitherto. Though the texture may be Vaughan Williams with a Bebop superimposition and all very pretty, the final effect becomes parody of self-parody, the artist's realest danger. Though probably even the holy Beatles must be permitted an occasional stillborn child.)

The Beatles have, so to speak, brought *fiction* back to music, supplanting criticism. No, they aren't new, but as tuneful as the Thirties with the same exuberance of futility that Bessie Smith employed. They have removed sterile martyrdom from art, revived the sensual. Their sweetness lies in that they doubtless couldn't care less about these pedantic explications.

If (and here's a big if) music at its most healthy is the creative reaction of, and stimulation for, the body, and at its most decadent is the creative reaction of and stimulation for the intellect—if, indeed, health is a desirable feature of art, and if, as I believe, The Beatles exemplify this feature, then we have reached (strange though it may seem as coincidence with our planet's final years) a new and golden renaissance of song.

DERYCK COOKE

The Lennon–McCartney songs

The Listener, 1 February 1968

My recent confession that I'd finished with post-Schoenberg music, because it had rejected the musical vernacular, was apparently taken in some quarters as an attack on Schoenberg himself, and a call for a return to musical 'sanity'. In fact, it was neither. It was a statement of a personal dilemma, which seemed worth making since it's clearly the dilemma of others as well.

No musician likes living entirely in the past. He wants to follow the development of present-day music towards the future; and I've no quarrel with genuine followers of the Schoenberg-to-Stockhausen line. It's just that I can't breathe in a world where the common musical language evolved by humanity at large has been abandoned for the private language invented by a single individual. So I follow the development of the vernacular by composers like Britten and Shostakovich—but this hardly leads to the future, since young composers everywhere dismiss the vernacular as 'exhausted', and follow the non-vernacular path. At which point I face a cul-de-sac—or I would do if I weren't aware that all music is music, not just the 'serious' kind, and that the vernacular is still far from exhausted—self-renewing, rather—in the world of popular music which gave it birth.

Of course, in turning to popular music, one risks reproach from colleagues for debasing standards. But the only realistic standard is the one which operates on all levels—that of creative genius, manifest in ultimate durability. The only English Victorian composer still alive today is Sullivan; the only Austrian one, except Bruckner, is Johann Strauss; Gershwin seems certain to outlive his 'serious' American contemporaries. And my guess is that Lennon and McCartney will still be remembered when most of our 'modern composers' are forgotten by everybody except musical historians.

Some 'serious' musicians have already acclaimed these song-writers—notably Hans Keller [music critic, 1919–85], William Mann and Wilfrid Mellers. But Keller apart (in television appearances), they haven't explained what is so special about them. There has been too much concentration on harmony, following Mann's original dovecot-fluttering *Times* article of 1963, with its references to 'pandiatonic clusters' and 'flat-submediant key-switches'. A purely harmonic analysis is misleading, and only invites misleading retorts: Sir Jack Westrup [musicologist, 1904–75], damning all pop music in the current *Music and Letters*, talks of 'harmonic ingenuities which serious critics mistakenly attribute to the singers instead of the expert musicians who write the "backing"'. Actually, this cannot apply to Lennon and McCartney, whose harmonic originality is evident in several songs written before they entered the commercial pop world, but it's irrelevant anyway, since an outstanding pop song is a structural fusion of harmonic, rhythmic and melodic originality, like any other outstanding piece of music.

Still, Mann was accurate; others have since fared worse. Glenn Gould [pianist, composer, broadcaster, 1932–82], writing in the November 1967 *High Fidelity*,* attributes the appeal of the Lennon–McCartney songs to a 'happy, cocky, belligerently resourceless brand of harmonic primitivism'. According to him, 'the chromatic bent that infiltrated big-band arrangements in the Thirties and Forties ran its course' and the reason for Lennon and McCartney's success is 'our

* 'The Search for Petula Clark'; reprinted in *The Glenn Gould Reader*, ed. Tim Page (London: Faber, 1987)

need of the common chord as purgative'; however, they themselves are 'entirely incidental' in this situation, since 'almost all pop music today is relentlessly diatonic'. He then compares their songs unfavourably with four by Tony Hatch—'Down town', 'Sign of the times', 'My love' and 'Who am I'—saying that although in these 'the harmonic attitude is relentlessly diatonic,' nevertheless 'for Tony Hatch tonality is not a worked-out lode.'

Which only shows how far astray a general harmonic approach can lead. The big-band arrangement is in an entirely different category from the popular song, which has always been relentlessly diatonic and based on common chords; but Lennon and McCartney continually juxtapose these chords, and others, in surprising new relationships, mingling major, minor, Dorian, Aeolian, Lydian and blues progressions in unprecedented ways. It's for them that tonality isn't a worked-out lode, and it's Hatch who is harmonically resourceless and primitive, since he uses little but the most conventional major progressions.

What his songs do have is appealing tunes—and that is the crux of the matter, since a popular song is primarily an appealing tune. Melodic appeal is impossible to analyse, but it's easy to identify, since any song which has it catches on, however banal its rhythm and harmony, whereas the most ingenious rhythm and harmony can't save a tune which lacks it. Even so, an appealing tune which has no rhythmic or harmonic originality soon wears out. The four Hatch songs mentioned have neither, except for 'Down town', with its tense syncopated approach to its climax—and in fact this song is wearing best. But an appealing tune which does have rhythmic or harmonic originality lasts infinitely: the characteristic Lennon–McCartney song has so much of both as to need a few hearings for its appeal to register, but then it survives any number of hearings.

Rhythmic originality is the most important, especially as regards bar-periods, since popular song has long been confined to an appalling eight-bar monotony. An eight-bar section, repeated; a 'middle eight' and the first eight again: only the finest songs have overcome this crippling restriction, by sheer melodic and harmonic inspiration. One or two nearly escaped, without realising it: 'Stormy weather' has a genuine seven-bar first section, spoiled by Harold Arlen's mechanical addition of an unnecessary instrumental bar to make up the eight. But Lennon and McCartney have broken completely free: sections of five, seven, nine, 11 and 13 bars are nothing to them. Particularly remarkable, as Keller pointed out, is 'Strawberry Fields', with its nine-bar first section divided into 1½, 2, 2, 1½ and 2, the penultimate bar being in 6/8 instead of 4/4, quaver equalling quaver. Of course, it's the individual melody and harmony which determines these irregular bar-periods, creating the structural fusion of harmonic, rhythmic and melodic originality I mentioned above. Here, after a delaying six-beat major phrase harmonised by the tonic chord ('Let me take you down 'cos I'm going'), the tune plunges fiercely on to the flat seventh, harmonised by the minor seventh on the dominant, for a solidly rhythmic eight-beat phrase ('*to* Strawberry Fields').

Equally subtle is the poignant 'Yesterday'. The seven-bar first section divides into 1 ('Yesterday'), 2 ('all my troubles seemed so / far away'), 2 ('Now it looks as if they're / here to stay'), and 2 ('Oh I believe in / yesterday'). The first bar sounds isolated—it's more like an end than a beginning, being a cadential appoggiatura (G-F-F over the tonic F major chord). But the following pair of two-bar phrases (D minor, F major again) innocently assume complete regularity as if a bar had just been mislaid somewhere at the beginning; and bar six ends with a dominant seventh on G, ready to cadence conventionally on the dominant, C, in bar seven. We expect the final 'yesterday' will be something like F-E-E over a C major chord; and since the previous two-bar phrases haven't entirely erased the feeling of being one bar short, we also expect an eighth (instrumental) bar, probably echoing the voice with D-C-C over a dominant seventh on C, ready to go back to the beginning. But the dominant expectations of bar six are rudely disappointed: bar seven contradicts the G dominant seventh with its complete opposite, the subdominant chord of B flat major, which cadences immediately on the tonic F major. Very strange—and even stranger, the tune doesn't cadence at all: it rises expectantly F-A-A— with no eighth bar to follow. Or rather, amazingly, the missing bar is discovered the moment the repeat begins. That first isolated bar now reveals the point of its cadential character, acting as the final eighth bar of the first statement—yet of course simultaneously as the opening bar of the repeat. More amazing still, bar seven of the first statement is now felt to be absorbed by the repeat to supply the bar missing at the beginning.

Yet when the repeat is over, the missing-bar effect still remains, naturally, and so the situation continues into the 'middle eight'. This is ostensibly orthodox, with two nearly identical four-bar phrases, each moving from D minor to F minor. But since it promptly loans its first up-beat bar ('Why she') to the first section, to supply the missing bar, it really starts with its second bar. And so the periods become four bars ('had to go I don't / know, she wouldn't / say; / I said') and three bars ('something wrong, now I / long for yester / day'). Again a tonic cadence is reached on the word 'yesterday', and again a bar is missing. Inevitably, with the return to the beginning, the first bar of all supplies the need once more. But when the final repeat of the first section is over, and the song ends, the bar is still missing. Bars have been loaned backwards and forwards, but one is continually and finally lost, like the obsessive 'yesterday' of the lyric.

Lennon and McCartney are genuine creators of a 'new music'. Strangely enough, a few 'serious' composers of 'new music' admire them, and some will say it shows you can enjoy the best of both worlds. Others will maintain it only shows that both types of music are rubbish. I wonder myself whether it isn't that the avant-garde are fascinated to find mere pop composers doing such creative things with the 'exhausted' vernacular.

JOSHUA RIFKIN

On the music of The Beatles

I wrote the following article for Edward E. Davis's anthology *The Beatles Book* (New York, 1968) but withdrew it when the publishers could not obtain copyright clearance for the music examples; for its belated appearance, I have undertaken some minor cosmetic surgery—a nip in the argumentation here, a tuck in the prose there—but left it otherwise unchanged. This means, first of all, that I have resisted the temptation to expand or update the coverage; although I subsequently presented, in various forums, discussions of such matters as the interlocking tempos and tonalities of *Abbey Road*, side two, I have not tried to weave any of this additional material into the existing fabric. More important, my decision to let my observations of almost 20 years ago stand—unamplified, unqualified, unchallenged—pays tribute to the fact that a considerable, perhaps unbridgeable gap separates what I wrote then from what I might say now.

No one who remembers that heady blend of Schenker, Schoenberg and logical positivism once so prevalent in certain academic corners of the American musical landscape will fail to recognise my article as an attempt at justifying The Beatles in terms of a particular ideology and, in so doing, to encompass them safely within its boundaries. But anyone aware of such things will also know how much the grip of that ideology has now slackened on even some of its most enthusiastic adherents. Ironically, for me, as for not a few of my friends and colleagues, The Beatles themselves played no little role in that slackening process. The very passion that we conceived for them provoked troubling questions: how could these musically unlettered kids, operating more or less collectively, produce something that we could see as somehow conterminous with the products of those fearsomely learned individuals who alone, we imagined, could create 'serious art'? Faced with such contradictions, we could either abandon the passion, try to reconcile it with the aesthetic and other paradigms to which we knowingly and unknowingly subscribed, or start to wonder about the paradigms themselves. We couldn't do the first; for a while, as my article attests, some of us tried the second; but ultimately, and perhaps inevitably, most of us wound up with the third. Not that The Beatles alone, of course, changed the entire belief system of a generation, or even that curious subset of it practising composition, theory or musicology at some American universities. But they certainly helped.

Hence the distance with which I now view the piece resurrected here. I would still feel that the sort of analysis to which I subjected The Beatles' music has insights to yield, and I would not take serious issue with most of my results, so far as they go. But the embracing claims of such analysis, the pantheon of critical values to which those claims belonged, even the notion of a critical pantheon: I see all that, and the rest of the whole implicit package, rather differently now—thanks, as I have indicated, in no small measure to the very music on which my article turned its modest positivistic light.

*   *   *

This may seem a rather sober article for such a lively subject. However, the vast quantity of prose concerning The Beatles, which has at one time or another focused on just about every other conceivable aspect of their art, their impact and their personalities, has somehow neglected to provide any serious analytic discussion of their music—which not only, after all, lies at the root of the entire phenomenon but also, as I shall try to show here, possesses a depth and richness that repay just such discussion.

This curious state of affairs has a twofold explanation: first, The Beatles' unique status as a collective cultural icon, which has made them fair game for writers of every persuasion and has also inspired perhaps more speculation on the broader effects of their work than on the work itself; and second, more important still, the fact that the language of musical analysis remains a hermetic mode of discourse even to an intelligentsia—and a journalistic corps—reasonably familiar with the critical and technical vocabularies of poetry, fiction, painting, drama and film.

Most criticism of pop music thus contents itself with breathless accounts of the writer's responses to the pop scene; critics who have attempted to deal with actual music usually betray a comprehension so severely limited as to obscure rather than clarify the subject at hand. Of course, not everyone wants things clarified: a widespread school of thought has it that we should not analyse popular music—not 'be academic' about it—at all, but just listen to it and enjoy it. But does not any experience of value survive analysis happily and even benefit from it? Analysis simply means getting to know something better; and 'being academic' in one's analysis—dealing with formal problems and expressing observations in the language that most suitably handles those problems—indicates only that one is taking the most efficient route to understanding and the most direct path to communication. In the present article I have, however, tried to keep specialised terminology to a minimum, so that readers with little or no musical training may infer at least a large part of the argument. Frequent musical examples should help unravel otherwise obscure points; and those who cannot read music may find the numerous textual references useful in guiding them to the recordings themselves.

I should point out that the following discussion is concerned only with the music of The Beatles as it appears on those recordings, irrespective of how it got there. The reader will find no elucidation of arcane instrumental or electronic effects, except when this appears particularly relevant, nor any rhapsodies about 'innovations' such as the introduction of the sitar or the electronics in *Sgt Pepper*; in music, at least, the use made of a medium may still be considered more important than the medium itself. I shall not spend any time on subtle differences between the songs of the Lennon–McCartney team—and in the present context, we might as well consider them a team even if one or the other is the sole author of a particular song—and those of George Harrison. The more important question of the role played by producer George Martin will likewise be ignored—for no one seems to know very much about this subject nor does it really affect our analysis.

I hope that readers of this article will return to The Beatles' music with a greater awareness of what has gone into it—and thus, of course, a greater awareness of what they can get out of it.

*   *   *

The style of The Beatles' music has remained consistent and individual from their very first recordings. Its essence resides less in the specific materials from which the music is fashioned than in the manner of handling these materials—an underlying unity of approach that has provided a coherent context for compositional development and refinement, made possible the organic absorption of external influences and enabled The Beatles to cover such a wide range of idioms without ever losing their own distinctive profile.

At the nerve-centre of the music lies a remarkable economy of means and organisation. On one level, this manifests itself in the generally compact dimensions of individual pieces and the tight integrative control over detail; on another, in the prevailing transparency of texture and in a spare harmonic palette that avoids both the 'bendings' of the blues and the ubiquitous added-note chords of older pop styles.

Ex.1a

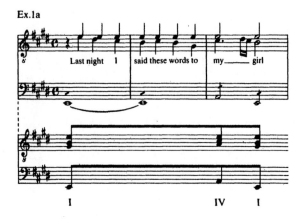

Ex.1b

PLEASE, PLEASE ME (J. Lennon/P. McCartney) Reproduced with permission © 1962 Dick James Music Ltd.

The fundamentals appear as early as 'Please please me', the title song of The Beatles' first album. The vocal lines are clear, the bass solidly contrapuntal; drumming helps to articulate the structure—note the changes of pattern at 'Come on, come on . . .' and 'I don't want to sound complaining . . .'—and timbres are sharply demarcated. Melody and harmony achieve a special consistency through a recurrent emphasis on the subdominant (Exx. 1a and 1b), and 'incidental' details are fastidiously handled: note, for instance, how the little instrumental figure that links the first two lines of the tune (Ex. 2a) generates the 'tag' that ornaments the final tonic (Ex. 2b).

Ex.2a　　　　　　　　　　　　　Ex.2b

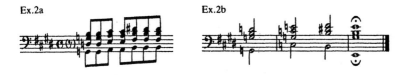

This instrumental figure merits attention for another reason as well: its momentary shift out of the prevailing diatonicism of the song through the introduction of G major, the chord of the lowered third degree. Juxtaposition and intermingling of chords and keys a third apart form one of the most characteristic elements of The Beatles' harmonic language. Their songs move between major and relative-minor keys—the most common third-relationship—with striking fluidity (for example, 'I want to hold your hand', 'Things we said today', 'Another girl', 'Your mother should know'), sometimes to the point of veiling tonal motion in harmonic ambiguity ('A day in the life'); parallel major and minor come into frequent contact as well ('Things we said today', 'I'll be back', 'Fixing a hole', 'The fool on the hill').

Third relationships also enrich the harmony by generating non-key chords and progressions not accountable for as dominant embellishments ('All my loving', 'It won't be long'). In some later songs, these can perform a more subtle and structurally significant role, as in 'You're going to lose that girl', where a 'pivot chord' of D major (a third away from the preceding F-sharp minor) acts as both the dominant of G major (the lowered third degree of tonic E major) and—at the close of the piece—the subdominant of the tonic subdominant (Exx. 3a and 3b). Third-related chords in 'Lucy in the sky with diamonds' mediate smoothly between A major, B-flat major and G major in an astonishingly short space of time (Ex. 4); indeed, in this song, as in several others ('You're going to lose that girl', 'Dr Robert',

Ex.3a

Ex.3b

YOU'RE GOING TO LOSE THAT GIRL (J. Lennon/P. McCartney) *Reproduced with permission* © 1965 *Northern Songs under licence to SBK Songs Ltd.*

Ex.4

LUCY IN THE SKY WITH DIAMONDS (J. Lennon/P. McCartney) *Reproduced with permission* © 1967 *Northern Songs under licence to SBK Songs Ltd.*

'Penny Lane', 'I am the walrus'), the constant interchange of modes leads to a strong tonicisation of more than one key, creating virtual dual tonal centres of a kind often found in 17th-century music.

The rhythmic life of The Beatles' music derives as much from their counterpoint and kaleidoscopically shifting textures as it does from Ringo Starr's always relevant drumming—not by accident, clearly, have they managed so successfully to produce a substantial number of pieces employing minimal percussion or none at all ('Yesterday', 'Eleanor Rigby', 'For no one', 'She's leaving home'). An agile bass line keeps 'A little help from my friends' on its toes; in 'Think for yourself', the fuzz bass vies with the singers for prominence and establishes a tensile propulsive force with its broad triplets cutting across the path of the melody. 'Good morning, good morning' receives a jolting impetus from its chorus of saxophones, while pulsating ostinatos sustain 'I want to tell you'. Melodies often fall into phrase lengths other than the usual four and eight bars, as witness the 10- and 15-bar lines of 'If I fell' or the subtly elided 12-bar stanza of 'I've just seen a face'. 'We can work it out' also proceeds in 12-bar units, those of the outer lines divided into equal parts, the 'bridge' into eight and four; 'Good day sunshine' contrasts regular eight-bar stanzas against a six-bar chorus consisting of three two-bar groups with an internal beat pattern of 3, 3, 2.

Variable metres make their first appearance in 'She said she said', the middle section of which ('She said, "You don't understand . . ."') moves from 4/4 to 3/4 and back to 4/4 without any break. Subtle variable metres also enhance 'Strawberry Fields forever', 'I want to tell you' and 'Within you without you'. Much of 'All you need is love' is built on a not-quite regular alternation of 4/4 and 3/4. The Beatles' metric experiments reach their apogee in 'Good morning, good morning', whose hard-rock exterior conceals an extraordinary structure based on irregularly phrased 5/4 bars constantly interrupted by bars of other lengths. 'Lucy in the sky', 'Being for the benefit of Mr Kite' and 'A day in the life' also deserve mention in this context, as they employ different, though related, tempos within one piece. 'A day in the life'—which originated as two separate songs—handles this in particularly impressive fashion: the second, faster section ('Woke up, got out of bed . . .') is twice the speed of the opening, and when the initial material returns ('I read the news today oh boy / Four thousand holes . . .'), the accompaniment maintains its quicker pace in ghostly contrast to the slower tempo of the disembodied voice line.

*   *   *

Let us take a closer look—at two songs, markedly different on the surface but linked by a number of underlying similarities.

'Strawberry Fields forever', released early in 1967, represents a peak in The Beatles' development and has probably received more critical attention than any other composition of theirs. One of the most complex products of all pop music, it achieves remarkable success in integrating a seemingly discrete sonic fabric into a coherent, tightly knit whole. For easier reference, we may present a diagram of the song as in Ex. 5.

Although, somewhat atypically, harmonic progression does not play a strong generating role in 'Strawberry Fields', it nevertheless reflects The Beatles' usual tendency towards unification through

Ex.5

Introduction (b)	A¹	B¹	A²	B²	A³	B³	Coda I (to fade)	Coda II
	Let me take you down . . .	Living is easy . . .		Always know . . .		No-one I think . . .		

consistent procedure. As in 'Please please me', a pervasive emphasis on the subdominant—the tonic, for instance, is reached only through plagal cadences—plays out the implications of the most prominent melodic figure (Ex. 6). Harmony, too, serves as the principal agent of

Ex.6

Let me take you down ...

STRAWBERRY FIELDS FOREVER (J. Lennon/P. McCartney) Reproduced with permission © 1967 Northern Songs under licence to SBK Songs Ltd.

another characteristic detail, the 'telescoped' presentation of the B sections in the brief introduction (Ex. 7). A further, less strictly

Ex.7

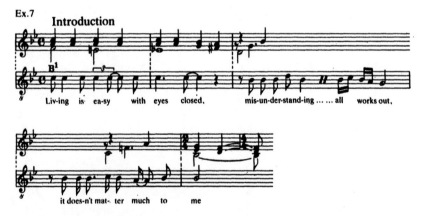

Introduction

Liv-ing is ea-sy   with eyes   closed,   mis-un-der-stand-ing ... ... all   works out,

it does-n't mat- ter   much   to   me

STRAWBERRY FIELDS FOREVER (J. Lennon/P. McCartney) Reproduced with permission © 1967 Northern Songs under licence to SBK Songs Ltd.

'harmonic' detail extends the integrative process to an even deeper level. If we reduce the melodic line of the A section as seen in Ex. 8a, we obtain the succession of five pitches shown in Ex. 8b; this

Ex.8a

Ex.8b   Ex.8c

STRAWBERRY FIELDS FOREVER
(*J. Lennon/P. McCartney*) *Reproduced
with permission © 1967 Northern
Songs under licence to SBK Songs Ltd.*

succession in turn, amplified by a reiteration of its first three pitches at the lower octave, yields the Indian-harp punctuations following A^2 and A^3 (Ex. 8c; the last three notes of the figure may also be interpreted as deriving from the melodic reduction, as shown by the dotted stems and beams in Ex. 8a)—which thus become not merely an 'interlude' but a kind of summation, or gloss, of the entire preceding chorus.

In counterbalance to its relative de-emphasis of harmony, 'Strawberry Fields forever' shows an unusually careful and thoroughgoing organisation of texture, particularly around a variety of repeated-note patterns—pitched and unpitched, periodic and aperiodic. Pitched quaver repetitions frame the main body of the piece, underlying A^1 (in the guitar) and A^4 (cellos and basses). B^1 and B^2 proceed against unpitched crotchet pulsations (produced, to the best of my knowledge, by a reversed tape of a cymbal), which increase their speed to quavers towards the end of the section. Aperiodic note-repetitions generate the brass figures in A^3 and A^4, and reiterated chords at crotchet speed form the accompaniment to the B sections as well as coming to the fore in the two codas—a point to which I shall return. The slow trills in Coda I also reflect, if more obliquely, the repeated-note motive, as do the vocal lines in the declamatory setting of 'Living is easy with eyes closed . . .' and—more distantly still—at the words 'Strawberry Fields/Nothing is real . . .' and 'Strawberry Fields forever'.

The two codas—the first with its hypnotic slow disintegration, the second seemingly rising out of nowhere and taking us into another world entirely—have perhaps occasioned more comment than any other aspect of 'Strawberry Fields'. 'The Beatles sink into the ground in London and pop to the surface again at Bombay', writes Albert Goldman;[1] yet while he and others may wish chiefly to emphasise how radically the scenery has changed, careful listening offers an unexpected reminder that the action unfolding before the backdrop remains essentially the same. Two elements stabilise the first coda: a double-time drum figure, already present in A^2, A^3 and A^4 but at a low dynamic level that can easily escape notice; and crotchet repetitions of a B-flat major triad whose internal balance gradually alters to bring the lowest note, B-flat, to the fore. Not only do these same elements reappear in Coda II (although the triad has withered away to leave only the B-flat), but they maintain themselves uninterruptedly through the fade-out and fade-in that link the two codas—although they become momentarily inaudible, their rhythmic motion does not cease. The only apparently new element in the second coda is the repetitive electronic figure heard above the background of the drums and repeated notes; and perhaps this, too, will turn out on further inspection to derive from the body of the song.

If 'Strawberry Fields forever' offers one of the finest examples of The Beatles' recurrent preoccupation with unifying the most disparate elements, 'Hello goodbye', released less than a year later, typifies another central aspect of their style: the refinement and elaboration of basically straightforward musical formations through careful plotting of detail.

As in many comparable Beatles songs, the primary field of concern is the accompaniment and its relationship to the main vocal line: the structure of 'Hello goodbye' derives largely from the way in which nominally subordinate material shifts between instruments and voices, assuming new importance with each transformation. The ascending scale that accompanies the words 'Hello, hello, / Every time you say goodbye . . .' (Ex. 9a)—and that reverses the descending scale heard beneath the words '. . . and I say go, go, go . . .' in the preceding section (Ex. 9b)—undergoes what we might describe as a cyclic metamorphosis of function, starting as a subsidiary element,

Ex.9a

Ex.9b   Ex.9c

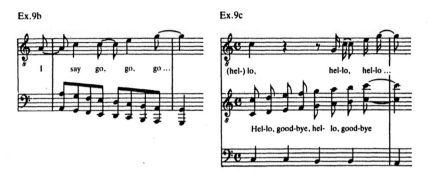

HELLO GOODBYE (J. Lennon/P. McCartney) Reproduced with permission © 1967 Northern Songs under licence to SBK Songs Ltd.

becoming a prominent counterpoint and then receding once more into the background. First presented rather quietly on the guitar, the scale motive next appears dually intensified: sung, to the words 'Hello goodbye, hello goodbye', and doubled at the octave (Ex. 9c; the octave doubling is prefigured by a similar doubling of the preceding downward scale); in subsequent appearances, it returns to the instruments and unison presentation, and declines in dynamic level until it reassumes its original subordinate role (Ex. 10). Voices and instruments also change places when the former accompany the latter in the 'break'; and in the final statement of the section 'You say yes . . .', the voices again provide a counterpoint to themselves, with the background words commenting on the main text. This same passage, finally, sees the voices take over the small guitar figure that previously anticipated the words 'Oh no . . .'.

Ex.10

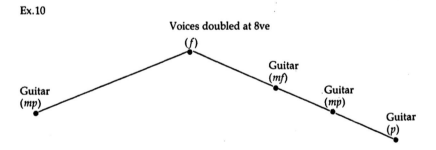

The procedures observed in 'Strawberry Fields forever' and 'Hello goodbye' hardly belong to those songs alone. 'I am the walrus', with its pervasive rocking figures ('I am he as you are he . . .') resembles 'Strawberry Fields' in its organisation of complex textures. 'Ticket to ride', in which the double-time drumming of the 'bridge' section ('I don't know why she's riding so high . . .') returns in the coda ('My baby don't care . . .'), forecasts the manner in which 'Strawberry Fields' joins its second coda to the rest of the song. Like 'Hello goodbye', 'Yesterday' unobtrusively shifts material between voice and instruments (Ex. 11), and 'Lady Madonna' is similarly distinguished

Ex.11a

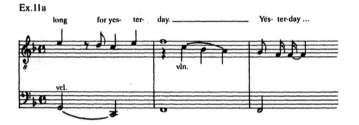

Ex.11b

YESTERDAY (J. Lennon/P. McCartney) *Reproduced with permission © 1965 Northern Songs under licence to SBK Songs Ltd.*

by its varied use of an accompanimental figure and its sometimes instrumental handling of the voices.

*   *   *

Writing in the late 1950s, Milton Babbitt stated that a popular song 'would appear to retain its germane characteristics under considerable alterations of register, rhythmic texture, dynamics, harmonic structure, timbre and other qualities'.[2] Perhaps the most significant innovation of The Beatles—and one that has not yet received adequate attention—is that they have created a popular music that resembles 'formal' or 'serious' music in the relevance of every detail to the identity of the composition. The music of The Beatles consists of far more than text, melody and implied harmonic succession. 'Michelle', for example, is just as much 'about' the superimposition of differing vocal lines above the same instrumental figure (Ex. 12) and the way in which a small guitar solo, built upon the harmonic progression that opens the song (Ex. 13), reappears in the coda, as it is about the

Ex.12a

Ex.12b

MICHELLE (J. Lennon/P. McCartney) Reproduced with permission © 1966 Northern Songs under licence to SBK Songs Ltd.

Ex.13

MICHELLE (J. Lennon/P. McCartney) Reproduced with permission © 1966 Northern Songs under licence to SBK Songs Ltd.

attempts of a young man to convey his love to a girl who does not speak his language. And the strategic placement of John Lennon's sighing interjections in 'Ticket to ride' is as essential to the song as the emotions that the sighs convey. 'Getting better' would not really be the same piece without those obsessive Gs, reaching their climax in the amazing sonority at the words 'I used to be cruel to my woman . . .'; and an absence of recorders, flutes and bells would transform 'The fool on the hill' into something altogether different.

The Beatles revolutionised the very molecular structure of pop music, transforming a language of strong appeal but apparently limited resources into a viable means of subtle artistic expression. They have created the first popular music that not only sustains detailed analysis but even demands it. Their unprecedented richness and structural depth have lent consistency and strength to their always surprising development: each successive product has not only brought a new advance or refinement but also confirmed the clarity, the force and the fascination of the music of The Beatles.

NEIL SINYARD

The English army had just won the war

> 'I saw a film today oh boy,
> The English Army had just won the war.
> A crowd of people turned away,
> But I just had to look
> Having read the book.'

It is hard to think of the John Lennon verse quoted above without automatically associating it with Richard Lester's film, *How I Won the War* (1967), which appeared some months after the release of the *Sergeant Pepper* album and in which Lennon plays a significant supporting role. The remarkable thing about the lyric as it relates to the film is its prophetic accuracy, amounting almost to a sneak preview. In retrospect, the 'crowd of people' that 'turned away' is an anticipation of the hostility of the public to *How I Won the War*, the film sinking through adverse word-of-mouth publicity after the initial attraction of Lennon's and Lester's name. 'Having read the book', the narrator-poet of 'A day in the life' would indeed be intrigued by the film, since it is a fantasised annihilation of a militaristic novel by Patrick Ryan which Lester and his writer, Charles Wood, heartily despised.

How I Won the War, to my mind, is Lennon's most important film. But to understand its significance, one has to see it in the context of the Lester/Beatles collaborations that preceded it: *A Hard Day's Night* (1964) and *Help!* (1965). The former is still widely regarded as the best-ever pop musical. By contriving witty one-liners for the boys rather than anything more extensive and complicated, Alun Owen's script had the dual effect of disguising their acting inexperience and giving the impression of snap ad-libbing worthy of the Marx Brothers. The sizzling spontaneity of Richard Lester's direction conveyed both a documentary immediacy and a technical virtuosity that not only captured the youthful originality of the music but arguably flattered them as musicians. This was witty reportage rather than wet romance and the comparable cinematic efforts of Elvis Presley, Cliff Richard, Tommy Steele and others seemed soggy indeed.

John Lennon was later to suggest that the contributions of Owen and Lester had been overrated, and that he and The Beatles ought to have been given more credit for the overall concept of the film. There is some justice in that. The Beatles were insistent about playing themselves and were quite precise about the kind of pop film they did *not* want to make, which invariably involved teenage romance and a contrived integration of songs: in that way, they undoubtedly extended Lester's and Owen's range of options. In fact, as Lester has acknowledged, it was Lennon who gave him and Owen the basic idea of the film when, to Lester's query about how he liked Stockholm, Lennon had replied: 'Fine—it was a room, a car, a concert and a sandwich.' Everything in the film flows from that: their protection from screaming fans, the limits on their freedom despite their ostensible power and, by contrast, the enormous release of energy when they escape from their shackles and lark about in a field to the bouncy strains of 'Can't buy me love'. The euphoria of that scene and the ecstasy of the final concert carry the optimism and confidence of Beatlemania, just as the images of claustrophobia and the sharp characterisations of spongers and media parasites carry a latent, more ominous message.

Groucho Marx complained about *A Hard Day's Night* that he could not tell one Beatle from another. The film is, in fact, careful to distinguish them, though that distinction was taken further in *Help!* and in George Dunning's animated feature, *Yellow Submarine* (1967). Basically, Paul is soft and sexy, Ringo lovable, George reserved and mean, and John clever and sarcastic. In *A Hard Day's Night*, it is John who sends up the pompous businessman on the train ('Give us a kiss'); sardonically consoles a sulking Ringo ('If I fell . . .'); talks back to his manager; and satirises the phoniness of previous pop musicals in his shout: 'Hey kids, I've got an idea—let's have the show right here!' It is also Lennon's lyric for the title song, written in one evening and encompassing the themes of work and love, that catches the film's astute blend of realism and romanticism. It is a sanitised picture of The Beatles, of course—their lives at that time, according to Lennon, were closer to Fellini's *Satyricon* than to *A Hard Day's Night*. Lester was less interested in them as people than in what they stood for as a group: a classless confidence and boundless vitality that were not only sweeping the country but upending years of social and political conservatism.

Help! was less well received by press and public and by The Beatles themselves, who complained about being guest-stars in their own film. Restrictions placed on permissible subject-matter by manager Brian Epstein, which excluded both their working lives (because that had been done) and their private lives (because that might be too sensational) led Lester and Wood to come up with the idea of using The Beatles as innocent bystanders in an extraordinary plot (roughly, Wilkie Collins's *The Moonstone* updated to the era of James Bond). It is a less integrated film than *A Hard Day's Night* but a more interesting one because more ambitious and audacious. Whereas *A Hard Day's Night* placed The Beatles in the context of the youth culture of contemporary Britain, *Help!* places them against a much larger context that alludes extensively to British Imperialism (the pastiche *Gunga Din* narrative), the British Establishment (significant action in Scotland Yard and Buckingham Palace) and Harold Wilson's new-technology Britain (represented by two brain-drain scientists, Victor Spinetti and Roy Kinnear). The significance of this is its implicit comment on the assimilation of the Beatles phenomenon into social convention. In the year of *Help!*, The Beatles themselves became part of the Establishment when Harold Wilson made them Members of the British Empire.

Some commentators have talked about the desperate frenzy of the film's style, but frenzied desperation is what *Help!* is about. 'And how long do you think you'll last?' says the Scotland Yard man (Patrick Cargill) to The Beatles. Although Lennon's response is suitably insolent ('What about the Great Train Robbery then?'), *Help!* seems to anticipate their imminent destruction. It stresses the theme of sacrifice and loss; it puts them in outrageous disguises which uncannily predict how they will look in five years' time (particularly true of Lennon); and it makes them part of a vehicle in which they are not the driving force, but the driven. Just as his lyric for *A Hard Day's Night* caught the spirit of the film, Lennon's title song for *Help!* is similarly astute in catching the film's underlying sense of desperation and disillusionment.

If one takes The Beatles' films and *How I Won the War* as a trilogy, one can see a clear line of progression. Either implicitly or explicitly, all three films are about class war. In *A Hard Day's Night*, the class enemy, whether it be the pompous businessman on the train or the patronising journalists at the press conference, is instantly put down as a new age is dawning. In *Help!*, The Beatles are encircled by Empire and Establishment and, although they are not cowed, their rebellion seems fragmented and precarious: the new age is curdling into conventionality. In *How I Won the War*, Lennon's working-class obedience to his superiors will get him killed: it might be set during the time of World War Two, but the bitterness is definitely that of a betrayed younger generation in the late 1960s, as the older values return. The films chart a spiral of increasing despair which is unquestionably connected to a deep disappointment with what is happening in Britain and America, notably the failed promises of Harold Wilson and the growing global concern over the Vietnam conflict. The confidence of *A Hard Day's Night* gives way to the confusion of *Help!* which is in turn displaced by the cynicism of *How I Won the War*, which looks back and forwards in anger.

How I Won the War is a black farce exposing the lunacy of war and the obscenity of war movies. It explodes minefields under the notions of leadership and courage. When it first appeared, it was praised by Arthur Schlesinger Jr, who compared it to Kubrick's *Dr Strangelove* (*Vogue*, December 1967); and was attacked, incredibly, by Bosley Crowther in *The New York Times* (November 9, 1967) for failing to acknowledge that 'war isn't funny'. Equally incredibly, John Coleman in the *New Statesman* (October 20, 1967) applauded it as 'magnificently funny nonsense', while *Films in Review* (November 1967) referred to its producers as degenerate and treacherous 'mod-monsters'. Even today, the film still looks fresh, challenging and unsettling. It is not surprising that the CND magazine, *Sanity* (November 1986), while being depressed by the current popularity of *Top Gun* (1986), finds something bracing and topical about the style and attitudes of *How I Won the War* when it gets another, inconspicuous airing on British television.

Drawing on his feelings about the Vietnam war, Lester intended the film to operate on two levels. First, it would be an anti-war film, pulling no punches in its depiction of the horror of slaughter and the mad insensitivity of commanders who treat war as a game. To that end, it sets its absurdist plot about a mission to establish a cricket pitch behind enemy lines within the framework of a stylised reconstruction of four of the bloodiest battles of World War Two—Dunkirk, Dieppe, Alamein and Arnhem. The jagged farce of the plot is matched by a screenplay (by Charles Wood) that is full of inspired flashes of lunatic logic ('There's been some marvellous advances in surgery—thanks to war').

On a second level, *How I Won the War* functions as a film that attacks war films, particularly reacting against the contemporary nostalgia for war films such as *The Great Escape* (1963) and *633 Squadron* (1964). Accordingly, Lester ridicules the whole notion of the military mission; pours scorn on the cliché of the camaraderie of the platoon (in Lester's film, the men hardly talk to one another); and makes contemptuous reference to supposed anti-war films like *The Bridge on the River Kwai* (1957) and *Paths of Glory* (1957) which, in Lester's view, only try to conceal suspect militaristic attitudes under a spurious 'nobility' and 'humanity'. Most controversially, he deliberately sets out to remove the conventional excitement or involvement of war films by a series of alienating devices that are designed to eliminate inappropriate identification—tinted images, direct addresses to the camera, actors wandering across actual newsreel footage. It is a remarkable *tour de force*, resulting in a film bristling with intelligence and ideas. There are few more searching interrogations of media images of war and the ideology of war movies in the history of the cinema.

For the first time playing a part that is not himself, John Lennon is cast in the role of Gripweed, a fair-weather Fascist with a schoolboyish sycophancy towards authority, reflected in his obsessive collecting of medals and insignia. At his first appearance at the symbolic cricket match, where Lieutenant Goodbody (Michael Crawford) opens the bowling and the platoon members take up appropriately subservient positions in the outfield, Gripweed sidles up to Goodbody and solicitously enquires, 'May I rub your ball, sir? It would give me great pleasure.' As in The Beatles' films, Lennon's acting inexperience is cleverly protected by giving him one-liners and eliminating any complicating romantic interest (when asked if he is married, Gripweed replies: 'No, I play the harmonica'). Within those limits, Lennon is very effective. Indeed, it is a brave, unsentimental performance of a character with few redeeming features.

This raises the question of Lennon's casting in the role and its effect, both at the time and in retrospect. 'I wanted first of all, in choosing the platoon,' said Lester (*Movie* No. 16, Winter 1968/69), 'to have people who in acting styles were as different one to the other as I could find, and so got the classical actor, all the different types that used to be in war films: the Irishman, the clown, the sex-mad Cockney. John seemed to be so different because he wasn't an actor, and I wanted the chemistry of having a platoon who all worked in their own separate styles.' He explained the concept of the film to Lennon on the phone (at the time there was no script) and, on that basis, Lennon agreed to appear. Perhaps its immediate significance is that it indelibly marked Lennon's difference from the other members of The Beatles, and the nature of that difference. No other Beatle could have appeared in *How I Won the War* without incongruity; but Lennon seemed quite at home amidst the film's surreal comedy, its cutting cleverness, its controversial tone and message, and its fearless anti-authoritarianism. It is a film that anticipates Lennon's more overt gestures of protest in the following years.

From the perspective of today's cinema, it is interesting that Lester chose not to play on the mythic associations of the pop superstar, which, for example, were to condition Nic Roeg's use of Mick Jagger's persona in *Performance* (1970) and Oshima's use of David Bowie in *Merry Christmas, Mr Lawrence* (1983). In *How I Won the War*, Lennon subordinates his personality to the modest and rather despicable figure of Gripweed. If the film is Lennon's feature film testament, it is, curiously, not so much because of his acting but because the film, more than any other, seems to have an outlook (irreverent, interrogatory, iconoclastic) and a form (audacious, experimental, unsettling) that one associates with Lennon's music at its best. Seen today, his presence in the film looks less like a performance than an endorsement. The film's savagery against the weapons of war still carries a powerful charge, and something of its enduring, influential spirit can be sensed in a recent drama by a fellow Liverpudlian who would be proud to claim kinship with John Lennon—Alan Bleasdale's *The Monocled Mutineer*.

CHARLES MAROWITZ

The Beatles' home movie

Village Voice, 4 January 1968

Cutting through the soft white pastry of Christmas 1967 like a dose of laudanum came the *Magical Mystery Tour*, a 50-minute television film conceived, written, directed, composed, edited, and shot (off-the-cuff) by The Beatles. In a medium that makes a great point of slicking back its hair and cleaning under its fingernails, The Beatles' jump-cutting, hand-held home movie came over as a calculated affront to professionalism.

The day after, the po-faced critics complained of anarchy and confusion, of fashionable avant-garde techniques mindlessly applied, of self-indulgence and even effrontery. Others who recognised they were dealing here with *the* trendsetters of our time, patted the film cautiously, deciding (ultimately) it had better be approved of for qualities it *probably* possessed although not apparently to the uninitiated, meaning themselves. (Unbeknownst to them, that included most everyone.) No one was particularly rude. No one was particularly enthusiastic. Everywhere there was a sense of occasion. The first film made by The Beatles themselves (one paper compared it with Welles's debut on *Citizen Kane*) and everywhere one was conscious that the occasion had not quite ushered in an event.

The next day, answering their TV critics, the put-upon lads from Liverpool explained: 'We tried to present something different . . . We thought we would not underestimate people and would do something new. It is better being controversial than purely boring.' But controversial usually means passionate pros and equally passionate cons, whereas the general consensus was negative to indifferent. Even the *Guardian* critic, who alone of all the dailies was not disappointed, praised the film for being an alternative to the glossy packages jutting out of all the other network stockings—rather than an achievement in its own right. The next day, however, finding himself drafted to carry the banner, he damned all the downputters for missing the point which, 24 hours and two television discussions later, he was able to expound.

The film is a kind of *collage-cauchemar* which starts with Ringo buying a ticket for a Mystery Tour and then proceeds to document the discontinuous odyssey of a bus-load of merry-makers who encounter what four magicians (The Beatles) devise from their metaphysical control tower above. (The necessity to provide enchantment for the customers being a subtle indictment of the public's expectations of its idols.) There are set pieces in which numbers from their latest album (a poor relation of *Sgt Pepper's Lonely Hearts Club Band*) are illustrated with trick photography, out-of-focus panning, jump-cuts, and endless footage of what actually happened to the people on the bus. There is an unexceptional strip-number, and a fascinating sequence in which George Harrison, quadruply projected, sits in the lotus position and sings a mildly Westernised Indian ballad. Victor Spinetti does a rough-and-ready imitation of the square-bashing act he did in *O What a Lovely War* and Ivor Cutler, a lachrymose composer-cum-comedian, looks mournfully at one and all. There are a few refreshing subliminal flashes during the musical numbers, but more often than not the pictures mickey-mouse the lyrics. Despite a poverty of visual imagination, the picture captures the frolicsome atmosphere its makers induced in their cast, and that is probably its most vital asset.

The *Magical Mystery Tour* is based on the now-fashionable principles of indeterminacy, chance-selection, and improvisation, without the guiding intelligence that men like Cage or Cunningham bring to the same principles. Being divided among four sensibilities (each of The Beatles was allowed to shoot whatever appealed to him), no uniform vision links the disconnected imagery, and the disparity of temperaments among the four makes the film divide rather than coalesce. Many of the images, like four English bobbies holding hands in a dance formation which is the exact duplicate of the anti-riot squad position, are slyly chosen and memorable. The bus trip, which may be a metaphor for a drug trip (although giving The Beatles the benefit of the doubt, I wouldn't expect them to be that obvious), shuttles from anarchy to fantasy without creating rich confusion or refreshing otherworldliness. In spite of a maniacally fleet rhythm, the result of brutal chop-cutting, the film is slow in many places because it lingers on shots—not for effect but from uncertainty as to where to go next.

What I liked about the film was its relentless privacy; its naive assumption that what it found interesting would interest others, and if it didn't, *tant pis*. It is not an artistic success, but why should a home-movie expect to be? The unconscious 'magical' concept in the picture was The Beatles' magical belief that anything they did was bound to come off, because they were The Beatles and, in some magical way, all the usual criteria for artistic achievement would be temporarily in abeyance. If one complains of the film (and one does) it is not because one expected plot, characters, and situation (The Beatles' lame defence the other night) but because it didn't realise its own surreal potentialities.

Brainwashed by the Maharishi and committed blindly to the Cage–Cunningham principle that what is is art and the less the organising-mind interferes the better, The Beatles have had a bash. What they failed to realise is that some underlying instinct—call it taste or talent, it remains an invisible thermostat regulating the artist's unconscious—is an indispensable part of the creative process, and without it no principles, no matter how fashionable, can possibly work.

However, it is ridiculous to discuss the film in these terms. It is another foray in the battle for anti-art, and I am not at all sure we have developed the criteria by which such works can be judged.

PAULINE KAEL

Metamorphosis of The Beatles

The New Yorker, 30 November 1968

From the nursery to the boutique is now a very short path; *Yellow Submarine* travels it with charm and ease. The Beatles, represented by cartoons, go to the rescue of the people of Pepperland and save them from the Blue Meanies, their weapons being (who'd have guessed it?) music and love—but what is so pleasant about *Yellow Submarine* is its lighthearted, throwaway quality, and the story seems as disposable as the banter and the images. If the movie tried to be significant, if it had 'something to say', it might be a disaster. One of the best characters is a gluttonous consumer with a vacuum snout, who devours the universe, yet the movie itself sucks up an incredible quantity of 20th-century graphics. If *Yellow Submarine* were not so good-natured and—despite all the 'artistic' effects—unpretentious, one would be embarrassed; its chic style can't support much more than the message of 'love'. You could almost make a game of how many sources you can spot, but, because of the giddy flower-childishness of it all, this not only seems all right but rather adds to one's pleasure. The eclecticism is so open that it is in itself entertaining—we have the fun of a series of recognitions. A little Nolde here, a bit of Klimt there, the hotel corridor from *The Blood of a Poet*, with *The Mysteries of China* now become Indian, and good old Birnam Wood moving once again—it's like spotting the faces in Tchelitchew's *Cache-Cache*.

The movie is extravagantly full of visual puns and transformations, but not too full (though there are places where one might wish for an extra instant to savour what is going by). The Beatles' non-singing voices are not their own, but they're good. The verbal jokes invite comparison with Edward Lear but can't sustain it. The movie seems to get its spirit back each time one of The Beatles' songs (sung by The Beatles) comes on . . . and this is not just because of the richer verbal texture but because the animation, ingenious as it is, is not much more than a shifting series of illustrations. The movie works best when the images (even though they don't quite connect with the meaning of the lyrics) are choreographed to the music.

In animation, anything can turn into anything else, and children love it for the illogic that is a visual equivalent of their nursery rhymes and jingles and word games. Recent American commercial cartoons have been so undistinguished visually and limited so much of the time to the reversibility of destruction that *Yellow Submarine* with its bright

Pop flourish and inventiveness, restores the pleasure of constant surprise, which has always been the fun of good animation. Yet what will probably make *Yellow Submarine* a great success is its superlogical development: The Beatles walk by, and flowers grow out of them. They're no longer the rebellious, anarchistic Pop idols that parents were at first so outraged by; they're no longer threatening. They're hippies as folk heroes, enshrined in our mythology. The name 'Beatles' no longer suits them; they have become quaint—such gentle, harmless Edwardian boys, with one foot in the nursery and the other in the boutique, nothing to frighten parents. The movie is a nostalgic fantasy—already nostalgic for the happy anarchism of 'love'. It finally goes a bit flat because love is no longer in bloom.

No doubt we can all do with less threat and less stress in the environment, and yet there's something depressing about seeing yesterday's outlaw idols of the teenagers become a quartet of Pollyannas for the wholesome family trade. And if one looks at a list of the merchandise being promoted in conjunction with the movie, one may long for the simpler days of Mickey Mouse watches. That omnivorous consumer had better get ready to suck up seven different *Yellow Submarine* books and a die-cast submarine and clocks and masquerade costumes and sweatshirts and stuffed dolls and inflatable swim toys and posters and lunchboxes and pillows and aprons and lamps and about 50 other products. Wasn't all this supposed to be what The Beatles were *against*? The way attacks on the consumer society become products to be consumed is, to put it delicately, discouraging. The Beatles had already become part of a comic-strip world in *Help!* By now, they have replaced Mickey Mouse as symbols of the union of art and popular success. Their loss of corporeality seems perfectly natural and right.

Movies are treacherous. I don't fully respect what the director, George Dunning, has done in *Yellow Submarine*; I don't truly admire much of what the chief designer, Heinz Edelmann, has done. And yet the movie is charming. They have done what hasn't been done before in animation—at least, not on anything like this scale. And if it's derivative, so was the Disney style—though not so obviously, since it was more unified. Despite all the enthusiasm registered in the press for animated features, this is one of the handful of palatable ones.

Without human characters, an animated feature is likely to be a bore, but animated human figures have never quite worked. Erwin Panofsky provided a reasonable explanation: 'The very virtue of the animated cartoon is to animate; that is to say, endow lifeless things with life, or living things with a different kind of life. It effects a metamorphosis, and such a metamorphosis is wonderfully present in

135

Disney's animals, plants, thunderclouds, and railroad trains. Whereas his dwarfs, glamorised princesses, hillbillies, baseball players, rouged centaurs, and *amigos* from South America are not transformations but caricatures at best, and fakes or vulgarities at worst.' Still, this may be a little too pat. In the arts, one can never be altogether sure that the next artist who comes along won't disprove one's formulations. *Yellow Submarine* does not exactly disprove Panofsky, but one sequence, the dancing couple for 'Lucy in the sky with diamonds', is a stunning use of stylised human figures—an apotheosis of Rogers and Astaire. Rather surprisingly, Edelmann follows the Disney and UPA artists very closely in most of the human characters, making The Beatles as limply boneless and sweet as Snow White, and the Meanies grisly caricatures constantly displaying their cruel teeth. Even so, they shake Panofsky's formulations a bit, because in *Yellow Submarine* this weakness is not as crucial as in the Disney films. Where there is so much to choose from and the style is a collection of rejectable items, something bad may not matter very much. Aesthetic theories don't always allow for the variety of what we enjoy; we may like a certain amount of caricature and grisliness, and I preferred Popeye and Mr Magoo to most animal characters in cartoons, because they were wittier. The Beatles provide a frame of reference that holds this movie together, though as cartoons they are weak facsimiles, with less character than the movie's fish, who are like windup toys, and its strange made-up monsters, or even its professorial little Boob. The single worst sequence in the movie—even worse than the addendum of filmed live Beatles—is the montage of photographed cities as the cartoon Beatles leave Liverpool; it disrupts the fantasy. But raiding the arts—shooting the works in animation—succeeds. It becomes an equivalent of the way kids dress now—cutting through the anxieties about what is appropriate and the class structure of good taste, wearing what they feel like wearing, and making life a fancy-dress ball. The movie has something of this freshness; throwing in a multiplicity of styles—even a couple of startling Op sequences—is a fluke solution to a problem that more rigorous-minded men have failed to solve.

. . . The Disney artists' animation was pre-Pop pop of a simple, consistent, and often stupid kind, and this was true, oddly, of *Animal Farm*, the last animated feature to come from England. But Pop has now become a *style; Yellow Submarine* uses Pop heroes and Pop Art deliberately, and with sophistication. And it works. But it is merely a further development of what ads and commercials have already been doing. People who want to make animated features may now have an easier time getting backing, but the aesthetic problems haven't been solved. Animators can't just keep on ravaging the art of the

20th century; after the orgy of *Yellow Submarine* it's going to look worn out.

Notes

1.   Albert Goldman, 'The emergence of rock', *New American Review* 3 (New York, 1968) p. 129

2.   Milton Babbitt, 'Who cares if you listen', *High Fidelity* viii/2 (February 1958) p. 39

FIVE

I'm Stepping Out

JOHN JONES

Meeting Yoko Ono

Yoko Ono's critics—perhaps less vindictive in the years since Lennon's death—have often blamed her for the break-up of The Beatles, though it appears the group's days were numbered even before John Lennon met her. What is certainly untrue is the notion that she used John to break into the art world: she was, in fact, well known in avant-garde circles long before. Lennon's celebrity simply brought her a wider, if not wholly appreciative, audience.

In September 1965, I began a year's research in New York which involved recording interviews with American artists. We lived in Greenwich Village. I probably first read about Yoko Ono in the Village newspaper which I searched for artistic events that would give me quick access to the art scene. I remember getting up in the dark to attend a rooftop 'happening' at dawn. I found the house but couldn't bring myself to knock on the door. I imagined the occupants might not take kindly to being woken by a foreigner who wanted to get on to the roof 'for a happening'.

'For a *what*?'

'A happening.'

'Listen buddy—you know what time it is?' . . .

I waited in the street for another art lover to show up who would know the form but no one came and I went back to bed. Later I was told that I could have pushed open the door and a staircase would have taken me all the way to the roof where the sun's first rays caught Yoko seated at a table. On it was laid out a row of similar pebbles which were priced at 5c, 50c, $5, $50, $500, $5,000 . . . They were clearly soliciting the question 'Why are these virtually identical stones priced so differently?' The answer was that buying them would give them their value. A pebble you gave five cents for became a 5c pebble; one you paid five thousand dollars for became a $5,000 pebble. It was a neat observation about art in the market place, a sort of dealers' sequitur to Duchamp's frequent declarations that art is simply what we agree to call art. But it was recognisably Yoko's. One of her recurring themes at that time was the affirmation that things are only what we think they are, that 'it's all in the mind'.

That year there were many 'happenings'; the word covered a multitude of spectacles which had in common little except the excitement of trying out alternatives to conventional theatrical and musical performances.

Yoko was already a well established exponent of this genre. She gave a concert at Carnegie Hall in 1961, toured Japan with John Cage [avant-garde composer, born 1912], and her New York appearances were frequent.

I think the first time I actually saw Yoko was at a programme which included Alan Kaprow spreading the floor with something (newspapers?) and then sweeping them up—a tall stepladder was involved; and Charlotte Moorman who had trouble with the police for public appearances in which it was claimed she wore nothing but the 'cello she was playing. It was probably one of the occasions when Yoko invited people to come from the audience and, with scissors, to snip off bits of the dress she was wearing. They could cut off as much or as little as they liked. At the time I wasn't sure what this particular piece 'meant'. The inverted commas recognise that 'meaning' was not a necessary feature of happenings. In them was the spirit that informed Susan Sontag's wise essay 'Against Interpretation'.

But many of Yoko's inventions had what you might call a 1960s version of a 'moral'. The dress-cutting seemed more enigmatic, but it generated considerable dramatic suspense. At first there was a relatively jocular audience reaction which sounded like 'O.K. You asked for it' and young men pretended eagerness to come forward and denude her. But when eventually volunteers had the scissors in their hands and were poised to cut, the oddness of the situation—and perhaps the powerful and inescapable thoughts of public rape—rendered them hardly able to cut at all. As I remember, they made a joke of it, cutting a mere centimetre or two, or, say, a decorative button. The private thoughts that were generated in the audience must have ranged from cruel, violent and erotic fantasies to feelings of apprehension about what was about to happen, which focused real hostility on the volunteer with the scissors (could they be sure he was sane?). And that was surely the point of it. With a minimum of stimulus the audience found itself experiencing that variety of

142

sympathetic and disturbing emotions that far more complex theatre aspires to awaken.

I can't remember asking to interview Yoko but I did and she talked about how some of her childhood experiences had survived to inform her current inventions. Hiding from visitors in a bag, for instance. She mentioned 'Fluxus' which was a kind of neo-Dada group, not easy to describe, which organised 'Fluxfests'—performances of happenings—and which published related material and sold 'irrational' art manifestations by mail order. Through them I got a sales list of Yoko's works and bought a loop of tape she'd prepared on which, it turned out, nothing was recorded. That may be misleading. Reading her list again I see that I may have bought: 'Soundtape of the Snow Falling at Dawn . . . 25c per inch. Types: a. Snow of India, b. Snow of Kyo, c. Snow of Aos.' Playing it again I can no longer be sure which snow mine is.

From the same list I could have bought custom-made underwear in vicuna to 'accent your special defects'. There was a crying machine 'which drops tears and cries for you when coin is deposited . . . $3,000'; and, for half that price, a Sky Machine which 'produces nothing when coin is deposited'.

I do have a set of cards on which were printed do-it-yourself happenings, one a day for two weeks. '1st, 2nd and 3rd day: Breathe. . . . 10th day: Swim in your dreams as far as you can.' It's almost a Beatles song title. One can understand John Lennon's frequent assertion that when he met Yoko Ono at London's Indica Gallery in 1966 he recognised a kindred spirit, one that matched that maverick, fantasist side of him, already ill-at-ease under the restraints of Epstein's respectability.

In 1964, Yoko published a book of her 'works' called *Grapefruit*. She gave me a copy. The title was chosen because she understood that a grapefruit was a hybrid of a lemon and an orange, the consequence of a collaboration between man and nature. Her inventions likewise aspired to combine the natural and the man-made. She quoted the sky-line as another metaphor or example of the coming together of nature and human contrivance. Opening the book at random I read 'Map piece: Draw a map to get lost.'

One of Yoko's injunctions was to give someone a present that you would like to receive yourself, so when she invited us to dinner I presented her with a book I found in the Village. It was old and well-bound but wordless, its pages having been neatly pierced in delightful patterns of holes. It wasn't Braille and I never guessed its purpose or point. I thought it a wonderful, mysterious find and gave it away with reluctance. She didn't seem quite as captivated by it as I'd hoped. I wonder if she still has it.

I'd been back in England a year or so when I heard that she and her husband Tony were coming to Leeds to perform at the art college and they accepted my invitation to stay, bringing their small daughter Kyoko with them.

Their performance included two items, the principal one being the Black Bag, and another which was a version of the party game in which a sentence is passed in whispers along a row of people. In the game the message is quite garbled by the time it reaches the last person. Yoko put her mouth to the ear of a speaker at the end of the front row of seats and instructed him to 'pass it on' along all the rows to the last seat at the back of the theatre, whilst she got on with something else. Later she asked what had arrived at the end and at various points en route. Strangely dissimilar words, tunes and noises emerged. It was then revealed that Yoko had whispered—you've guessed it—nothing at all.

The black bag was roomy enough for two people to climb into it easily. Once inside and lying on the floor, Yoko and Tony closed the entrance. For a while nothing much happened. A lecture theatre full of people gazed in expectant silence at a black lump on the platform. When those in the bag moved the audience began to speculate about their actions. It did look as if they might be undressing. The bag writhed and fidgeted. Were they naked now? Were those projections knees or elbows? Was it an embrace? Another long pause. . . . Now they seem to be struggling. They can't be making love. *Can they?* It went on for at least half an hour. When they finally came out of the bag they were just as they had been when they went in. Whatever had gone on in the bag had only happened in the spectator's thoughts. Just as it had invented the whispered 'message', the imagination of the audience had written the script of the bag. On another occasion Tony summed it up as 'trying to involve the audience in the creative process itself'.

Yoko and Tony were undemanding guests, not expecting, or even wanting, to be taken to see the sights of Yorkshire. They ate an inordinate amount of brown rice. Yoko entertained my children—all of us—by making superb Origami birds and animals. We strung them on a thread where, in the weeks that followed, the cat played with them and finally tore them to shreds. I wish I had kept them.

Yoko was planning a film and needed some cash to start it. I lent her £50. My contribution was acknowledged in the titles of that underground masterpiece *Bottoms* in which a hundred people's behinds are filmed, each for 20 seconds as they 'walked' on an endless belt. The cinema screen was divided by a wobbly cross of shadow into four areas of softly undulating flesh. No two actors' performances were the same. The variety of forms of the human hind-quarters has to be seen to be appreciated. The film has everything: a riveting theme with a hundred variations, formal consistency, human interest and a laugh a minute.

Actors had been recruited by advertising for people to take part in an avant-garde film production, and when interviewed they had talked, some quite fulsomely, about their suitability for and experience of experimental theatre. Not all took kindly to it when told what role they were being asked to perform. The soundtrack of the film was made up from these interviews but, hilarious as this accompaniment was, it could just as well have been a Bach fugue, so exquisite was the formal rhythm of the thing.

Before the film came out, Yoko sent me a cheque repaying half the debt and later Tony directed me to collect the other half from Apple. I waited one morning in the shadow of Paul McCartney with the teeny-bopper fans and was given £25 in cash by The Beatles' new financial manager.

Months later a delivery man looked for me in the office of my department in the university and was sent by the secretary to my home. To my wife he delivered a huge bouquet of white flowers among which nestled another £25 cheque and a card which read 'Love and Peace. John and Yoko'.

I posted this extra cheque back to Yoko at Apple. A week later it returned, stamped 'Not known at this address'.

MICHAEL WOOD

John Lennon's schooldays

New Society, 27 June 1968

A heavy man with glasses sits on a chair looking at a green monster with four legs. Caption? 'An adult looks at a Beatle.' The caption is mine, but the drawing is John Lennon's. It appears in his second book, *A Spaniard in the Works*.

There are four-legged things everywhere in Lennon's drawings: sheep, cats, cows, Sherlock Holmes on his knees. The first book, *In His*

Own Write has a huge Wrestling Dog ('But who would fight this wondrous beast? I wouldn't for a kick off'), and a piece called 'Liddypool' is accompanied by a sketch of chatting quadropuses.

It is a child's world, or a world that Thurber might have drawn for a child. Animals and freaks have comic dignity while adults look silly and too big, bending over and crawling. A double suggestion runs through the writing in both books: adults *are* silly, they give children rubbish to read and expect them to like it; and left to themselves, adults are worse than children—they talk jabberwocky about politics and colour and religion, and they believe what they say.

So we get Enig Blyter's famous five—ten of them taking off for Woenow Abbey—' "Gruddly Pod, Gruddly Pod," the train seemed to say, "Gruddly Pod, we're on our hollidays".' There is a trip to Treasure Ivan with Large John Saliver, Small Jack Hawkins, Cpt Smellit and Squire Trelorgy. But Prevelant ze Gaute also appears, and Docker Adenoid along with Harrassed MacMillion and the late Cassandle of the Mirror on the Wall. The Bible, hymns, newspapers, the telly, bad films: the world shrinks to the nonsense of a book for small children.

The trick is simple, a standard schoolboy game. You retreat to baby talk, to mock-childishness, to the linguistic pranks of Lewis Carroll and Edward Lear. This is your revenge on all the language, life and literature that people are asking you to take seriously. You bend and break what they teach you; you make their world sound like Wonderland. Vile ruperts spread through a village, an old man leaves his last will and testicle, there is dirty weather off Rockall and Fredastaire. A day is a red lettuce day.

The jokes are John Lennon's, but they have already seen good service in most grammar schools in this country. The grammar school is the place for this intelligent, informed and infantile humour, I think; and school may have been more important for Lennon and McCartney than either home or Liverpool, whatever sociologists and trendmen say. Grammar school pupils are alert, disciplined and frightened. Their pleasures are psychological—torturing a nervous teacher—and fairly secret.

I remember a joke that ran for months when I was at school. Whenever a teacher left the room, someone would draw a head, side view, on the blackboard. It would be a policeman in a huge helmet or a guardsman in a vast busby. At the side of this would appear a drawing of the policeman or guardsman without his helmet or busby. His head would be exactly the same shape as his hat. Another version showed a grotesque club-foot—with or without a shoe, it looked the same.

Thinking back, I can see two things in our enjoyment of those gruesome gags. First, a hope that the world would stay simple, that our fears of mess and complication might prove to be unfounded. Just think. If the mask should fall to reveal a face just like the mask, if the truth about life, which parents and teachers hinted at so darkly, should turn out to be exactly like the façade, then they would be the fools with their conspiracy theories, and we would be right in our scared simplicity. And, secondly, I think we were fascinated by disease and deformity, which represented the future ugliness of life itself. If we could keep that at the level of a joke, if we could tame it in the safeness of school, everything would be all right.

All this is in Lennon. The adult world makes him larf, and his books are a vengeance. He has verbal forms of the club-foot joke—Mr Borris Morris, in the story of that name, has a happy knack of being in the right place at the right place—and a splendid visual version. Two beggars stand side by side, each complete with stick, trumpet, dog and begging tin. One of them has dark glasses, and his dog has dark glasses too. The man carries a placard on his chest saying: 'I am blind'. The other man also has a placard. It says: 'I can see quite clearly'. Thus does the world shed its secrets for the innocent. Although for the person who can make such a joke, as for the boys who could laugh at our drawings, innocence is already a fantasy, an incipient nostalgia, no longer a state of mind.

But most strikingly Lennon sets up a gallery of deformed and violent people, a literal menagerie of creatures born on the blackboard during a break. A man clubs his wife to death. A friendly little dog ('Arf, Arf, he goes, a merry sight') is put to sleep. Eric Hearble, who has a growth on his head, loses his job teaching spastics to dance ('"We're not having a cripple teaching our lads," said Headmaster'). Randolph is killed at Christmas by his pals ('At least he didn't *die* alone did he?') and a girl wonders about flowers for her wheelchair at her wedding— luckily her father comes home and cancels the husband. Little Bobby, 39 years old, gets a hook for his missing hand as a birthday present. Only the hook is for the wrong hand, his good left hand, and they have to chop that off to fit the hook.

It is absurd to compare Lennon to Joyce. Lennon's puns are piecemeal, scattered and unequal. Joyce's punning in *Finnegans Wake* is a system, a metaphysic for melding worlds. When Joyce writes of the flushpots of Euston and the hanging garments of Marylebone, the Bible and London really collide. But Lennon has some fine effects. A pun is what Durkheim in another context called a logical scandal, it is an escape from linear meaning. It is language on holiday, and Lennon occasionally gets the authentic glee of this.

'Anything you say may be used in Everton against you.' 'Father Cradock turns round slowly from the book he is eating and explains that it is just a face she is going through.' People dance with wild abdomen, and send stabbed, undressed envelopes.

Why is there so little of all this in the songs Lennon writes with Paul McCartney? McCartney's sobering influence? Hardly. More likely both are being tactful towards their public. They know that people are offended by nonsense, by things they can't understand; they know that people tend to take jokes that baffle them as a personal insult, a calculated exclusion. And their songs after all are a commercial enterprise—Lennon and McCartney have written well over 100 songs since 1962, and their work has been recorded by almost everyone you can think of.

Certainly there are occasional puns—'It won't be long / Till I belong to you.' 'A hard day's night', the nonsense title of a film and a song, comes from a Lennon story called 'Sad Michael'. There are all the double meanings concerning pot and LSD on the *Sgt Pepper* album, there is the sound play of by, buy, bye-bye in the song 'She's leaving home'. And the songs have developed towards complexity.

Lennon and McCartney's early lyrics were thin and conventional. There was rain in the heart, there were stars in the sky, birds were always threatening not to sing. The tunes were good, some of them as good as those of Rodgers or Leonard Bernstein. But the gap between words and music in pieces like 'If I fell', 'And I love her', 'Ask me why', 'Not a second time', was embarrassing for anyone who wanted to take the songs seriously. The best lyrics, which went with up-tempo numbers like 'I feel fine', 'All my lovin'', 'Can't buy me love', were the ones which said the least. They said yeah, approximately. I'm not suggesting that Lennon and McCartney didn't know how conventional they were being, or that they couldn't have done better. But they didn't do better, presumably because they weren't interested.

Now they are interested. We get the sharpness of 'Your day breaks / Your mind aches', where the rhyme really does something. People, characters, begin to take the place of the anonymous lover of the early songs, shouting, sobbing, missing, losing, promising his standardised love. We get Rita the meter maid, and the man who wants to be a paperback writer. We get Eleanor Rigby and all the lonely people, and the sights and sounds of Penny Lane. To say nothing of Billy Shears, Sgt Pepper and Mr Kite. And we get the complex compassion of songs like 'Wait' ('If your heart breaks / Don't wait') and 'She's leaving home', where the girl going off writes a note 'that she hoped would say more', and her parents moan their incomprehension: 'We gave her most of our lives . . .' The whole work develops a sense of waste, of 'tears cried for no one', as one song has it.

But still, the music has developed more than the language, and the language is not a main attraction in these songs. Lennon and McCartney's words are still less important than those of Bob Dylan, or Lorenz Hart, or Cole Porter, or Ira Gershwin. We have to look elsewhere for the link between the songs and Lennon's stories.

The link is not hard to find. It takes us back to school, and Lennon and McCartney's repeated flights into the past. Think of the titles: 'Yesterday', 'The night before'. Think of the nostalgia in songs like 'Things we said today', or 'In my life': 'There are places I'll remember all my life'. Think of the echoes of melodrama and music hall in the *Sgt Pepper* album, the jaunty George Formby tone of 'When I'm sixty-four'. In 'Good morning, good morning' we take a walk past the old school—'Nothing has changed, it's still the same'—and 'She said she said' flings a bewildered boy out of the classroom on to a hard life. The girl tells him that she knows what it's like to be dead, and he can only reply, 'No no you're wrong when I was a boy everything was right . . .'. Lennon and McCartney in their songs do indeed 'live the past in the present', as Richard Poirier wrote about them in *Partisan Review* last year. But it is a personal and sentimental past, not a historical one—it is the specific past of good school days, when the world was simpler and adults looked like fools. Lennon and McCartney are not naïvely nostalgic, but they are nostalgic. Their songs and Lennon's stories express the *good child's* hostility to grown-ups. That is what we mean by the youth of The Beatles, an attitude, not an age—after all, they were in their twenties when they began to make it around 1962. The attitude is not dangerous, at worst it deserves a detention, and this is why adults have been so keen to endorse The Beatles. This is safe play for children, mild naughtiness, and much better than breaking up Margate or digging up Paris.

The Beatles are a middle generation between the old conformers and the new rebels, between those who find it hard to believe that the world will change and those who know it's got to. Lennon and McCartney protest against the world adults have made, of course. They hate its pain and loneliness. But their protests are quiet, and their only answer so far has been escape into dope or India.

But the question remains. The Beatles have by-passed adulthood, and this links them with the revolutionary students who are asking why they should grow up when growing up means napalm, treachery, compromise and Porton Down. For years we have sold maturity as a virtue, we have preached the careful ethic of the status quo. But The Beatles are nearly 30 and wildly successful on anyone's terms. If they haven't grown up yet, why should they now?

ADRIAN MITCHELL

Beatles

The Listener, 3 October 1968

William Huskisson, President of the Board of Trade, was standing between the lines in Liverpool welcoming the first train. 'I declare this railway well and truly—AARAGH!' SPLAT! It was the best death scene since an eagle dropped a tortoise on the head of Aeschylus (THUNK!) but it only rates 21 words in Hunter Davies's *The Beatles*, although however already this official biography is a long trudge compared with Michael Braun's sprinting Penguin (*Love Me Do*), yet notwithstanding perhaps there's some fair scenery along the way, especially when Mr Davies shows how various songs were fitted together. So much for criticism.

The average Englishman wakes up one morning to find himself born,
and starting to explore
what his body is for
finds there's rhythm and blues
in his shoes
and that's news
because a few years ago
the average British toe
could only go
slow slow quick slow slow.
Now the offbeat of the heartbeat
is the children's choice
and the human voice
can shake while it sings and twist and shout
because some of the fear's flown out.

Most of us are mostly afraid—
Murder Incorporated has to be paid
and there's terror in the bone
because of Al Capone
from Canterbury, Baby-Face Calvin
and the spiritual Chicago of Rome.
And though you chain up the door
of your rentokilled home—
Matthew Mark Luke and John

surround the bed that you lie on with dread,
each of them armed with a nuclear warhead.

But the Beatles roared along
at the wheel of an independently suspended song
and they saw the rows of English feet
and they knew that feet without a beat are just meat,
so they rolled down the windows to let the word be heard
and every time they passed a naked human has-been
they all shouted out—it's a clean machine.
Jehovah, Jesus, Holy Ghost and Ringo Starr,
Four-faced jubilee weeping in the public bar,
Suddenly flowering home-made submarine—
Shift all the slag heaps from Aberfan to Esher Green.
I'm not trying to paint you a quartet of saints
or musical Guevaras.
But the standard of loving has
plopped through the bottom of the graph.
So the few who do any kind of thing
that shakes out the horrors
are quadruply welcome
especially if they make us laugh.

The fashion-go-round of the underground
may forsake them,
the Army or the CIA may take them,
but we'll meet again . . .

So to the point as fast as possible. When Allen Ginsberg was last over here, he gave a reading of Blake and Ginsberg at the Roundhouse, Chalk Farm, at a time when all honest chalk farmers were in bed dreaming of the sprouting pink, blue and white lengths of chalk which decorate the dusty fields around the blackboard forest. Between poems Ginsberg talked about fear. He said that 10 or 15 years ago he had been full of fear, but that he'd worked at cutting down his terror ration and had changed until he was hardly afraid of anything. I sat in the audience and felt the lump of fear which I always carry diminish.

The Beatles appear to be moving, zigzag, in the Ginsberg direction. They've already shown some courage in a traditionally cowardly trade—for in pop music the aim is to be loved by everyone, villains included. Maybe it was foolhardiness when they filmed their own *Magical Mystery Tour*. It contained some images—policemen holding hands on top of a concrete bunker or shelter while The Beatles played below in Disney masks—which were way beyond the heads of most of the critics. The progress of their songs from 'Please please me' (instantly likeable and who, at that time, could ask for anything more) to 'Penny Lane' (poetry) and 'A day in the life' and 'I am the walrus' (adventurous poetry) has been an exciting voyage to follow. After all, everyone knew Francis Chichester wasn't going to fall off the edge of the world, but The Beatles might.

Snipers from the press will keep trying to shoot them down and keep missing, because The Beatles have more to offer than the press. Most people, without envy, wish them good luck on their journey. More than that, many people hope that their courage increases, and not just for the sake of their art. There are obviously more important issues.

Take one of these. For many years England has been unofficially, sometimes shamefacedly and often silently racialist. Then along came Enoch Powell, strumming on the nerves of the nation, speaking the language of cold sweat. Suddenly he became the first popular politician since the war—has anyone else so rallied the Right? Enoch Powell has changed and will continue to change English politics from blatantly selfish to patently lunatic. The weakness of both Heath's and Wilson's responses proves how scared they are.

I'm not suggesting that Powellism could be stopped if The Beatles applied their considerable wits to a record called *Enoch*. But they would be heard. They would also lose votes. They would be subject to a great deal of hatred. They have taken risks in the past, but this would be a higher risk, one that might mean imprisonment (in a bad future) or might, by amplifying the small chorus of brave voices, mean that the future might be less bad.

WILLIAM MANN

The new Beatles album

The Times, 22 November 1968

The most important musical event of the year occurs today. It is, of course, the publication of the new two-disc album from, by, and simply entitled, *The Beatles*. Thirty tracks by those four—one by Ringo, three by George Harrison, the rest by that prodigiously inventive two-headed magic dragon still identified as Lennon–McCartney, though devotees may now have begun to attribute their songs to one or other ('Fool on the hill' was by Paul, 'I am the walrus' by John, don't you agree?) and will confidently continue so to divide their music on the new album.

It is the first Beatles collection of songs since *Magical Mystery Tour*, and their first LP since *Sgt Pepper*; but it does not include any of the songs newly composed for the *Yellow Submarine* film—a pity, especially since some of the tracks on *The Beatles* are scrappy or pot-boilers. The album comes from Parlophone on The Beatles' own Apple label, has a plain white sleeve, but inside includes a huge colour poster of snapshots and a new colour photograph of each. The words of all the songs are printed on the back of the poster and the poetic standard varies from inspired ('Blackbird') through allusive ('Glass onion') and obscure ('Happiness is a warm gun') to jokey, trite, and deliberately meaningless.

The Lennon–McCartney songs are as provocative as ever. Nine of the 26 are superbly inventive and in the same class is George Harrison's 'Long, long, long', a melting love song in slow, waltz tempo—though, as with several other tracks, I am in two minds how much of the appeal is due to the brilliant scoring of George Martin (whom some regard as, not the fifth, but the first Beatle). I say inventive rather than creative. Even more than in *Sgt Pepper*, the Lennon–McCartney numbers retrace charted territory either to mock or to explore further. There are overt references to their own earlier songs (brilliant and delightful in 'Glass onion', especially the touch of recorders for 'Fool on the hill'), to Bob Dylan ('Yer blues'), Chubby Checker and The Beach Boys ('Back in the USSR'), the Ska of Desmond Dekker and the Aces ('Ob-la-di, ob-la-da').

There are near-quotes from Alan Price's 'Simon Smith', 'The Harlem Shuffle', and from Indian and Greek poetry. Some songs adopt the style of talking blues, shouting blues, rock 'n' roll (especially Elvis Presley), The New Vaudeville Band (itself a pastiche of old-style pop), the quasi-improvisatory songs of The Incredible String Band, Nashville country and western, Latin American calypso, Indian traditional music (inevitably), *musique concrète*, flamenco and even the slushy ballad. ('Good night' had me collapsed in laughter, but I suspect that it will be a regular request for The Jimmy Young Show—it is as well constructed a ballad as any that won Sinatra or Humperdinck a golden disc, though obviously genuine pistachio.) There are doubtless other allusions and pastiches and quotations that I haven't yet identified— several fleeting reminiscences had me smiling but stumped for recognition. And there are, as in *Sgt Pepper*, a quantity of musical and verbal references to drug-taking and hippy experiences, some less communicative to my antacid self than others.

The flip side of 'Hey Jude' was an up-tempo song called 'Revolution'. Side four of the new LP includes a slow version, slightly varied in places, called 'Revolution 1', and a Cage-style indeterminate montage of assorted sounds (interesting, narcotic, but rather too long—though the stereo recording, as with the whole album, adds artistic point and detail that mono listeners will miss) entitled 'Revolution 9'—a private reference is implied, since the credit titles list acknowledgement to all at No. 9.

There are too many private jokes (they remind me of the Before-the-Fringe revues) and too much pastiche to convince me that Lennon and McCartney are still pressing forward with their race against other progressive composers. The genius is all there, though. The girls emerge well. Prudence, Martha, Julia, Sadie and Mother Nature, not to mention Sexie Sadie and Desmond's Mollie. Nature is figured as well, with the blackbird, and the piggies (are they Chicago police or just company directors?), the son, my monkey, the eagle who picks my eye, the elephants and tigers, in 'Bungalow Bill', the lizard on a window pane. There is a gourmand's banquet in 'Savoy truffle'. John Lennon's 'Helter skelter' [*sic*], a rock number, is exhaustingly marvellous, a revival that is willed by creativity (yes, the word is apposite here) into resurrection, a physical but essentially musical thrust into the loins.

It is, once again, a brilliant feat of invention. The next Lennon–McCartney anthology must, imperatively, look forward rather than back. But these 30 tracks contain plenty to be studied, enjoyed, gradually appreciated more fully, in the coming months. No other living composer has achieved so much this year.

A. MARTYNOVA

A fairy tale about a present-day Cinderella

Sovetskaya Kultura, 3 December 1968

The four 'Cinderellas' are George Harrison, Paul McCartney, John Lennon and Ringo Starr. After the stunning success of their first songs they travelled all over the hemisphere, released mountains of records and drove crowds of teenagers out of their minds; they brought to life hundreds of similar ensembles, earned millions of dollars, and returned home to Great Britain where the Queen received and congratulated them. Tears of adoration appeared in the eyes of millions of admirers—it is, after all, moving to see such simple and pleasant fellows get such high honours; it's as if they had rewarded you also. And so you sit by the TV or listen to records: 'Yesterday, all my troubles seemed so far away . . . . Oh, I remember yesterday . . . .'

You're at peace in your soul—they say that the English treasury's been enriched, but now you have heroes that aren't imaginary, ones who're always with you. . . .

[From 1963,] first-hand reports, covers of magazines with circulations in the millions, and mountains of souvenirs, shirts, suspenders, lighters—the market began to work for The Beatles, fanning the flame of Beatlemania. And, according to the steel logic of economics, The Beatles began to work for the market. Both sides were winners. Who, then, was on the losing side at that time? During the first stage in this escalation of success, it seemed that no one was.

Aside from unfortunate parents, perhaps, the spiritual tragedies bothered no one . . . [as] . . . thousands of crazed teenagers stupefied by the unceasing 'yeah-yeah' rushed towards their idols with the despair of the condemned. Only some time later did sociologists busy themselves with this problem, and it came to the surface that idol-worship is not merely a 'disease of an age' but that it is a direct result of the spiritual, but more exactly spiritless atmosphere of bourgeois society in which youth seeks out its 'gods' in order to protest against the canonised 'gods'. It appeared that Power, Money, Career, and Well-being no longer instilled children, even of bourgeois families, with great respect. Furthermore, they rejected these values and sought their own.

It is not accidental that at the beginning of the Sixties young people tossed about the expression 'don't trust anyone older than 30!' Upon consideration, it's not as eccentric as it appears at first glance—not to trust anyone when you're 16 is not only difficult, but even unnatural. Is it possible that children simply stopped loving their parents and became egoists before their time? As is well known, each family has its black sheep, but in recent years in America and Europe there have been far too many families that have given rise to 'black sheep' who have become vagabonds, criminals, dope addicts, so that it has become necessary to sound the alarm.

The phenomenon of youth abandoning the bourgeois family is spreading so rapidly and unpredictably, and at times takes on such ugly forms, that its essence becomes obscured. Beatlemania and after that 'mods', 'rockers', 'hippies', 'yippies', 'diggers'—what a number of incredible movements and anti-movements have sprung up during some 10 years in the life of one society . . . When they first appeared they brought on condescending laughter; when one's young, one's green; they'll get over sowing their wild oats! Later people began to observe more closely and became alarmed.

Beatlemania was one of the symptoms. Kindled by radio, movies, TV and the press, Beatlemania mangled spirits while 'grown-ups' looked on in bewilderment. As soon as The Beatles reached the height of their success, that is, when they were transformed from 'Cinderellas' into idols, the fairy tale, as one is wont to say, comes to an end. Even if they sing about 'love which is not for sale' or compose romantic ballads or shout 'yeah-yeah'—it no longer matters, for now everything will be swallowed up just the same. It wasn't only the songs written by The Beatles that stopped belonging to them, but they themselves—after all, they also had their own lives.

. . . Conversing with The Beatles, Hunter Davies noticed that they're confused, that they're looking for something; what that is they themselves can't understand, but basically they're looking for themselves. For they haven't had time to think; it turned out that they simply didn't have sufficient elementary knowledge to understand and appraise what was going on. Confusion led to despair—at one time The Beatles planned to renounce everything and go off to an uninhabited island, but then they abandoned this idea which wouldn't have been so easy to realise.

Then a new idea was born, more acceptable to the society in which they live: the creation of their own stock company—Apple. This also is an 'island' of a sort, but one with a solid economic foundation. The shareholders have already got down to business—they have monopoly rights on any performance of their compositions. Moreover, fans recording their music are obliged to pay a fee to the company, Apple. The Beatles no longer perform for the public; everything that's done by them is recorded in a studio equipped with the most modern equipment, only on records and only for enormous sums of money.

Thus The Beatles have become businessmen. This activity now takes up the greater part of their time. True, records of their new songs from time to time appear on the market, and even with quite a bit of commotion. For instance, take the last record, *Two Virgins*. It went like hot cakes, and here's why: on the cover there was a photograph of John Lennon with his new girlfriend, Yoko Ono—both nude. Again there were headlines in the newspapers, again a 'sensation'. You can't get away from it. Without arousing the interest of the public, both Apple and the songs, however they were intended, won't last long.

It turns out that there's very little of the fantastic in the fairy tale but more and more numbers and calculations. True, some good songs remain, but they're not the ones that the young people sing when they go out into the streets to protest the war, violence and legalised slavery. They sing the songs of civil fortitude composed by Bob Dylan, Pete Seeger, Joan Baez, and others, those who are truly popular youth singers. Their success, by the way, was in no way affected by Beatlemania. The Beatles have always been proud of their being apolitical and of their non-participation in the governmental machine. They invited one into the world of love, nature and pure feelings; in short, into another world, one separated from the surrounding one. Yet they didn't find such a world, even with the help of narcotics. Instead, they became the property of another world—of pop-art, the market, and business.

WILLIAM MANN

Those inventive Beatles

The Times, 5 December 1969

If adverse reviews elsewhere have dissuaded you from buying *Abbey Road*, The Beatles' new LP, do not hesitate any longer. It teems with musical invention—mostly by Lennon and McCartney, though all four contribute songs—and the second side, as a piece of musical construction, is altogether remarkable and very exciting indeed. The stereo recording will be called gimmicky by people who want a record to sound exactly like a live performance: how can that guitarist (presumably George Harrison) in 'Here comes the sun' hop three or four yards sideways so quickly? He can't, but the effect is agreeable and adds a non-visual drama to the music. Like the back-tracked horns [*sic*] in 'Maxwell's silver hammer', and the electronic distortion of voice in 'Oh! darling', the stereo manipulation is used for a musical purpose, not just the sound ravey.

The first two songs on side one, 'Come together' and Harrison's

'Something', have been put out as a single. Nice as they are—especially the lazy ostinato bass in the former—they are minor pleasures in the context of the whole disc. For mass appeal I would have pinned greater hopes on 'Maxwell', a neo-vaudeville comic song about a jocular murderer, and Ringo Starr's 'Octopus's garden' which might be called Son of Yellow Submarine and, like 'Maxwell', delights the teenybopper in all of us. Side one ends with a long piece, 'I want you', which is really two alternating tunes: the second of these (actually heard first as an instrumental prelude), 'She's so heavy', is built on a haunting ground-bass that eventually monopolises a grand build-up, in the manner of 'Hey Jude', growing and proliferating and getting louder until the only solution was to cut the tape dead when the side is full. Most exciting.

But not as marvellous as side two. This begins with George Harrison's slow, torrid 'Here comes the sun', much the most powerful song he's written so far, only hinted at for the moment. It melds into 'Because', not Guy d'Hardelot but Lennon–McCartney, mind-blowing close harmony (it reminds me of 'This boy' all those years ago, though the harmonies are more subtle nowadays) over an asymmetrical 3 plus 5 rhythmic pulse. Then a wistful romantic tune, 'You never give me your money' with a down-to-earth second half in honky-tonk style that fades into a further instalment of 'Sun King' with words in a mixture of Spanish and Italian. This blends into a whole series of rock 'n' roll songs that seem to find their tunes in developments of the same initial mood and musical invention.

Some have called this a medley but the effect is more dramatic, more structural; to tie the music further together there is even a back-reference to the ground-bass of 'She's so heavy'. The last portion of the side begins softly with a new tune to the old words 'Golden slumbers kiss your eyes': towards the end of The Beatles' double LP there was a send-up ballad called 'Goodnight' and 'Golden slumbers' is a companion to it, but straight rock ballad, not send-up cyclamate.

It merges into a new refrain with a heavy rock beat, 'Boy you're gonna carry that weight', and this includes a reprise, with full symphony orchestra, of the 'You never give me your money' tune that got lost a long way earlier: its return is as satisfying as the discovery of a ten-bob note you've been missing for a week. The tempo steps up for a one-line tune that never gets as far as line two because guitar and drums go off on their own in an inspired duet until quick piano chords introduce the last song-epigram: 'And in the end the love you take is equal to the love you make'. The record seems to be over but the long pause is followed by a mini-tribute to 'Her Majesty' in which voice and guitar walk slowly across the room.

A pity the words of the songs aren't supplied with the record. John Lennon has said that *Abbey Road* is an attempt to get away from experiment and back to genuine rock 'n' roll, so I suppose they don't want us to study the words: a pity because learning by ear isn't as accurate. In any case, when anyone is as naturally inventive as The Beatles to try non-experimentation is a forlorn hope.

RICHARD CROSSMAN

The Diaries of a Cabinet Minister

from: Vol 3 (1968–70)

Wednesday 31 December 1969
Last night Patrick [Crossman's son] and I stayed up at 10.30 to see another programme where they were choosing the man of the decade. Alistair Cooke put forward the case of our friend John Kennedy, with the theme that we have never recovered from the shock of his death. Then there was a ridiculous scene with Mary McCarthy, whom I last remember meeting at [London publisher] George Weidenfeld's dinner party, lecturing us that Ho Chi Minh was the man of the decade, the man who is against technology, the man who speaks for the small people and for participation against the wickedness of the modern world. It was absolute nonsense. Then there was a curious piece with Desmond Morris, the fellow who has made a tremendous success with a couple of bestsellers about sex and the human race. He had John Lennon as the man of the decade. Well, some days ago I saw on *24 Hours* an extraordinary interview with John Lennon, who is now a kind of Jesus Christ figure. Here he was again and, do you know, he was the only person who said that it hadn't been a bad decade, that we'd made enormous advances and that a lot of people were happier than ever before. In their own way he and The Beatles were saying 'We disown the whole Establishment not out of utter depression and pessimism, but because we are confident of the future and that we can take over and create a world of peace and amity.'

In his strange fashion, looking through those spectacles, with his beard and his odd Japanese wife, he was, I must admit, the only person in all these programmes with a gospel, a hope and a belief.

BERNARD LEVIN

The isle is full of noises

from: *The Pendulum Years—Britain and The Sixties*

Most celebrated of all the experimenters in other-worldly ways of life were some of those very Beatles, one of whom, towards the end of the decade, caused great offence to many by going to bed in public with his new bride, a Japanese lady who was variously described as a sculptress and a film-maker, though none could remember seeing any sculpture by her, and the only film she was known to have made consisted entirely of shots of naked buttocks moving, with more or less grace, away from the camera. Mr and Mrs John Lennon, then, having been married, elected to spend their honeymoon entirely in bed, a custom which was, after all, not entirely original. What made their honeymoon different from most is that it was spent in conditions of extreme public exposure, in a suite at the Hilton Hotel, Amsterdam, to which reporters, interviewers, newspaper and television photographers and other interested parties were free to come, and in suitable cases invited to join them in the bed, and there celebrate with the loving couple what was supposed to be the point of the entire proceedings, to wit a demonstration on behalf of personal and international peace. To this end, the walls of the bedroom were decorated with signs reading 'Bed Peace', 'Hair Peace', 'Stay in Bed', and 'Grow Your Hair', and the peaceful two argued, reasonably enough, that if everyone stayed in bed, occupying themselves in growing their hair, there would be no wars. To the question, what would happen if most stayed in bed and grew their hair but a few of the more ruthless declined to do so, they had clearly not addressed themselves, for the philosophy behind the performance was summed up by Mr Lennon, who said that all would be well if the Vietnamese, both North and South, would only take their trousers off, followed by the Arabs, the Israelis, the Russians and the Americans, while Mrs Lennon unwittingly touched upon the fallacy in the argument by proclaiming that their mood could be summed up in the words: 'Remove your pants before resorting to violence.' It might, of course, be objected that this is the spirit which in practice presumably guides every rapist, but granting that Mrs Lennon meant to say that he who removes his pants will be unable to resort to violence, it still left unresolved the problem of what to do about those whose pants stayed resolutely on, and still more the problem of how to deal with those who had learnt to do violence while naked from the waist down, or up, or even both . . .

. . . It cannot be denied that much of the nonsense talked by the young idols, in particular Mr and Mrs Lennon, invited much of the criticism, though as against that one might reflect that the intimate conversation of the newly married is not usually expected to be either coherent or profound, though as against *that* one might reflect that the intimate conversation of the newly married is not usually expected to be filmed, recorded and made public. Nor can it be denied that much of the nonsense, even when it was not so extreme or so obtrusive as to invite the more extreme or obtrusive criticism, was still nonsense. Nevertheless it differed from most of the nonsense talked, under the guise of philosophy, by those who were in the business of making money out of popular entertainment in two crucial particulars. First, there was nothing either proselytising or pernicious about it; second, it was gentle, introspective, and pacific. A deep sense of unease afflicted many of those who studied this phenomenon, so much so that their unease took the form of extreme hostility to it; it seemed as though they feared for their ordered, aggressive and interfering world, though in truth there was little danger to it from the young people who sat cross-legged on the floor in caftans . . .

WILLIAM MANN

Strong as ever

The Times, 8 May 1970

Ghoulish rumour-mongers are putting it about that *Let It Be* is The Beatles' last LP together, and this is why the record sleeve, accompanying book (much too fat to be called a booklet) and outer cover are black-edged, and may be why the album costs so much. Let us attend the funeral when life is pronounced extinct: at the moment the corporate vitality of The Beatles, to judge from *Let It Be*, is pulsating as strongly as ever.

The album takes its title from a recent single written by Lennon and McCartney, performed here in a slightly more elaborate version; *Let It*

Be is also the title of the new Beatles film to be shown later this month. The fat book of colour photographs and conversations is called *The Beatles Get Back*, slightly confusing since 'Get back' is another recent Beatles single (also included, a little abbreviated, on the LP) and was, for a time, the projected name of the film. All will be sorted out eventually, no doubt.

Meanwhile the LP is a sort of trailer for the film's music. As such it does not attempt any large-scale musical construction such as distinguished side two of *Abbey Road*; there are, on the other hand, several very short tracks, snatches of music that may recall things in Paul McCartney's solo LP. Of the 12 tracks there are two by George Harrison, one fragment of a rude Liverpool song about Maggie Mae, another fragment, 'Dig it', ascribed to all four Beatles, and the rest are by Lennon and McCartney.

The first of the two sides is the stronger, containing at least three lovely new songs. 'Across the universe' follows the manner of 'Strawberry Fields' and 'Glass onion', worthily so. The refrain, 'Nothing's gonna change my world', is really haunting, and the instrumentation (with acoustic guitars and a distant choir) has great character—but this is true of other tracks as well, and the stereo placing of sound is consistently fascinating. 'Dig a pony' has a captivating refrain too, as well as relaxed, imaginative harmony and construction. George's 'I me mine', a slow rock number, took my fancy immediately with its easy switches of musical metre.

As we may now expect, there is a slow ballad by Paul, 'The long and winding road', good of its kind, perhaps not specially distinctive. Also on the second side is a pleasant 12-bar blues by George, 'For you blue', which features Hawaiian effect and some chat during the music; and an early Lennon–McCartney, 'One after 909', recorded now for the first time. A slowish, quiet blues called 'I've got a feeling' has that gently insinuating quality of some other Lennon–McCartney songs ('Let it be' is another) which at first seem ordinary but gradually take complete possession of the listener's inner ear. Not a breakthrough record, unless for the predominance of informal, unedited live takes (Phil Spector is the producer); but definitely a record to give lasting pleasure. They aren't having to scrape the barrel yet.

SIX

Carry That Weight

Power to the people: John Lennon and Yoko Ono talk to Robin Blackburn and Tariq Ali

Red Mole, 8–22 March 1971

TA: Your latest record and your recent public statements, especially the interviews in *Rolling Stone* magazine, suggest that your views are becoming increasingly radical and political. When did this start to happen?

JL: I've always been politically minded, you know, and against the status quo. It's pretty basic when you're brought up, like I was, to hate and fear the police as a natural enemy and to despise the army as something that takes everybody away and leaves them dead somewhere. I mean, it's just a basic working class thing, though it begins to wear off when you get older, get a family and get swallowed up in the system. In my case I've never not been political, though religion tended to overshadow it in my acid days; that would be around '65 or '66. And that religion was directly the result of all that superstar shit—religion was an outlet for my repression. I thought, 'Well, there's something else to life, isn't there? This isn't it, surely?' But I was always political in a way, you know. In the two books I wrote, even though they were written in a sort of Joycean gobbledegook, there's many knocks at religion and there is a play about a worker and a capitalist. I've been satirising the system since my childhood. I used to write magazines in school and hand them around. I was very conscious of class, they would say with a chip on my shoulder, because I knew what happened to me and I knew about the class repression coming down on us—it was a fucking fact but in the hurricane Beatle world it got left out—I got farther away from reality for a time.

165

TA: What did you think was the reason for the success of your sort of music?

JL: Well, at the time it was thought that the workers had broken through, but I realise in retrospect that it's the same phoney deal they gave the blacks, it was just like they allowed blacks to be runners or boxers or entertainers. That's the choice they allow you—now the outlet is being a pop star, which is really what I'm saying on the album in 'Working class hero'. As I told *Rolling Stone*, it's the same people who have the power, the class system didn't change one little bit. Of course, there are a lot of people walking around with long hair now and some trendy middle class kids in pretty clothes. But nothing changed except that we all dressed up a bit, leaving the same bastards running everything.

RB: Of course, class is something the American rock groups haven't tackled yet.

JL: Because they're all middle class and bourgeois and they don't want to show it. They're scared of the workers, actually, because the workers seem mainly right-wing in America, clinging on to their goods. But if these middle class groups realise what's happening, and what the class system has done, it's up to them to repatriate the people and to get out of all that bourgeois shit.

TA: When did you start breaking out of the role imposed on you as a Beatle?

JL: Even during the Beatle heyday I tried to go against it, so did George. We went to America a few times and Epstein always tried to waffle on at us about saying nothing about Vietnam. So there came a time when George and I said 'Listen, when they ask next time, we're going to say we don't like that war and we think they should get right out.' That's what we did. At that time this was a pretty radical thing to do, especially for the 'Fab Four'. It was the first opportunity I personally took to wave the flag a bit. But you've got to remember that I'd always felt repressed. We were all so pressurised that there was hardly any chance of expressing ourselves, especially working at that rate, touring continually and always kept in a cocoon of myths and dreams. It's pretty hard when you are Caesar and everyone is saying how wonderful you are and they are giving you all the goodies and the girls, it's pretty hard to break out of that, to say 'Well, I don't want to be king, I want to be real.' So in its way the second political thing I did was to say 'The Beatles are bigger than Jesus.' That really broke the scene, I nearly got shot in America for that. It was a big trauma for all the kids that were following us. Up to then there was this unspoken policy of not answering delicate questions, though I always read the papers, you know, the political bits. The continual awareness of what was going on made me feel ashamed I wasn't saying anything. I burst out because I could no longer play that game any more, it was just too much for me. Of course, going to America increased the build up on me, especially as the war was going on there. In a way we'd turned out to be a Trojan horse. The 'Fab Four' moved right to the top and then sang about drugs and sex and then I got into more and more heavy stuff and that's when they started dropping us.

RB: Wasn't there a double charge to what you were doing right from the beginning?

YO: You were always very direct . . .

JL: Yes, well, the first thing we did was to proclaim our Liverpoolness to the world, and say 'It's all right to come from Liverpool and talk like this'. Before, anybody from Liverpool who made it, like Ted Ray, Tommy Handley, Arthur Askey, had to lose their accent to get on the BBC. They were only comedians but that's what came out of Liverpool before us. We refused to play that game. After The Beatles came on the scene everyone started putting on a Liverpudlian accent.

TA: In a way you were even thinking about politics when you seemed to be knocking revolution?

JL: Ah, sure, 'Revolution'. There were two versions of that song but the underground left only picked up on the one that said 'count me out'. The original version which ends up on the LP said 'count me in' too; I put in both because I wasn't sure. There was a third version that was just abstract, *musique concrète*, kind of loops and that, people screaming. I thought I was painting in sound a picture of revolution— but I made a mistake, you know. The mistake was that it was anti-revolution. On the version released as a single I said 'when you talk about destruction you can count me out'. I didn't want to get killed. I didn't really know that much about the Maoists, but I just knew that they seemed to be so few and yet they painted themselves green and stood in front of the police waiting to get picked off. I just thought it was unsubtle, you know. I thought the original Communist revolutionaries coordinated themselves a bit better and didn't go around shouting about it. That was how I felt—I was really asking a question. As someone from the working class I was always interested in Russia and China and everything that related to the working class, even though I was playing the capitalist game. At one time I was so much involved in the religious bullshit that I used to go around calling myself a Christian Communist, but as Janov says, religion is legalised madness. It was therapy that stripped away all that and made me feel my own pain.

RB: This analyst you went to, what's his name . . .

JL: Janov . . .

RB: His ideas seem to have something in common with Laing in that he doesn't want to reconcile people to their misery, to adjust them to the world but rather to make them face up to its causes?

JL: Well, his thing is to feel the pain that's accumulated inside you ever since your childhood. I had to do it to really kill off all the religious myths. In the therapy you really feel every painful moment of your life—it's excruciating, you are forced to realise that your pain, the kind that makes you wake up afraid with your heart pounding, is really yours and not the result of somebody up in the sky. It's the result of your parents and your environment. As I realised this it all started to fall into place. This therapy forced me to have done with all the Godshit. All of us growing up have come to terms with too much pain. Although we repress it, it's still there. The worst pain is that of not being wanted, of realising your parents do not need you in the way you need them. When I was a child I experienced moments of not wanting to see the ugliness, not wanting to see not being wanted. This lack of love went into my eyes and into my mind. Janov doesn't just talk to you about this but makes you feel it—once you've allowed yourself to feel again, you do most of the work yourself. When you wake up and your heart is going like the clappers or your back feels strained, or you develop some other hang-up, you should let your mind go to the pain and the pain itself will regurgitate the memory which originally caused you to suppress it in your body. In this way the pain goes to the right channel instead of being repressed again, as it is if you take a pill or a bath, saying 'Well, I'll get over it'. Most people channel their pain into God or masturbation or some dream of making it. The therapy is like a very slow acid trip which happens naturally in your body. It is hard to talk about, you know, because you feel 'I am pain' and it sounds sort of arbitrary, but pain to me now has a different meaning because of having physically felt all these extraordinary repressions. It was like taking gloves off, and feeling your own skin for the first time. It's a bit of a drag to say so, but I don't think you can understand this unless you've gone through it—though I try to put some of it over on the album. But for me at any rate it was all part of dissolving the Godtrip or father-figure trip. Facing up to reality instead of always looking for some kind of heaven.

RB: Do you see the family in general as the source of these repressions?

JL: Mine is an extreme case, you know. My father and mother split and I never saw my father until I was 20, nor did I see much more of my mother. But Yoko had her parents there and it was the same . . .

YO: Perhaps one feels more pain when parents are there. It's like when you're hungry, you know, it's worse to get a symbol of a cheeseburger than no cheeseburger at all. It doesn't do you any good, you know. I often wish my mother had died so that at least I could get some people's sympathy. But there she was, a perfectly beautiful mother.

JL: And Yoko's family were middle-class Japanese but it's all the same repression. Though I think middle-class people have the biggest trauma if they have nice imagey parents, all smiling and dolled up. They are the ones who have the biggest struggle to say, 'Goodbye mummy, goodbye daddy'.

TA: What relation to your music has all this got?

JL: Art is only a way of expressing pain. I mean the reason Yoko does such far out stuff is that it's a far out kind of pain she went through.

RB: A lot of Beatle songs used to be about childhood . . .

JL: Yeah, that would mostly be me . . .

RB: Though they were very good there was always a missing element . . .

JL: That would be reality, that would be the missing element. Because I was never really wanted. The only reason I am a star is because of my repression. Nothing else would have driven me through all that if I was 'normal' . . .

YO: . . . and happy . . .

JL: The only reason I went for that goal is that I wanted to say: 'Now, mummy-daddy, will you love me?'

TA: But then you had success beyond most people's wildest dreams . . .

JL: Oh, Jesus Christ, it was a complete oppression. I mean we had to go through humiliation upon humiliation with the middle classes and showbiz and Lord Mayors and all that. They were so condescending and stupid. Everybody trying to use us. It was a special humiliation for me because I could never keep my mouth shut and I'd always have to be drunk or pilled to counteract this pressure. It was really hell . . .

YO: It was depriving him of any real experience, you know . . .

JL: It was very miserable. I mean apart from the first flush of making it—the thrill of the first number one record, the first trip to America. At first we had some sort of objective like being as big as Elvis—moving forward was the great thing, but actually attaining it was the big let-down. I found I was having continually to please the sort of people I'd always hated when I was a child. This began to bring me back to reality. I began to realise that we are all oppressed which is why I would like to do something about it, though I'm not sure where my place is.

RB: Well, in any case, politics and culture are linked, aren't they? I mean, workers are repressed by culture not guns at the moment . . .

JL: . . . they're doped . . .

RB: And the culture that's doping them is one the artist can make or break . . .

JL: That's what I'm trying to do on my albums and in these interviews. What I'm trying to do is to influence all the people I can influence. All those who are still under the dream and just put a big question mark in their mind. The acid dream is over, that is what I'm trying to tell them.

RB: Even in the past, you know, people would use Beatle songs and give them new words. 'Yellow submarine', for instance, had a number of versions. One that strikers used to sing began 'We all live on bread and margarine'; at LSE we had a version that began 'We all live in a Red LSE'.

JL: I like that. And I enjoyed it when football crowds in the early days would sing 'All together now'—that was another one. I was also pleased when the movement in America took up 'Give peace a chance' because I had written it with that in mind really. I hoped that instead of singing 'We shall overcome' from 1800 or something, they would have something contemporary. I felt an obligation even then to write a song that people would sing in the pub or on a demonstration. That is why I would like to compose songs for the revolution now . . .

RB: We only have a few revolutionary songs and they were composed in the 19th century. Do you find anything in our musical traditions which could be used for revolutionary songs?

JL: When I started, rock and roll itself was the basic revolution to people of my age and situation. We needed something loud and clear to break through all the unfeeling and repression that had been coming down on us kids. We were a bit conscious to begin with of being imitation Americans. But we delved into the music and found that it was half white country and western and half black rhythm and blues. Most of the songs came from Europe and Africa and now they were coming back to us. Many of Dylan's best songs came from Scotland, Ireland or England. It was a sort of cultural exchange. Though I must say the more interesting songs to me were the black ones because they were more simple. They sort of said shake your arse, or your prick, which was an innovation really. And then there were the field songs mainly expressing the pain they were in. They couldn't express themselves intellectually so they had to say in a very few words what was happening to them. And then there was the city blues and a lot of that was about sex and fighting. A lot of this was self-expression but only in the last few years have they expressed themselves completely with Black Power, like Edwin Starr making war records. Before that many black singers were still labouring under that problem of God; it was often 'God will save us'. But right through the blacks were singing directly and immediately about their pain and also about sex, which is why I like it.

RB: You say country and western music derived from European folk songs. Aren't these folk songs sometimes pretty dreadful stuff, all about losing and being defeated . . ?

171

JL: As kids we were all opposed to folk songs because they were so middle-class. It was all college students with big scarfs and a pint of beer in their hands singing folk songs in what we call la-di-da voices—'I worked in a mine in New-cast-le' and all that shit. There were very few real folk singers you know, though I liked Dominic Behan a bit and there was some good stuff to be heard in Liverpool. Just occasionally you hear very old records on the radio or TV of real workers in Ireland or somewhere singing these songs and the power of them is fantastic. But mostly folk music is people with fruity voices trying to keep alive something old and dead. It's all a bit boring, like ballet: a minority thing kept going by a minority group. Today's folk song is rock and roll. Although it happened to emanate from America, that's not really important in the end because we wrote our own music and that changed everything.

RB: Your album, Yoko, seems to fuse avant-garde modern music with rock. I'd like to put an idea to you I got from listening to it. You integrate everyday sounds, like that of a train, into a musical pattern. This seems to demand an aesthetic measure of everyday life, to insist that art should not be imprisoned in the museums and galleries, doesn't it?

YO: Exactly. I want to incite people to loosen their oppression by giving them something to work with, to build on. They shouldn't be frightened of creating themselves—that's why I make things very open, with things for people to do, like in my book (*Grapefruit*). Because basically there are two types of people in the world: people who are confident because they know they have the ability to create, and then people who have been demoralised, who have no confidence in themselves because they have been told they have no creative ability, but must just take orders. The Establishment likes people who take no responsibility and cannot respect themselves.

RB: I suppose workers' control is about that . . .

JL: Haven't they tried out something like that in Yugoslavia; they are free of the Russians. I'd like to go there and see how it works.

TA: Well, they have; they did try to break with the Stalinist pattern. But instead of allowing uninhibited workers' control, they added a strong dose of political bureaucracy. It tended to smother the initiative of the workers and they also regulated the whole system by a market mechanism which bred new inequalities between one region and another.

JL: It seems that all revolutions end up with a personality cult—even the Chinese seem to need a father-figure. I expect this happens in Cuba too, with Che and Fidel . . . In Western-style Communism we would have to create an almost imaginary workers' image of *themselves* as the father-figure.

RB: That's a pretty cool idea—the Working Class becomes its own Hero. As long as it was not a new comforting illusion, as long as there was a real workers' power. If a capitalist or bureaucrat is running your life then you need to compensate with illusions . . .

YO: The people have got to trust in themselves.

TA: That's the vital point. The working class must be instilled with a feeling of confidence in itself. This can't be done just by propaganda— the workers must move, take over their own factories and tell the capitalists to bugger off. This is what began to happen in May 1968 in France . . . the workers began to feel their own strength.

JL: But the Communist Party wasn't up to that, was it?

RB: No, they weren't. With 10 million workers on strike they could have led one of those huge demonstrations that occurred in the centre of Paris into a massive occupation of all government buildings and installations, replacing de Gaulle with a new institution of popular power like the Commune or the original Soviets—that would have begun a real revolution but the French C.P. was scared of it. They preferred to deal at the top instead of encouraging the workers to take the initiative themselves . . .

JL: Great . . . but there's a problem about that here you know. All the revolutions have happened when a Fidel or Marx or Lenin or whatever, who were intellectuals, were able to get through to the workers. They got a good pocket of people together and the workers seemed to understand that they were in a repressed state. They haven't woken up yet here, they still believe that cars and tellies are the answer. . . . You should get these left-wing students out to talk with the workers, you should get the school-kids involved with *The Red Mole*.

TA: You're quite right, we have been trying to do that and we should do more. This new Industrial Relations Bill the Government is trying to introduce is making more and more workers realise what is happening . . .

JL: I don't think that Bill can work. I don't think they can enforce it. I don't think the workers will co-operate with it. I thought the Wilson Government was a big let-down but this Heath lot are worse. The underground is being harrassed, the black militants can't even live in their own homes now, and they're selling more arms to the South Africans. Like Richard Neville said, there may be only an inch of difference between Wilson and Heath but it's in that inch that we live. . . .

TA: I don't know about that; Labour brought in racialist immigration policies, supported the Vietnam war and were hoping to bring in new legislation against the unions.

RB: It may be true that we live in the inch of difference between Labour and Conservative but so long as we do we'll be impotent and unable to change anything. If Heath is forcing us out of that inch maybe he's doing us a good turn without meaning to . . .

JL: Yes, I've thought about that, too. This putting us in a corner so we have to find out what is coming down on other people. I keep on reading the *Morning Star* (the Communist newspaper) to see if there's any hope, but it seems to be in the 19th century; it seems to be written for dropped-out, middle-aged liberals. We should be trying to reach the young workers because that's when you're most idealistic and have least fear. Somehow the revolutionaries must approach the workers because the workers won't approach them. But it's difficult to know where to start; we've all got a finger in the dam. The problem for me is that as I have become more real, I've grown away from most working-class people—you know what they like is Engelbert Humperdinck. It's the students who are buying us now, and that's the problem. Now The Beatles are four separate people, we don't have the impact we had when we were together . . .

RB: Now you're trying to swim against the stream of bourgeois society, which is much more difficult . . .

JL: Yes, they own all the newspapers and they control all distribution and promotion. When we came along there was only Decca, Philips and EMI who could really produce a record for you. You had to go through the whole bureaucracy to get into the recording studio. You were in such a humble position, you didn't have more than 12 hours to make a whole album, which is what we did in the early days. Even now it's the same; if you're an unknown artist you're lucky to get an hour in a studio—it's a hierarchy and if you don't have hits, you don't get recorded again. And they control distribution. We tried to change that with Apple but in the end we were defeated. They still control everything. EMI killed our album *Two Virgins* because they didn't like it. With the last record they've censored the words of the songs printed on the record sleeve. Fucking ridiculous and hypocritical—they have to let me sing it but they don't dare let you read it. Insanity.

RB: Though you reach fewer people now, perhaps the effect can be more concentrated.

JL: Yes, I think that could be true. To begin with, working class people reacted against our openness about sex. They are frightened of nudity, they're repressed in that way as well as others. Perhaps they thought 'Paul is a good lad, he doesn't make trouble'. Also when Yoko and I got married, we got terrible racialist letters—you know, warning me that she would slit my throat. Those mainly came from Army people living in Aldershot. Officers. Now workers are more friendly to us, so perhaps it's changing. It seems to me that the students are now half-awake enough to try and wake up their brother workers. If you don't pass on your own awareness then it closes down again. That is why the basic need is for the students to get in with the workers and convince them that they are not talking gobbledegook. And of course it's difficult to know what the workers are really thinking because the capitalist press always only quotes mouthpieces like Vic Feather [1908–76; General Secretary of the TUC, 1969–73] anyway. So the only thing is to talk to them directly, especially the young workers. We've got to start with them because they know they're up against it. That's why I talk about school on the album. I'd like to incite people to break the framework, to be disobedient in school, to stick their tongues out, to keep insulting authority.

YO: We are very lucky really, because we can create our own reality, John and me, but we know the important thing is to communicate with other people.

JL: The more reality we face, the more we realise that unreality is the main programme of the day. The more real we become, the more abuse we take, so it does radicalise us in a way, like being put in a corner. But it would be better if there were more of us.

YO: We mustn't be traditional in the way we communicate with people—especially with the Establishment. We should surprise people by saying new things in an entirely new way. Communication of that sort can have a fantastic power so long as you don't do only what they expect you to do.

RB: Communication is vital for building a movement, but in the end it's powerless unless you also develop popular force.

YO: I get very sad when I think about Vietnam where there seems to be no choice but violence. This violence goes on for centuries perpetuating itself. In the present age when communication is so rapid, we should create a different tradition, traditions are created everyday. Five years now is like 100 years before. We are living in a society that has no history. There's no precedent for this kind of society so we can break the old patterns.

TA: No ruling class in the whole of history has given up power voluntarily and I don't see that changing.

YO: But violence isn't just a conceptual thing, you know. I saw a programme about this kid who had come back from Vietnam—he'd lost his body from the waist down. He was just a lump of meat, and he said, 'Well, I guess it was a good experience.'

JL: He didn't want to face the truth, he didn't want to think it had all been a waste . . .

YO: But think of the violence, it could happen to your kids . . .

RB: But Yoko, people who struggle against oppression find themselves attacked by those who have a vested interest in nothing changing, those who want to protect their power and wealth. Look at the people in Bogside and Falls Road in Northern Ireland; they were mercilessly attacked by the special police because they began demonstrating for their rights. On one night in August 1969, seven people were shot and thousands driven from their homes. Didn't they have a right to defend themselves?

YO: That's why one should try to tackle these problems before a situation like that happens.

JL: Yes, but what do you do when it does happen, what do you do?

RB: Popular violence against their oppressors is always justified. It cannot be avoided.

YO: But in a way the new music showed things could be transformed by new channels of communication.

JL: Yes, but as I said, nothing really changed.

YO: Well, something changed and it was for the better. All I'm saying is that perhaps we can make a revolution without violence.

JL: But you can't take power without a struggle . . .

TA: That's the crucial thing.

JL: Because, when it comes to the nitty-gritty, they won't let the people have any power; they'll give all the rights to perform and to dance for them, but no real power . . .

YO: The thing is, even after the revolution, if people don't have any trust in themselves, they'll get new problems.

JL: After the revolution you have the problem of keeping things going, of sorting out all the different views. It's quite natural that revolutionaries should have different solutions, that they should split into different groups and then reform, that's the dialectic, isn't it—but at the same time they need to be united against the enemy, to solidify a new order. I don't know what the answer is; obviously Mao is aware of this problem and keeps the ball moving.

RB: The danger is that once a revolutionary state has been created, a new conservative bureaucracy tends to form around it. This danger tends to increase if the revolution is isolated by imperialism and there is material scarcity.

JL: Once the new power has taken over they have to establish a new status quo just to keep the factories and trains running.

RB: Yes, but a repressive bureaucracy doesn't necessarily run the factories or trains any better than the workers could under a system of revolutionary democracy.

JL: Yes, but we all have bourgeois instincts within us, we all get tired and feel the need to relax a bit. How do you keep everything going and keep up revolutionary fervour after you've achieved what you set out to achieve? Of course Mao has kept them up to it in China, but what happens after Mao goes? Also he uses a personality cult. Perhaps that's necessary; like I said, everybody seems to need a father figure. But I've been reading *Khrushchev Remembers*. I know he's a bit of a lad himself—but he seemed to think that making a religion out of an individual was bad; that doesn't seem to be part of the basic Communist idea. Still people are people, that's the difficulty. If we took over Britain, then we'd have the job of cleaning up the bourgeoisie and keeping people in a revolutionary state of mind.

RB: . . . In Britain unless we can create a new popular power—and here that would basically mean workers' power—really controlled by, and answerable to, the masses, then we couldn't make the revolution in the first place. Only a really deep-rooted workers' power could destroy the bourgeois state.

YO: That's why it will be different when the younger generation takes over.

JL: I think it wouldn't take much to get the youth here really going. You'd have to give them free rein to attack the local councils or to destroy the school authorities, like the students who break up the repression in the universities. It's already happening, though people have got to get together more. And the women are very important too, we can't have a revolution that doesn't involve and liberate women. It's so subtle the way you're taught male superiority. It took me quite a long time to realise that my maleness was cutting off certain areas for Yoko. She's a red hot liberationist and was quick to show me where I was going wrong, even though it seemed to me that I was just acting naturally. That's why I'm always interested to know how people who claim to be radical treat women.

RB: There's always been at least as much male chauvinism on the left as anywhere else—though the rise of women's liberation is helping to sort that out.

JL: It's ridiculous. How can you talk about power to the people unless you realise the people is both sexes.

YO: You can't love someone unless you are in an equal position with them. A lot of women have to cling to men out of fear or insecurity, and that's not love—basically that's why women hate men . . .

JL: . . . and vice versa . . .

YO: So if you have a slave around the house how can you expect to make a revolution outside it? The problem for women is that if we try to be free, then we naturally become lonely, because so many women are willing to become slaves, and men usually prefer that. So you always have to take the chance: 'Am I going to lose my man?' It's very sad.

JL: Of course, Yoko was well into liberation before I met her. She'd had to fight her way through a man's world—the art world is completely dominated by men—so she was full of revolutionary zeal when we met. There was never any question about it: we had to have a 50–50 relationship or there was no relationship, I was quick to learn. She did an article about women in *Nova* more than two years back in which she said, 'Woman is the nigger of the world'.

RB: Of course we all live in an imperialist country that is exploiting the Third World, and even our culture is involved in this. There was a time when Beatle music was plugged on Voice of America. . . .

JL: The Russians put it out that we were capitalist robots, which we were I suppose . . .

RB: They were pretty stupid not to see it was something different.

YO: Let's face it, Beatles was 20th-century folksong in the framework of capitalism; they couldn't do anything different if they wanted to communicate within that framework.

RB: I was working in Cuba when *Sgt Pepper* was released and that's when they first started playing rock music on the radio.

JL: Well I hope they see that rock and roll is not the same as Coca-Cola. As we get beyond the dream this should be easier: that's why I'm putting out more heavy statements now and trying to shake off the teeny-bopper image. I want to get through to the right people, and I want to make what I have to say very simple and direct.

RB: Your latest album sounds very simple to begin with, but the lyrics, tempo and melody build up into a complexity one only gradually becomes aware of. Like the track 'My mummy's dead' echoes the nursery song 'Three blind mice' and it's about a childhood trauma.

JL: The tune does; it was that sort of feeling, almost like a Haiku poem. I recently got into Haiku in Japan and I just think it's fantastic. Obviously, when you get rid of a whole section of illusion in your mind you're left with great precision. Yoko was showing me some of these Haiku in the original. The difference between them and Longfellow is immense. Instead of a long flowery poem the Haiku would say 'Yellow flower in white bowl on wooden table' which gives you the whole picture, really.

. . . *TA*: How do you think we can destroy the capitalist system here in Britain, John?

JL: I think only by making the workers aware of the really unhappy position they are in, breaking the dream they are surrounded by. They think they are in a wonderful, free-speaking country. They've got cars and tellies and they don't want to think there's anything more to life. They are prepared to let the bosses run them, to see their children fucked up in school. They're dreaming someone else's dream, it's not even their own. They should realise that the blacks and the Irish are being harassed and repressed and that they will be next. As soon as they start being aware of all that, we can really begin to do something. The workers can start to take over. Like Marx said: 'To each according to his need'. I think that would work well here. But we'd also have to infiltrate the army too, because they are well trained to kill us all. We've got to start all this from where we ourselves are oppressed. I think it's false, shallow, to be giving to others when your own need is great. The idea is not to comfort people, not to make them feel better but to make them feel worse, to constantly put before them the degradations and humiliations they go through to get what they call a living wage.

WILFRID MELLERS

Imagine

Music and Musicians, January 1972

The composing duo of Lennon and McCartney is as impressive as it is mysterious; and if one doesn't push the metaphor too far, one might say that John is the negative, Paul the positive, pole. Opposite poles generate electricity: between John and Paul the sparks flew. John's fiery iconoclasm was tempered by Paul's lyrical grace, while Paul's wide-eyed charm was toughened by John's resilience. Even though they didn't, we are told, compose together after the first few years, it is clear that, creatively, they needed one another. Now that they are separated and Beatle mythology is deflated, they are as composers put to a stern test. The evidence suggests that John, at least, will be equal to it.

His new solo LP *Imagine* is a remarkable achievement. To appreciate it adequately we must consider it in relationship to his earlier solo disc, *Plastic Ono Band*. This deals, like Paul's *McCartney*, with personal love as against corporate activity; but, whereas McCartney's verbally minimal approach makes for a happy sophisticatedly innocent music, Lennon's underground songs start from words which stimulate a music both primitive and deeply melancholy. Yet Lennon has his own kind of sophistication, for the sequence of songs is planned—no less than *Sgt Pepper*—as a whole. We begin with 'Mother' which cuts the ties of family, saying goodbye in successive stanzas to mother, father and children, in a rigidly frozen metre so slow that it seems liable at any moment to cease. The vocal line is hard, rudimentary, with pentatonic riffs like a gospel shout; and it, too, is fragmented, threatened with complete stasis. The variety of nuance and inflection in the 'goodbyes', though pervasively Lennonesque and English, is worthy of the finest negro soul singer. The sense of imminent breakdown leads to a coda that scarily reverses the verbal meaning of the stanzas. With a change in rhythm, John lurches into a desperate ululation, 'Mamma don't go, Daddy come home', which rises to a scream and then fades out as they take no notice.

Left alone he tells us, or rather tells himself, to 'Hold on', and if he does 'it's gonna be all right' and, with Yoko's help, 'We're gonna win the fight'. But the beat—still handled by Ringo incidentally—is nervously jittery, and the tune, though lyrical, is still fragmented, breaking the sense of the sentences, so that we hang precariously in the middle of the 'gonna be all right' phrase, wondering if we'll ever land. The pentatonic melismata on 'Hold on' are tender, yet tentative.

So the positive qualities of this lovely song are exploratory rather than assured; and it is abruptly succeeded by 'I found out', a song which *is* assured, but only in denunciation. If 'Mother' had exploded family ties, this song blows up the brother-friend relationship, for he's seen through junkies, Jesus, Hare Krishna and has found out that it 'can do you no harm to feel your own pain'. Musically the piece is very primitive, pre-harmonic, almost pre-pentatonic in monodic chant style, with fierce beat. 'Working-class hero' is also musically rudimentary, an anglicised Bob Dylan talking blues, with drone-like triadic accompaniment and a vocal line for the most part undulating between adjacent tones. The words are about Them (who 'hurt you at home and hit you at school . . . kept you doped with religion and sex and TV . . . 'til you think you're so clever and classless and free') and Us, the young, whose alienation is complete.

'Isolation' is, indeed, the title of the last song on Side 1: an (again anglicised) version of negro piano blues, beginning with an ostinato and a texture recalling the great Jimmy Yancey. The piano's bare, open fifths touchingly suggest the emptiness of isolation ('we're afraid to be alone'), whilst the scrunchy, dense, passing dissonances convey an intensity of pain as the music sounds, timeless, through the silent night. The bluesy tune is infinitely sad, its phrases broken, separated by silences, the melismata on 'afraid' lyrically aspiring, yet at the same time stifled. The middle section ('you're just a human, a victim of the insane') becomes rhythmically more agitated with soul-style yells, but the final stanza, seeing our fear against the world's impermanence and the sun's eternity, re-establishes the music's blue gravity which, whatever the words say, withstands terror. In this most moving song Lennon has done something which The Beatles in their togetherness couldn't have done. He has created an English, 1970 equivalent of the negro blues, which was an urban folk art of the solitary heart. In this his achievement as an Englishman is collateral with Bob Dylan's as a white American.

The second side of the disc precisely mirrors but also intensifies the first side. 'Remember' again describes childhood and youth; Mum's and Dad's dreams for you were no less phoney than the myths of radio or silver screen. The music is here minimal, for the almost pre-pentatonic vocal line is splintered, the sense of the words shattered by silences; and we're conscious mainly of the loud, remorselessly nagging beat—which ends, however, by knocking us *un*conscious, and literally blowing up the past. After that, the song advising us to 'hold on' for love's sake is almost impotent. The old-fashioned piano ballad imperceptibly steals in on us from far away. When the vocal line begins to sing of 'Love', it's for real, as the tenderly floating, folk-like phrase suggests, reinforced by disturbing triadic shifts on the words 'feeling', 'reach' and 'you'. Nonetheless the folk-like phrase never manages to become a fulfilled song: once more the line is broken, and the ballad dissolves on the antique parlour piano, an intimation of reality, although too dreamy to survive the world we're born into.

In any case the dream is dismissed by the next song, ironically titled 'Well, well, well', a sinister beat number obliterating all pentatonic Edens. Melodically the song is African in its primitivism, and the stanzas are monophonic, the vocal being doubled by raucous fuzzbuzz instruments, unharmonised, but with an aggressively thumping beat. The 'well, well, well' refrain has triadic harmony, but in African antiphonal style, with no progression. The words concern a failed love-relationship, set not in a childish or adolescent past but very much in the immediate present. He takes his love out to dinner, where they talk of revolution and Women's Lib; they go into a big field to 'watch the English sky'. Yet 'we both were nervous, feeling guilty, and neither one of us knew just why', so a cannibalistic impulse ('she looked so beautiful I could eat her') gains ascendancy, the primitive beat and the monophonic yells build up cumulatively, until the music becomes a voodooistic nightmare. The final repetitions of 'well, well, well' are a series of screams.

Left alone again, he turns inward, enquiring 'Who am I? What am I supposed to be?' This invitation to 'Look at me' is gentle, with folk-like guitar and a tune that might be a folk song if ever it got going. But it revolves round and round on itself, failing to sing, sometimes petering out into silence, and an attempted modulation sharpwards doesn't come off. The refrain 'Oh my love, oh my love' is a bemused appeal—which might possibly offer some kind of release, since in the last stanza the question 'Who am I?' is modified to 'Nobody else can see, just you and me, who are we? Oh my love, Oh my love'. But hope—if that's what it is—is frail: as is evident in the next and climacteric song 'God' which, in emotional weight, balances the 'Isolation' song of Side 1. 'God' begins as a song of total rejection: for having told us in soul-style monodic plaint that 'God is a concept by which we measure our pain', the central body of the number consists of a catalogue of 'don't believes' in quasi-monodic incantation, with cumulatively intensifying percussion. The list covers I Ching, the Bible, Tarot, Hitler, Jesus, Kennedy, Buddha, Yoga, kings, ending with 'I don't believe in Beatles'. This is followed by a brief, intently silent silence; and then, unaccompanied, in lyrical pentatonicism 'I just believe in me, Yoko and me, and that's reality'—the last three words being spoken. The final section of the song is again lyrical and basically pentatonic, but with a somewhat minatory ostinato on percussion. It tells us that 'the dream is over' and dismisses Beatle mythology: 'I was a dream-weaver . . . I was the Walrus . . . but now I'm John.' The tiny epilogue, however, prevents our taking this self-reliance with easy optimism: 'My mummy's dead' may express the release he asked for in the first song of the cycle, yet does so in a sickening cross between nursery rhyme (it opens with the descending scale of 'Three blind mice') and television jingle. If it takes us back to the childhood The Beatles had started from, it's utterly disabused and disillusioned: 'I can't explain so much pain, I could never show it. My mummy's dead.'

Impressive though this disc is, one might have been tempted to take it as a fiery valediction. The new disc, however, proves that its uncompromising honesty was in fact a spring-board for new life. The title song, 'Imagine', takes up the theme of rejection from the earlier disc, asking us to imagine that there's no heaven, no hell, no possessions; then it transforms the theme into a positive vision of peace and the brotherhood of Man. If this sounds pretentious—as the words, without the music, of some of the songs on *Plastic Ono Band* sound self-indulgent—the music makes the vision incarnate. From an introverted, brooding piano texture of rocking arpeggios a folk-like vocal line flowers and proliferates. The melismata on the words 'some day' and 'join us' suggest potentiality, waiting to be fulfilled; strings halo the voice with modal gravity, but with no hint of cinematic gloss.

From this vision *in potentia* we descend with a bump to 1920-ish barrelhouse rag. 'Crippled inside' uses the inane eupeptism of this style to contrast the masks we wear in public with our crippled inner selves. The effect depends on a collusion of words with music, on a recognition that our disguises are comparable with those of the black-faced minstrel, and that we employ them for similar ends. The farce of the conventionally rhetorical coda in half time (arms outstretched, grin wider then ever) is slightly horrendous as well as funny; and lest we might think that he's referring only to the other guy as crippled inside, John follows this with a song of personal insecurity. Thematically 'Jealous guy' sometimes recalls 'A day in the life', that mythic song of a generation; but it's also related to the 'lost' songs of *Plastic Ono Band*. Its musical materials are again rudimentary: a stepwise phrase in echoing repetition, a mere rising scale to convey loss of control and a 'shivering inside'. Yet again the permutations of rhythm and of vocal inflection suggested by the words, and the unexpectedly related triads that make us 'cry', are oddly positive in effect, building up to an almost jaunty, whistling refrain and to a line that—in comparison with the fragmented utterances of *Plastic Ono Band*— might be called lyrically sustained. Similarly, though 'It's so hard' is saying precisely that—living and loving are both difficult and painful—the barrelhouse piano style is primitively potent, the ostinato compulsive, the gospel-style vocal line doubled with fuzzbuzz, so that the sonority has a harsh rock-bottom reality comparable with that of the genuine blues. The potential we detected within 'Isolation', on the previous disc, is being fulfilled.

As it is still more impressively in the big song that concludes Side 1. In a sense this is again a song of rejection: 'I don't want to be a soldier' (sailor, failure, rich man, poor man, beggar, thief, churchman), these rejections being chanted in an even-rhymed undulation, a tone up and a tone down, around a nodal point. The monodic incantation, primitively liturgical in flavour, is sustained against a remorseless beat and non-harmonic, pentatonic instrumental figurations that build up a furious hubbub resembling a voodoo ceremony at full tilt. The world outside indeed seems to be demoniacally possessed, and finally expires in electrophonic tweets and judders. Yet the vocal chant survives, and indeed grows stronger, so that the ultimate rejection of its 'Oh no, no' refrain (in African homophony) becomes, paradoxically, a triumph.

The first two songs on the second side repeat, but modify, the previous pattern. 'Gimme some truth' is again a hard-driving rock song of rejection, denouncing 'up-tight, short-sighted, narrow-minded hypocrites' with a wit comparable with Dylan's. Again hard physical energy becomes life-enhancing. 'Oh my love' takes up the theme of the two-way love relationship against society. Parlour piano substitutes for barrelhouse piano, for the song is balladic, with no jazz or blues elements. Its corniness, however, is superficial, and it isn't an old-world dream, like the piano ballad on the earlier disc. The melismata on the phrases 'My eyes can see' and 'For the first time in my life' enact a new birth, hopefully, doubtfully, in our ears and heart. And what is here tentative is consummated in 'How do you sleep?', which on the surface seems a vicious anti-Paul song. Apparently *Sgt Pepper* took Paul by surprise: he lives with straights, jumps when his momma speaks to him, and makes a pretty sound which is no more than muzak to John's ears. Yet whatever the personal malice and malignity, the music redeems it, and gives to the words a generalised application. *Pepper* took us *all* by surprise, and the question 'How do you sleep at night?' is pertinent to us all. In this sense the song contrasts the masks we present to the world—which other songs on the disc have torn asunder—with the reality within the subconscious, and in sleep. This may be why the tune, beginning with assertive repeated notes, expands into pentatonic arabesques, and ends with sustained strings (also pentatonic) burgeoning over a potent beat. The song acquires a grave nobility, almost an heroic quality, worthy of comparison with the finest songs of Dylan in this vein. As an account of Paul's music, it's vitiated by rancour; as a statement about the human condition, it's highly impressive—and an experience that, to be fair, we must suspect to be beyond Paul's range.

Characteristically, this sustained affirmation is followed immediately by another song of doubt: 'How can I go forward when I don't know which way I'm facing? How can I feel something if I just don't know how to feel?' Again the entirely diatonic song is basic in its musical material: a descending scale which unexpectedly stops, is punctured with thumping cadential chords, tries again, but ends in an 'Oh no, no' refrain that is also truncated with instrumental cadences separated by brief pregnant silences. Paradoxically again, the firmly diatonic and cadential nature of these broken phrases makes them quite different in effect from the fragmentary stumblings of the comparable songs on *Plastic Ono Band*. Indeed, they make an affirmation out of their however hesitant honesty, and strings derive from these chordal energies a soaring lyricism. This being so, the song can run into the final number: an unambiguous pæan of love for Yoko. The rhythmic pulse is continuous with a talismanic refrain that, however simple, doesn't need to be self-defensively ironic; and although the song is not intrinsically among the more interesting, its effect in the context of the whole disc is powerful. Its happiness seems at once tipsy (and therefore dangerous) and true; and if it finally takes off into a Dylan-like electronically distorted whining of harmonicas, we know that this Eden has been won through to, and will need to be won through to again and again.

WILFRID MELLERS

Infantilism

New Statesman, 27 October 1972

In their glorious heyday, The Beatles were a foursome that created a communal mythology of the young, pertinent and potent because their songs also sprang from individualised experience. John and Paul, the two leading Beatle composers, were complementary not in the sense that they composed together—after the early days they seldom did—but because they were opposite poles that generated electrical sparks that in turn fired and flamed. Now that they're separate, but still creating, we can see more clearly what each offered; and can also realise how difficult it is for one to function without the other. McCartney, with his new group Wings, produces pleasant songs more than competently executed; though they sometimes have topical themes such as conservation or pollution, they're turned outward to the world, seldom emotionally involved. With Lennon's first solo LP, on the other hand, personal involvement was everything, for the songs were directly autobiographical and an extension of the primal therapy which John and Yoko had recently undergone.

In infantile hysteria John yelled for the lost maternal breast, yet in the process obliterated the Mother and struck the Father dead. Nonetheless, his personal frenzy was metamorphosed into rudimentary art; into the young white blues of affluence and possession, as against the old black blues of poverty and dispossession; and the integrity of his 'British' blues technique—both in composition and in style of performance—was strong enough to allow his pain to 'stand for' that of the urban young everywhere.

On his second solo LP, *Imagine*, it seemed that he would be able to build on this personal catharsis, for the autobiographical elements, though still powerful, were less obtrusive, and the total effect of the still-savage songs was curiously and courageously affirmative. Interestingly enough, this was most impressively manifest in the big new-voodoo song of negation 'I don't wanna be a soldier', and in the explicitly anti-McCartney number 'How do you sleep?' To have achieved this tough maturity must have called for considerable spiritual stamina; that it couldn't be long sustained was hardly surprising. In any case, it isn't sustained on the new double album *Some Time in New York City*; for here John relinquishes personal experience in favour of the easier option of the public gesture. As William Blake and the earlier Beatles knew, generalities signify only in relation to particularities; and for the particularities of the first two Lennon solo LPs the political themes of *Some Time in New York City* are no adequate substitute. There's a hint of the former interior energy in the Women's Lib song 'Woman is the nigger of the world'; but the opening phrase, which has the tension of true jazz and stimulates some fine instrumental soloing, eventually dissipates in ramble and repetition, and in harmonic shifts that cease to surprise because the tune lacks direction. The more successful songs, such as the Irish troubles number 'Sunday Bloody Sunday', come off more through the remorselessness of their violence and the sheer decibel content of their presentation than through musical character or quality. Other songs rely on other extra-musical means, such as a presumably ironic contrast between the grim glumness of the words and the obvious corn of the music; thus John's 'The luck of the Irish' verbally demolishes the beastly English to a music-hall tune that is all lyrical blarney, while Yoko's 'We're all water'—verbally the closest approach to wit and poetry on the disc—also works, rather effectively, the same way. But I don't know what to make of her 'Sisters O sisters', for if the mind-boggling triteness of the tune is a joke against Utopianism we're left with utter nihilism, whereas if it isn't intended ironically I can only be glad that I'm unlikely to survive to taste the 'new world it's never too late to build'. There's a difference between what's simple and what's moronic. On the two earlier discs John's subjective infantilism was a process of painful self-discovery—for himself, for today's young, and vicariously for ourselves. On this disc undifferentiated rage on behalf of all radical causes spends itself in thin air; and political—unlike personal—infantilism, since it cannot be psychologically transcended, is as dangerous as it is ineffective.

The companion disc, *Live Jam*, is even more depressing than *Some Time in New York City*. Here there are no political gestures; but what we're left with, in live, mostly improvised performance, is little more than a public scream. Since the screamers include people as talented as Lennon and Zappa (and Yoko has yelled well enough from time to time), there are bound to be some interesting noises on and off. Self-indulgence could hardly be carried further, however, since to *this* infantilism there is neither artistic catharsis nor passionate (if intellectually half-baked and musically irrelevant) political conviction. Compositional silence and social-political action is presumably the next step, for Lennon as for some representatives of music's avant-garde. Let's hope it will be more responsible than these discs suggest.

JON WIENER

John Lennon versus the FBI

New Republic, 2 May 1983

Is rock 'n' roll revolutionary? The question sounds foolish at a time when Ronald Reagan is instructing James Watt on the true meaning of

The Beach Boys. But rock and politics added up to a burning issue in 1971 and 1972, and the connection was taken as seriously by Richard Nixon's White House as it was by the counterculture—maybe more so. And the rock star most feared by the Nixon gang was the singer-songwriter who had first won fame as the 'clever Beatle', John Lennon. As a result, Lennon became the only rock 'n' roller the government ever tried to deport because of the political power of his music. This strange story appears in the 26 pounds of FBI and Immigration files recently released to me under the Freedom of Information Act.

The Nixon Administration learned in February 1972 that Lennon was thinking about mounting a concert tour that would combine rock music with radical politics. Lennon's friend, Jerry Rubin, hoped to end the tour with a 'political Woodstock' outside the Republican National Convention, where Nixon was to be renominated. This information came to the White House from a rather improbable source on concert bookings, Senator Strom Thurmond, who had written to Attorney General John Mitchell about Lennon's plans. Thurmond sent a secret memorandum, drafted by the staff of his Subcommittee on Internal Security, to both Mitchell and the White House. The memo noted that 'radical New Left leaders' who were 'strong advocates of the program to "dump Nixon"' were planning 'to hold rock concerts in various primary election states for the following purposes: to obtain access to college campuses; to encourage 18-year-olds to register; to press for legislation legalising marijuana; to finance their activities; and to recruit persons to come to San Diego during the Republican National Convention in August 1972. . . . [Rennie] Davis and his cohorts intend to use John Lennon as a drawing card to promote their success. . . . If Lennon's visa is terminated it would be a strategic counter-measure.'

This was precisely the sort of thing that had been contemplated by John Dean, the counsel to the President, in his famous August 1971 memo: 'We can use the available political machinery to screw our political enemies.' Mitchell passed Thurmond's suggestion along to the Immigration and Naturalization Service; the next month, the INS, relying on Lennon's 1968 British misdemeanour conviction for marijuana possession, ordered him deported.

Lennon's main file in the FBI's Central Records System in Washington, DC, is a '100 case file'. '100' is the classification number for 'domestic security' investigations. Lennon's main file has 288 pages; the Reagan Justice Department has refused to release 199 of them, largely under the claim that they have been 'properly classified in the interests of national defense or foreign policy'. (Could this have something to do with the Lennon–McCartney song 'Back in the USSR'?) The pages that have been released are riddled with deletions on the same grounds. In some cases 'released' pages have been completely blacked out except for the headings.

Many of the documents in Lennon's FBI file are coded teletypes, a form reserved for sensitive messages because they require complicated encrypting and decrypting. Others are 'LHMs', Letterhead Memos, prepared for dissemination to other government agencies, reporting on Lennon's activities and plans. In Lennon's case, confidential LHMs were distributed by the 108th Military Intelligence Group in New York, the Secret Service, Naval Intelligence, the Immigration and Naturalization Service, the State Department, the US Attorney for New York, and the CIA. Many of the reports are addressed to, or sent by, J. Edgar Hoover, who is never mentioned by name but only by the awesome title: 'Director'. (Hoover died in May 1972, and L. Patrick Gray became Acting Director.)

The FBI documents are written in a bizarre language: 'From SAC, New York, to DIRECTOR, FBI: ReBuairtel 1/26/72, captioned Project "Yes" IS-NL, OO:NY, enclosed for the Bureau are 10 copies of an LHM captioned as above. Copies are being designated for those offices having PCPJ in their Divisions'. Fortunately, the Fund for Open Information and Accountability has published a phrase book to help readers translate such documents: *Are You Now or Have You Ever Been in the FBI Files?*, by Ann Mari Buitrago and Leon Immerman (Grove Press, 1981). 'SAC' is the Special Agent in Charge of the field office; 'ReBuairtel' refers to an internal Bureau communication sent by air mail. Project 'Yes' was Yoko Ono's 'Youth Election Strategy', the media arm of the planned 1972 tour. The FBI classified 'Yes' under 'Internal Security—New Left', and the origination office ('OO') was New York. PCPJ was the People's Coalition for Peace and Justice, an umbrella organisation coordinating plans for demonstrations at the Republican National Convention. When the FBI described Lennon in file captions, they didn't list him as 'ex-Beatle' but rather as 'SM-REVACT', Hooverspeak for 'Security Matter-Revolutionary Activities'.

The FBI maintained files on Lennon not only at FBI HQ in the SOG ('Seat of Government'), but also in FBI field offices, especially in New York, the 'OO' that had primary responsibility for the Lennon investigation. The OO file contains the most valuable documents, including virtually all such original materials as surveillance logs, interviews with informers, agents' memos on following leads, and details about how information is received and how agents are to proceed with an investigation. That file is also riddled with deletions.

The FBI has a conspiratorial conception of its enemies; it maintains massive files not just on individuals, but especially on organisations. Several hundred additional FBI Lennon pages are located in a file on a paper organisation that existed for no more than a month or two: the 'Election Year Strategy Information Committee', which apparently consisted of Rennie Davis at a desk in the basement of the Lennon–Ono apartment in Greenwich Village, working to set up Lennon's prospective concert tour.

The bulk of the Lennon files, however, came not from the FBI but from the Immigration and Naturalization Service. The record of the deportation proceedings takes up thousands of pages, in which Lennon's brilliant lawyer Leon Wildes ran circles around the INS's struggling chief trial attorney, Vincent Schiano. The administrative memos by various Immigration Service officials, who were trying to figure out how to get Lennon deported before the Republican National Convention, take up hundreds of pages. The correspondence file grew to several thousand pages, as Senators, celebrities, and Beatle fans requested information and took stands. Letters from Bob Dylan (who wrote, '[they] put an end to this mild dull taste of petty commercialism that is being passed off as artist art by the overpowering mass media. Hurray for John and Yoko!') and John Updike (who wrote, 'They cannot do this great country any harm, and might do it some good') are filed next to letters from adolescents in Ohio protesting Lennon's 'exportation' and 'deportment'.

The Nixon Administration's effort to deport Lennon made headlines during the wild political spring of 1972. In May, Nixon ordered the mining of Haiphong Harbour and massive new bombing raids, setting off a week of unprecedented antiwar mobilisations and civil disobedience, more frenzied and despairing than ever before. John and Yoko spoke at a midtown Manhattan antiwar rally, then headed off to their first immigration hearing. Nixon wanted them deported, Lennon told reporters in his Liverpool accent, 'because we're peaceniks'. The Mayor of New York, John Lindsay, and *The New York Times* expressed their support for Lennon and Ono. Beatle fans across the nation joined a letter-writing campaign around the theme, 'Let them stay in the USA'. Although the Immigration Service was falling all over itself in its haste to deport the Lennons, it maintained publicly that the case was perfectly routine. The falsity of that claim did not become clear until three years later when the Thurmond memo to Mitchell was unearthed well after Nixon himself had been deported from Washington. The Thurmond memo helped convince a federal judge to overrule the Immigration authorities and grant Lennon permanent residency in 1975. The rest of the story, told in the FBI files, has not been known until now.

The deportation case had its roots in a concert-rally John and Yoko gave in Ann Arbor, Michigan, in December 1971—a benefit for a local activist named John Sinclair, who had served two years of a 10-year sentence for selling two joints of marijuana to an undercover cop. Lennon and his movement friends regarded the Sinclair concert as a trial run for their proposed national tour. They wanted to see how a typical rock audience would respond to a rally that combined music with radical politics. The FBI was interested in precisely the same question. Its undercover agents were salted among the 15,000 excited Midwestern college kids who came to Crisler Arena to see John and Yoko and their friends.

The concert-rally began with Allen Ginsberg, who led the crowd in chanting 'Om-m-m-m-m'. Phil Ochs sang a song about Nixon. A local band played Elvis Presley's 'Jailhouse rock' for the man behind bars, and a version of Chuck Berry's 'Nadine', with new words about Bernadine Dohrn, a member of the Weather Underground: 'Bernadine, sister is that you?/Your picture's in the post office/But the people are protecting you'.

Jerry Rubin gave a speech explaining the rally's trial balloon purpose. 'A lot of events like this one will take place up and down the country between now and San Diego', he said, and called for 'a million of you to turn up at the Republican National Convention to humiliate and defeat Richard Nixon'. Dave Dellinger talked about 'a people's convention at San Diego next summer'. Rennie Davis talked about Vietnam. Bobby Seale called on the audience to 'start attacking the monster of capitalism'. Stevie Wonder, a surprise guest, sang and played 'For once in my life', and delivered a brief speech attacking Nixon and Agnew.

At 3 am, seven hours after the concert-rally began, John Lennon appeared. Despite the lateness of the hour, no one had left. For this was a major event: Lennon's first concert appearance in the United States since The Beatles waved goodbye at San Francisco's Candlestick Park five years earlier. 'We came here to show and to say to all of you that apathy isn't it, that we *can* do something. OK, so flower power didn't work. So what. We start again.' 15,000 people cheered. Then he sang the new song he had written for the occasion: 'John Sinclair'.

The undercover FBI men in the audience took it all down, scribbling even more furiously than the reporters from *Rolling Stone, Village Voice,* and the *East Village Other*—and sent a 26-page report to the Director, 'five (5) copies of a LHM setting forth information regarding captioned rally'. The FBI at first refused to release the full report in response to my Freedom of Information Act request, citing their authority to withhold 'investigatory records compiled for law enforcement purposes, the release of which would constitute an unwarranted invasion of the personal privacy of third parties'. The Assistant

Attorney General for Legal Policy eventually ruled in favour of my appeal and sent the withheld portion.

The section began with a complete set of the lyrics to 'John Sinclair', which the FBI had classified 'Confidential', even though they were in due course printed on the sleeve of Lennon's next album, *Some Time in New York City*. It wasn't great poetry (sample: 'It ain't fair, John Sinclair/In the stir for breathing air. . . Was he jailed for what he done/Or representing everyone?'), but it was no secret, either. Copies were forwarded to the FBI field offices in Boston, New York, Chicago, Milwaukee, San Francisco, and Washington, DC. Perhaps this was the FBI's understanding of the itinerary Lennon and Rubin had planned for the tour.

Meanwhile, back in Ann Arbor, the concert had an aftermath no one had anticipated: 55 hours after John and Yoko left the stage, John Sinclair was set free. A board of appellate judges released him on bond. Jerry Rubin was ecstatic, calling the release 'an incredible tribute to the power of the people. . . . We won!' He called for 'two, three, four, many more Ann Arbors!' No wonder the FBI was treating the lyrics to Lennon's song with such superstitious respect.

Lennon's FBI file for January and February 1972, the months preceding the deportation order, is bulging with reports on the 'Election Year Strategy Information Committee', Rennie Davis's effort to set up the concert tour. Stew Albert's name appears repeatedly in the EYSIC files. Every document mentioning him explains that 'Albert was arrested on April 12, 1966, at Berkeley, California', at a demonstration sponsored by the Progressive Labor Party. The next paragraph invariably explains that the PLP 'was founded in 1962 by individuals expelled from the Communist Party, USA, for following the Chinese Communist line'. Both those statements are true, but the implication that Albert was a member or sympathiser of the PLP is not. In fact Albert was known to the press as Jerry Rubin's 'Yippie lieutenant', a bitter antagonist of the humourless PLPers. When I asked him about his 1966 Berkeley arrest, he dismissed it as 'a youthful indiscretion'.

The first mention of EYSIC in the FBI files is dated January 28, 1972: 'The public will soon become aware of its existance [sic] and purpose—anti-Calrep activities' (i.e., demonstrations outside the California Republican convention). Several hundred pages later, a confidential LHM explains that 'the organisation ceased to exist approximately the first of March, 1972', one month after its founding. The INS ordered Lennon deported on March 6; thus EYSIC's dissolution did not come in response to the deportation order. Nor did the deportation order change Lennon's plans, as J. Edgar Hoover himself noted in a memo dated April 10: 'Subject continues to plan activities directed towards RNC and will soon initiate series of "rock concerts" to develop financial support.' (The FBI's use of 'quotes' was always curious.)

Given Lennon's refusal to change his plans, Hoover ordered his New York office to 'promptly initiate discreet efforts to locate subject'. The problem was that the FBI files showed his 'temporary residence' to be the 'St Regis Hotel, 150 Bank Street, New York City'. Bank Street is in Greenwich Village; every New York cop and cab driver knows the St Regis is in midtown, at 55th Street and Fifth Avenue. In fact, the agents who couldn't find any big hotels on Bank Street were quite close to their quarry. At the time, the Lennons were living in a two-bedroom apartment at 105 Bank Street, having checked out of the St Regis several months earlier.

The FBI worried about everything. In a coded teletype headed 'urgent', the Special Agent in Charge of the New York FBI informed J. Edgar Hoover, 'a source who is in a position to furnish reliable information advised that subject has been offered a teaching position with New York University during the summer . . . officials presume that subject will accept.' Like the Bank Street St Regis, this scrap of intelligence never quite panned out.

None of the documents that has been released was sent to or from Richard Nixon himself. But Nixon's chief of staff, H. R. Haldeman, was kept informed about the progress of the FBI's campaign to 'neutralise' Lennon. The contents of an April 25, 1972, memo to Haldeman have been obliterated in their entirety, under the national security exemption. But the memo's postscript refers Haldeman to a fuller report sent by E. L. Shackelford to E. S. Miller. Those agents' names have appeared in the news in a different connection. Miller (along with Mark Felt) was found guilty of breaking and entering in the FBI investigation of the Weather Underground. He and Felt are the only FBI agents ever to be convicted of crimes committed on the job. (They were pardoned by Ronald Reagan in 1981.) Their supervisor on that case was E. L. Shackelford. Do the withheld portions of Lennon's file contain evidence that the FBI committed the same kinds of illegal acts against Lennon that the same people were convicted of having committed in the Weather Underground case?

Hoover stated in another memo that Lennon was 'in US to assist in organising disruption of RNC'. That was absurd. The Lennons left London and moved to New York for a variety of reasons. For instance, they wanted to try to get custody of Yoko's American daughter by a previous marriage. But above all they came to America because it was the land of the free, the home of rock 'n' roll.

Still, it isn't hard to understand the Nixon Administration's fear of Lennon's political potential. In Ann Arbor, Lennon had shared the stage with the same people who had organised the Chicago demonstrations against the Democrats in 1968. In terms of attendance, Chicago had been a flop; only 20,000 showed up. The following fall, a quarter of a million came to Washington for the Vietnam Mobilisation, and half a million went to hear music in Woodstock that summer. Only Mayor Daley's police riot made the Chicago demonstrations a historic event. None of the big rock stars had come to Chicago.

If Lennon topped the bill at a 'political Woodstock' outside the 1972 Republican National Convention, Rubin and his friends reasoned, they would bring together the two strands of the '60s: counterculture and New Left, rock and radical politics. Robert Christgau, writing about Lennon in *Newsday* that summer, declared, 'if rock and roll is to continue to function politically, it must continue to liberate its audience—to broaden fellow-feeling, direct energy, and focus analysis'. That's exactly what Lennon and Rubin wanted to achieve. Nor were the counterculture, the New Left, and the FBI alone in believing in the political power of rock music. In 1969, *Time* magazine wrote that rock was 'not just a particular form of pop, but . . . one long symphony of protest . . . basically moral . . . the proclamation of a new set of values . . . the anthem of revolution'. The underground press never made a stronger claim. For once, Nixon wasn't being paranoid—or at least his deliriums were shared by others.

Lennon's lawyers successfully delayed the deportation order, and apparently advised him to cancel his rock tour plans. But the FBI still worried that he would lead demonstrations against Nixon at the convention which had now been moved to Miami (hence his 'anti-Mirep activities'). By the summer of 1972, the FBI was searching for a way to strengthen what the INS now privately admitted was a 'very loose case'. The FBI wrote in July that 'LENNON is reportedly a "heavy user of narcotics" known as "downers". This information should be emphasised to local Law Enforcement Agencies . . . with regards to subject being arrested if at all possible on possession of narcotics charge.' If such an arrest were made, Lennon 'would become more likely to be immediately deportable'.

FBI agents do not enforce the laws making possession of narcotics a crime. (Judging from this memo, they don't even know that 'downers'—barbiturates—are not narcotics.) That's why they had to get the local cops to try. And that's why this memo sounds like a proposal to set Lennon up for a drug bust to prevent him from leading antiwar demonstrations at the Republican convention.

Lennon never was busted on drug charges, and never appeared in any of the Miami news reports. But the FBI was haunted by the fear that he might have secretly demonstrated against the Republican convention. Acting Director L. Patrick Gray was informed in September by the Miami SAC that 'local authorities have furnished no information to indicate the presence of the subject in Miami Beach, Florida, at any time during the summer of 1972'. Nevertheless, just to make sure, the FBI decided to do an extraordinary thing: 'On 8/22/72 and 8/23/72 approximately 1,200 individuals were arrested in Miami Beach by local authorities during protest demonstrations against the Republican National Convention. The records relating to these arrests were photographed by the Miami Office and the film is currently being processed by the FBI Laboratory. When the arrest records become available, they will be reviewed to determine whether subject may have been arrested during the above convention.'

If John Lennon had been arrested for demonstrating against Richard Nixon, it would have been one of the biggest events in the history of counterculture politics. The FBI's belief that Lennon could have demonstrated against Nixon and then been arrested, *without anyone finding out about it*, provides a ludicrous ending to the story. Two months of work by the Miami FBI 'failed to reflect that the subject was one of those arrested'. L. Patrick Gray was informed. On 8 December, 1972, 'in view of subject's inactivity in Revolutionary Activities . . . captioned case is being closed in the NY Division'.

Thus the John Lennon files that have been released make the FBI look more like the Keystone Kops than the Gestapo. But the campaign to 'neutralise' Lennon wasn't a joke; it was a crime. Lennon spoke out against the war at rallies and demonstrations. He associated with leading antiwar activists. But the files contain no evidence that Lennon committed any criminal acts: no bombings, no terrorism, no conspiracies. His activities were precisely the kind protected by the First Amendment. The files show that he was a victim of an Administration obsessed with its 'enemies', and abusing the power of the Presidency in violation of the Constitution. And the two-thirds of Lennon's main FBI file which has been withheld in its entirety is likely to contain evidence of additional dirty tricks and interference with the Lennons' private lives.

Soon after his re-election, Nixon had bigger things to worry about than John Lennon, but the INS kept Lennon in court for three more years. By the mid-1970s, rock politics proved to be more flexible, and more available to work within the system, than Lennon and his friends could have imagined in 1971 and 1972. The 1976 Democratic primary candidates relied on rock concerts for much of their fundraising. Jerry Brown had Linda Ronstadt, Jackson Browne, The Eagles, and Chicago.

Sargent Shriver had Neil Diamond and Tony Orlando. Birch Bayh had Stephen Stills. Hubert Humphrey had James Brown(!). Arlo Guthrie and Harry Chapin sang for Fred Harris. And Jimmy Carter had The Allman Brothers.

By 1980 a new group of rock musicians were playing a new kind of political concert: the *No Nukes* film showed the Madison Square Garden concert starring Bruce Springsteen, Graham Nash, Jackson Browne, Bonnie Raitt, and others. Some of these stars appeared at the peace demonstrations in New York's Central Park and the Rose Bowl in Los Angeles in June 1982, where hundreds of thousands of demonstrators sang John Lennon's 'Imagine'. The recent peace movement concert-rallies have been much tamer than what Lennon and Rubin had in mind in 1972, but they certainly helped to mobilise youthful opposition to the Reagan Administration. Perhaps the parallel between Lennon's activities and those of today's politically active rock stars may help explain the Reagan Administration's action on the Lennon FBI files.

The Reagan Administration's withholding of the Lennon FBI file is part of a larger policy hostile to public access to government information. Under the Carter Administration, documents could be classified 'confidential' and exempted from release under the FOIA only if their disclosure would cause 'identifiable damage to national security'. If this policy was already too vague, the recent Reagan executive order on classification made it worse. Reagan has removed the word 'identifiable' from the definition. Now, an FBI classification officer can withhold documents even if the threat they pose is unidentifiable.

Among the many emotions that were released by rock music in the late 1960s was a feeling for revolution. The experiences of anger and exaltation that rock music provided for countless Americans were not in themselves political experiences. Lennon knew that. He also knew that rock could become a potent political force when it was linked to real political organising, when, for example, it brought young people together to protest the war. In 1971 and 1972 he made a commitment to test this political power. The 26 pounds of files reveal the government's commitment to stop him.

We don't know the full extent of their effort, because so many of the files have been withheld. Was Lennon really a threat to the national security, as the Reagan Administration now claims? Or are Reagan's people trying to conceal the full story of the government's harassment of an antiwar activist? The ACLU of Southern California and I hope to find out: we filed suit in federal court on March 22 [,1983] to win release of the classified pages of John Lennon's FBI file.

PAUL HODSON

John Lennon, Bob Geldof and why pop songs don't change the world

Youth is the future. If we can get inside their minds and tell them to think in favour of non-violence, we'll be satisfied. What's the point of getting fame as a Beatle and not using it? (John Lennon, 1969)[1]

Pop music and politics

Quite a lot of pop music has been political, going against the middle- and working-class grain of traditional boy–girl relationships, the patronage and oppression of people who aren't white, the codes of proper behaviour. Less often, pop has tackled politics itself, trying to change the actions of national and international institutions. When pop musicians play politics they are good at using lyrics and concerts to express their unhappiness with the state of the world, but they do little to change it. When it is the politicians who start the relationship with pop, they use it as an instrument for their politics. There's a gap in the market, between expression and instrumentalism, for an honest pop politics. John Lennon tried to bridge the gap.

The Specials, formed as the British recession reached Coventry in the late 1970s, are a perfect example of a band using pop to express their political ideas. In songs like 'Ghost town' (1981) ('This town/Is coming like a ghost town/All the clubs have been closed down') they describe easily how they feel about where they come from. The glory of their 'Free Nelson Mandela' (1984) has been seized on by young black people striding through South Africa's current collapse. The band itself—black and white musicians—gave the lie to the claims of skinhead racism in Coventry ('Why must the youth fight against itself?'—'Ghost town').

The Specials use pop to tell stories about people, showing accurately how the band feels and showing their like-minded listeners that others feel the same. They do this well. But however clearly expressed, the spread of these feelings among those who have no power does not have any effect on the powerful. 'Free Nelson Mandela' is beautiful, but ''Ere we go, 'Ere we go, 'Ere we go' served the striking miners just as well in 1984–85. If the South African comrades win where the miners lost, it is not the quality of their tunes that will make the difference.

Mainstream politicians, on the other hand, are usually too old and overworked to give a damn for any pop music since 'Peggy Sue' and 'Blue suede shoes'. As Paul Johnson put it in his 1964 attack on Beatlemania (see p. 42), 'The boys and girls who will be the real leaders and creators of society tomorrow never go near a pop concert. They are, to put it simply, too busy. They are educating themselves.'[2] Across the years and the parties, the interest in pop of the 'real leaders and creators of society' has been as a propaganda instrument which they believe can win the hearts and control the heads of the young electorate. Harold Wilson proposed The Beatles for an MBE in 1965 because he thought the band had 'a transforming effect on the minds of youth, mostly for the good. It kept a lot of kids off the street'.[3] Conservative ministers responded to the 1981 riots in English cities by offering black people money for rehearsal studios and recording cooperatives. Neil Kinnock, elected Labour Party leader in 1983, publicised the party's new look by teaming up with an association of artists called Red Wedge, described by Simon Frith and John Street in *Marxism Today* as 'part of an electoral strategy. . . . The use of musicians to give emotional support to politicians'.[4] The Trotskyite Militant Tendency, seeking to keep their grip on the Labour Party's Young Socialist organisation, staged their 1986 Rally at the Albert Hall like a pop concert—dry ice included. The strategy worked, according to an article in the *Militant* newspaper: 'Karen was so determined that she get to this year's rally that she sold her ticket to a UB40 concert. "It's a big sacrifice," says Karen, "but I'm sure it will be well worthwhile just to hear the comrades from South Africa and Derek Hatton." '[5] But as Alex Bennett, a community activist in Militant-dominated Liverpool, put it, 'They went for pop in a big way at the Albert Hall. But it's purely functional. If they can capitalise on a concept they will.'[6]

The problem with The Specials' expressive approach to politics is that it does nothing to change the politicians. The instrumental approach adopted by both Kinnock and the Militant has the same problem. Pop music is about using the body, being active, feeling good. Somewhere between the dance floor and the back rooms of power all this gets lost. Politicians use pop like they use trade unions, kidney machines and patriotism—as another counter in the dull attempt to gain votes and buy off trouble.

Let's take it to the bridge—John Lennon and politics

It's hard, then, to use pop honestly as a force for change. There's a gap between the unheeded accuracy of The Specials and the untouchable efficacy of the Militant. Lennon wanted to bridge this gap, to use pop and his pop star status to change the world.

The political targets Lennon chose were the big ones, the ones that

199

affect the lives of millions—war ('Happy Xmas war is over'), the class system ('Working class hero'), racism and sexism ('Woman is the nigger of the world'). Where his songs proposed solutions these were universal and Utopian ('Imagine', 'Give peace a chance'). His political tactics were centred on people, not organisations. He aimed to find ways to bridge the gap by connecting individuals' behaviour and political change.

The first bridge Lennon found depended on his abiding recognition of the links between personal and political issues. This recognition is the central theme of Jon Wiener's book *Come Together: John Lennon in his time*. Wiener concludes by quoting Lennon's assertion that 'your way of life is a political statement' and adds, 'From "Working class hero" to "Watching the wheels" he struggled to make the personal and the political come together.'[7] Sometimes, for example in 1968 and 1975–80, Lennon focused his political imagination almost entirely on his own mind and the way he lived. But even when that imagination was most outwardly directed, in the early 1970s, he still deployed it through the self-exposure of the *John Lennon/Plastic Ono Band* LP. On this record, just as on 'Revolution' and *Double Fantasy*, he states the political connections he sees in his own life in order to urge political self-examination on others.

The second way Lennon tried to link individuals and politics was by writing songs for the people of 'the movement': 'Newspaper songs, you know, when you write about something instant that's going on right now.'[8] 'Power to the people' and 'Give peace a chance' are newspaper songs: 'That's what my job is, our job is, to write for the people now.'[9]

Did the tactics of self-examination and newspaper songs succeed in building a bridge between the lived experience of the pop generation and the experienced manipulators of political power? Did John Lennon change the world? In 1966 he hoped he could: 'Although the youngsters may be asked to fight I'll stand up there and try to tell them not to.'[10] By 1970, speaking about 'Working class hero', he thought he'd found the way: 'I'm saying it's a revolutionary song, you know, not the song itself, it's a song for the revolution.'[11] Looking back in 1980 he described his and Yoko Ono's role in the peace movement in grand style: 'We felt our duty or our position was—to keep on about peace, until something happened, you know, and it was in the tradition of Gandhi, only with a sense of humour.'[12]

Lennon's political commitment is a catchphrase of the public image of the 1960s. Many commentators have taken his work at face value as proof of the possibility of an honest bridge between pop and politics. Ray Coleman describes Lennon as 'a catalyst and a dream-weaver for a generation's ideals';[13] the peroration of Jon Wiener's assessment of Lennon's political career asserts more moderately that 'politically, he was important because he made himself part of the movements seeking an end to the Vietnam War and freedom and equality for blacks and women. He shared the movements' hopes, arguments, confusions and occasional triumphs. He joined in.'[14] Paul McCartney, according to David Stuart Ryan, 'said after Lennon's death that people would remember that Lennon had helped to speed up American withdrawal from Vietnam and that was how Lennon would like to be remembered—as a peace campaigner.'[15] Ryan himself claims that in 1968 Lennon 'could have turned a youth feeling its power . . . into an army of dedicated revolutionaries'.[16]

Many of Lennon's critics are equally convinced of his political effectiveness. Writing in *The Spectator*, Colin Welch argues that The Beatles (assisted by 'their numberless imitators and heirs'), 'abducted' our children, 'obliterated' their awareness of present reality ('whatever disagreeable facts remain may be sung, wished, loved or dreamed away') and encouraged them to 'render themselves unemployable'. 'How far', he asks, 'are The Beatles' teachings and example responsible for the ruin of their native city?'[17] Lennon, 'the man who "stood for peace"', is also one of the principal villains of Tony Tyler's attack on 'Rock and rollers, wearing their "committed" hat, [who] have dabbled disastrously—and with a self-righteousness absolutely unparalleled in recent annals—in contemporary politics'. The most disastrous piece of dabbling, for Tyler, is Vietnam. 'Far away in Indo-China, what the North Vietnamese army could never have done unaided, the Now Generation of America now did for them. The American government decided . . . that the domestic unrest provoked by the Vietnam war was in the long term a greater threat to national stability than the loss in overseas American prestige.'[18]

Despite the claims of Lennon, his supporters and his critics, he did not 'bridge the gap'. If he had sung only about love and drugs, if he'd left the state of the world alone, political life today would not be perceptibly different. Lennon's political songs were not an instrument for change, just an expression of the need for it. In part this is an assertion about the limited role great women and men play in history. But it is more than that. The main obstacle to pop stars who want to change the world is the fact that powerful political institutions— businesses, parties, governments—have insulated themselves against easy influence from the rest of society. The analysis and strategy needed to blast through this seal, or sneak past it, have eluded pop's political hopefuls.

Tyler is right to say that American withdrawal from Vietnam was hastened by the opinion of the folks back home. The formation of that opinion was a slow and complex process. Tyler, like Paul McCartney, implies that a high proportion of folk reached this opinion because Lennon told them to give peace a chance. There is simply no evidence for this, no evidence for Welch's suggestion that it was The Beatles and not the international economy that did Liverpool down, and no evidence for Ryan's claim that Lennon—or indeed anyone else in Britain or America, in the 1960s or since—had an army of followers awaiting only his word to become 'dedicated revolutionaries'.

Critics and supporters alike use Lennon to personalise and symbolise the political attitudes and impact of the 1960s 'counter-culture'. This is dangerous, short-cut thinking which exaggerates the impact of political pop. To change the world you need to change the institutions that hold power. And to change *them*, even in minor ways, a movement needs an analysis of the current situation; objectives; a strategy for change; knowledge of the movement's own strengths and weaknesses; a mechanism for communication between the movement's leaders and supporters.

Lennon's politics remained expressive, rather than an instrument for change, because he rejected on principle concepts like political analysis, strategy and communication. He made this clear when interviewed by Andy Peebles in 1980.

> It got down to all we were saying was, Give peace a chance. Not 'we have any formula' or 'communism or socialism will answer it' or 'any "-ism" could answer it'. We didn't have a format or a . . . we couldn't give you a plan . . . but just consider the idea of . . . not having this war, just consider it. So that's what we, in a nutshell, were saying.[19]

Lennon's public analysis of the political situation was vague. It was constrained by a tendency to think either in universals ('woman', 'the people', 'the world', 'the establishment') or in individual terms ('You better change your mind instead'). These terms provide a weak foundation for political action when compared with the vocabulary of class or of institutions. Lennon's stated objectives were predominantly Utopian, untranslated into attainable goals; his strategic thinking blew about in the wind, as suggested by the fact that on one version of 'Revolution' he substituted 'don't you know that you can count me in' for 'count me out'. Given his claim that 'your way of life is a political statement', he showed surprisingly little concern about the weakness of his own position—as Tyler points out, the 'Imagine' promotional film showed that 'those who urged the no-possession option upon their admirers and followers were themselves visibly richer than Croesus'.[20] Lennon's privileged isolation, the scale of the political targets he chose and the size of the movements he joined combined to make any communication with members of the counter-culture strictly one-way—and that mainly in the one-dimensional form of pop lyrics.

These handicaps to Lennon's search for political impact reproduce the weaknesses of the counter-culture itself. As Robert Hewison argues in *Too Much*,

> The ideological divisions within the counter-culture were too great for it ever to have constituted a real threat. The values of 'peace and love' could not sit easily with the earnest endeavour of the political radicals. . . . The more hedonistic elements of the counter-culture were incapable of the discipline necessary to achieve revolution.[21]

The glamour of populism

John Lennon's political songs express his views clearly. Many contemporaries shared these views. But despite Lennon's reputation as 'a catalyst for a generation's ideals', there is no evidence that his songs caused any political change. Lennon's political analysis was vague, his strategy was nothing more than to 'keep on about peace until something happened', and the culture with which he aligned himself was itself equipped more for expressive witness to evil than effective action for good.

In the 1980s, pop's quest for a bridge between expression and instrumentalism has a new symbol—Bob Geldof, who set pop stars to fighting African famine with a number one single (by Band Aid, 1984), two enormous concerts (Live Aid, London and Philadelphia, 1985) and an international fun run (Sport Aid, 1986). Geldof, who was lead singer with The Boomtown Rats, played organiser rather than musician to this movement. Unlike Lennon, he saw that he must borrow some of the bureaucrats' tactics—and he turned himself into an international politician too.

The claims made for the political impact of the Band Aid movement extravagantly echo those made for Lennon.

> By its very existence, let alone its triumphant success, Live Aid gashed a great gaping hole in the contemporary Conservative portrait of the modern malaise (David Edgar, *Marxism Today*).[22]

> Its greatest success has been to change the national and, to a rather lesser extent, the international political agenda. . . . It placed new and quite dramatic pressure on the government to take the aid question seriously and to act (Stuart Hall and Martin Jacques, *Marxism Today*).[23]

Many commentators concentrate on the movement's tactics, exulting in the fact that it provided the bridge the latest pop generation needed to exploit its political potential:

Sport Aid, with its royal patronage and its celebrity trappings, may be a long way removed from the radicalism of Sixties counter-culture, but its version of a different way of getting things done is still recognisably an 'alternative' one . . . capable of mobilising what is now a growing spectrum of opinion that finds no expression in conventional party politics (Michael Poole, *The Listener*).[24]

In pop history, 1985 will always go down as the year when pop's protagonists became fed up with merely urging others ever onwards and actually got on with doing something themselves (Fred Dellar, *New Musical Express*).[25]

Geldof and Band Aid avoided many of the weaknesses of Lennon's political stance. They had two clear objectives: to raise money to feed starving people, and to raise public awareness to put pressure on governments. There was a clear strategy of avoiding party politics, involving the apathetic and seeking broad alliances to reach these objectives. There was analysis and exploitation of the strengths of the movement's pop roots: as Hall and Jacques point out, Geldof's 'rock credentials *were* his political credentials, a guarantee to the fans that . . . they were unlikely to hear a replay of the old-style lyrics of the professional politicians'.[26] And Geldof knew the limits of what he could achieve:

There's no doubt we stopped thousands of people dying, but there's also no doubt it was a drop in the ocean. The famine will come again, because the political and the environmental conditions don't change. . . . The most important thing we did was to raise the issue.[27]

In other words, it's back to the crowded ghetto of traditional instrumental politics. But there are signs of greater sophistication in that camp too, at least in the Labour Party. The party magazine *New Socialist* was relaunched in May 1986 in a style to make sense to young people, with fashionable *Face* journalist Robert Elms attacking 'the appalling elitism of puritans who despise popular culture' and asserting that 'style and the left were once synonymous, a style that came from the root of our radicalism. We were the right stuff because we had the hearts and voices of a people, we had the glamour of populism.'[28] A month later in *New Socialist*'s competitor *Marxism Today*, Simon Frith and John Street thoughtfully contrasted the ambiguous position of the Red Wedge popsters, 'constrained around the electoral needs of the (Labour) party', with an alternative pioneered by the Labour-controlled Greater London Council: financial support for 'the concept of "cultural industries", the political realisation that the arts aren't just a matter of moral uplift or community identity but involve job opportunities, a chance for people to have material control of their culture'.[29]

Pop's political objectives, Lennon-vague or Geldof-defined, have almost always been 'progressive' or 'libertarian', concerned with equality, democracy and the need to align means and ends. Pop musicians have tried both to express their ideas and to change the world. The weakness that has stopped them achieving the second aim has been flawed communication. Stars with large followings have sought political influence in a most undemocratic way. Instead of finding ways to talk about ideas and tactics with their supporters, their stance has been 'take my word for it'. Worse, this word has been communicated by means—lyrics and concerts—which are incapable of carrying the sophisticated analysis world-changing needs. Frith and Street quote Julie Burchill—'There's no safer way to castrate a political view than to express it to a throbbing backbeat'—and a *Smash Hits* interview with someone leaving a Red Wedge concert: 'We didn't come here for the politics. They passed us by. I mean, I don't like things like racialism, but the only thing it really changed my mind about was The Smiths. I didn't used to think much of them.'[30]

If pop politics *is* to change the world, it needs to stop messing with the national and international elites of pop stars and politicians, and to concentrate—like the GLC—on small local initiatives where musicians and their ideas can rub up against the people they aim to liberate. Feminists have learnt this. Pop must too.

> Anger and struggle against oppression and subordination are necessary, but not adequate alone, for we must develop resources to bring the new social order into being, not merely resist the old. This must involve not only the slogans of rebellion but more profoundly . . . a lived cultural transformation (Sheila Rowbotham, *Granta*).[31]

Notes

1. Ray Coleman, *John Lennon* (London, 1984) p. 318

2. Paul Johnson, 'The menace of Beatlism', *New Statesman* (28 February 1964) p. 327. Reprinted in this collection

3. Quoted, Coleman *op. cit.* p. 246

4. Simon Frith & John Street, 'Party music', *Marxism Today* (June 1986)

5. 'Why I'm coming to the rally', *Militant* (14 November 1986)

6. Alex Bennett in conversation with the author (December 1986)

7.   Jon Wiener, *Come Together: John Lennon in his time* (London, 1985) p. 306

8.   *The Lennon Tapes:* John Lennon and Yoko Ono in conversation with Andy Peebles, 6 December 1980 (London, 1981) p. 42

9.   Jann Wenner, ed., *Lennon Remembers—The Rolling Stone Interviews* (New York, 1970) p. 110

10.   Coleman *op. cit.* p. 255

11.   Wenner *op. cit.* p. 110

12.   Peebles *op. cit.* p. 46

13.   Coleman *op. cit.* p. xi

14.   Wiener *op. cit.* p. 306

15.   David Stuart Ryan, *John Lennon's Secret* (London, 1982) p. 245

16.   *ibid.* p. 156

17.   Colin Welch, 'Beatlemania', *Spectator* (17 December 1983) p. 32

18.   Tony Tyler, *I Hate Rock 'n' Roll: An Illustrated Diatribe* (London, 1984) pp. 49, 125

19.   Peebles *op. cit.* p. 22

20.   Tyler *op. cit.* p. 117

21.   Robert Hewison, *Too Much—Art and Society in the Sixties* (London, 1986) pp. 167–8

22.   David Edgar, 'Why Aid came Live', *Marxism Today* (September 1985) p. 26

23.   Stuart Hall & Martin Jacques, 'People Aid—a new politics sweeps the land', *Marxism Today* (July 1986)

24.   Michael Poole, 'Beating Time—Riot 'n' Race 'n' Rock 'n' Roll' (book review) *The Listener* (5 June 1986)

25.   Fred Dellar, 'Review of 1985', *New Musical Express* (21–28 December 1985)

26.   Hall & Jacques *op. cit.*

27.   John Mortimer, interview with Bob Geldof, *Spectator* (8 November 1986)

28.   Robert Elms, 'Ditching the Drabbies—a style for socialism', *New Socialist* (May 1986) pp. 12–14

29.   Frith & Street *op. cit.*

30.   *ibid.*

31.   Sheila Rowbotham, 'Lance', *Granta* 9 (Cambridge, 1983) p. 167

John Lennon, Hamburg 1960 (*courtesy Astrid Kirchherr/Redferns*)

John Lennon (right) with George Harrison (left) and Stuart Sutcliffe in a Hamburg fairground in 1960 *(courtesy Astrid Kirchherr/Redferns)*

John Lennon during the shooting of *How I Won the War* (1967) *(courtesy National Film Archive/Richard Lester)*

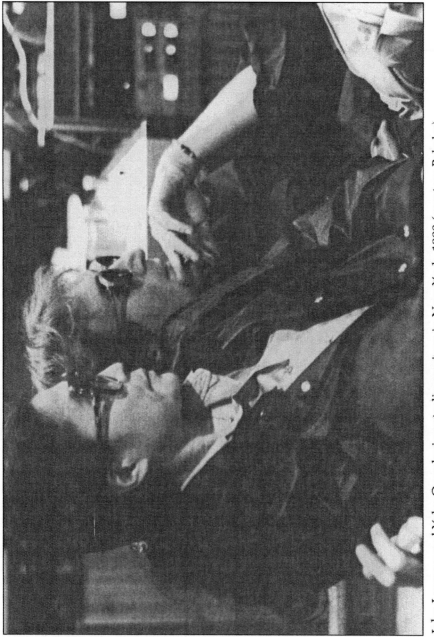

John Lennon and Yoko Ono during studio sessions in New York, 1980 *(courtesy Polydor)*

SEVEN

Tomorrow Never Knows

BEN GERSON

Together again: Walls and Bridges

Rolling Stone, 21 November 1974

Walls and Bridges shows John Lennon to be as mercurial as ever. I anticipated an unbearable suffering occasioned by the collapse of one of this century's most public love affairs—after all, Yoko Ono was presented as the membrane between agony and peace for Lennon, between illusion and reality. Yet the relative clear-headedness of this album suggests that she may have been only the most recent in a series of causes from which Lennon is extricating himself with customary agility. He seemed more pugnacious, more doctrinaire, more vulnerable when Yoko was supposedly supplying him with bliss than he is today.

For the first time since the formation of The Beatles, Lennon is on his own and, remarkably, he seems to find that tolerable, though half the numbers on *Walls and Bridges* record his pangs of loss. 'Going down on love' is characterised by a confusion of emotions, honestly rendered, rather than Lennon's notoriously wide oscillations between paranoid megalomania and Edenic composure. A mixture of penitence, anger, perseverance, feelings of justice, feelings of injustice, the song discards the programmatic righteousness of earlier Lennon efforts—to its own musical detriment.

'What you got', part Sly, part Isley Brothers, harnesses Lennon's rambunctious sense of rhythm to soul phrases chosen for their relevance to him and Yoko. Here, pure physical exertion is intended as an outlet. Nonetheless, on this cut and others, Jim Keltner's drums lack the requisite punch.

The dreary 'Bless you' attempts an accommodation, but mainly succeeds in oozing false humility. In imagery reminiscent of 'Julia', Lennon betrays his continued possessiveness. His advice to Yoko's current lover, that he be 'warm and kind hearted' but that he should remember that his and Yoko's love is undying, strikes me as intentionally emasculating. The purported magnanimity of the Reverend Fred Ghurkin (the self-mocking pseudonym John assigns himself in the credits) is the obverse of wounded male vanity. Only 'Scared' throbs with the primal fear and sense of confinement of his earlier solo LPs.

'Whatever gets you thru the night' is really side one's gateway to the palmier regions of side two. John is so happy to have won the right to blind pleasure that the misery which is the pretext almost gets forgotten. It's the ice cream that follows a tonsillectomy. Elton John's vocal harmony and keyboards are very assertive but Bobby Keys's off-key blowing weakens Elton's efforts.

The first two songs on side two, '# 9 dream' and 'Surprise surprise (Sweet bird of paradox)' prove that Lennon is resilient and can still love. They make his claims of suffering in some sense pro forma, and they make *Walls and Bridges* diverse and spirited. Untouched by the recriminations and breast beating of side one, these songs display the musical as well as lyrical evidence of John's new lease on life. Whereas the soft edges to Lennon's band elsewhere rob his music of its necessary incisiveness, on '# 9 dream' they contribute to a perfect meringue of sound. 'Surprise surprise', whose pungent harmonies and fade-out recall 'Drive my car', pulses with equally strong vital signs.

Superficially, the viciousness of 'Steel and glass' contradicts these high spirits. With a melody, arrangement and psychological motive virtually identical to the earlier 'How do you sleep?' it falls into what could be called John's sacrificial mode. I find it boring and needless, but its unalloyed hatred is peculiarly compatible with the optimism of the previous two selections. At least the sides are clearly drawn.

On the cover of the lyric sheet Lennon is wearing a big smile. Adorning the inside of the sheet are various drawings he made at age 11. The back cover has a genealogy of the name Lennon—the first time he has acknowledged his patrimony. The closing song on *Walls and Bridges* is Lee Dorsey's 'Ya ya', 'starring Julian Lennon on drums and Dad on piano and vocals', Julian being the son who remained in England while the Lennons crisscrossed this country in search of Yoko's daughter Kyoko. By slowing it down and overenunciating, Lennon makes 'Ya ya' into a children's song. Coming at the end of the record it seems a companion piece to the infantile, macabre 'My mummy's dead' on *Plastic Ono Band*.

On 'Scared' John asserts that love and peace were only an ill-fitting mask for his old stand-bys, hatred and jealousy. On 'Nobody loves you (when you're down and out)' he sings with a typically Lennonesque compression of language (a highlight of the album) and his voice is superbly malleable and ferocious. He comments on the necrophilia of hero worship, the dilemma of the ageing rock star and the bankruptcy of rock mythology: 'All I can tell you is it's all showbiz.' Even love can be a symptom of narcissim, a media creation which its 'possessor' can feel only when it's made public.

The insights are reformulations of the lessons of *Plastic Ono Band*, with this difference: on *POB* the tearing away of veils only revealed another face to Lennon's Utopianism. Then (keeping in mind his crucial inconsistency in idealising his relationship with Yoko) illusionlessness seemed the ultimate liberation. Today Lennon knows that neither dreams nor their puncturing is the answer. There is no neat answer. When one accepts one's childhood, one's parenthood and the impermanence of what lies between, one can begin to slog along. When John slogs, he makes progress.

ERIC TAMM

Beyond Strawberry Fields: Lennon's later style

Melody, harmony, rhythm and form—in these aspects of his musical craft, John Lennon underwent no major developmental changes from the period of 'Strawberry Fields forever' to the end of his recorded output. But making rock records involves a good deal more than writing songs. Unlike composition in the Western art music tradition, where the written score represents the ideal version of the piece, rock songs are fixed in vinyl, and thus one specific performance or realisation becomes the 'ideal'. In rock, it is often the sheer *sound* that grabs the listener and makes the decisive musical statement: many a mediocre song has been redeemed through a compelling, original arrangement; conversely, it takes a very fine song indeed to defeat the effects of a dull, lifeless, unimaginative production. After the release of *Plastic Ono Band* in 1970, Lennon's concern with arrangement and production values declined, often with disastrous effects. With *Walls and Bridges* (1974) and, especially, *Double Fantasy* (1980), he once again seemed to devote attention to the sound as well as the spirit of the music. ·

Melody, harmony, rhythm and form

John Lennon knew how to write a rock melody. Rock tunes tend not to share the classical qualities of 'melody' so often extolled in music text books—lyricism, seamless continuity, floating grace, a sense of ongoing development to a point of climax and a return to rest. Since songwriters such as Chuck Berry penned songs like 'Sweet little sixteen' and 'Roll over Beethoven', the classic rock melody has consisted of short phrases intimately mated to the rhythms and accents of speech, often revolving closely round a very few notes (frequently drawn from a pentatonic scale), with a good deal of repetition built into the structure. This structure may feature its own form of the tension–release principle, frequently derived from the dominant–tonic relationship inherent in the standard blues chord progressions (*qv* Chuck Berry). Yet a certain static quality prevails in the archetypal rock melody, based on playful motivic arabesques that do not 'go' anywhere.

Many of Lennon's post-'Strawberry Fields' melodies have this static, reiterative, ritualistic quality. Each phrase of 'Lucy in the sky with diamonds', for instance, employs a three-note melodic cell just ripe for Retian analysis.[1] The main melody of 'I am the walrus' is virtually a chant on two notes, with short phrase-endings that function like the endings of medieval Psalm Tones, rounding off the musical thought in a formulaic manner. Other Lennon tunes that are little more than embellishments of one or two notes appear in 'Dear Prudence', 'Julia', 'Across the universe', 'Dig it', 'Come together', 'New York City', and 'Give me some truth'. Only slightly more complex are the melodies of 'Polythene Pam', 'Remember', 'Attica State', 'Sunday Bloody Sunday', and 'Going down on love'. All such songs take on something of the character of poetry recited or chanted to simple, effective formulas.

After he left The Beatles, Lennon relied increasingly on characteristic vocal melismas to embellish his melodic skeletons: in 'Mother', 'God', 'How do you sleep?', 'Oh Yoko!', 'Mind games', 'I know (I know)', 'Bless you', and 'Watching the wheels', the melodic flourishes at phrase-ends proliferate to the point of mannerism. Another Lennon technique is the prolongation or repetition of a syllable or word for purposes of emphasis: 'isolation' in the song of the same title; 'gotta' in 'John Sinclair'; 'ever' in 'Dear Yoko'; 'do it' in 'Bring on the Lucie (Freda Peeple)'; and the huge melismatic prolongations of phrase ends in 'Steel and glass' ('and your New York *talk* . . .').

Lennon had a pronounced gift for writing hooks—perfect combinations of verbal and musical phrases, often with in-built repetition and often serving as a song's refrain. Almost all his songs—even the bad ones—have one, and among the more memorable are those found in 'Lucy in the sky with diamonds', 'Baby you're a rich man', 'Bungalow Bill', 'New York City', 'Whatever gets you through the night', and '(Just like) Starting over'. That Lennon speciality, the rock anthem—songs with solemn, uplifting, political or philosophical overtones—employ specially powerful hooks: 'All you need is love', 'Across the universe', 'Give peace a chance', 'Instant karma', 'Imagine' and 'Grow old with me', among others.

By the time he wrote 'I am the walrus', Lennon had reached a plateau of harmonic understanding which was not to evolve significantly in his remaining works. It did not have to. He had an intuitive grasp of the way chords—primarily triads and seventh chords—work together, the way they colour a melody and contribute to musical tension–release effects. Indeed, given the static quality of many of his melodies, it's left to the harmony and rhythm to provide the sense of motion or forward thrust. In 'I am the walrus', for instance, the reiterative melody is propelled by its jumpy rhythm and by the ominous, unusual chord root movements—a cork bobbing on powerful ocean swells.

Lennon's systematic exploration of remote modulations and higher discords such as ninths and elevenths has had few parallels in the rock idiom—such harmonic complexities don't mesh well with the spirit of rock. What Lennon did intuitively was to stake out certain harmonic realms to which he returned repeatedly. Some of his songs are based on pure or only slightly elaborated blues progressions ('Yer blues', 'Beef jerky'). Many more are based on the full gamut of primary and secondary major and minor triads in a given major or minor key, enhanced by frequent borrowings from related keys. A handful draw on the characteristic mellow sound of the major chord with added sixth, a favoured cadential tonic chord in the early Beatles' style ('Sun king', 'Hold on John', 'You are here', and 'Beautiful boy'). The distinctive, pointed sound of the augmented triad, not much used in rock as a whole though found frequently enough in The Beatles' early work, retains its place in Lennon's harmonic vocabulary in songs like 'Isolation', 'Nobody loves you (when you're down and out)' and 'I'm losing you'. In a number of songs, 'strange' harmonic progressions and modulations are derived empirically. Sometimes they work ('I am the walrus', 'Julia', 'Remember', '#9 dream'); sometimes they don't ('Out the blue', 'Bless you').

Among Lennon's most successful post-'Strawberry Fields'

compositions are those in which he employs an ostinato as a kind of harmonic underpinning. Familiar from Beatles' technique in such songs as 'Day tripper' and 'Lady Madonna', ostinatos unify a piece and provide a counterpoint against the vocal line. The Baroque, *style brisé* [literally 'broken', arpeggiated] electronic instrumental line in 'Lucy in the sky with diamonds' sets off the revolving-door melody perfectly; with its chromatic descent, the guitar's repeated accompanimental pattern in 'Dear Prudence' creates a mesmeric harmonic framework; the inexorable guitar ostinatos in 'Give me some truth' and 'Mind games' have unifying functions, even as they clash magnificently with the harmonic changes beneath. Lennon could also use a simple piano motive to give character to a whole track—for instance the throbbing pedal note in 'Remember', or the little roulade in 'Watching the wheels'.

In the realms of rhythm and form, Lennon felt even less need to depart from rock norms. His rhythmic genius lay not in innovation but in matching the inflections and accents of speech with the contours of his melodies. Practically every Lennon song displays this quality. Very occasionally, he uses an unusual metre for a bar or two (5/4 in 'Good morning' and 'Across the universe', 7/4 in 'All you need is love'), but the result is completely unforced, flowing out of natural speech rhythms. Formally, standard patterns of verse, refrain, and bridge are the rule. Exceptions are found in 'Happiness is a warm gun' (whose multi-sectional, multi-metric structure is simply the result of several different elements being thrown into the creative mix), 'Mother' (which lacks a bridge section but is articulated formally through the lyrics, with verses beginning 'Mother', 'Father', and 'Children'), and '#9 dream' (which consists of two long, multi-sectional verses, each with refrain).

Production and arrangements

The music of The Beatles was outstanding because they consistently achieved a rare balance between art and artifice, content and form, song and arrangement. With The Beatles, John Lennon had the privilege of working with a highly gifted songwriter, arranger and bassist in Paul McCartney, a brilliantly imaginative and resourceful producer in George Martin, and two creative and often underrated instrumentalists in George Harrison and Ringo Starr. As Lennon's personal development led him to relax his team commitment, he was increasingly thrown back on his own resources. It turned out that he was less concerned with making great rock records than with making brutally direct and honest personal statements through his lyrics. Music, he seemed to feel, had to be more than a seductively beautiful or intellectually stimulating sound: it had to *say* something as well.

Lennon's mistrust of music's ability to speak for itself cost him: however successful his drive toward creative and personal freedom, the recorded versions of many of his 1970s songs do not approach those of the 1960s in impact and quality. John Lennon's own musical personality emerged during and after the breakup of The Beatles, and he stood before the public, as he had intended, naked.

By mid-1967, the time of *Sgt Pepper's Lonely Hearts Club Band*, The Beatles were pooling their creative ideas in the studio with George Martin, but Lennon and McCartney had been writing more or less independently for some time. Only four songs on that album can be firmly attributed to Lennon: 'Lucy in the sky with diamonds', 'Being for the benefit of Mr Kite', 'Good morning', and the outer sections of 'A day in the life'. These are great pieces, but owe much of their greatness to the sparkling purposefulness and cleanliness of their arrangements—the electronic keyboard, intelligently active bass lines and timbral contrasts of 'Lucy'; the special effects of 'Mr Kite'; the exhilarating horns, electric guitars and massed voices of 'Good morning'; and the spare, moody textures of Lennon's portions of 'A day in the life'.

Lennon's single sides just before and after *Sgt Pepper* were similarly unique soundscapes: 'Baby you're a rich man' was an experiment in varieties of percussive treatment, echoed piano chords and the ubiquitous careenings of a screeching double-reed instrument, while the chugging, churning string-section sound of 'I am the walrus' was so powerfully evocative that it ultimately inspired the formation of a band, The Electric Light Orchestra, built entirely around that particular sonority.

As soon as these epochal experiments were completed, however, Lennon began to have doubts about so-called 'art rock', and his next group of songs abandoned all electronic/symphonic trappings in favour of a back-to-rock-basics approach. That approach is evident in the double album *The Beatles*, the Lennon-composed singles surrounding it ('Revolution', 'Don't let me down', and 'The ballad of John and Yoko') and in the tracks that would be released only in 1970 as *Let It Be*. In all these works, special effects are minimised and The Beatles are heard playing their own music with very few overdubs. There are few frills—just well-rehearsed songs, well-realised arrangements, and characteristic gestures and riffs defining the shape of each piece. 'Dig a pony' is a good example of this approach: it has a simple yet powerfully surging triadic/pentatonic instrumental introduction that later serves as a break, and a carefully controlled flux of dynamic levels; it achieves its spacious, hyper-pop effects by taking best advantage of the talents of a creatively integrated four-member rock ensemble.

On Side One of The Beatles' last studio album, *Abbey Road*, Lennon's contributions—'Come together' and 'I want you (She's so heavy)'—have stood up very well over the years. While it is mind-boggling today to reflect on a record that contains 'I want you' side by side with 'Maxwell's silver hammer' and 'Octopus's garden', it is to The Beatles' credit that their creative collective could produce music of such elegant form yet minimalistic power as 'I want you' with Lennon in charge.

Lennon finally broke out of The Beatles production and music-making team and made *Plastic Ono Band* in 1970, an album produced by 'John and Yoko and Phil Spector', and featuring only three primary instrumentalists: Lennon himself on guitar and piano, Ringo Starr on drums, and Klaus Voorman on bass. He said that The Beatles had 'died as musicians' when Epstein put them in suits and sent them on tours playing the same 20-minute set every night; he criticised 'that sort of dead Beatles sound, or dead recording sound' that he thought characterised the group's albums. *Plastic Ono Band* went at least one or two steps beyond *The Beatles* and 'I want you' in the direction of rock minimalism, and some of the final cuts were recorded in as little as two takes. It is an elemental, confessional musical statement; it works because of its spontaneity, yet also because almost every note and gesture is necessary, vital and musically significant. In 'Mother', the melody unfolds over a drum, piano, and bass accompaniment so spare that, as in the music of Webern or Cage, the silences between beats seem charged with electricity. On 'I found out' and 'Well well well', the trio lays down a groove of unembellished simplicity, drive, and commitment, powered by Lennon's dirty, distorted, yet finely controlled electric guitar—a sound anticipating punk by half a decade. The soft ballads—'Love', 'Hold on John', 'Look at me'—are as musically convincing as the brutal rock numbers not just because they are good songs, but because the instrumentation is uncluttered, unpretentious, and purposeful (though there are moments of sloppiness in the guitar playing on 'Look at me' that would not have been allowed on a Beatles record). Spector's role in the album's production is unobtrusive, with a nice touch here and there, such as the return of the piano at the end of 'Love'.

The story is very different on *Imagine*, Lennon's next album. The Spector strings are evident yet innocuous enough in the title track; the arrangement of this grand, yet understated, rock hymn has a classical purity and simplicity, even if it is a bit on the dull side. In 'I don't want to be a soldier', Spector's so-called Wall of Sound rears its head, with echoed drums and a cavernous quality given to the whole ensemble; the ritualistic intonations of the vocal line are drowned in the sonic soup. The high point on the album is 'Give me some truth', where every instrumentalist makes a distinct and important contribution to the sound.

The studio-recorded half of *Some Time in New York City*, the final Lennon–Spector co-production (aside from part of the oldies collection *Rock 'n' Roll*), succeeds in so far as Spector does not swamp the straightforward, well-rehearsed rock of the Plastic Ono Elephants Memory Band.

Lennon produced and arranged his next album, *Mind Games*, by himself. By and large, it is an engineering and mixing failure: the mixes are marred by a lack of spaciousness and acoustic presence, sounding dry, woody, and unprofessional; the instrumental sounds bleed together; there is far too much inessential musical information, indicating Lennon's inability or unwillingness at this point to undertake creative, constructive arranging and editing. Songs like 'Aisumasen', 'Bring on the Lucie (Freda Peeple)', and 'Meat city' succeed only because they are fine songs; for the rest, botched production makes it very difficult to tell how good they really are.

By the time he produced *Walls and Bridges*, Lennon had learned, or re-learned, how to exert control over the mix, and the result was such outstanding and sophisticated production jobs as '#9 dream' and 'Nobody loves you (when you're down and out)'. Similar care was taken six years later in the making of *Double Fantasy* (co-produced with Ono and Jack Douglas)—state-of-the-art as far as production was concerned. '(Just like) Starting over' is a model of musical clarity, with its immaculate mix, simple yet considered arrangement, and transparent rhythmic counterpoint. In 'I'm losing you', as in most of the songs on *Double Fantasy*, a few repeated riffs give character and organisation to the backing tracks with enough acoustic space around each instrument to allow the individual parts of the interacting whole to be heard.

In 'God', on *Plastic Ono Band*, Lennon renounced the role of the 'dream-weaver'. Part of his commitment to being just 'John' involved approaching music with fewer self-conscious attempts at the kind of dazzling artifice so evident in Beatles tapestries like *Sgt Pepper*: artifice creates an illusory world, and the reborn John wanted only truth. But in the end, Lennon seemed to accept the inherently 'artificial' nature of music, and to accept his role as a craftsman capable of making artifacts that were simultaneously admirable in form and honest in content.

217

A. LOPUKHIN and V. PAKHOMOV

Five shots end the life of the famous singer and composer

Komsomolskaya pravda, 12 December 1980

John Lennon, singer, composer and poet, has died at a murderer's hands. His name is linked with The Beatles quartet, which he founded, a group that was the public's idol in the 1960s. Radio and television stations [in Britain] immediately interrupted their broadcasts to announce John Lennon's tragic death. The songs and music of The Beatles—four simple lads from Liverpool—are being heard once again in Britain. . . .

Senseless murders are becoming more and more common in New York and throughout the United States. Murdering famous people has become the fashion. The motives for the crime are usually primitive and inhuman: to become famous, if only for a day, and see one's name in screaming newspaper headlines, in order to escape the emptiness and hopelessness of one's life. The reason that impelled 25-year-old Mark Chapman, who is unemployed, to take up a pistol is not yet known. . . . Right now, the murderer is in New York's Bellevue Hospital, where he is undergoing a forensic psychiatric examination.

The bitter irony of this tragedy is that a person who devoted his songs and music to the struggle against violence has himself become its victim. . . .

John Lennon was the most exploratory and inventive member of the [Beatles] group. Many of his best songs are deeply lyrical. John Lennon's art had flights of inspiration, it had periods of stagnation, it had mistakes; however, he remained a person of integrity who did not compromise. He did not want to become a slave to public success, and in the late 1960s he rejected much of what he had previously advocated in his art.

Lennon's song 'Give peace a chance' became the anthem of the young people's antiwar movement in the West. It was sung by participants in mass demonstrations against the US war in Vietnam. In 1969, as a sign of protest against the British government's support for the American aggression in Vietnam, John Lennon returned to Buckingham Palace the Order [*sic*] of the British Empire that had been awarded to him. His biting and witty statements often confounded journalists and were not always liked by members of the ruling classes. Lennon's songs are still banned in the Republic of South Africa, a country whose racist regime he passionately spoke out against.

The fatal shots struck John down at the moment of his return to creative life. After a five-year silence, he had put out an interesting album, *Double Fantasy*, which won immediate popularity. Friends who saw him on the eve of his death say that Lennon was full of creative plans and had never looked on life so optimistically.

Crushed by what had happened, Paul McCartney had difficulty finding words: 'He will be remembered for his unique contribution to music, art and the cause of peace throughout the world.'

M. BEGLOV

On John Lennon's death

Sotsialisticheskaya industria, 12 December 1980

Blowing up this tragic event to the proportions of a supersensation, American newspapers, including the most 'respectable' ones, have been devoting whole pages to articles about the life of this famous singer, poet and composer. Radio stations and television networks have been zealously recounting the particulars of the murder, dwelling on pages from Lennon's biography and going to great lengths in a search for details about his killer. J. Lennon, to whom America had paid almost no attention in recent years, is now being elevated virtually to the rank of a spiritual leader of several generations of Western youth.

However, what lies behind the furore that the American press has whipped up over Lennon's murder is clearly nothing but an elementary desire to profit from his death. Interest in the records made by Lennon and other members of the long-disbanded Beatles, records for which there had been little demand in the US in recent years, has been artificially inflated to incredible proportions. Lines form at music stores early in the morning. Lennon's latest album, *Double Fantasy*, which American critics have unanimously called the most unsuccessful of his works, is selling like hot cakes.

During the 1960s, American show business squeezed everything it could out of the rapid rise of John Lennon and his comrades. John Lennon's life is a typical example of the cruel exploitation of talented Western musicians who rise to the apex of success. First come frenzied popularity, kindled by noisy advertising, contracts for many millions of dollars, and exhausting concerts. Then come narcotics, disillusionment with life, and feverish attempts to stay atop the wave of popularity.

Lennon experienced all of this. He died a multimillionaire. According to some reports, his wealth is estimated at $150 million to $250 million. However, people here prefer not to mention how many millions of dollars, pounds sterling and marks are lying in the safes of record companies, his advertising agents and other wheeler-dealers in the music field in various countries, just as people are keeping quiet about how much American show business hopes to make from the musician's death.

By the way—and some American publications have been compelled to admit this—for the US, the fact of Lennon's murder, in and of itself, is not at all remarkable but commonplace. He is merely the 701st victim of an armed assault in New York this year. In the US as a whole, 10,700 people died from gunshot wounds last year. They were all victims of the cult of violence that is flourishing in the US, and of the unrestricted sale of firearms.

The current furore in the US is very much reminiscent of events that occurred here a few years ago when another of America's musical idols, Elvis Presley, died from narcotics abuse. Like Lennon today, he was then a candidate for 'sainthood', but it wasn't three years before the name of E. Presley had been consigned to oblivion. After making millions of dollars on his death, the bosses of American show business relegated him to the archives.

MARTIN AMIS

Lennon—from Beatle to househusband

The Observer, 14 December 1980

In my teens I had a friend called Barry who resembled John Lennon to a disconcerting degree: the fluted nose, the beaked mouth, the eyelids thin and insolent.

Barry's method of accumulating girlfriends was laborious but original. All day he studied the 'Pen Pals' section of *Beatles Monthly*. He selected the girls who lived preferably no more than a few hundred yards from his parents' flat, and wrote to them enclosing a photograph of himself (complete with peaked Lennon cap; later with rimless spectacles) and the signature 'Barry Lennon'—or 'Buddy Lennon', depending on his mood.

In crew-necked Beatles jacket and Chelsea boots with Cuban heels, I often made up the foursomes that Barry would subsequently arrange. He would present himself now as Lennon's kid brother, now as his cousin, now as some more exotic relation (co-foundling, for instance)—sometimes, I think, as Lennon himself. Now the charade has sinister overtones; but it seemed innocent then.

Barry was well up on Beatle lore. He knew that John was 5 feet 11 inches (as were Paul and George: mascot Ringo, of course, was 5 feet 8 inches), that his taste in clothes encompassed 'anything casual', the sort of jellybabies he liked, the characteristics of his wife and his child—who was Barry's little nephew, after all. Considering his other plentiful demerits, Barry's success with his pen pals was very consistent. As I went along with it all, as Barry Lennon's sidekick and gofer, I sensed that the girls—though unquenchably gullible—really saw through Barry's imposture. But they didn't want to break the illusion of proximity, and neither did I.

John Lennon was born in 1940. Barry and I were born in 1949, and so were well placed to have our teenage years utterly dominated by The Beatles and their music. As a 13-year-old, I witnessed their first ever TV appearance—on some innocuous news and views show that I usually watched on my return from school. They sang 'Love me do'. I knew at once that they would become a part of my life. Shortly afterwards I made a five-shilling bet with my father, who claimed that The Beatles would be more or less forgotten within a year. When the time came for him to pay up, he confessed to a liking for one or two of their songs. By then my mother was a devoted fan. Everyone was.

Initially regarded as wanton and subversive figures—after all, they reinvented long hair—The Beatles quickly established their family appeal, an appeal nurtured by their manager Brian Epstein. The lovable moptops, the Fab Four, turned out to be nice lads really—to nationwide sighs of parental relief. . . . But John Lennon remained a wayward and unpredictable element, thwarting the homogenisation that Epstein clearly had in mind. Musically and personally, Lennon gave The Beatles their edge.

He mugged to camera and taunted compères. He coined, or at any rate popularised, the phrase 'Little girls should be obscene and not heard.' In interviews he could be very funny or, alternatively, very unfunny. He published two books of prattling word-play, *In His Own*

Write and *A Spaniard in the Works*. He got drunk and caused scuffles in restaurants and clubs.

As songwriters and lead singers, Lennon and McCartney captured and divided the fans, while George and Ringo were merely innocent by-standers. There was something over-cute and chirpy about Paul: he wanted to be loved not only by your mother, but by your grandmother too. Preferring Paul to John was like preferring Cliff Richard to Elvis Presley, or Donovan to Dylan. John was the leader; he was his own man. After their musical summit in the late Sixties, with the LPs *Rubber Soul*, *Sgt Pepper* and the 'White Album', it became clear to me and a million other anxious readers of the rock press that The Beatles' days were numbered. And we all knew that it was John who was breaking away.

In the old days Barry reminded me of Lennon. Later on Lennon reminded me of Barry—trend-crazed Barry, a fantasist, a chameleon. Barry was now having a terrible time trying to stay abreast of Lennon's startling changes in appearance and philosophy. Having created the Swinging Sixties, Lennon became a hold-all for the thronging credulities of the next decade, a decade whose demise coincided with his own.

Lennon's career in the early Seventies reads like a telex of banal headlines and captions. Lennon returns his MBE; meets with Pierre Trudeau; John and Yoko take out advertisements praising peace; they consort with the Maharishi, Timothy Leary, assorted minor gurus; LSD, cocaine, heroin; beard, shades, crew-cut, scalplock; bed-ins, bag-ins, be-ins, in-ins. . . .\Then Lennon 'got tired of waking up in the papers'. He succumbed to depression and hermitism. He became a 'househusband', rearing his son and baking bread at home while Yoko went out acquiring real estate. Their dream was to buy up the whole of the Dakota, the *Rosemary's Baby* mansion block on Central Park West. When questioned about this, Yoko once said, 'The thing is, John never had a house of his own.'

Separated from the melodic balance of The Beatles, Lennon's music became harsh and spiky, occasionally memorable and moving but more often strident and sloganising. He died just as his lyric talent seemed to be rejuvenating. What took him to America was a desire not just for (comparative) anonymity, but also for the teeming classlessness of New York. His murder was very typical of the city—flukey and meaningless. Deaths of this kind are what happens when the Warhol catchphrase—Everyone a Star—teams up with psychopathology, with the wrong kind of Barry.

Like countless others I played The Beatles' records into the turntable. They measured out my teens. Any Beatles track instantly transfers me to a specific segment of my past. When I heard of Lennon's death I felt a sense of shock well beyond what I felt at the deaths of the Kennedys and Luther King. I suffered this shock as it were helplessly. I thought of Barry—dreaming Barry, who bought two copies of 'Strawberry Fields' in case he broke one on the way home. I can only guess at his present sufferings. For both of us the past will never be the same again.

GEORGE MELLY

John Lennon

Punch, 17 December 1980

Reading the newspapers, listening to the radio and television, you get the impression that everybody loved and has always loved John Lennon. Well they didn't. They loved Ringo and respected George and were seduced by Paul, but after the original honeymoon period with 'The Fab Four', they recognised, quite correctly, that John couldn't be bought, wouldn't compromise, tried to change the world through a series of gestures which, because they were seriously intended but expressed symbolically, were bound to fail and could be dismissed with contemptuous laughter. Only a week or two ago the news that he never went out, but baked bread every day and looked after his son, seemed good enough for a few snide paragraphs. Lennon, the rich hippy with his six apartments and that ugly Japanese wife. Lennon, the cock-flasher, acorn-sender, bed-in freak. Lennon, the Howard Hughes of rock.

Well, Lennon had just begun to go out again, was making a new album, and had renewed his love affair with New York as a city, 'the safest on earth', and then a psychopath who identified with him pulled a gun and shot him dead. 'I just shot John Lennon,' he told the janitor. 'Ungrammatical,' said my friend Derek Taylor with angry despair. He believes a contempt for language shows a contempt for life. Lennon respected language.

Difficult to remember, ploughing through the eulogies in every newspaper, that Lennon was for a long time trapped in an enormous cage called the United States. If he left, they told him, he wouldn't be allowed back, so despite a great deal of pressure he wouldn't leave, and anyway he knew and they knew it wasn't the marijuana bust as they pretended. It was his opposition to the war that had enraged the Nixon administration.

Lennon was always the awkward one. There was the tremendous fuss when he said that at that moment The Beatles were more famous than Jesus Christ, which was in a sense true. He didn't say better or holier or eternally more famous, just more famous *then*; a statement of fact for which they burnt his records.

And yet I wouldn't exactly accuse the media of hypocrisy. They do, and I'm writing this only two days after his death, feel outrage because they sense that he was someone who was part of a whole generation's youth, someone who changed the sensibility of almost everybody, who proved, together with a few other key figures, that poetry was not an esoteric art but available for all. A newspaper today printed the famous photograph of Yoko and him showing their bare bottoms. At the time the response was outrage or ridicule. Now they look only vulnerable, only human.

The boy who killed him wanted attention. 'Happiness', The Beatles once sang with satirical phallic intentions, 'is a warm gun.' The boy took it literally. The boy is happy. He is, for a moment, as famous as his victim. What Tom Wolfe called 'The Me Decade' has found its pathetic spokesman.

I met Lennon several times and sometimes we got on and sometimes we didn't. I was one of the trad generation and he hated that because he felt that initially the jazz men had treated him with contempt, blocked his way and that of the music he believed in. When his first book, *In His Own Write*, was published I reviewed it favourably but at the publisher's party we nearly came to blows because I insisted, and would still insist, that the Black origins from which his very early songs derived were superior. He seemed to me arrogant. I suspect, with some reason, that he found me patronising. He was a hard man then, not at all the 'happy little rocker' of the publicity handouts.

I didn't meet him again until after The Beatles had broken up when he and Yoko were on the same chat show. They were very quiet and benign and we had a friendly if rather disorientated conversation of some length. With his long hair and granny glasses, his gentle and affectionate manner, it was hard to recognise the tight-mouthed aggressive young man of five years earlier. We parted with much of that bear-hugging which was the fashion of the time. I had just published a book which was critical of what I felt were their rather *déjà vu* activities. I felt guilty about it. They seemed so at peace, and I thought Yoko was lovely.

Then they broke up and John had his hair cut and in the company of the singer, Harry Nilsson, that most seductive of ravers, hit the town again. They were known as 'The Vampires' because they only came out at night. Rumours of shattered picture windows reached me. The old Lennon had surfaced with a vengeance.

I was in LA with Derek Taylor, formerly The Beatles' PRO and some time later a director of the ill-fated Apple. We were trying in vain to persuade Warner Brothers, for whom he was working, that there was a reason to invest some money in a middle-aged jazz-singer who had just gone back on the road. We were staying in a bungalow which was an annexe of the Chateau Marmont, that grotesquely beautiful example of Spanish Hollywood kitsch. I got up one morning and came out of the bedroom to confront Derek and John returning, with steam coming out of their ears, from a night on the tiles. It was a little tentative to start with. This was no longer the loving hippy but the old aggressive scouser full of drink and God knows what else; the rocker who had made it facing the trad-singer who'd tried to block his way. However, there was something we shared in common. We were both Liverpudlians and Liverpool is the most chauvinist place in the world. 'Liverpool', wrote Alun Owen, who also wrote *A Hard Day's Night*, 'scars its children for life.'

Somehow we got on to a scouse wrestler who spanned both our childhoods. His name was Jackie Pye and his speciality was throwing snot at the referee. With the palm trees of LA looming up through the smog outside, we recreated those nights in the smoky Liverpool stadium of 20 years before when Jackie Pye, to the delighted outrage of the crowd, performed his gimmick. It was an hysterical and unforgettable couple of hours.

He was less sympathetic in New York a few months later when I was singing there. Derek and I were staying in The Algonquin. Lennon and Nilsson showed up there 'baying for broken glass'. John rang up my publicity agent at 2 am and demanded carnal knowledge. She was not best pleased, and, perhaps to his surprise, made it clear.

His separation from Yoko didn't work out. They found they needed each other too much and the long rave-up was over. In their ever-growing complex of apartments Lennon became a recluse. He was only just ready to come out.

John Lennon offered an insoluble paradox. His huge fortune reduced the value of his gestures (he and Yoko once arrived in a white Rolls to fast on the steps of a church), and yet without his fame those same gestures would have passed unnoticed. He showed at all times great courage and indifference to mockery, but what he wanted— peace, goodwill, love—remain as elusive as ever. He was not ashamed to show that he had a penis and that he loved his wife, but his lasting value is in his music both before and after The Beatles broke up. Here he was both tough and tender, exact and universal, funny and tragic.

The sheer bulk of his obituaries is mysterious, beyond logic. Nothing he hoped for came about: wars rage, people hate, a young man buys a gun and waits outside the Dakota building; and yet everyone, it seems, feels diminished by his death.

ROBERT CHRISTGAU

Symbolic comrades

Village Voice, 14–20 January 1981

'Death of a Beatle', phooey—he'd been the most outspoken *ex*-Beatle for 10 stubborn, right-headed years. 'End of the '60s', asinine—if the decade wasn't finished on 31 December 1969, then it bit the dust a few weeks earlier at Altamont, or a few years later with McGovern. Yet there is a sense in which John Lennon's death does bring back our collective past, because it's the first genuine pop event to hit America in a very long time. In England they've had The Sex Pistols, but Stateside it's back to Dylan's 1974 tour, or maybe Rolling Thunder in 1975. The nearest we've come since then to rock and roll news that inspired the mass imagination, that momentarily melded a disparate, casual-to-fanatic audience into something like a community, was (don't hold your breath) *Saturday Night Fever*.

What's frightening, of course, is that this pop event was an assassination, one that may feel of a piece with Kennedy and King but has more in common structurally with Valerie Solanas's attempt on Andy Warhol (crucial difference: Solanas was a rival not a fan) and more in common historically with such recent headlines as the murders of Allard Lowenstein and who knows how many black schoolchildren in Atlanta. But for me, what's just as scary is that the community catalysed by Lennon's loss is obviously so momentary, partial, and (to use my fave '70s cliché) fragmented. The polarities aren't always mutually exclusive—contradictory feelings are the essence of our era—and don't divide into neat sets of parallels, but they indicate real divisions nonetheless. Here are those who've always regarded John as a symbolic comrade, there those who've always regarded him as an actual leader. Here are those who've aged with him, there those so young they revere him as the spirit of an Edenic prehistory. Here are those secretly relieved to put the quietus on the '60s, there those who hope somehow to revive them. Here are those who moon about all-you-need-is-love and give-peace-a-chance, there those who (like Stephen Holden in *Rolling Stone*) are reminded once again that 'love doesn't stop bullets'. Here are those who lament The Beatles as avatars of their faded youth, there those whose hearts go out to the wife and son that John the ex-Beatle left behind.

We feel these divisions musically, too. We hear more late Beatles than early Beatles, more 'Imagine' than 'Instant karma', and we know that *Double Fantasy*—which still trailed Bruce Springsteen on *Cash Box*'s airplay chart the week Lennon's death catapulted both album and single to number one in sales—will never saturate the radio (and the air itself) like *Sgt. Pepper*. Richard Goldstein's notorious Sunday *Times* pan of *Sgt. Pepper* had no constituency, although many critics (not me) agree with it now. But the regretful reviews of *Double Fantasy* that appeared in the *Boston Phoenix* (Kit Rachlis) and were withdrawn in the wake of the tragedy from the *Times* (Stephen Holden), *Rolling Stone* (Tom Carson), and the *Voice* (Geoffrey Stokes) spoke for John's more demanding fans. Saleswise, the comeback was a major success—sure to do even better than the most famous (as opposed to popular) ex-Beatle might expect. It produced a hit single, which was no foregone conclusion. But many found it fatuous, and I'm sure some young punks go along with *Soho News* club columnist (Ira Kaplan) who opined that Lennon's death meant less to 'rock 'n' roll, present and future' than the heroin ODs of Raybeat George Scott and Germ Darby Crash, who was so cool he died *on purpose*.

That would be a rank stupidity even if the album were a lot worse than its critics believe. I think it's a lot better, and I was beginning to think so before 8 December. The simplistic words and less than adventurous music were off-putting at first. But John sounded wonderful, and the times (or I) had caught up with Yoko's singing, so I kept playing the thing, a good sign with a record that resists final judgment. About meaning, of course, there could be no hesitation— this was John and Yoko's love album. The title made me think of Marco Vassi's great porn novel, *Mind Blower*, which is dedicated to the proposition that no matter how good the sex gets your minds will always be in different places. John and Yoko were denying this— gratuitously, perhaps, but I identified with the urge.

Not everyone did, or does—many of John's symbolic comrades find the couple's mutual self-involvement unrealistic and embarrassing. In the 25 November *Boston Phoenix*, Kit Rachlis confessed himself 'annoyed' by the artists' assumption 'that lots of people care deeply about John Lennon and Yoko Ono'. Sounded reasonable at the time, but since then the argument has become null, at least for a few years. *Double Fantasy* itself is now a pop event; its slightest moments have gained pathos, impact, and significance. The most devastating transformation occurs in 'Beautiful boy', John's lovely lullaby for his son Sean, which seems destined to become one of the kid's most vivid connections to his dead father: 'Have no fear/The monster's gone/He's on the run and your daddy's here.' But Yoko's 'Every man has a woman who loves him', the least distinguished piece of music on the album, runs a close second: 'Every man has a woman who loves him/In rain or shine or life or death,' she tells us. And later on reverses genders in the same couplet.

Oh Yoko. In a surprisingly astute analysis of 'Yoko and John' for *Rolling Stone*, Susan Brownmiller suggests that 'coming to terms with Yoko Ono, even in this hour of her personal loss, may be forever beyond the emotional capacity of some of John's loyal, bereft fans.' This is probably true, though I do wonder how many of his fans will come to terms with John himself—he remains a thorny case. Anyway, no matter how much mass self-pity was mixed in with the first outburst of grief—and mourners do always feel a little sorry for themselves—Yoko is now a cynosure, a focus of public empathy. So much so, in fact, that the relationship which was (to quote Brownmiller, who undervalues Yoko's career and is right on nevertheless) Yoko's 'major conceptual piece of art' is in danger of being sentimentalised into an ideal marriage for the Age of Survival, played to the distant strains of 'We can work it out' and the looped theme of 'Yellow submarine'. It was for suggesting such a script that *Double Fantasy* offended some people.

A very sharp critique of the marriage and the album was written for the *Voice*. Geoffrey Stokes's pan was palpably reluctant—he loved John, respected Yoko, and wanted to like their record. But to him the evidence seemed incontrovertible, and it was summed up by the title we chose: 'The Infantilisation of John Lennon'. Stokes was so broken up by the assassination that for a while he didn't even want me to quote him, but Annie Leibowitz's *Rolling Stone* cover photo—naked John clings foetally to clothed, impassive-looking Yoko—changed his mind. For Stokes, *Double Fantasy* is a concept album on a 'basically misogynist' theme: 'vampire-woman-sucks-life-out-of-man-who-enjoys-every-minute-of-his-destruction'. From the nursery-rhyme reversal of 'Cleanup time'—the queen counts the money while the king makes the bread and honey—to the passive-active combo of

(John's) 'I'm losing you' and (Yoko's) 'I'm moving on' to the abject abstraction of 'Woman' to the father-and-son equation of 'Beautiful boy' to the acute separation anxiety of 'Dear Yoko' to 'Hard times are over', a finale in which Yoko becomes 'a multi-tracked choir, engulfing all that goes before her', the album celebrates a love 'so all-fired powerful it exists without (present) pain, without conflict'. Even worse, it celebrates a love that doesn't involve, or permit, 'a functioning, adult John Lennon'.

Many post-moderns reject the whole notion of passionate monogamy—it's said to be reactionary, or dishonest, or corny (never, hmm, threatening). But Stokes, I happen to know, is passionately monogamous himself—what bothers him about John-and-Yoko is their, or its, absoluteness. The marriage seems as self-contained as a tautology, and as useless; it trivialises a great artist and deifies a dubious one. I use the present tense to refer to the relationship as art, as music and pop event, and in fact I think there's more tension, eccentricity, and humour in this art than might first appear. Nevertheless, Stokes is right in many ways. As a victim of separation anxiety myself, I regard the modern practice in which husbands and wives sleep apart, for sexual *or* professional (i.e. travel) reasons, as one of the barbarisms of the age, but if I felt myself 'wilt just like a faded flower' after an hour alone, I'd tell it to my shrink, not my muse. When John croons about 'the little child inside the man', he's articulating a bedrock assumption of the marriage, and while I'd call his matrifying mythicisation of Yoko 'basically sexist' rather than 'basically misogynist', I'm no less suspicious of what it suggests—the Earth Mother twaddle that has deradicalised so much left-wing feminism.

But all this is to fall into the old trap of expecting leadership from symbolic comrades—specifically, of expecting ideology from a rock star, or for that matter an avant-garde adept. Unlike most rock stars, Lennon actually consorted with ideologues for a while, and some movement retirees seem unaware that he ever went away, but in fact he was never a very impressive politico, given as he was to grandiose bouts of philosophical idealism and a baldness of rhetoric that was more effective when his mood was confessional rather than propagandistic. Politically, his indelible value was the way the abrasive anger that always lay just beneath his surface was transmuted into joy and hope. And this transmutation only occurred when first his group, then his wife shielded him from the aloneness he dreaded before anything else in life.

Make no mistake—this does appear to have been a rather neurotic marriage. But why do we always assume that neurosis must be defeated, transcended, escaped? John Lennon learned not merely to make do with his compulsions but to make something fairly miraculous out of them. The marriage itself, first of all—neurotic, but also, as we used to say, liberated, with male and female roles confounded, not just reversed. Very few matriarchs get to run a $150 million counting house unless it is bequeathed to them, and stay-at-home fathers who can afford live-in help rarely attend to parenting with John's care and intense devotion. But anyone who believes Yoko 'dominated' her husband should locate David Sheff's superb *Playboy* interview, in which Lennon both credits Yoko with saving his life and finds it difficult to let her get a paragraph in edgewise. And anyone who wants to dismiss Yoko—with her astrology, her peace-is-here-if-you-want-it—as a paramystical crackpot should find me somebody else who can manage a fortune like she was playing chess, learn to sing rock and roll, and make a genius happy all at the same time. This marriage was a saga of autotherapy with few parallels in our obsessively psychodramatic culture. It was also a great romance.

And then there's the minor miracle of the music. With its rich, precise sound, its command of readymades from New Orleans R&B to James Brown funk, and from magical mystery dynamics to detonating synthesizers, *Double Fantasy* is one of the two albums released in 1980 (Poly Styrene's dreamlike *Translucence* is the other) to put the anonymous usages of studio rock to striking artistic purpose. The music sounds somehow economical even when 24 (or is it 40?) tracks are humming; it doesn't just frame or set the voices, it projects them. And what voices. When he last essayed this sort of thing on *Walls and Bridges*, during his separation from Yoko, John sounded confused and unconvinced. Here he sounds sweet, tough, pained, reflective, calm, and above all soulful. When Yoko last tried to go pop on *Approximately Infinite Universe* (though compare 'Why?' on her experimental *Plastic Ono Band* to Material or Blood Ulmer and renew your faith in prophetic avant-gardism), she sounded like a bad Buffy Sainte-Marie imitator. Now her speed and sexuality, her forced rhythms and peristaltic gutturals, add a new-wavish edge to John's confident professionalism. The elementary device of alternating cuts between the two spouses (no duets) makes their union come alive more than any of the often one-dimensional lyrics. But I ought to admit that for the most part I like the lyrics, especially John's. I liked the lyrics on his *Plastic Ono Band*, too, not so much for what they said or how they said it but for what they said *about* how they said it—that John's commitment to the outspoken and straightforward knew no bounds. Nine years later, though he's more mature, more amiable, happier, that commitment is unchanged. I use the present tense, of course, to refer to art. I hope there's at least a little more.

A great album? No, but memorable and gratifying in its slight, self-limited way—connubial rock and roll is hard to find. I wouldn't think of patterning my own marriage on anyone else's, but like any good art *Double Fantasy* transcends specifics, even its status as a pop event. It helps me remember what I cherish. And it helps me cherish the two people who made it as well.

ELIZABETH THOMSON

Lennon's epitaph

The Listener, 8 March 1984

Fate decreed that *Milk and Honey* be John Lennon's final epitaph;[2] it could have been his rebirth. Had Lennon had time to polish his lyrics and to mix final tracks, this could have been a compelling opus. *Double Fantasy*, released just weeks before his death in 1980, contained some good songs, but its endless celebration of domestic bliss was ultimately cloying. The new album shares these failings—but the complacency is here tempered by moments of wry humour and a broader view of life and the world outside the Dakota.

Inevitably, Lennon's 20 minutes'-worth is swamped by his widow's indulgent packaging and her own redundant songwriting. Her six songs (recorded when?) are lyrically idiosyncratic, trite and unmemorable, delivered in that inimitable if repellent screech. (Curious how one feels well disposed toward Yoko until she opens her mouth to sing.) She fares best with her native tongue in 'Your hands'. Yoko must also be held responsible for the inadequate documentation of the album. What we have here is a ragbag of unfinished cuts, demos and home recordings, none of which is sufficiently explained in the notes. Instead, we get a stream of Ono consciousness and a set of unannotated and frequently inaccurate lyric transcriptions.

As for the musicians, the line-up is much the same as on *Double Fantasy* with the inexplicable addition of Bowie's sideman, Carlos Alomar, on backing vocals. Three 'omissions' could give rise to some speculation: in September 1980, *Rolling Stone* reported that Rick Nielson, Bun E. Carlos and Robin Zander, of Cheap Trick, had been among the coterie of musicians in the studio with the Lennons. But none of them is credited, either on *Double Fantasy* or on *Milk and Honey*. Are they nameless for contractual reasons or do they really not appear on the albums? In which case, are there other tracks still in the can on which they do appear?

In general, there is little evidence of production. Raw and unadorned, 'I'm stepping out' is an optimistic rocker that gently re-asserts Lennon's sense of identity. 'I don't wanna face it', perhaps the album's most fully realised track and certainly its heaviest, shows Lennon at something like his best—self-aware and lyrically assured:

> Say you're looking for a place to go
> Where nobody knows your name,
> You're looking for oblivion
> With one eye on the Hall of Fame;
> Say you're looking for some peace and love
> Leader of a big old band
> You wanna save humanity
> But it's people that you just can't stand.

The single, released from the album, 'Nobody told me', is a deftly ironic catalogue of life's contradictions. It rolls along purposefully enough, despite a 'vamp-till-ready' quality in the instrumental work: Ono declined to overdub guitar breaks.

'Borrowed time' is catchy and faintly twee; Lennon offers us a gently reggaefied reworking of sentiments first voiced in 'Help!' (1965). Similar in style, '(Forgive me) My little flower princess' is the album's nadir; it is not improved by gaping holes in lyrical and instrumental texture. Perhaps it would have been kinder to leave this one in the vault from which 'Grow old with me' was allegedly stolen. The version here is crudely recorded on home cassette; Yoko has added nothing but a touch of reverb. Lennon had intended a lush production ballad—'a standard, the kind they would play in church every time a couple get married'. Instead, McCartneyesque over-indulgence is held in check. Lennon's piano work recalls that on 'Imagine'. The melody is haunting; the words sentimental but poignant.

Thus Lennon's epitaph is sadly ironic: 'fate decree(d)' John and Yoko could not 'grow old' together. *Milk and Honey* adds to our portrait of the artist at 40: a man who's arrived at middle age, with a sense of inner peace and a certain optimism. A man who's still aware, if no longer angry.

Notes

1. Rudolph Réti: music theorist whose analysis was based on the concept of motivic 'cells'. See *The Thematic Process in Music* (New York, 1951)
2. Yoko decreed otherwise: 1986 saw the release of *John Lennon Live in New York City*, an ineffectual remix of the charity concert held in Madison Square Garden, 30 August 1972; and *Menlove Ave.*, out-takes from Lennon's *Walls and Bridges* (1974) and *Rock 'n' Roll* (1975)

EIGHT

Remember

JOHN ROCKWELL

For $325, a chance to assess the legacy of The Beatles

The New York Times, 24 October 1982

The Beatles were the most: the most influential group in the history of rock, the most successful, the most idolised, the most idealised and, almost without question, the most talented.

The band broke up in 1970, but all through the past decade, people nurtured the hope they would reunite. No matter that any reunion would have been almost destined to disappoint; the hope remained. But now, with John Lennon's murder in late 1980, all these hopes are past. The three remaining solo Beatles will continue to pursue their varied careers. But 'The Beatles' have been frozen into time, a distinct historical entity that began in 1962 and ended forever eight years later.

Even before Mr Lennon's death, The Beatles nostalgia and memorabilia industry was in full swing. There were Beatles books, Beatles song-books, Beatles bootleg and live and greatest-hits albums, Beatles conventions, Beatles Broadway shows, Beatles discographies and bibliographies, even a Beatles concordance.

With Mr Lennon's demise, the industry escalated into 24-hour shifts. In recent months we have seen a flood of Beatle-abilia, including several more handsome books and still further record recyclings. Just this week, to celebrate the 20th anniversary of the first Beatles British single, 'Love me do', released on 5 October 1962, Capitol issued an LP of the 20 top-selling Beatles songs.

But all of these pale before a massive 14-disc, ominous-looking black box that has been released in a limited 5,000-copy edition for the holiday season. It is called, portentously, *The Beatles: The Collection*, is issued by Original Master Recordings (BC-1) and carries a suggested list price of $325.

All you need is cash and for the Beatles fan who has, or wants, everything, the price may well be worth it. What we have here are the basic British Beatles albums—what might now be called the canonical collection—in audiophile super-fidelity, cut with the half-speed process direct from EMI's master tapes. The album comes with a booklet that includes colour reproductions of the individual album jackets, plus a 'Geo-Disc' to align your cartridge so that these sonic wonders may be heard as wondrously as possible.

The huge black box recalls CBS's 31-disc Stravinsky retrospective that came out last year. Both sets have a clumsy, cocktail-table ponderousness, fraught with a solemn significance that pop fans may find inappropriate. But both make the case for their artists as cultural icons, figures of such importance that they shaped their age. In Stravinsky's case, that was transparently true, and it was true for The Beatles as well.

If any one person or group defined that whole spectrum of dreams, accomplishments, failures and creative confusion we call the 60s, it was The Beatles. An entire generation grew up singing these songs, and mating to them. Quite apart from their intrinsic musical value, which is considerable, an astonishing number of Beatles songs retain their power to transform roomfuls of early-middle-aged people into weepy nostalgists. Given the fact that this baby-boom generation counts as the most numerous among us, there are plenty of weepy nostalgists out there to whom The Beatles still mean a great, great deal.

A sequential listening to these recordings, in their pristine sound, does not significantly alter one's memory of what The Beatles achieved; it only reinforces one's admiration for that achievement.

Yes, George Harrison's songs are often banal, Ringo Starr was not a virtuoso drummer, Paul McCartney had (and has) his sentimental side, and Mr Lennon could lapse into self-indulgent ranting. And yes, George Martin, too, without whose farsighted arrangements and production techniques The Beatles would have been a lesser band, could revert to prosaicness without their inspiration, as in the movie-music orchestrations that clutter side two of *Yellow Submarine*.

But all that pales beside the seemingly endless flow of memorable songs. The evolution over these eight years and 14 discs is remarkable, from vital yet simple early-60s rockers to affecting ballads, stirring anthems, bold experiments and complex mini-operas. After 1966, The Beatles were strictly a studio band, and by late in the decade, they and Mr Martin were pioneering production styles that have yet to be surpassed, and that sound absolutely comtemporary today.

As much as anything else, this lasting contemporaneity defines the greatness of the band. For all their epitomisation of their time, they seem to have tapped some secret of universality. Even such songs as 'All you need is love' or 'Come together', which might seem impossibly dated, still ring fresh.

They achieved this universality by their innate talent and by the fact that their evolution, still denounced by some as a betrayal of rock, really amounted to an abandonment of rock's parochialism in favour of a broader, more lasting popular sensibility.

The basis of any pop song is its melody and its words. On both counts, The Beatles, individually and collectively, were masters of the pop genre, and remained so throughout the life of the band. Ringo's few songs are cute, but of course the basis of The Beatles songbook are those by 'Lennon–McCartney'. We now know that the bulk of those songs were written by one or the other. But hearing them all together again makes one realise the closeness of their collaboration. Often songs by Mr Lennon are sung by Mr McCartney, and vice versa. Mr McCartney, justly famous for his ballads, could also write biting rockers, and Mr Lennon had his soft side. If any one thing can be said to define their compositional gift, it is the way they managed to adhere to basics yet to transcend crude simplicity by all manner of deft extensions and dislocations of the expected.

In their later years as a group, The Beatles could lapse into excess or eccentricity, and they certainly did so as solo artists in the 70s. But even when they were dealing with subjects far removed from their fans (for example, 'Taxman'), or when they had wandered into Indian exotica and visionary idealism, they retained the common touch. An essential innocence pervades these songs, right up to the end; if anything, with 'Let it be' and the other great McCartney ballads of the late 60s, it dominates as never before, purifying all the pretensions.

In their cellar-dwelling Hamburg years, and even on their first couple of LPs with Ringo, The Beatles were a fierce little rock and roll band, one that could match the young Rolling Stones blues lick for blues lick. Later, as they expanded into a cultural phenomenon, their commitment to the narrow, strict directness of rock lessened, and for that they have been excoriated by rock purists.

But it was that very diversification that ensured their universality. Their evocations of an older British music-hall tradition, their modest but ingenious formal experiments, and above all their willingness to reach out to a mass audience that craved pop ballads rather than the ruder passions of rock, allowed them to speak to almost everyone.

Reaching out to everybody may not be a central goal for an elitist, but The Beatles were the best and greatest of populists. They and their decade believed not simply that the finest art is the most popular art, but that any art is exalted if it resonates universal concerns, reinforcing and clarifying the otherwise incoherent desires of everyday people. By reaching wide, The Beatles reached deep. It was the accuracy of their articulation of their age that allowed them to transcend that age, and to speak to us as powerfully and privately today as they did two decades ago.

The Original Master Recordings box is not flawless. Ironically, the excellence of the sound may not be an absolute advantage; it allows all sorts of disconcerting inner details and even tape hiss to be heard as never before. . . . A similar stricture applies to the choice of the British albums over their American counterparts. Americans grew up with the American albums, and may feel disoriented by the British versions. The American albums were usually different from the British originals, especially in the first few years. The British albums had more songs, with the Americans squeezing out extra albums from singles and tracks left off earlier US releases. Nostalgia aside, however, it is clearly preferable, in a supposedly definitive set like this, to go back to the 'official' British originals.

But there are still problems. 'Magical mystery tour', for instance, came out in December 1967 in Britain as a two-disc, 45-rpm extended-play set. A month earlier, the American version had been released as an LP with several singles not included in earlier British albums on side two. It was not until 1976 that EMI issued that same LP in Britain. Original Master Recordings was thus faced with a dilemma. In a collection of British LPs, *Magical Mystery Tour* was not really part of the canon. Yet to leave it off would be to do without some of the great Beatles songs.

The rather odd solution is to insert the British version of the American version as disc 13, between *Abbey Road* and *Let It Be*. This is not chronological or even very logical. But a company official argued that since both this version of *Magical Mystery Tour* and *Let It Be* were pieced together with minimal Beatles involvement, those two albums had been appended to the first 12, which are in fact arranged chronologically.

Eventually . . . it would be nice to get a genuinely complete Beatles collection of all the studio-recorded *songs* arranged in exact chronological sequence. By limiting this set to albums, even British albums, over 15 songs that did not appear on these 14 LPs are missing—'Hey Jude', to cite one particularly grievous omission. Those albums that were intended as conceptual statements could still be heard as such, since their songs would have been recorded at the same time. But a song collection would answer the ultimate Beatlemaniac's needs better than the present set manages to do.

Still, this particular black box is worth hearing and having, if you can afford it. The Beatles industry will rumble on, producing every manner of artifact associated with the Fab Four. But in the recording era, with musicians who compose by ear using not just their instruments but the most sophisticated instrument of all, the recording studio, records become the true legacy, more permanent and meaningful than notated scores arranged dutifully by others.

Thus Beatles records *are* The Beatles, the centre of their achievement and what we will always remember them by. On the aural evidence of this wonderful-sounding collection, those memories deserve to be as loving as nostalgia has already ordained.

PETER SCHICKELE

Say, John . . .

A few memories and reflections:

Times Square, walking down Broadway, past one of those camera, wristwatch and souvenir stores that are forever about to go out of business, and out of which music blares on to the street. 'I wanna hold your HAAAAAAAAAAND. . . .' I was hooked right then and there, stood there on the sidewalk through several repetitions of the song before moving on. An immediate fan.

Next to music in my heart comes movies; I first saw *A Hard Day's Night* in Berkeley, California, and by the time my wife and I had driven back across the country to New York City we had seen it several more times in vastly varied towns and cities. During the following decade it overtook *Beat the Devil* and *Shoot the Pianist* as my most-often-seen movie; I lost count somewhere around 14 or 15. As a sort of 'Real movie person' I am well aware of the film's silliness and other should-be flaws, but every time I see it the visceral joy produced by that one-time flash alchemy of director and 'talent' sets me to dancing in my seat, and renders dispassionate comment irrelevant, as is the case with the best Marx Brothers and W. C. Fields movies. (The songs in *Help!* may be even better than those in the first film, but things were already getting self-conscious by then.) In the wake of *A Hard Day's Night* grown men and women were acting like teen fans, going around asking each other, 'Who's your favourite Beatle?' The most interesting people usually answered either 'It's a silly question', or 'John Lennon'.

I was teaching at Juilliard at the time. Juilliard is a very performance-oriented school, but there was one real musicologist on the faculty then, a man whose speciality included the Renaissance masses in which composers built elaborate polyphonic edifices around popular songs of the day, the latter usually sung in long notes in the middle of the musical texture. A mutual faculty friend told me that the musicologist had seen *A Hard Day's Night*, had loved it, and had exclaimed that he could imagine future composers writing masses based on some of those songs. Whether future composers actually do that or not, I know what he means: it's the combination of strong melodic profile and simple rhythmic values in songs like 'I should have known better' that makes for good *cantus firmus* fodder. This aspect of some of the early songs seems largely Lennonesque. Come to think of it, the melismas (more than one note to a single syllable) of 'Not a second time' on the first American album sound positively Gregorian.

The English side of my wife's family used to refer to certain people as being 'not quite nice'. Lennon was nowhere near quite nice. But he has not been the only artist with a strong mean streak to articulate tenderness more ravishingly than have many other, much nicer, artists. Not to mention how well he articulated his mean streak.

Was there really 'so much left to say?' That was one of the fascinating things about Lennon: no matter how wrong-headed and self-indulgent he got, you could never write him off for good. One never knew, did one?

JOHN TAVENER

John and Yoko

I remember being invited to an American's house in Hereford Square for dinner; he said John and Yoko were coming. Soon after I arrived a white limousine drew up and John and Yoko came in, equipped with their own *macrobiotic* dinner. Yoko I had known from before, but John I had not met. John wanted to hear tapes of my music—and we spent the evening on the floor (as I remember) listening to each other's tapes. It was from this meeting that Apple Records signed me up as their first 'classical' composer.

It may seem a curious thing to say—but what I remember most about them was their 'unworldliness'.

If they had not been like this, I don't think we would have got on so well. One felt that both John and Yoko were intuitively aware of the transcendent.

Whether they could have *defined* this, I doubt, but enough that they knew they were on a journey. For John the journey is continuing, but in a 'greater light' and he has left us richer for his brief span on earth.

LUKAS FOSS

Night music

Night Music for John Lennon: Prelude, Fugue and Chorale
In memory of 8 December 1980

I began to work on a commission by the Northwood Symphonette for brass quintet and chamber orchestra the morning of the day that John Lennon was killed. Admittedly, this influenced the composition. There are no quotations, not even stylistic similarities to Beatle music, but the tonal nostalgia of the Prelude, the use of the electric guitar, the particular use of major chords (though put into serial order) in the

243

Fugue, and the homage implied by the final Chorale all point to the tragic event of 8 December 1980.

I do not claim to be a rock music authority, but there have been rock elements in previous compositions (like *America Cantata*)—in fact, more so than in the work under discussion. What I love about The Beatles is that theirs is a genuinely 'young' music. Many composers have a healthy love-envy for folk expression. Our music is, at best, ageless: it is never young. Brahms loved and envied Johann Strauss's waltzes their quality of youth. Bartók spent his life trying to fuse the freshness of gypsy folk elements with his highly erudite musical expression, and in the 1920s every composer had a love for, or a lover's quarrel with, early jazz.

Finally, I think that John Lennon—more than anyone else— deserves credit for bringing 'poetry' back to popular music—poetry rather than 'lyrics'. It is a small miracle that something as uncommercial as Lennon's art became a huge commercial success. We needed something fresh and idealistic and it came at the right time.

MELOR STURUA

Murder on 72nd Street

Znamya V (1983)

On Palisades Boulevard in the suburbs of Los Angeles, surrounded by giant tropical palm trees, stands the studio of the famous Australian sculptor Brett Strong. The first thing that strikes the visitor's eye is an imposing bronze statue nearly three metres tall. Strong, a man not devoid of a sense of humour, and an ironic sense of humour at that, has dubbed his creation 'Statue about Freedom'. Not 'Statue to Freedom', but very much 'About Freedom'.

The story of its name is revealing. First a brief word about the sort of statue that it is. Strong cast a statue in bronze of his deceased friend John Lennon. He proposed to give the sculpture as a gift to the city of New York; it would be positioned in Central Park in the part that is named Strawberry Fields in memory of Lennon. Ed Koch, the mayor of New York, politely—even effusively—thanked the sculptor for his generous gift, but refused outright to accept it.

'Why?' Strong queried, completely bewildered.

'The thing is that we're as poor as church mice. We can't allow ourselves a luxury like this. We haven't the means to look after a statue.'

The mayor of New York is also a great humorist.

'But surely a bronze Lennon won't need a lot of looking after.'

'Well, but there you are,' answered Koch, with a note of impatience already in his voice. He was in a hurry to go off to Israel at the invitation of Begin. They had prepared a hectic programme for Koch in Tel Aviv. He was to visit the occupied West Bank of the Jordan, East Jerusalem, and then—in a military helicopter and with a heavy security guard— south Lebanon. In short, Koch was not in the mood to deal with Strawberry Fields and a statue of Lennon. Blood-stained deserts and other statues were waiting for him.

Bewildered and offended, the sculptor returned to Los Angeles. Later, he set out to the city hall and made a similar proposition to Bradley, the mayor of Los Angeles. Bradley agreed enthusiastically; then a few days afterwards, clearly embarrassed, he went back on his agreement. It had turned out that the city fathers were categorically opposed. Unlike the hypocritical Koch they did not resort to pleading poverty, but declared straight out that they would not tolerate Lennon as a neighbour—even in bronze—because the ideas that he propounded were not to their taste.

And so the Lennon sculpture returned again to the sculptor's studio on the seafront boulevard of Pacific Palisades, surrounded by giant tropical palm trees, where it stands to this day. And Strong, remembering the troubles he had been through with it, tagged it 'Statue about Freedom'.

The story of how official America turned its back on the 'bronze colossus'—the statue does indeed weigh three tons—is not a new one. American reaction has more than once taken a cruel and humiliating revenge on the memory of those artists whose work steps outside the framework of its normal socio-political creed. That is why it would be more true to call the statue 'Freedom in Chains' than to call it 'Statue about Freedom'. Strong intends to destroy it and melt it down. This is a pity. This unwanted statue, this statue without a home, as Lennon himself once was, has already become a distinctively original monument to the society of violence and conformism. A memorial which stands in accusal. . . .

It is possible to understand the New York and Los Angeles city fathers. Brett Strong's gift seemed no doubt like a Trojan horse and they were afraid of it. The modern American Troy is fearful of forces which may penetrate it and 'undermine the foundations of society'.

Some New York city hall employees told me quite frankly: 'If we'd have accepted Strong's gift and placed the statue of Lennon in Central Park, we'd have attracted all sorts of new problems and concerns, and we've got more than enough as it is. You don't need to be a prophet to see that Strawberry Fields would pretty soon become a place of pilgrimage for all the anti-war demonstrators, for the nuclear disarmament movement, for the protesters against the carrying and sale of fire-arms, for the movement to help feed the starving nations of Africa, and for all sorts of dissidents.'

. . . But America after all is a country of astounding paradoxes. The bronze Lennon has been condemned to the sculptor's studio, while it seems that Mark David Chapman, the murderer of Lennon, will soon be given his freedom.[?] Famous and rich. American Herostratuses win not only fame but a fistful of dollars too . . .

In the same way, practically all the heroes of the Watergate scandal have become millionaires. They spent behind bars just the time necessary to write their memoirs. The gospel according to Chapman is awaited with special impatience. It seems that the content will be full of Freudian meaning. Chapman, you see, imagined himself to be Lennon—complete with a Japanese wife—and so the act of murder for this degenerate creature was not a crime but an act of suicide!

. . . Lennon said that violence is pornography, and war is the most extreme, the most repugnant and the most cynical form of pornography. He likened the Pentagon to a giant brothel, and the generals to its occupants. And this is another reason why there proved to be no room for a bronze Lennon on American soil. The land where they put up monuments to general-avengers, to general-executioners, to general-aggressors, where they place on a pedestal the works of MacArthur and Westmoreland, Ridgeway and Rogers, Abrahams and Haig; this is not the place for a 'peacenik' asking 'give peace a chance' for humanity to survive. And now the Pentagon, this brothel of aggression, plans to establish in Western Europe, including the country of Lennon's birth, its Pershings and its guided missiles. Were Lennon still alive he would, no doubt, be raising his voice against this new threat as once he did against the presence on English soil of the Polaris missiles, a far cry from the happy, life-giving childlike joy of 'Yellow submarine'.

. . . For great and boundless is God's chosen land of America! Fifty states are spread over its land, from the Atlantic Ocean to the Pacific, from New York in the East to Los Angeles in the West. But nowhere, absolutely nowhere at all, could there be found a place for the 'Statue about Freedom', for there is no freedom in the great, boundless, God's chosen land of America. Yet all the same I will not be mistaken if I say that the bronze Lennon will not finish its days in the sculptor Brett Strong's studio on the fabled and beautiful boulevard of Pacific Palisades, surrounded by giant tropical palm trees, bathed in the sun and the salt of the sea. I will not be mistaken and I will not be surprised if I see John—the man and the statue—at an anti-war meeting in New York's Central Park or at a protest demonstration of Mexican Chicanos in Eastern Los Angeles. I will recognise his stooping figure amongst those taking part in an Aldermaston march in his native England or in the avant-garde of the 'spring offensive' in the homeland of his Japanese wife, Yoko Ono. With his guitar at an angle, screwing up his shortsighted eyes with gentle irony, he will lead his young son Sean by the hand and demand in his name, and in the name of all the children on our planet who love and who sing his songs:

—Give peace a chance!

PHILIP LARKIN

Fighting the fab

The Observer, 9 October 1983

. . . Only of course they were not altogether ordinary young men. The music that made them famous was an enchanting and intoxicating hybrid of Negro rock and roll with their own adolescent romanticism. The Lennon–McCartney collaboration produced a series of love songs that appealed to the highest in the land as directly as to the Liverpool typists in the Cavern at lunchtime, in a manner that constituted the first advance in popular music since the war. This cannot be gainsaid.

. . . At the same time, they remained individuals. Instead of riding their early successes on ever-more-deafening tours, they defiantly 'went private' to concentrate on doing their own thing, or Lennon and McCartney's own things, in the recording studio. 'Please please me' was displaced by surreal lyrics, mystic orientalia, peace messages and anti-American outbursts. The trouble was that as surrealists, mystics or political thinkers The Beatles were rather ordinary young men again. Their fans stayed with them, and the nuttier intelligentsia, but they lost the typists in the Cavern.

. . . The decade from their break-up in 1970 until the murder of Lennon in 1980 makes a sorry, fragmentary story. . . . All four Beatles continued to make records, but never has a whole been greater than its parts.

. . . So gigantic a success as theirs seems like the tapping of some unsuspected socio-emotional pressure that when released swept them completely away from their natural artistic context to perish in the rarefied atmosphere of hagiolatry. The four tiny figures, jerking and gesticulating inaudibly at the centre of larger and larger stadiums of screaming, were destroyed (in Lennon's case literally) by their own legend.

When you get to the top, there is nowhere to go but down, but The Beatles could not get down. There they remain, unreachable, frozen, fabulous.

ADRIAN HENRI

New York City Blues

(*for John Lennon*)

You do not cross the road
To step into immortality
An empty street is only the beginning

The words will still flow through you
Even on this cold pavement,
Are heard in some far place
Remote from flowers or flash-bulbs.

In that city, on Gothic railings
Dark against the snowy park
Still a dead flower, a faded letter,
Already one month old.

'Life is what happens to you
When you're busy making other plans,'
This empty street
Is only the beginning.

Remember

Here, in your other city,
Riot vans prowl the December dark,
Remember angry embers of summer,
Familiar ghost guitars echo from stucco terraces.

Meanwhile, in the Valley of Indecision,
We rehearse stale words, store up expected songs,
Celebrate sad anniversaries.
Flowers and flash-bulbs. Cold pavements.

You do not cross the road
To step into immortality
At the dark end of the street
Waits the inevitable stranger.

Afterword 2003

When *The Lennon Companion* was originally put together, some fifteen years after the apparent end of The Beatles, we aspired to 'show it like it was' without the benefit of too much hindsight. The group's reputation and influence appeared to have settled down; commentators anticipated a certain plateauing-out beyond the sales boost spawned by the advent of compact discs. Now that a further fifteen years have elapsed, a period nearly as long as John Lennon's entire creative life, we can see that his stature has continued to grow in ways both inevitable and surprising. As individual band members depart—never quite in the right order, as someone unkindly quipped—they leave the bookshelves and CD racks heaving with third-age Beatlemania. And above the fray looms St Lennon the martyr. The year 2002 saw Liverpool's Speke Airport renamed after him and 'above us only sky' re-Imagined as a marketing tool.[1] A BBC TV poll cited him as one of the Greatest Britons.[2] First a victim, then a posthumous beneficiary of the cult of celebrity, Lennon's artistic legacy can seem almost secondary to his role as a secular icon. If this isn't the kind of immortality he craved, it is nevertheless a big part of the status he now enjoys.

The cultural climate has changed too, and in ways that we could not have anticipated in 1987. As music lovers, most of us feel instinctively that music has a unique capacity to synchronise emotional, communicative and motor skills not only within our own brains but with the minds and bodies of others. Its mysterious spell is woven through a complex interaction of background expectation and foreground innovation. But does this apply across the board? Michael Berkeley sees The Beatles' legacy this way:

> Popular music is the art of repetition, so it is essential that the repeated
> motif is top-notch, and with them it nearly always was. Plus their songs
> often take unexpected twists and turns, like the best music in all genres.[3]

Whatever your take on the relative ephemerality of 'popular'
music—an alien, pre-masticated imposition according to the high cultural pessimists of the post-Frankfurt School, but a vital eruption from
below for those seduced by the denim-clad immediacy of a Bruce
Springsteen—it is, or was, possible to think about listening to it as an
experience of 'placing', of being 'drawn, haphazardly, into affective
emotional alliances with the performers and with the performers'
other fans'.[4] Western art music, on the other hand, is, or was, about
something else again: something older, something absolute. When, in
the 1960s, William Mann and Wilfrid Mellers heaped praise on The
Beatles, they were seeking to appropriate their output for a Great Tradition. So, in a sense, were we.

Since 1987, the cultural hierarchy has been melting and shifting,
whether through the unfettered power of consumer capitalism or a
genuine desire to give other musics their place in the sun. In an apho-
rism of Norman Lebrecht's, 'the loudest noise in World Music is the
clattering of generic fences'.[5] We have moved on from the artificial
Keats versus Dylan feud created by the British media from October
1991,[6] but today's flabby consensus between cultural critics and
broadsheet journalists that the division between 'high' and 'low' art
doesn't matter any more, that sees Beethoven's Ninth and Carl
Perkins' 'Blue suede shoes' as equally valuable cultural texts, is no
more helpful. The rock-influenced American composer Christopher
Rouse put it like this:

> I'm not going to talk about rock and roll any more. It doesn't need my
> help. It's not that I no longer like that music, but I feel the wagons have
> been circled, and I'm going to stick with my high-falutin', élitist, dead
> white European male brethren and, if necessary, go down fighting.[7]

Where does this leave the legacy of Lennon the musician?

Also in flux in recent years is the reputation of Yoko Ono. Long excoriated as an alien import on several levels, her risk-taking conceptual art looks much less threatening these days, particularly in the
UK, where influential collectors with big budgets have pushed an indigenous blend of installation art towards the mainstream. In November 1997, a major retrospective exhibition at Oxford's MoMA

(Museum of Modern Art) helped clear the air, and today her work is found alongside that of Fluxus artists at London's Tate Modern. Her curious brand of naïvety, charm and business nous remains a problem for some, and her wholehearted embrace of the market, surely worlds away from Lennon's own political inclinations, has allowed her to sanction the use of his work in promotional campaigns and TV ads. She must see this as a means of keeping his name before a younger public—it's not as if she needs the income—but it's something The Beatles themselves have more often sought to avoid. Now entering her eighth decade, Yoko joins forces with The Pet Shop Boys on a new dance version of her most enduring song, the uncomfortably prophetic 'Walking on thin ice'. Their chic anonymity of style meshes well with her own. Would Lennon have become the atheist's messiah without her? Probably not. She was not cited as co-writer on 'Imagine', but her fingerprints are all over a text which amounts to little more than an appeal for people to be nice to one another. On a more practical level, she recently paid out to ensure that control of John's childhood home, his Aunt Mimi's house in Liverpool, was passed to Britain's National Trust. As she recognises, it doesn't exactly support the myth. 'John was the working-class hero because he felt that way, but you could say he was more middle class, and living in a nice part of town'.[8] What of that myth?

As with John F. Kennedy, everyone of a certain age remembers where they were and what they were doing when they heard that Lennon had been shot. The death of Elvis Presley, three years earlier, though perhaps less of a shock, was universally mourned. But Lennon's assassination had particular impact as a cultural marker, not just the premature end of an established legend but the start of a new one. In Liverpool and New York, the two cities with a greater claim on him than any other, there were spontaneous acts of mass-mourning. Television stations played and replayed footage of The Beatles in their magnificent heyday; *A Hard Day's Night* and *Help!* reminded us of a kinder, gentler, more innocent time. On the radio, the world united to 'Imagine' and 'Give peace a chance'. In the years since, as Anthony Elliott writes in *The Mourning of John Lennon* (1999), he has become

> strangely representative of loss in our culture—an object of mourning, of fantasy, of intense feelings of hope and dread. Lennon is for many a figure of idealisation. Inside the myth of the Fab Four, the moptops, Lennon reigns supreme. He is championed as a musician, poet, avant-garde artist, political radical, and world peace activist.[9]

'Outside the myth', Lennon—like, say, Diana, Princess of Wales—sometimes elicits a more negative response: 'he is a fraud or phony. . . . At once idolised and denigrated . . . ambivalence pervades our memory of him'.[10]

In a global village shrunk and wired beyond Marshall McLuhan's wildest imaginings, the scale and intensity of the response to the death of Princess Diana were unprecedented. She, too, became a martyr—'unreachable, frozen, fabulous', much like Larkin's Beatles. Yet, 'the Diana effect' as a mass-phenomenon was remarkably short-lived. Even when whipped into hysterical frenzy by a ravenous media industry on a 24-hour feeding schedule, the genuine sadness left no lasting cultural legacy. Concentrating on the post-Beatle years, Elliott's 'metabiography' explores these

> interconnections between fantasy and culture—in particular the ways in which celebrities are imagined and, thereby, symbolically 'used' by people in their everyday lives.[11]

Lennon as cultural icon was 'an intimate companion' throughout Elliott's childhood, a sense of identification irrevocably assaulted in December 1980. 'Shock, confusion and horror' gripped him, and with hindsight he wonders

> how loss connects to the broader dynamics of culture. For whom, exactly, is the mourner mourning? Are we mourning some aspect of ourselves? How might the mourning self relate to cultural mourning? How does contemporary culture mourn?[12]

In part by rushing out to buy books and CDs, as if the handing over of money demonstrates our love for the departed and ownership makes us part of the family. Thus, Kurt Cobain's *Journals*[13] are published with due solemnity after an appropriate interval, his scribblings promoted as a creed for the new millennium.

Lennon himself has been commemorated in less orthodox ways. In New York's Central Park, just outside the Dakota Building where he lived and died, Ono created a small memorial garden, Strawberry Fields, where fans stand in quiet contemplation, often leaving flowers. In a Liverpool which once shunned formal recognition of 'four lads who shook the world',[14] John, Paul, George and Ringo are now honoured with exhibitions, plaques and sundry items of statuary. Tourists who have long come to the city to gaze at 'the shelter in the middle of a roundabout' can now visit 251 Menlove Avenue, where Lennon lived with his Auntie Mimi and rehearsed with The Quarry Men, and 20 Forthlin Road, where McCartney grew up.

These days the worship is nowhere more fervent than in the Far East. The Beatles aren't just big in Japan: thirty years after they broke up, Beatlemania lives. Sunao Ashihara, a novelist who made his debut with a story about a Japanese high school band, wrote 200 pages on his pilgrimage to Liverpool,[15] while critic Rûytarô Monobe contributed a comparative study of Lennon and Akutagawa Rûynosuke, the early twentieth-century short story writer who also died young.[16] Shinko Music of Tokyo is able to feed the voracious appetites of Japanese fans with a seemingly endless supply of previously unpublished photographs. And while Britain boasts a handful of lookalike, soundalike bands who make a living at Beatle conventions and, occasionally, in London's West End, some of their Japanese counterparts even have their own imitators! The most successful of the 'originals' are The Parrots, who can fill Abbey Road, Tokyo's premier Beatle venue, five nights a week with their three-hour show. In addition to Abbey Road, there's the Cavern, which has branches in Osaka and Kyoto as well as Tokyo, and the world's first John Lennon museum in Saitama, north of Tokyo, which houses a concert venue and an exhibition space featuring items loaned by Ono. Japan also boasts countless study groups and scores of Beatle shops, selling all manner of memorabilia.[17]

Nor are Australians immune. The fixation began in 1964, when The Beatles seduced a nation that had been in total thrall to American culture. Their first tour is regarded as the 'greatest entertainment coup Australia has ever witnessed'.[18] Closer to home, The Beatles remain a potent force in Eastern Europe. In the former Czechoslovakia, the 'John Lennon Peace Wall', spontaneously created in a quiet corner of Prague's diplomatic quarter shortly after his death, became a focal point for dissident graffiti and a symbol of non-violent rebellion; the success of Václav Havel's Velvet Revolution turned it into a tourist attraction.

Insofar as the UK market was concerned, it was the mid-1990s that saw a recrudescence of Beatlemania: whether by accident or design, The Beatles 'reunion' campaign was exquisitely timed. Perceiving a dim echo of the political and cultural atmosphere of the early 1960s, A&R men of a certain age had begun signing up the 'indie' bands that would create the soundtrack for the dying days of an unpopular Conservative government. The localised pop renaissance that became known as Britpop didn't last—check out today's indigenous stars, barely distinguishable one from another and often fabricated through the medium of star-making TV shows—but bands such as Supergrass, Suede, Blur, Pulp and, above all, Oasis did constitute some sort of second coming, bringing back a unanimity to the British pop-buying audience that hadn't been seen for decades. The music itself was guitar-based and, to a greater or lesser extent, indebted to The Beatles. For the Gallagher brothers behind Oasis, John Lennon was a presiding deity and, with Johnny Rotten of The Sex Pistols, the main influence on Liam's incendiary vocals—even if the material did sound more like Status Quo! It is claimed that some 2.5 million people, about five per cent of the UK population, applied for tickets for Oasis at Knebworth in 1996, Britpop's Woodstock.[19] Though these groups did not make the same impact in the US, they transformed the domestic scene. Or was it *The Beatles Anthology* series that validated their own efforts? One can't be sure which came first, except to recall that Oasis was seldom criticised for imitating The Beatles; rather they won plaudits to the extent that they resembled them. With Blur and Oasis battling it out for the top spot in the singles chart, Beatles-versus-Stones comparisons proved irresistible.

The Beatles' most recent compilation, a collection of their number ones, has sold spectacularly.[20] But it was the mid-1990s release of archive material, much of it previously in circulation on bootleg, which—in the wake of Britpop's *homage*—raised The Beatles to a new level of cultural omnipotence. First came *Live at the BBC* (1994), more than fifty songs recorded between 1962 and 1965 for radio programmes such as *Saturday Club*. The release was given a fanfare, EMI inviting 250 journalists from around the world to the BBC's Maida Vale studios where the songs were originally set down. Yet despite that, the company underestimated demand, and the 200,000 initial pressing sold out virtually overnight. EMI's share price rose 14 points in expectation of windfall profits.

Twelve months later came the first of the much-heralded *Beatles Anthology* sets and an accompanying TV series, later released on video and DVD. The surviving Beatles and George Martin participated in the project, Martin calling it 'a historical outlook on the music'.[21] Volume 1 disappointed many, with its inclusion of Hamburg-era recordings of such chestnuts as 'Besame mucho' and 'Ain't she sweet', though 'Free as a bird', the opening number, attracted a good deal of attention. Recorded by Lennon at his New York home in 1977 on to mono cassette, it was completed in 1994 with vocals, guitar and drums by

McCartney, Harrison and Starr overlaid on Lennon's voice and piano. Once again, a Beatles single entered the Christmas chart, notwithstanding earthbound production work by Jeff Lynne.

The second and third collections, released in 1996, allow us to eavesdrop on the evolution of classics like 'A day in the life' and 'While my guitar gently weeps'. Such previously unreleased cuts as 'What's the new Mary Jane' also received their first official outing in a belated drive to trump the bootleggers. A reworking of another Lennon home demo, 'Real love', featured on Volume 2 and made for a further hit single. But even after *Anthology*, might there be more to come? Peter Doggett recently listed as many as twenty unrealised projects.[22]

Inevitably, Yoko was keen to ensure that there would be Lennon— and Ono—compendia to rival The Beatles' own, and her four-CD Lennon tribute is an artwork in itself. There is disconcertingly little in the way of new material, although it was interesting to find Lennon burlesquing Harrison and Dylan with quite such gleeful venom. There are demos and outtakes, but most of the set consists of more or less finished versions of songs already released in alternative guises in the manner of *Menlove Ave.* In some cases, the *John Lennon Anthology* versions are superior to those given disc space at the time. The presence of Cheap Trick[23] gives a rockier edge to 'I'm losing you', and George Martin provides a lush orchestral framework for the home recording of 'Grow old with me'. The mainstream 1970s production values of *Walls and Bridges* were not to all tastes, so the inclusion of stripped-down versions of some of its songs may be appreciated by collectors. Meanwhile, the absence of the out-of-tune backing vocals on 'One day at a time' from *Mind Games* is an unmixed blessing. That the couple's early experimental albums have been transferred to CD will be of little interest to non-fanatics, but the second-generation CD remasterings of *Imagine* and *Mind Games* are rather different, stealing a march on The Beatles' own catalogue. As with the *John Lennon Anthology*, opulent packaging tends to take the edges off Lennon's radicalism, positing a friendlier, more domesticated image for an older if not wiser audience, but the sound is cleaner with generally punchier vocals. That said, the higher-fi of the revamped *Mind Games* brings a degree of crispness that is not always helpful when its production is less strong to start with; the title track in particular relies on its smudgy, post-hallucinogenic haze.

*   *   *

Since *The Lennon Companion* was first published in 1987, the flow of books about The Beatles as a band, and John, Paul, George and Ringo as individuals has reached new heights. Standard works by Hunter Davies and Ray Coleman have appeared in new editions, while Jann Wenner's celebrated post-Beatle interview, *Lennon Remembers,* was re-transcribed thirty years on with Ono's blessing, its long-excised indiscretions now restored. Lennon was remembered in *Stuart Sutcliffe: The Beatles' Shadow and His Lonely Hearts Club Band* (2001). Written by Pauline Sutcliffe, this account of The Beatles' Hamburg days and the friendship between Lennon and the author's brother prompted some lurid headlines. In fact the book itself sets the record straight in a cool and unsensational manner. As Sutcliffe says in her introduction,

> My family have lived with none of the benefits but all of the enmities and rivalries, and sometimes the horrors, of our founding association with the most popular musical group of all time.[24]

As the late and largely unlamented Albert Goldman discovered in 1988, when he finally published *The Lives of John Lennon,* few people want their heroes, working-class or otherwise, knocked from their pedestals like so many Soviet statues. A lesson he might have learned a few years earlier with his deconstruction of *Elvis* (1981). Of course, he claimed to regret the fact that the Lennon he came to know during his arduous researches was not the Lennon he'd hoped to find, just as Presley had failed to match up to the good doctor's exalted standards. The feigned intimacy of the opening pages sets the tone:

> Lennon has confined himself to his room for the past three years. Save for summer holidays in Japan, he rarely leaves his queen-size bed, to which he clings like a sailor aboard a life raft. Much of the time, he sleeps, perhaps half the day, in two- to four-hour spells. The balance of the day he spends sitting in the lotus position, his head enveloped in a cloud of tobacco or marijuana smoke . . .[25]

By the end of the next page, we have learned that he is an anorexic—one whose morning retching is heard by the man who drops by to keep Yoko in her $5000-a-week habit. Even Lennon's 'weak, hooded eyes, so sensitive to light that he complains of the glare from the tiny bulbs on the Christmas tree'[26] are grist for the mill, evidence for the prosecution, somehow his fault. At some 700 pages, Goldman's book was heavy but certainly not heavyweight and, while his most lurid 'revelations' inevitably made headlines on both sides of the Atlantic, Beatle fans largely ignored it. Ono, to her credit, maintained a dignified silence. It was Goldman's academic credentials that made *The Lives of John Lennon* especially difficult to stomach. The former Professor of English and Comparative Literature at Columbia University, New York, responsible for one of the first Ivy League courses on popular culture, was a man with studies of Wagner and Thomas De Quincey to his credit. And surely *someone* should have been able to point out to him that nothing by The Beatles ever played at 78 rpm!

McCartney has lived a life less open to Goldmanesque parody, though an overweening self-confidence has at times threatened to undermine his likeable public image. Detractors would say he is simply less interesting than John and, despite his undeniable melodic genius, somehow less talented. Always the cute Beatle in every sense, his decision to appoint Barry Miles as his authorised biographer ensured that nothing too grotesque would spill out. Portentously packaged, *Paul McCartney: Many Years from Now* (1997) shed no new light on the relationship between Lennon and McCartney (or McCartney and Lennon), though Paul did acknowledge that the sum was greater than the parts.

> A body of work was produced that I don't believe he alone could have produced, or I alone could have produced . . . So much of it was team effort, joint effort, there really was so much of it.[27]

'What would we be listening to today had Paul McCartney not met up with John Lennon in July 1957? Fortunately, we will never know.'[28]

The recollections of press officer Derek Taylor, a man 'at the centre of the revolution stemming from The Beatles',[29] are an altogether more engaging read. *It Was Twenty Years Ago Today* (1987) finds the Beatles loyalist looking back to the so-called Summer of Love and the making of the album that defined it, *Sgt Pepper's Lonely Hearts Club Band*. The LP was revisited by its producer, George Martin, in *Summer of Love: The Making of Sgt Pepper* (1994). Alas, the man whose catalytic effect on The Beatles as musicians and Lennon and McCartney as composers can scarcely be denied has produced a cliché-ridden account of the 700 hours it took to get it all together. Even so, this is an essential read for anyone with a serious interest in how the music was made.

Also no great shakes as a literary stylist, the redoubtable Mark Lewisohn supplied both the research for and the notes accompanying

The Beatles Anthology series. Lewisohn's obsession with The Beatles began when, as a four-year-old, his mother played him 'Please, please me'. A former BBC finance clerk turned journalist, he has written books too numerous to mention, including *The Complete Beatles Recording Sessions* (1988), which is based on Abbey Road data and interviews with some seventy people associated with Beatle recordings. Five years later, *The Complete Beatles Chronicle* combined much of that volume with material from an earlier title, *The Beatles Live!* George Martin's foreword describes it as being 'as accurate as it is detailed', though Tim Riley was irritated by the book's 'offhand references'[30] and description which 'evades the effect of the creative process'[31] and 'begs elucidation'.[32] That's true, but Lewisohn's books are superior to similar volumes on, say, Bob Dylan and an essential contribution to Beatle lore. Such exhaustive day-by-day diarising of everything The Beatles did in the studio, on tour, and for radio and TV is unlikely to be surpassed. Lewisohn is perhaps the one man who has heard all the tapes in EMI's archive.

Available in various forms, Doug Sulpy and Ray Schweighardt's *Get Back: the unauthorised chronicle of The Beatles Let It Be disaster* (1997) goes into incredible, minute-by-minute detail to give a completist's chronology of the *Let It Be* sessions and the songs performed. They out-Lewisohn Lewisohn, only less accessibly and with less deference to EMI in their tale of 'Drugs, divorce and a slipping image'.

Michael Bryan Kelly took a wide-angle lens to *The Beatle Myth* (1991), not so much an attack on the group as a revisionist take on the extent of their penetration of and influence on the US market. With its unconventional, middle-American perspective, Kelly's book sets up some Aunt Sallys for convenient demolition, but it also provides a useful reminder that American Beatlemania was fundamentally an East Coast phenomenon. Rejecting as myth the traditional version of events that he traces to Lillian Roxon's *Rock Encyclopedia*, Kelly deploys contemporary *Billboard* charts to demonstrate the limits of the British invasion.

Once associated with the British weekly *New Musical Express*, Ian MacDonald's perspective could not have been more different. The author was perhaps fortunate that his wildly ambitious contextual study, *Revolution in the Head* (1994), appeared on the crest of the wave of resurgent Beatlemania. Most of the book is devoted to a song-by-song breakdown of everything the group released—there can be several pages on each number, including, in the updated edition, a rare perusal of the quasi-posthumous *Anthology* compositions. His evaluations, while patently sincere and sometimes seductive, are obstinately individualistic. His negative appraisal of 'Across the universe' is but one example that will enrage long-standing fans, though it is worth remembering that it took Phil Spector to make it work. 'Here, there and everywhere' is dismissed as 'chintzy and rather cloying',[33] though most of us would regard it as among the best of McCartney. 'All you need is love' is full of 'comfortable self-indulgence'.[34] Maybe—but since it was written to be performed on the world's first satellite link-up at what was by any standards a comfortable and self-indulgent time, surely that was the point. And are the alternating bars of 4/4 and 3/4 time *really* 'inelegant'? Isn't the verse's irregular metre precisely what makes the song original by undercutting the apparently bland reassurance of the text? One is reminded of MacDonald's efforts on behalf of Dmitri Shostakovich in *The New Shostakovich* (1990), an enthusiastic, perhaps intentionally shrill attempt to portray the Soviet composer as a thoroughgoing dissident. Yet, just as that overstated treatise provoked fresh debate about the meaning of his work, so MacDonald's pontifications here remind us that this is music that really means something in the context of the culture and history of our own civilization. His drive to reclaim the social and philosophical accomplishments of the Sixties strikes a chord with music lovers bemused by the long-standing demonisation of 'their' decade by right-wing politicians.

> It is difficult to overestimate The Beatles' impact and influence. Purely in terms of pop, they invented the idiom as later generations came to know it, revolutionising pop songwriting, studio production, video promotion, general presentation and instrumental styles . . . Beyond these accomplishments, The Beatles dominated and defined their time, reflecting every culturally significant shift in their kaleidoscopic decade in ways so acute, and at time prescient, that it occasionally seemed to their contemporaries that the group caused some of the major changes of the 1960s. In fact this was not so, but it was a testament to the scale of their real achievements that a quartet of popular musicians should be credited with so fundamental a contribution to late 20th-century culture.[35]

Like MacDonald, Mark Hertsgaard blends musical, technical and historical comment in *A Day in the Life: the music and artistry of The Beatles* (1995), weaving a chronological narrative that gives a sense of The Beatles' development both as musicians *per se* and as musical technicians. Hertsgaard, whose book grew out of a *New Yorker* article which alerted the world to the making of *Anthology*, contends that their music was in short, high art for the mass public. And remarkably enough, it was recognised and embraced as such virtually from the moment it first reached a wide audience. Yet precisely because The Beatles were such a gigantic popular success, there will always be those who refuse to accept that the music they produced might qualify as high art.[36]

In his recently updated *Tell Me Why—The Beatles: album by album, song by song, the Sixties and after* (2002), Tim Riley offers a more succinct critique than his title might suggest, although, unlike Mac-Donald and Hertsgaard, he finds room to look at The Beatles solo. For him, the promise of *Double Fantasy* (1980), Lennon's last finished album, neatly counterpoints the torment of his first, *Plastic Ono Band* (1970). Going along with the conventional notion of Lennon as risk-taker, musically and socially, he nevertheless points out that, without McCartney, he could sound 'all too risky, in unattractive ways'. The Lennon and McCartney partnership, Riley suggests, 'provided him with a musical reckoning, the same way he intimidated Paul lyrically'.[37]

It was a sign of the times that Phaidon Press's *20th Century Composers* series should include The Beatles in its flashy, post-modernist embrace, but Allan Kozinn's *The Beatles* (1995) proved a genuinely helpful introduction to their work, again eschewing the usual ragbag of anecdote and reportage. Here, the Sixties backdrop is covered only insofar as it provides the context for the group's musical evolution. One might object that the author tends to avoid showing 'the boys' in anything other than a charmed light so that factors relating to misjudgment or failure, public or private, are downplayed whatever their relation to the group's development and eventual fracture. Hence, The Beatles' refusal to attend a reception given by Imelda Marcos—indicating not only their growing sense of superiority and inviolateness but also an increasing unwillingness to tour and resentment at the constant intrusion of an adoring public—is dismissed merely as a scheduling mix-up. The strength and purpose of the book lie in its elucidation of the band's musical efflorescence; the New Yorker's arm's-length viewpoint restores a certain objectivity.

In 1997, the arrival of Allan Moore's *Cambridge Music Handbook* on *The Beatles: Sgt Pepper's Lonely Hearts Club Band* was another benchmark, posing a host of pertinent questions. How could pop or rock music properly 'belong' in this prestigious Cambridge University Press series if its chronicling could only take place within shifting parameters of taste and commerce where each new fad requires a rewrite, a conscious re-evaluation of what has gone before? Perhaps it is a weakness that Moore still feels he has to justify the writing of it, wrapping himself up in defensive sociological flummery when he is actually at his most persuasive and acute in analysing the songs themselves. While he is not the first to treat them with respect (he makes conscientious reference to Wilfrid Mellers and Ian MacDonald), the detail is new, the focus sharper. Why has he chosen *Sgt Pepper*? Because that LP is still usually represented as the pinnacle of the group's achievement, the definitive 'concept' album in which a more 'classical' form of unity is achieved through the sophisticated—poetic, musical and conceptual—interlinking of tracks. But is this apparent primacy any more than a product of good salesmanship, with Peter Blake's artwork, the elision of one song into the next and the printed-out lyrics combining to trump the claims of rival Beatle album cycles, notably *Revolver* (1966)? In the end, staggering under the weight of all those rotten concept albums of the 1970s, Moore sees *Pepper*'s chief legacy as a sort of 'failed striving for legitimacy', but he shows how it resonates on many other levels. He has his own methodology for identifying particular passages in the absence of the definitive measures of classical music's full score: he uses CD timings instead. Even at this distance he is too beguiled by Lennon's dissembling to admit that 'Lucy in the sky' is an out-and-out LSD song, perhaps overly concerned to document what everyone else has said. Nevertheless, anyone committed to the notion that the death of post-Schoenbergian modernism has opened the floodgates to alternative forms of expression, or that popular song matters *per se*, will want to, indeed have to, get to grips with these arguments.

Combining the forensic skills of the academic researcher, the exhaustive documentary impulse of Lewisohn and the musical insights of Moore and company, Walter Everett, Associate Professor of Music at the University of Michigan, has produced the last word on the musical architecture of Beatle songs. Not that he is as readable or as passionate as some of his predecessors: *The Beatles as Musicians*—the first of its two volumes appeared in 1999—doesn't have one overarching theory to prove and its hype-free scene-setting is fairly basic. Rather, The Beatles are presented as composers/poets/performers fit for theoretical inquiry, with fresh ideas about melody, harmony, counterpoint, rhythm, form and colour. Everett's analyses can be dense and he himself suggests that his ideal reader should have several years of college-level music training. That doesn't render his work useless to the notationally challenged. It just means picking and choosing the bits one understands. Once again, every significant song is covered, only the level of detail is unprecedented, and, on a purely technical level, this must be counted the 'best' study yet published. Previous commentators might be as familiar with the contemporary magazine literature but Everett knows his guitar technique (as well as how to document it), he knows who played what, and he also displays an awareness of the outtakes. Even so, not everyone will respond positively to an approach which arguably sidesteps what makes the music so great in the first place: the way limited, rebellious musicianship leads on to innovation and its own distinctive brand of mastery. When the growth and influence of recording in our own society provide a neat and not necessarily judgmental explanation for the increasing appeal of circular, non-developing structures based on sound (as distinct from the older, intellectual tradition encouraged by the infinite possibilities of notation), is it right to use the methodologies of the one to analyse the other?

In Russell Reising's *Every Sound There Is: The Beatles' Revolver and the transformation of rock and roll* (2002), the Everett problem (naturally, he contributes a chapter) is present again. The fourteen writers range in age from 20 to 60-plus and hail from around the globe, yet several of them seem inclined to keep the discussions in house, refining essentially unoriginal observations into the terminology of their own academic disciplines rather than throwing fresh light on the album's creation and reception history. The book is well-produced, in part a spin-off from the Beatles 2000 conference in Jyväskylä, Finland, but it shows the limitations as well as the strengths of the new, interdisciplinary musicology that embraces elements of literary and sociological theory and issues of identity, subjectivity and gender.

Generally speaking, the popular music studies fraternity continues to shy away from discovering what makes an oeuvre intrinsically great, insisting that we should give primacy to the listening context through which it has been perceived and its meaning socially constructed. What analysis there is tends to canonise by complexity, but at least the most prestigious institutions are now in on the act. At Yale, Mark Stuart Spicer's study of 'British pop-rock in the post-Beatles era' includes numerous transcriptions and graphic analyses. He identifies the 'intertextual' tendencies in the band's own work as the source of compositional forms made possible by the rapid advances in recording technology since 1966. At Princeton, Virgil Edwin Moorefield looks at the changing role of the producer in pop, with special reference to George Martin and Phil Spector. 'From the illusion of reality to the reality of illusion' includes an original composition designed to throw further light on the issues discussed in the text. Here again, the author sees technology and artistic creation as increasingly inter-dependent in our culture. Whether it's his supposed public or private persona that is being evoked, John Lennon himself is just as often used as an archetype in the elucidation of some extra-musical socio-logical theory.

Back in the mainstream, the official line is summed up by *The Beat-les Anthology* (2000), a belated literary offshoot from those mid-Nineties CD sets. Here, the voices of John, Paul, George and Ringo come alive again and, while this lavish, magical mystery tour of a book offers little that's genuinely new, it does, to an unprecedented degree, draw the reader into The Beatles' insular world. For more than a decade, they really were a band of brothers and, like any broth-ers, they argued and fell out. Until his death, Lennon remained deeply ambivalent about The Beatles and that ambivalence is, of ne-cessity, reflected in *The Beatles Anthology*. One can't help but wonder how time and the new-found happiness with Yoko and Sean might have led him to remember things differently.

There are more and more books about Lennon himself. Too easily overlooked, John Robertson's *The Art and Music of John Lennon* (1990) is another title organised in terms of session dates, while seeking also to relate music-making to personal development. In rejecting both the of-ficial Ray Coleman/Yoko Ono version of Lennon's life and the destruc-tive revisionism of Albert Goldman, Robertson never forgets that the music ought to come first. He offers a corrective to the notion that Lennon's Lost Weekend period was in any sense creatively fallow (*Walls and Bridges* is highly rated) and he is at pains to show that Lennon was working during the supposed house husband years. The final spasm of creativity in 1980, presented here as the sweeping-up of ideas developed over the years, is itself part of the myth, whether self-created or media-driven. In contrast, Paul Du Noyer's *We All Shine On* (1997), both detailed and dispassionate, breaks little new ground.

Jon Wiener, who documented Lennon's battles with the US govern-ment in his illuminating study *Come Together: John Lennon in his time* (1985), was finally able to tell the full story of what he calls 'a kind of rock 'n' roll Watergate'[38] in *Gimme Some Truth: the John Lennon FBI files* (1999). It reproduces a hundred of 'the most significant' pages ob-tained by the author after his fourteen-year struggle under the terms of President Carter's strengthened Freedom of Information Act, a fight he took all the way to the Supreme Court.

There can be no Beatles reunion now, but rumours continue to pour forth, often in response to purely local conditions. The bizarre allegation that 'Hey Jude' might be an antisemitic reference to Bob Dylan could only arise from the controversy surrounding the public use of the word 'Jew' in today's Germany.[39] McCartney remains as anxious as ever that his part in the creative miracle of The Beatles be properly documented, hence the perverse row over label credits that surfaced again with his latest live album. This lists nineteen Beatles songs as written by 'Paul McCartney and John Lennon', reversing the Lennon–McCartney namecheck ingrained in the collective unconscious. More productively, it was agreed to release an ostensibly de-Spectorized version of *Let It Be*. It is not the intention of *The Lennon Companion* to denigrate McCartney's achievement:

> Melodic consonance versus harmonic dissonance; energetic optimism in uneasy cahoots with sedentary sarcasm; [these are] the archetypal conflicts which lent the Lennon–McCartney partnership both its musical distinction and its mythic edge. . . .[40]

George Harrison's death prompted new encomiums:

> Life seemed to speed up as The Beatles turned pop music on its head, dragging it almost overnight from a teenage diversion into an art form, while never seeming to take themselves seriously. They were gods and fellow mortals at the same time, dazzlingly skilful and doggedly self-deprecating: a very British combination. The Beatles made us feel better about ourselves in a way that went beyond the music. They brought the country to life, liberating a generation weaned on the smothering burdens of war and a collapsing empire. They carved through barriers, uniting north and south, and upper, middle and working classes. The Beatles could not be condescended to, dismissed or kept in place. They were too powerful a force and as hit followed hit the momentum increased to the point where everyone could share in their success without feeling threatened by it.[41]

While Michael Palin's words are resonant, Hanif Kureishi's earlier evaluation remains unusual in its genuine warmth towards the post-Beatle Lennon:

> In the Seventies, the liberation tendencies bifurcated into two streams— hedonism, self-aggrandisement and decay, represented by the Stones;

and serious politics and self-exploration, represented by Lennon. He continued to be actively involved in the obsessions of the time, both as initiate and leader, which is what makes him the central cultural figure of the age, as Brecht was, for instance, in the Thirties and Forties. But to continue to develop, Lennon had to leave the containment of The Beatles and move to America. He had to break up The Beatles to continue to lead an interesting life.[42]

Elizabeth Thomson and David Gutman
London, April 2003

Notes

1. The newly extended airport was renamed Liverpool John Lennon Airport in a ceremony performed by the Queen, with Yoko Ono in attendance, on 25 July 2002.
2. The final shortlist included William Shakespeare, Elizabeth I, Isambard Kingdom Brunel, Diana, Princess of Wales and Winston Churchill, eventually voted Greatest Briton.
3. quoted in Robert Sandall, 'All their yesterdays, today and tomorrow', *Sunday Times* (15 January 1995)
4. Simon Frith, 'Towards an aesthetic of popular music' in *Music and Society*, eds. Richard Leppert and Susan McClary (Cambridge: Cambridge University Press, 1987) pp. 139–40
5. Norman Lebrecht, 'Tomorrow, the world', *Evening Standard* (13 November 2002)
6. In a celebrated incident on BBC TV's *Late Show*, the playwright Sir David Hare had warned against ranking Bob Dylan alongside the poet Keats.
7. quoted in Ann McCutchan, *The Muse that Sings* (New York: Oxford University Press, 1999) p. 131
8. Yoko Ono interviewed by Michael Bracewell in 'The Thursday Interview: Creativity in a cold climate', *Independent* (21 March 2002) p. 7
9. Anthony Elliott, *The Mourning of John Lennon* (Berkeley: University of California Press, 1999) p. 1
10. ibid., p. 1
11. ibid., p. 9
12. ibid., p. 11
13. Kurt Cobain, *Journals* (London: Viking, 2002)
14. wording on a sign commemorating the original Cavern in Mathew Street
15. Sunao Ashihara, *Beatles junrei* (Tokyo: Bungei-shunju, 1995)
16. Rûytarô Monobe, *John Lennon—to Rhyûnosuke* (Tokyo: Kindai-Bungeisha, 1994)
17. *see* Richard Lloyd Parry, 'Fab in the Far East', *Independent* (21 February

1999). Such devotion is all the more remarkable given that The Beatles visited Japan only once—in 1966. Their performance at Nippon Budokan, the Hall of Martial Arts built for the Tokyo Olympics two years earlier, was arranged only after delicate negotiations between the British Embassy and a Japanese government reluctant to sanction anything so frivolous. The Beatles' MBEs helped swing the case.

18. quoted in Lawrence Zion, 'The impact of The Beatles on pop music in Australia: 1963–66', *Popular Music* VI/3 (October 1987) p. 291

19. *see* Philip Norman, 'And the beat goes off', *Sunday Times* Magazine (16 February 2003) p. 32

20. *see* Robert Sandall, 'The day the music industry died', *Sunday Times* Magazine (16 February 2003) p. 26. Sandall comments: 'The Beatles' hits package, *1*, is thought to have sold more than 40m worldwide; an estimated half of those were bootlegs'.

21. quoted in Mark Hertsgaard, 'Letting it be', *New Yorker* (24 January 1994) p. 78

22. Peter Doggett, 'The lost Beatles albums', *Record Collector* (March 2003) pp. 20–33

23. George Small, Rick Nielsen, Tom Petersson and Bun E Carlos

24. Pauline Sutcliffe, *Stuart Sutcliffe: The Beatles' shadow and his lonely hearts club band* (London: Sidgwick & Jackson, 2001) p. 4

25. Albert Goldman, *The Lives of John Lennon* (London: Bantam Press, 1988) p. 13

26. ibid., p. 15

27. quoted in Barry Miles, *Paul McCartney: Many years from now* (London: Secker & Warburg, 1997) p. 596

28. Walter Everett, *The Beatles as Musicians: The Quarry Men through Rubber Soul* (New York: Oxford University Press, 2001) p. 343

29. George Melly, 'Derek Taylor: escape from the rock', *Guardian* (10 September 1997) p.15

30. Tim Riley, *Tell Me Why—The Beatles: album by album, song by song, the Sixties and after* (Cambridge, MA: Da Capo Press, 2002) p. 395

31. ibid., p. 394

32. ibid., p. 414

33. Ian MacDonald, *Revolution in the Head* (London: Fourth Estate, 1994) p. 168

34. ibid., pp. 209–10

35. Ian MacDonald, 'The Beatles' in *The New Grove Dictionary of Music and Musicians* (London: Macmillan, 2000) Volume 3, p. 23

36. Mark Hertsgaard, *A Day in the Life: the music and artistry of the Beatles* (New York: Delacorte Press, 1995) p. 317

37. Tim Riley, op. cit., p. 368

38. Jon Wiener, *Gimme Some Truth: the John Lennon FBI files* (Berkeley: University of California Press, 1999) p. 9

39. *see* Melvin J Lasky, 'Babel', *Prospect* (April 1997) p. 72

40. Robert Sandall, 'All their yesterdays, today and tomorrow', op. cit.

41. Michael Palin, 'George Harrison—no CD can play back his kindness, his generosity or his warmth', *Independent on Sunday* (2 December 2001) p. 21

42. Hanif Kureishi, 'Boys like us', *Weekend Guardian* (2–3 November 1991) p. 6

Selective bibliography

Volume numbers are given in roman numerals, issue numbers in arabic. A plus sign following a page number indicates that the article continues on unspecified pages later in the volume or issue. Items marked with an asterisk are represented in this book.

*Amis, Martin, 'Lennon—from Beatle to househusband', *The Observer* (14 December 1980) p. 25

Appleyard, Brian, 'An ordinary woman made myth', *Independent* (29 March 1990) p. 18

Aquila, Richard, 'Why we cried: John Lennon and American culture', *Popular Culture and Society* X/1 (1985) pp. 33–42

Ashton, John, 'Hearing Lennon's secret messages', *New Society* (18/25 December 1980) pp. 550–1

Attie, Jeanie and Brown, Josh, 'John Lennon', *Radical History Review* 24 (Fall 1980) pp. 188–90

Bacon, David and Maslov, Norman, *The Beatles' England* (London: Columbus Books, 1982)

Baird, Julia, *John Lennon, My Brother* (New York: Henry Holt, 1988)

Baker, Glenn A., *The Beatles Down Under: the 1964 Australia & New Zealand tour* (Glebe: Wild & Woolley, 1982; reprinted: Ann Arbor: Pierian Press, 1985)

Barber-Kersovan, Alenka, 'Tradition and acculturation as polarities of Slovenian popular music' in *Popular Music Perspectives: Papers from the First International Conference on Popular Music Research, Amsterdam,* June 1981 (Göteborg & Exeter: IASPM, 1982) pp. 174–89

Beatles, The, *The Beatles Anthology* (London: Cassell, 2000)

Beatty, John, 'Eleanor Rigby: structure in the arts', *Centerpoint* IV/2 (1980) pp. 14–35

*Beglov, M., 'On John Lennon's death', *Sotsialisticheskaya industria* (12 December 1980) p. 3

Beller-McKenna, Daniel, 'Beatle-John's "alter ego"', *Music and Letters* LXXX/2 (May 1999) pp. 254–68

Bellman, Jonathan, 'Indian resonances in the British invasion, 1965–1968', *Journal of Musicology* XV/1 (Winter 1997) pp. 116–36

*Berio, Luciano, 'Commenti al rock', *Nuova Revista Musicale Italiana* I (May/June 1967) pp. 125–35

Bernstein, Leonard, 'Introduction' to *The Beatles* by Geoffrey Stokes *(see below)*

Best, Pete and Doncaster, Patrick, *Beatle! The Pete Best Story* (London: Plexus, 1985)

Bird, Donald Allport, Holder, Stephen P., and Sears, Diane, 'Walrus is Greek for corpse: rumour and the death of Paul McCartney', *Journal of Popular Culture* X (1976) pp. 110–21

*Blackburn, Robin and Ali, Tariq, 'Power to the people', *Red Mole* (8–22 March 1971) pp. 7–10

Bowen, Phil, ed. *Things We Said Today* [poems about The Beatles] (Devon: Stride Publications, 1995)

Bracewell, Michael, 'Give Yoko a chance', *The Guardian* (20 January 1996) pp. 12–16

Bracewell, Michael, 'Imagine Yoko's own story', *Independent on Sunday* (12 December 1999) Review, pp. 4–5, 7

Bracewell, Michael, 'Yoko Ono: "I'm used to people not liking my stuff"', *Independent* (21 March 2002) Review, p. 7

Braun, Michael, *Love Me Do: The Beatles' progress* (London: Penguin, 1964)

Brocken, Michael, *Some Other Guys! Some Theories about Signification: Beatles cover versions* (Liverpool: Institute of Popular Music, 1996); reprinted in *Popular Music and Society* XX/4 (1996) pp. 5–40

Bromell, Nicholas Knowles, *Tomorrow Never Knows: rock and psychedelics in the 1960s* (Chicago: University of Chicago Press, 2000)

Brown, Peter and Gaines, Steven, *The Love You Make* (London: Macmillan, 1983)

Buckley, William F., 'The Beatles and the guru', *National Review* (12 March 1968) p. 259

Buckley, William, F., 'Count me out', *National Review* (19 November 1990) p. 62

Burchill, Julie, 'Frontlines', *Time Out* (14 November 1985) pp. 11–13

Burn, Gordon, 'All my loving: when the hits hit the fan', *Independent* (17 August 1991) Weekend, p. 23

Campbell, Colin and Murphy, Allan, *Things We Said Today: the complete lyrics and concordance to The Beatles' songs 1962–1970* (Ann Arbor: Pierian Press, 1980)

Carr, Roy and Tyler, Tony, *The Beatles: an illustrated record* (London: New English Library, 1975)

Castleman, Harry and Podrazik, Walter, *All Together Now: the first complete Beatles discography* (Ann Arbor: Pierian Press, 1975)

Castleman, Harry and Podrazik, Walter, *The Beatles Again* (Ann Arbor: Pierian Press, 1977)

Castleman, Harry and Podrazik, Walter, *The End of The Beatles?* (Ann Arbor: Pierian Press, 1985)

Chester, Andrew, 'For a rock aesthetic', *New Left Review* 59 (1970) pp. 83–95

*Christgau, Robert, 'Symbolic comrades', *Village Voice* (14–20 January 1981) pp. 31–2

*Clayton, Peter, 'Revolver', *Gramophone* (October 1966) p. 233

Clayton, Peter, 'Rubber Soul', *Gramophone* (February 1966) p. 414

*Cleave, Maureen, 'How does a Beatle live? John Lennon lives like this', *Evening Standard* (4 March 1966) p. 10

Cleave, Maureen, 'Lennon's bitter time of truth', *Evening Standard* (31 December 1986) p. 17

Cleave, Maureen, 'Old Beatles—a study in paradox', *The New York Times Magazine* (3 July 1966) pp. 10–11, 30–2

Cockrell, William Dale, 'The Beatles's *Sgt Pepper's Lonely Hearts Club Band* and *Abbey Road* Side Two: Unification within the rock recording' (diss. University of Illinois, 1973)

Coffin, Patricia, 'Art beat of the 60s: The Beatles', *Look* XXXII (9 January 1968) pp. 32–41

Coleman, Ray, *Brian Epstein: the man who made The Beatles* (London: Viking, 1989)

Coleman, Ray, *John Winston Lennon 1940–1966* (London: Sidgwick & Jackson, 1984)

Coleman, Ray, *John Ono Lennon 1967–1980* (London: Sidgwick & Jackson, 1984)

Comden, Betty, 'Letter from Liverpool . . . almost', *Vogue* [US] 146 (December 1965) pp. 120, 124+

Compton, T., 'McCartney or Lennon? Beatle myths and the composing of the Lennon–McCartney songs', *Journal of Popular Culture* XXII/2 (1998) pp. 99–131

Connolly, Ray, *John Lennon 1940–1980* (London: Fontana, 1981)

Conrad, Peter, 'Starfucker', *Quarto* (January/February 1981) p. 3

*Cooke, Deryck, 'The Lennon–McCartney songs', *The Listener* (1 February 1968) pp. 157–8; reprinted in *Vindications* (London: Faber, 1982) pp. 196–200

Cott, Jonathan, 'The Rolling Stone interview', *Rolling Stone* (23 November 1968) pp. 11–13+

Cott, Jonathan, 'She takes a trip around the world: A Hard Day's Night', *Ramparts* (October 1965)

Cott, Jonathan and Doudna, Christine, eds, *The Ballad of John & Yoko* (London: Michael Joseph, 1982)

*Coward, Noel, *The Noel Coward Diaries* ed. Graham Payn and Sheridan Morley (London: Weidenfeld & Nicolson, 1982)

Critchley, Julian, 'After the Beatles—an interest in all things British', *The Times* (21 November 1969) p. 11

*Crossman, Richard, *The Diaries of a Cabinet Minister Vol 3* ed. Janet Morgan (London: Hamish Hamilton & Jonathan Cape, 1977)

*Dallos, Robert E., 'Beatles strike serious note in press talk', *The New York Times* (23 August 1966) p. 30

Davies, Evan, 'Psychological characteristics of Beatle mania' *Journal of Historical Ideas* XXX/2 (1969) pp. 273–80

Davies, Hunter, *The Beatles* (London: Heinemann, 1968; revised edition: London: Jonathan Cape, 1985)

Davies, Russell, 'Lennon's confessions', *London Review of Books* (5–18 February 1981) pp. 17–18

Davies, Russell, 'Life with Aunt Mimi', *The Observer* (8 July 1984) p. 21

Davies, Russell, 'The onset of Ono', *The Observer* (4 November 1984) p. 25

Davis, Edward, ed., *The Beatles Book* (New York: Cowles Education Corporation, 1967)

DeCurtis, Anthony, 'Imagine remembered and remastered', *Rolling Stone* (30 March 2000) pp. 19, 76

Dhondy, Farrukh, 'An open letter to The Beatles', *The Listener* (7 September 1967) pp. 298–9

Difford, Chris, 'To be as good', *Rolling Stone* (16 February 1984) pp. 59–61

Dilello, Richard, *The Longest Cocktail Party* (London: Charisma Books, 1973; reprinted: Ann Arbor: Pierian Press, 1983)

Doggett, Peter, 'The lost Beatles albums', *Record Collector* (March 2003) pp. 20–33

Drake, David, 'Beatlefax and Beatle fans', *New Society* (30 September 1982) pp. 533–4

Du Noyer, Paul, *We All Shine On* (London: Carlton, 1997)

Du Noyer, Paul, 'John (Winston) Lennon' in *The New Grove Dictionary of Music and Musicians* (London: Macmillan, 2000)

Eagleton, Terry, 'New bearings: The Beatles', *Blackfriars* XLV/4 (1964) pp. 175–8

Edgar, David, 'Why Aid came Live', *Marxism Today* (September 1985) pp. 26–30

Eger, Joseph, 'Ives and Beatles!', *Music Journal* XXVI (September 1968) pp. 46, 70–1

Eisen, Jonathan, ed. *The Age of Rock: sounds of the American cultural revolution* (New York: Vintage, 1969)

Elliott, Anthony, *The Mourning of John Lennon* (Berkeley: University of California Press, 1999)

Epstein, Brian, *A Cellarful of Noise* (London: Souvenir Press, 1964; revised edition: Ann Arbor: Pierian Press, 1984)

Evans, Mike, *The Art of the Beatles* (London: Anthony Blond/Merseyside County Council, 1984)

Evans, Mike, ed. *The Beatles: literary anthology* (London: Plexus Publishing, 2003)

Evans, Mike and Jones, Ron, *In the Footsteps of The Beatles* (Liverpool: Merseyside County Council, 1981)

Everett, Walter, 'The Beatles as composers: the genesis of *Abbey Road, Side Two*' in *Concert Music, Rock, and Jazz Since 1945*, ed. Elizabeth West Marvin and Richard Herrmann (Rochester, NY: University of Rochester Press, 1995)

Everett, Walter, *The Beatles as Musicians: Revolver through the Anthology* (Oxford: Oxford University Press, 1999)

Everett, Walter, *The Beatles as Musicians: The Quarry Men through Rubber Soul* (Oxford: Oxford University Press, 2001)

Everett, Walter, 'Fantastic remembrance in John Lennon's Strawberry Fields Forever and Julia', *Musical Quarterly* LXXII/3 (1986) pp. 360–93

Farrell, Gerry, 'Reflecting surfaces: the use of elements from Indian music in popular music and jazz', *Popular Music* VII/2 (May 1988), pp. 189–205

Fawcett, Anthony, *John Lennon: One Day at a Time* (London: New English Library, 1977)

Feofanow, Oleg, 'Musik des Aufruhrs (VII): Zur Entstehung und zu Entwicklungstendenzen in der Rockmusik', *Musikforum* XXVIII/1 (1983) pp. 24–30

Fitzgerald, Jon, 'Lennon–McCartney and the middle eight', *Popular Music and Society* XX/4 (1996) pp. 41–52; reprinted in *The Beatles, Popular Music and Society: a thousand voices*, ed. Ian Inglis (New York: St. Martin's Press, 1999)

Fogo, Fred, 'Come together, over me: generational memory and social drama in the death of John Lennon' (diss. University of Utah, 1990)

Fogo, Fred, *I Read the News Today: the social drama of John Lennon's death* (London: Rowman & Littlefield, 1994)

Freed, Richard D., 'Beatles stump music experts looking for key to Beatlemania', *The New York Times* (13 August 1965) p. 17

French, Philip, 'Richard Lester', *Movie* 14 (Autumn 1965) pp. 5–11

Fricke, David, 'John Lennon's unheard masterpieces', *Rolling Stone* (10 December 1998) pp. 93–4, 137

Fricke, David and Ressner, Jeffrey, 'Imaginary John Lennon: the true story behind Albert Goldman's character assassination of John Lennon', *Rolling Stone* (20 October 1988) pp. 42–5, 93

Friede, Goldie, Titone, Robin and Weiner, Sue, *The Beatles A–Z* (New York: Methuen, 1980)

Frith, Simon, 'About a lucky band who made the grade', *New Society* (26 March 1981) pp. 554–5

Frith, Simon, 'John Lennon', *Marxism Today* (January 1981) pp. 23–5

*Frost, David, 'John's gospel', *The Spectator* (12 August 1966) pp. 12–13

Frontani, Michael Roy, 'The Beatles as sign: their transformation from moptops to Gramscian intellectuals' (diss. University of Ohio, 1998)

Gabree, John, 'The Beatles in perspective', *Down Beat* 34 (16 November 1967) pp. 20–2

*Gerson, Ben, 'Together again: Walls and Bridges', *Rolling Stone* (21 November 1974) pp. 44–6

Gillett, Charlie, *The Sound of the City* (London: Souvenir Press, 1970; revised edition, 1983)

Giuliano, Geoffrey, *The Beatles: a celebration* (London: Sidgwick & Jackson, 1986)

Gloag, Kenneth, 'All you need is theory', *Music and Letters* LXXIX/4 (November 1998) pp. 577–83

Goldman, Albert, 'The Beatles' Abbey Road', *Life* (1969); reprinted in *Freakshow* (New York: Atheneum, 1971) pp. 130–2

Goldman, Albert, 'The Beatles decide to Let It Be—apart', *Life* (24 April 1970) pp. 38–9; reprinted in *Freakshow* (New York: Atheneum, 1971) pp. 154–6

Goldman, Albert, 'The emergence of rock', *New American Review* 3 (1968); reprinted in *Freakshow* (New York: Atheneum, 1971) pp. 3–24

Goldman, Albert, 'Future past—an interview with John Lennon', *Charlie* (June 1971) pp. 24–7 and (July 1971) pp. 27–8, 58

Goldman, Albert, *The Lives of John Lennon* (London: Bantam Press, 1988)

Gopnik, Adam, 'Carry that weight', *New Yorker* (1 May 1995) pp. 80–5

Gottfridsson, Hans Olof, *The Beatles from Cavern to Star-Club: the illustrated chronicle, discography and price guide 1957–1962* (Stockholm: Premium Publishing, 1997)

Graustark, Barbara, 'The real John Lennon', *Newsweek* (29 September 1980) pp. 54–5

Grossel, Heinrich, 'Die Beat-Musik: Versuch einer Analyse', *Neue Sammlung* VII (1967) pp. 240–53

Grossel, Heinrich, 'Die Beat-Musik: Versuch einer Analyse', (version) *Das Orchester* XVII (December 1969) pp. 526–30

Gruen, Bob, *Listen to These Pictures: photographs of John Lennon* (London: Sidgwick & Jackson, 1985)

Gutman, David, 'John Winston Lennon/John Ono Lennon', *Brio* XXI/2 (Autumn/Winter 1984) pp. 69–70

Hames, A. and Inglis, I., 'And I will lose my mind: images of mental illness in the songs of The Beatles', *International Review of Aesthetics and Society* XXX (December 1999) pp. 173–88

Hamill, Pete, 'John Lennon: long night's journey into day', *Rolling Stone* (5 June 1975) pp. 46–8+

Harding, Jeremy, 'The groom stripped bare by his suitor', *London Review of Books* (4 January 2001) pp. 23–6

Harrison, George, *I, Me, Mine* (London: W. H. Allen, 1981)

Harry, Bill, *The Beatles 3: Paperback Writers* (London: Virgin, 1984)

Harry, Bill, *The Beatles 4: Beatlemania* (London: Virgin, 1984)

Harry, Bill, *The Beatles 5: Beatles for Sale* (London: Virgin, 1985)

Harry, Bill, *The Book of Lennon* (London: Aurum Press, 1984)

Harry, Bill, *The John Lennon Encyclopedia* (London: Virgin, 2000)

Harry, Bill, *Mersey Beat: The Beginnings of The Beatles* (London: Omnibus Press, 1977)

Harry, Bill, *The Ultimate Beatles Encyclopedia* (London: Virgin, 1992)

Heinonen, Yrjö, 'From experience to an idea: from an idea to music. A general model of the compositional process and its application to the songwriting and recording process of The Beatles' (diss. University of Jyväskylä, 1995)

Heinonen, Yrjö, *et al.*, *Beatlestudies 1: songwriting, recording and style change* (Jyväskylä: University of Jyväskylä, Department of Music, 1998)

Heinonen, Yrjö, *et al.*, *Beatlestudies 2: history, identity, authenticity* (Jyväskylä: University of Jyväskylä, Department of Music, 2000)

Heinonen, Yrjö, *et al.*, *Beatlestudies 3: proceedings of the Beatles 2000 Conference* (Jyväskylä: University of Jyväskylä, Department of Music, 2001)

Henke, James, *Lennon Legend* (London: Weidenfeld & Nicolson, 2003)

Hertsgaard, Mark, 'Letting it be', *New Yorker* (24 January 1994) pp. 78–87

Hertsgaard, Mark, *A Day in the Life: the music and artistry of The Beatles* (New York: Delacorte Press, 1995)

Herzogenrath, Wulf and Hansen, Dorothee, eds. *John Lennon: drawings, performances, films* [exhibition catalogue] (Bremen: Cantz Verlag, 1995)

Hewison, Robert, *Too Much: Art and Society in the Sixties* (London: Methuen, 1986)

Hoffmann, Dezo, *The Beatles Conquer America* (London: Virgin, 1984)

Hoffmann, Dezo, *John Lennon* (London: Columbus Books, 1985)

Hoffmann, Dezo, *With The Beatles: the historic photographs . . .* (London: Omnibus Press, 1982)

Hopkins, Jerry, *Yoko Ono* (London: Sidgwick & Jackson, 1987)

Horwitz, Margaret McBride, 'Persona and spectacle in the films of Elvis Presley and The Beatles' (diss. University of California–Los Angeles, 1990)

Howlett, Kevin, *The Beatles at the BBC: the radio years, 1962–70* (London: BBC Books, 1996)

Howlett, Kevin, *The Beatles at The Beeb: the story of their radio career, 1962–1965* (London: BBC, 1982; reprinted: Ann Arbor: Pierian Press, 1983)

Inglis, Ian, 'The Beatles are coming: conjecture and conviction in the myth of Kennedy, America and The Beatles', *Popular Music and Society* XXIV (Summer 2000) pp. 93–108

Inglis, Ian, 'Nothing you can see that isn't shown: the album covers of The Beatles', *Popular Music* XX/1 (January 2001) pp. 83–97

Inglis, Ian, 'Variations on a theme: the love songs of The Beatles', *International Review of Aesthetics and Society* XXVIII (June 1997) pp. 37–62

Inglis, Ian, ed. *The Beatles, Popular Music and Society: a thousand voices* (New York: St. Martin's Press, 1999)

Jackson, Jeffrey M. and Padgett, Vernon R., 'With a little help from my friend: social loafing and the Lennon–McCartney songs', *Personality and Social Psychology Bulletin* VIII/4 (December 1982) pp. 672–7

James, Clive, 'A Cavern in Arcadia', *Creem* XVII (October 1972) pp. 24–9, 44

*Johnson, Paul, 'The menace of Beatlism', *New Statesman* (28 February 1964) pp. 326–7

Jones, Dylan, 'I'll play that again', *The Sunday Times* (18 October 1998) 11, pp. 2–3

Jovanovic, Rob, *John Lennon Imagine* (New York: Schirmer Books, 2003)

*Kael, Pauline, 'Metamorphosis of The Beatles', *The New Yorker* (30 November 1968); reprinted in *Going Steady* (London: Maurice Temple Smith, 1970) pp. 187–92

Keller, Hans, 'Music ghettos', *The Listener* (7 February 1974) p. 183

Kelly, Michael Bryan, *The Beatle Myth: the British invasion of American popular music, 1956–1969* (London: McFarland, 1991)

Kesey, Ken, 'Now we know how many holes it takes to fill the Albert Hall'; reprinted in *Demon Box* (New York: Viking, 1986)

Kettle, Martin, 'MI5 helped FBI spy on Lennon', *The Guardian* (27 September 1997)

Kohl, P. R., 'A splendid time is guaranteed for all: The Beatles as agents of carnival', *Popular Music and Society* XX/4 (1996) pp. 81–8

Kopkind, Andrew, 'I wanna hold your head: John Lennon after the fall', *Ramparts* (April 1971) pp. 19, 55–6

Kozinn, Allan, *The Beatles* (London: Phaidon, 1995)

Kozinn, Allan, 'Widow of Lennon, guardian of myth', *The New York Times* (15 November 1998) 2, pp. 19–20

Kureishi, Hanif, 'Boys like us', *The Guardian* (2 November 1991) supplement, pp. 4–7

*Lahr, John, 'The Beatles', *New Republic* (2 December 1981) pp. 19–23; reprinted in *Automatic Vaudeville* (London: Heinemann, 1984) pp. 100–10

Lahr, John, 'Introduction' to *Up Against It* by Joe Orton (London: Methuen, 1979) pp. v–xvi

*Larkin, Philip, 'Fighting the fab', *The Observer* (9 October 1983)

Leigh, Spencer, *Let's Go Down the Cavern: the story of Liverpool's Merseybeat* (London: Vermilion, 1984)

Lennon, Cynthia, *A Twist of Lennon* (London: Star, 1978)

Lennon, John, 'Being a short diversion on the dubious origins of Beatles', *Merseybeat* 1/1 (6–20 July 1961) p. 1; reprinted in *Mersey Beat: The Beginnings of The Beatles* by Bill Harry *(see above)*

Lennon, John, 'The Goon Show scripts', *The New York Times Book Review* (30 September 1973) p. 6

Lennon, John, *In His Own Write* (London: Jonathan Cape, 1964); reprinted in *The Penguin John Lennon* (London: Penguin, 1965)

Lennon, John, *Skywriting by Word of Mouth* (London: Pan, 1986)

Lennon, John, *A Spaniard in the Works* (London: Jonathan Cape, 1965); reprinted in *The Penguin John Lennon* (London: Penguin, 1965)

*Levin, Bernard, *The Pendulum Years—Britain and The Sixties* (London: Jonathan Cape, 1971)

Lewisohn, Mark, *The Complete Beatles Chronicle* (London: Pyramid Books, 1992)

Lewisohn, Mark, *The Complete Beatles Recording Sessions: the official story of the Abbey Road years* (London: Hamlyn, 1988)

Lewisohn, Mark, *The Beatles—25 Years in the Life* (London: Sidgwick & Jackson, 1987)

Lisovsky, V., 'What we think and talk about: who is your idol?', *Izvestia* (17 January 1982) p. 3

*Lopukhin, A. and Pakhomov, V., 'Five shots end the life of the famous singer and composer', *Komsomolskaya pravda* (12 December 1980) p. 3

MacDonald, Ian, *Revolution in the Head: The Beatles' records and the Sixties* (London: Fourth Estate, 1994; revised edition, London: Pimlico, 1998)

MacDonald, Ian, 'The Beatles' in *The New Grove Dictionary of Music and Musicians* (London: Macmillan, 2000)

MacDonald, Ian, *The People's Music* (London: Pimlico, 2003)

*Mann, William, 'The Beatles revive hopes of progress in pop music', *The Times* (29 May 1967) p. 9

*Mann, William, 'The new Beatles album', *The Times* (22 November 1968) p. 9

*Mann, William, 'Strong as ever', *The Times* (8 May 1970) p. 9

*Mann, William, 'Those inventive Beatles', *The Times* (5 December 1969) p. 7

*Marowitz, Charles, 'The Beatles' home movie', *Village Voice* (4 January 1968) p. 23

Martin, Bernice, 'Not Marx but Lennon', *Encounter* LVI (June 1981) pp. 49–51

Martin, George, *All You Need is Ears* (London: Macmillan, 1979)

Martin, George with Pearson, William, *Summer of Love: the making of Sgt Pepper* (London: Macmillan, 1994)

*Martynova, A., 'A fairy tale about a present-day Cinderella', *Sovetskaya Kultura* (3 December 1968)

Marwick, Arthur, *The Sixties* (Oxford: Oxford University Press, 1998)

Masters, Brian, *The Swinging Sixties* (London: Constable, 1985)

McCabe, Peter, and Schonfeld, Robert D., *Apple to the Core: the unmaking of The Beatles* (London: Sphere, 1973)

McKeen, William, *The Beatles: a bio-bibliography* (New York: Greenwood, 1989)

McKinney, Devin, *Magic Circles: The Beatles in Dream and History* (Cambridge, MA: Harvard University Press, 2003)

Mehnert, Klaus, *The Twilight of the Young* (London: Secker & Warburg, 1978)

Mellers, Wilfrid, *Caliban Reborn: renewal in twentieth-century music* (London: Gollancz, 1968)

*Mellers, Wilfrid, 'Imagine', *Music & Musicians* (January 1972) pp. 30–2

*Mellers, Wilfrid, 'Infantilism', *New Statesman* (27 October 1972) pp. 614–15

Mellers, Wilfrid, *Twilight of the Gods: The Beatles in retrospect* (London: Faber, 1973)

*Melly, George, 'John Lennon', *Punch* (17 December 1980) p. 1130

Melly, George, *Revolt into Style* (London: Allen Lane, 1970)

Mendl-Schrama, Heleen, 'Schubert en de Beatles, wenen en Liverpool', *Mens en Melodie* XXXIX (November 1984) pp. 498–501

Merle, Pierre, *John Lennon, la ballade inachevée* (Paris: Archipel, 2000)

Middleton, Richard and Muncie, John, 'Countercultural style: the case of music', in *Popular Culture* (Open University, Block 5, Unit 20, 1981) pp. 77–85

Miles, Barry, *Paul McCartney: many years from now* (London: Secker & Warburg, 1997)

Miles, Barry, *The Beatles: a diary—an intimate day by day history* (London: Omnibus, 1998)

*Mitchell, Adrian, 'Beatles', *The Listener* (3 October 1968) p. 447

Moore, Allan F., 'Authenticity as authentication', *Popular Music* XXI/2 (May 2002) pp. 209–23

Moore, Allan F., *The Beatles: Sgt Pepper's Lonely Hearts Club Band* (Cambridge: Cambridge University Press, 1997)

Moorefield, Virgil Edwin, 'From the illusion of reality to the reality of illusion: the changing role of the producer in the pop recording studio' (diss. Princeton University, 2001)

Morris, Jan, 'The monarchs of the Beatle empire', *Saturday Evening Post* (27 August 1966) pp. 23–6

Morrison, Blake, 'The sound of the Sixties', *Times Literary Supplement* (15 May 1981) pp. 547–8

Mudge, Roberta Ann, 'Liszt, Chopin, Wordsworth and The Beatles', *Music Journal* XXIX (April 1971) pp. 35–6

Munn, Michael, *All Our Loving: a Beatles fan's memoirs* (London: Robson, 1999)

Narducy, Raymond Don, 'The films of The Beatles: a study in star images' (diss. Northwestern University, 1981)

Neaverson, Bob, *The Beatles Movies* (London: Cassell, 1997)

Neises, Charles P., *The Beatles Reader* (Ann Arbor: Pierian Press, 1984)

Norman, Philip, 'Life without Lennon', *The Sunday Times* (3 May 1981) p. 13

Norman, Philip, *Shout! The true story of The Beatles* (London: Hamish Hamilton, 1981)

O'Dell, Denis with Neaverson, Bob, *At the Apple's Core: The Beatles from the inside* (London: Peter Owen, 2002)

O'Grady, Terence J., 'The ballad style in the early music of The Beatles', *College Music Symposium* XIX/1 (1979) pp. 221–9

O'Grady, Terence J., *The Beatles: a musical evolution* (Boston: Twayne, 1983)

O'Grady, Terence J., 'The music of The Beatles from 1962 to Sgt Pepper's Lonely Hearts Club Band' (diss. University of Wisconsin, 1975)

O'Grady, Terence J., 'Rubber Soul and the social dance tradition', *Ethnomusicology* XXIII/1 (January 1979) pp. 87–94

Okun, Milton, music ed., *The Compleat Beatles* (2 vols) (London: Omnibus Press, 1981)

Ono, Yoko, *Grapefruit* (London: Sphere, 1970)

Ono, Yoko, *Yoko at Indica: Unfinished Paintings and Objects* (exhibition catalogue) (London: Indica Gallery, 1966)

Ono, Yoko, ed. *John Lennon: Summer of 1980* (photographs) (London: Chatto & Windus, 1984)

Ono, Yoko, *et al.*, 'Is that an apple? Yoko Ono in London', *Art Monthly* 212 (December 1997/January 1998) pp. 1–7

Palmer, Tony, *All You Need Is Love: the story of popular music* (London: Weidenfeld & Nicolson, 1976)

Palmer, Tony, 'Tomorrow and tomorrow', *London Magazine* (September 1967) pp. 73–7

Pang, May and Edwards, Henry, *Loving John: the untold story* (London: Corgi, 1983)

Parry, Richard Lloyd, 'Fab in the Far East for ever', *Independent on Sunday* (21 February 1999) p. 1

Patterson, R. Gary, *The Walrus Was Paul: the great Beatle death clues* (New York: Fireside, 1998)

Peebles, Andy, *The Lennon Tapes* (London: BBC, 1981)

Pelyushonok, Yury, *Strings for a Beatle Bass: the Beatles generation in the USSR* (Ottawa: PLY Publisher, 1999)

Pichaske, David R., *Beowulf to Beatles: approaches to poetry* (New York: The Free Press, 1972)

Podrazik, Walter, *Strange Days: the music of John, Paul, George and Ringo twenty years on* (Ann Arbor, MI: Popular Culture Ink, 1994)

Poirier, Richard, 'Learning from The Beatles', *Partisan Review* 34 (Fall 1967) pp. 526–46; reprinted in *The Performing Self: compositions and decompositions in the languages of contemporary life* (New York: Oxford University Press, 1971) pp. 112–40

Porter, Steven Clark, 'Rhythm and harmony in the music of The Beatles' (diss. City University of New York, 1979)

Potter, Keith, '. . . reflects on the significance of John Lennon', *Classical Music* (10 January 1981) p. 7

Price, Charles Gower, 'Sources of American styles in the music of The Beatles', *American Music* XV/2 (1997) pp. 208–32

Reek, David R., 'Beatles Orientalis: influences from Asia in a popular song tradition', *Asian Music* XVI/1 (1985) pp. 83–131

Reinhart, Charles, *You Can't Do That! Beatles Bootlegs & Novelty Records 1963–1980* (Ann Arbor: Pierian Press, 1981)

Reising, Russell, ed. *Every Sound There Is: The Beatles' Revolver and the transformation of rock and roll* (Aldershot: Ashgate, 2002)

Reynolds, Roger, 'Twilight of the Gods', *The New York Times* (22 September 1974) p. 39

Reynolds, Stanley, 'Big time', *The Guardian* (3 June 1963) p. 10

Reynolds, Stanley, 'The cruel and uncompromising working class hero', *The Guardian* (10 December 1980) p. 10

Riley, Tim, *Tell Me Why: a Beatles Commentary* (London: Bodley Head, 1988)

Robertson, John, *The Art and Music of John Lennon* (London: Omnibus, 1990)

Robinson, Lisa, 'Conversations with Lennon', *Vanity Fair* (November 2001) pp. 230–45

*Rockwell, John, 'For $325, a chance to assess the legacy of The Beatles', *The New York Times* (24 October 1982) pp. 19, 26

Rockwell, John, 'Leader of a rock group that helped define a generation', *The New York Times* (9 December 1980) p. B7

Roos, Michael E., 'The walrus and the deacon: John Lennon's debt to Lewis Carroll', *Journal of Popular Culture* XVIII/1 (1984) pp. 19–29

*Rorem, Ned, 'The music of The Beatles', *The New York Review of Books* (18 January 1968) pp. 23–7; reprinted in *Setting the Tone* (New York: Limelight Editions, 1984) pp. 337–45

*Rose, Lloyd, 'Long gone John: Lennon and the revelations', *Boston Phoenix* (10 December 1985) pp. 1, 6–10, 22

Rose, Lloyd, 'Remembering when film was fab', *Boston Phoenix* (28 August 1984) pp. 1, 5, 11

Saltzman, Paul, *The Beatles in Rishikesh* (New York: Viking, 2000)

Sandall, Robert, 'All their yesterdays, today and tomorrow', *The Sunday Times* (15 January 1995) 10, pp. 12–13

Sante, Luc, 'Beatlephobia', *New York Review of Books* (22 December 1988), pp. 30–5

*Sarris, Andrew, 'A Hard Day's Night', *Village Voice* (27 August 1964) p. 13

Sarris, Andrew, 'Help!', *Village Voice* (9 September 1965) p. 15

Sauceda, James, *The Literary Lennon: a comedy of letters* (Ann Arbor: Pierian Press, 1983)

Scaduto, Anthony, *The Beatles* (New York: Signet, 1968)

Schaefer, Oda, 'Beatlemania', *Melos (Zeitschrift fur Neue Musik)* (11 November 1964) pp. 334–41

Schaffner, Nicholas, *The Beatles Forever* (New York: McGraw Hill, 1978)

Schuler, Manfred, 'Rockmusik and Kunstmusik der Vergangenheit: ein analytischer Versuch', *Archiv fur Musik-Wissenschaft* XXXV/2 (1978) pp. 135–50

Schultheiss, Tom, *A Day in the Life: The Beatles day-by-day 1960–1970* (London: Omnibus Press, 1980)

Semmel, Keith David, 'The Pepperland perspective: a study in the rhetorical vision of The Beatles 1962–1970' (diss. Bowling Green State University, 1980)

Sheff, David, 'John Lennon & Yoko Ono: a candid conversation . . . ', *Playboy* (January 1981) pp. 75–6, 79+ *(see below)*

Sheff, David, 'John Lennon: his final words on The Beatles' music', *Playboy* (April 1981) pp. 179, 182+ *(see below)*

Sheff, David, *The Playboy Interviews with John Lennon & Yoko Ono* (London: New English Library, 1982)

*Shepard, Richard F., 'Stokowski talks of something called Beatles', *The New York Times* (15 February 1964) p. 13

Shotton, Pete and Schaffner, Nicholas, *John Lennon: In My Life* (London: Coronet, 1984)

Silva, Alberto Pulido, 'Estetica y Musica electronica', *Heterofonia* XIV/74 (1982) pp. 27–30

Simels, Steve, et al, 'Nine ways of looking at The Beatles 1963–73', *Stereo Review* (February 1973) pp. 57–63

Sinyard, Neil, *The Films of Richard Lester* (London: Croom Helm, 1985)

Souster, Tim, 'The Beatles in their prime', *The Listener* (15 April 1971) pp. 465–7

Souster, Tim, 'Rock, beat, pop-avantgarde', *The World of Music* XII/2 (1970) pp. 33–41

Spicer, Mark Stuart, 'British pop-rock music in the post-Beatles era: three analytical studies' (diss. Yale University, 2001)

Stannard, Neville, *The Beatles 1: The Long and Winding Road* (London: Virgin, 1982)

Stannard, Neville and Tobler, John, *The Beatles 2: Working Class Heroes* (London: Virgin, 1983)

*Steinem, Gloria, 'Beatle with a future', *Cosmopolitan* [US] (December 1964)

Stetzer, Charles W., 'Four aspects of the music of The Beatles: instrumentation, harmony, form and album unity' (diss. University of Rochester, 1976)

Stokes, Geoffrey, *The Beatles* (London: Omnibus Press/Star, 1981)

Storb, Ilse, 'Penny Lane—Modell einer Analyse', *Musik und Bildung* III (1971) pp. 189–92

Straus, Peter, '(Just like) starting over: John Lennon and the evolution of a paternal identity' (diss. Wright Institute, 2001)

*Sturua, Melor, 'Murder on 72nd Street', *Znamya* V (1983) pp. 181–207

Sullivan, Henry W., 'Paul, John and *Broad Street*', *Popular Music* VI/3 (October 1987) pp. 327–38

Sullivan, Mark, 'More popular than Jesus: The Beatles and the religious far right', *Popular Music* VI/3 (October 1987) pp. 313–26

Sulpy, Doug and Schweighardt, Ray, *Get Back: the unauthorised chronicle of The Beatles Let It Be disaster* (New York: St. Martin's Press, 1997)

Sutcliffe, Pauline with Thompson, Douglas, *The Beatles' Shadow: Stuart Sutcliffe and his lonely hearts club* (London: Sidgwick & Jackson, 2001)

Sweeting, Adam, 'Let it be—again', *The Guardian* (18 October 1995) supplement, pp. 2–4

Taylor, Alistair and Roberts, Martin, *Yesterday, The Beatles Remembered* (London: Sidgwick & Jackson, 1988)

Taylor, Derek, *As Time Goes By* (London: Abacus, 1974; reprinted: Ann Arbor: Pierian Press, 1983)

Taylor, Derek, *Fifty Years Adrift (in an open-necked shirt)* (Guildford: Genesis Publications, 1985)

Taylor, Derek, *It Was Twenty Years Ago Today* (London: Bantam Press, 1987)

Taylor, Rogan, *The Death and Resurrection Show* (London: Anthony Blond, 1985)

Terry, Carol D., ed., *Here There & Everywhere: the first international Beatles bibliography 1962–1982* (Ann Arbor: Pierian Press, 1985)

Theroux, Paul, 'Why we loved The Beatles', *Rolling Stone* (16 February 1984) p. 21

*Thomson, Elizabeth, 'Lennon's epitaph', *The Listener* (8 March 1984) p. 25

Thomson, Elizabeth, 'The literary Beatle', *Books & Bookmen* (January 1985) pp. 19–20

*[Times, The], 'Obituary: Dominant role in a pop music revolution', *The Times* (9 December 1980) p. 17

*[Times, The], 'Penny Lane for a song', *The Times* (1 April 1967) p. 11

*[Times, The], 'What songs The Beatles sang . . . ', *The Times* (27 December 1963) p. 4

Turner, Steve, *A Hard Day's Write: the stories behind every Beatles' song* (London: Little, Brown, 1994)

Turner, Steve, 'The ballad of John and Jesus', *Christianity Today* (12 June 2000), p. 86

*Tynan, Kenneth, 'Help!', from *Tynan Right and Left* (London: Longman, 1967) pp. 205–7

Udovitch, Mim, 'Let us now praise famous men', *The New York Times Book Review* (8 October 2000)

Villinger, A., *Die Beatles-Songs: Analysen zur Harmonik und Melodik* (Frieburg: Hochschulverlag, 1983)

*Wain, John, 'In the echo chamber', *New Republic* (7 August 1965); pp. 20–2

Welch, Colin, 'Beatlemania', *The Spectator* (17 December 1983) p. 32

Welch, Colin, 'Passing the torch', *The Spectator* (10 December 1983) p. 23

Wenner, Jan, 'John Lennon', *Rolling Stone* (21 January 1971) pp. 32–42 and (4 February 1971) pp. 36–43 *(see below)*

Wenner, Jan, ed. *Lennon Remembers: the Rolling Stone interviews* (London: Penguin, 1973; revised edition: London: Verso, 2000)

West, A. and Martindale, C., 'Creative trends in the content of Beatles' lyrics', *Popular Music and Society* XX/4 (1996) pp. 103–25

Wiener, Jon, *Come Together: John Lennon in his time* (London: Faber, 1985)

Wiener, Jon, 'Copyright as censorship', *The Nation* (22 May 2000) pp. 20–2

Wiener, Jon, *Gimme Some Truth: the John Lennon FBI files* (Berkeley: University of California Press, 1999)

Wiener, Jon, 'Give peace a chance', *The Nation* (20 October 1997) pp. 5–6

*Wiener, Jon, 'John Lennon versus the FBI', *New Republic* (2 May 1983) pp. 19–23

Wiener, Jon, *Professors, Politics and Pop* (London: Verso, 1991)

Williams, Allan, *The Man Who Gave The Beatles Away* (London: Elm Tree, 1975)

Willis, Ellen, 'The Big Ones', *The New Yorker* (1 February 1969) pp. 55–6+

Wolfe, A. S. and Haefner, M., 'Taste cultures, culture classes, affective alliances and popular music reception: theory, methodology, and an application to a Beatles song', *Popular Music and Society* XX/4 (1996) pp. 127–55

*Wolfe, Tom, 'A highbrow under all that hair?', *Book Week* (3 May 1964) pp. 4, 10

Wolper, David and Solt, Andrew, *Imagine: John Lennon* (London: Bloomsbury, 1988)

*Wood, Michael, 'John Lennon's schooldays', *New Society* (27 June 1968) pp. 948–9

Worsthorne, Peregrine, 'Beatles in a mystic grove', *The Daily Telegraph* (3 September 1967)

Yates, Robert, 'Backbeat', *Sight and Sound* (April 1994) pp. 35–6

Yorke, Ritchie, John, Yoko & year one', *Rolling Stone* (7 February 1970) pp. 14–18+

Zion, Lawrence, 'The impact of The Beatles on pop music in Australia 1963–66', *Popular Music* VI/3 (October 1987) pp. 291–311

Discography

This discography is selective. It does not attempt to detail every extant recording by The Beatles as a group or John Lennon as an individual. Rather, we have listed only the original releases together with those compilations which are useful in building a comprehensive collection in that they revive tracks only released as singles and/or give alternate takes. As regards Lennon's solo output, we have not documented his studio work as producer or session musician. We do however itemise songwriting credits for artists such as Ringo Starr and Harry Nilsson.

Discs are listed in UK release order, though some US-only issues are included where no domestic equivalent exists. Where two numbers are cited, the UK specification takes precedence. In some instances compilations are now more readily available than the original LPs; in these cases we have appended the relevant details. Most Beatles and Lennon albums have appeared on CD: again we have given the appropriate references, plus second-generation remasters.

Collectors seeking comprehensive coverage of the *oeuvre*, official and otherwise, should refer to the excellent discographical volumes noted in our bibliography.

Lennon with The Beatles

1963

Please Please Me: I saw her standing there; Misery; Anna (go to him); Chains; Boys; Ask me why; Please please me; Love me do; P.S. I love you; Baby it's you; Do you want to know a secret; A taste of honey; There's a place; Twist and shout

Parlophone PCS 3042
CDP 746 435 2 (CD)

With The Beatles: It won't be long; All I've got to do; All my loving; Don't bother me; Little child; Till there was you; Please Mr Postman; Roll over Beethoven; Hold me tight; You really got a hold on me; I wanna be your man; Devil in her heart; Not a second time; Money

> Parlophone PCS 3045
> CDP 746 436 2 (CD)

1964

A Hard Day's Night: A hard day's night; I should have known better; If I fell; I'm happy just to dance with you; And I love her; Tell me why; Can't buy me love; Any time at all; I'll cry instead; Things we said today; When I get home; You can't do that; I'll be back

> Parlophone PCS 3058
> CDP 746 437 2 (CD)

Beatles for Sale: No reply; I'm a loser; Baby's in black; Rock and roll music; I'll follow the sun; Mr Moonlight; Kansas City; Eight days a week; Words of love; Honey don't; Every little thing; I don't want to spoil the party; What you're doing; Everybody's trying to be my baby

> Parlophone PCS 3062
> CDP 746 438 2 (CD)

1965

Help!: Help!; The night before; You've got to hide your love away; I need you; Another girl; You're going to lose that girl; Ticket to ride; Act naturally; It's only love; You like me too much; Tell me what you see; I've just seen a face; Yesterday; Dizzy Miss Lizzy

> Parlophone PCS 3071
> CDP 746 439 2 (CD)

Rubber Soul: Drive my car; Norwegian wood (This bird has flown); You won't see me; Nowhere man; Think for yourself; The word; Michelle; What goes on; Girl; I'm looking through you; In my life; Wait; If I needed someone; Run for your life

> Parlophone PCS 3075
> CDP 746 440 2 (CD)

1966

Revolver: Taxman; Eleanor Rigby; I'm only sleeping; Love you too; Here, there and everywhere; Yellow submarine; She said she said; Good day sunshine; And your bird can sing; For no one; Doctor Robert; 1 want to tell you; Got to get you into my life; Tomorrow never knows

> Parlophone PCS 7009
> CDP 746 441 2 (CD)

A Collection of Beatles' Oldies (but Goldies): She loves you; From me to you; We can work it out; Help!; Michelle; Yesterday; I feel fine; Yellow submarine; Can't buy me love; Bad boy; Day tripper; A hard day's night; Ticket to ride; Paperback writer; Eleanor Rigby; I want to hold your hand

> Parlophone PCS 7016
> Parlophone FA 413 081 1

1967

Sgt Pepper's Lonely Hearts Club Band: Sgt Pepper's lonely hearts club band; With a little help from my friends; Lucy in the sky with diamonds; Getting better; Fixing a hole; She's leaving home; Being for the benefit of Mr Kite; Within you without you; When I'm sixty-four; Lovely Rita; Good morning good morning; Sgt Pepper's lonely hearts club band; A day in the life

> Parlophone PCS 7027
> Capitol SMAS 2653
> CDP 746 442 2 (CD)

Magical Mystery Tour [double EP]: Magical mystery tour; Your mother should know; I am the walrus; The fool on the hill; Flying; Blue Jay Way

Parlophone SMMT 1–2

Magical Mystery Tour [US origination]: Magical mystery tour; The fool on the hill; Flying; Blue Jay Way; Your mother should know; I am the walrus; Hello goodbye; Strawberry Fields forever; Penny Lane; Baby you're a rich man; All you need is love

EMI PCTC 255
Capitol SMAL 2835
CDP 748 062 2 (CD)

1968

The Beatles: Back in the USSR; Dear Prudence; Glass onion; Ob-la-di, ob-la-da; Wild honey pie; The continuing story of Bungalow Bill; While my guitar gently weeps; Happiness is a warm gun; Martha my dear; I'm so tired; Blackbird; Piggies; Rocky raccoon; Don't pass me by; Why don't we do it in the road; I will; Julia; Birthday; Yer blues; Mother Nature's son; Everybody's got something to hide except me and my monkey; Sexy Sadie; Helter skelter; Long long long; Revolution 1; Honey pie; Savoy truffle; Cry baby cry; Revolution 9; Good night

Apple PCS 7067–8
Apple SWBO 101
CDS 746 443 8 (CD)

1969

Yellow Submarine: Yellow submarine; Only a northern song; All together now; Hey bulldog; It's all too much; All you need is love; excerpts from film score composed and orchestrated by George Martin

Apple PCS 7070
Apple SW 153

CDP 746 445 2 (CD)

Abbey Road: Come together; Something; Maxwell's silver hammer; Oh! darling; Octopus's garden; I want you (She's so heavy); Here comes the sun; Because; You never give me your money; Sun king; Mean Mr Mustard; Polythene Pam; She came in through the bathroom window; Golden slumbers; Carry that weight; The end; Her Majesty

Apple PCS 7088
Apple SO 383
CDP 746 446 2 (CD)

1970

Let It Be: Two of us; Dig a pony; Across the universe, I me mine; Dig it; Let it be; Maggie Mae; I've got a feeling; One after 909; The long and winding road; For you blue; Get back

Apple PXS 1
Apple PCS 7096
Apple AR 34001
Capitol SW 11922
CDP 746 447 2 (CD)

1973

The Beatles 1962–1966: Love me do; Please please me; From me to you; She loves you; I want to hold your hand; All my loving; Can't buy me love; A hard day's night; And I love her; Eight days a week; I feel fine; Ticket to ride; Yesterday; Help!; You've got to hide your love away; We can work it out; Day tripper; Drive my car; Norwegian wood (This bird has flown); Nowhere man; Michelle; In my life; Girl; Paperback writer; Eleanor Rigby; Yellow submarine

Apple PCSP 717
Apple SKBO 3403
CDP 797 0362 (CD)

The Beatles 1967–1970: Strawberry Fields forever; Penny Lane; Sgt Pepper's lonely hearts club band; With a little help from my friends; Lucy in the sky with diamonds; A day in the life; All you need is love; I am the walrus; Hello goodbye; The fool on the hill; Magical mystery tour; Lady Madonna; Hey Jude; Revolution; Back in the USSR; While my guitar gently weeps; Ob-la-di, ob-la-da; Get back; Don't let me down; The ballad of John and Yoko; Old brown shoe; Here comes the sun; Come together; Something; Octopus's garden; Let it be; Across the universe; The long and winding road

Apple PCSP 718
Apple SKBO 3404
CDP 797 039 2 (CD)

1977

The Beatles at the Hollywood Bowl: Twist and shout; She's a woman; Dizzy Miss Lizzy; Ticket to ride; Can't buy me love; Things we said today; Roll over Beethoven; Boys; A hard day's night; Help!; All my loving; She loves you; Long tall Sally

Parlophone EMTV 4
Capitol SMAS 11638
EMI MFP 4156761

The Beatles Live! At The Star Club in Hamburg, Germany, 1962: I saw her standing there*; Roll over Beethoven; Hippy hippy shake; Sweet little sixteen; Lend me your comb; Your feet's too big; Twist and shout*; Mr Moonlight; A taste of honey; Besame mucho; Reminiscing*; Kansas City; Nothin' shakin' (but the leaves on the trees); To know her is to love her; Little Queenie; Falling in love again; Ask me why*; Be-bop-a-lula; Halleluja, I

love her so; Red sails in the sunset; Everybody's trying to be my baby; Matchbox; I'm talking about you; Shimmy shake; Long tall Sally; I remember you

These tracks are replaced on the US version by 'I'm gonna sit right down and cry (over you)'; 'Where have you been all my life'; 'Till there was you'; 'Sheila', respectively

Bellaphon LNL 1
Lingason LS 2 7001
Walters Records BDR 8001–2 (CD)

1978

Rarities: Across the universe; Yes it is; This boy; The inner light; I'll get you; Thank you girl; Komm gib mir deine hand (I want to hold your hand)*; You know my name (Look up the number); Sie liebt dich (She loves you)*; Rain; She's a woman; Matchbox; I call your name; Bad boy; Slow down; I'm down; Long tall Sally

On the US version, both these tracks are in English

Parlophone PSLP 261
Capitol SPRO 8969
Parlophone PCM 1001

1979

The Songs Lennon and McCartney Gave Away: I'm the greatest; One and one is two; From a window; Nobody I know; Like dreamers do; I'll keep you satisfied; Love of the loved; Woman; Tip of my tongue; I'm in love; Hello little girl; That means a lot; It's for you; Penina; Step inside love; World without love; Bad to me; I don't want to see you again; I'll be on my way; Cat call

EMI NUT 18

1980

The Beatles Rarities [US only]: Love me do; Misery; There's a place; Sie liebt dich; And I love her; Help!; I'm only sleeping; I am the walrus; Penny Lane; Helter skelter; Don't pass me by; The inner light; Across the universe; You know my name (Look up the number); the Sgt Pepper innergroove

Capitol SHAL 12060

1988

Past Masters Volume 1: Love me do; From me to you; Thank you girl; She loves you; I'll get you; I want to hold your hand; This boy; Komm gib mir deine hand; Sie liebt dich; Long tall Sally; I call your name; Slow down; Matchbox; I feel fine; She's a woman; Bad boy; Yes it is; I'm down

Parlophone CDP 790 043 2 (CD)

Past Masters Volume 2: Day tripper; We can work it out; Paperback writer; Rain; Lady Madonna; The inner light; Hey Jude; Revolution; Get back; Don't let me down; The ballad of John and Yoko; Old brown shoe; Across the universe; Let it be; You know my name (Look up the number)

Parlophone CDP 790 044 2 (CD)

1994

The Beatles Live at the BBC: From us to you; I got a woman; Too much monkey business; Keep your hands off my baby; I'll be on my way; Young blood; A shot of rhythm and blues; Sure to fall (in love with you); Some other guy; Thank you girl; Baby it's you; That's all right (mama); Carol; Soldier of love; Clarabella; I'm gonna sit right down and cry (over you);

Crying, waiting, hoping; You really got a hold on me; To know her is to love her; A taste of honey; Long tall Sally; I saw her standing there; The honeymoon song; Johnny B Goode; Memphis, Tennessee; Lucille; Can't buy me love; Till there was you; A hard day's night; I wanna be your man; Roll over Beethoven; All my loving; Things we said today; She's a woman; Sweet little sixteen; Lonesome tears in my eyes; Nothin' shakin'; The hippy hippy shake; Glad all over; I just don't understand; So how come (no one loves me); I feel fine; I'm a loser; Everybody's trying to be my baby; Rock and roll music; Ticket to ride; Dizzy Miss Lizzy; Kansas City/Hey-hey-hey-hey!; Match-box; I forgot to remember to forget; I got to find my baby; Ooh! My soul; Don't ever change; Slow down; Honey don't; Love me do

Apple CDP 8 31796 2 (CD)

1995

The Beatles Anthology 1: Free as a bird; That'll be the day; In spite of all the danger; Hallelujah, I love her so; You'll be mine; Cayenne; My Bonnie; Ain't she sweet; Cry for a shadow; Searchin'; Three cool cats; The Sheik of Araby; Like dreamers do; Hello little girl; Besame mucho; Love me do; How do you do it; Please please me; One after 909 [sequence]; One after 909; Lend me your comb; I'll get you; I saw her standing there; From me to you; Money; You really got a hold on me; Roll over Beethoven; She loves you; Till there was you; Twist and shout; This boy; I want to hold your hand; Moonlight bay; Can't buy me love; All my loving; You can't do that; And I love her; A hard day's night; I wanna be your man; Long tall Sally; Boys; Shout; I'll be back [demo]; I'll be back; You know what to do; No reply [demo]; Mr Moonlight; Leave my kitten alone; No reply; Eight days a week [sequence]; Eight days a week; Kansas City/Hey-hey-hey-hey!

Apple CDP 8 34445 2 (CD)

1996

The Beatles Anthology 2: Real love; Yes it is; I'm down; You've got to hide your love away; If you've got trouble; That means a lot; Yesterday [take one]; It's only love; I feel fine; Ticket to ride; Yesterday; Help!; Everybody's trying to be my baby; Norwegian wood (This bird has flown); I'm looking through you; 12-bar original; Tomorrow never knows; Got to get you into my life; And your bird can sing; Taxman; Eleanor Rigby [strings only]; I'm only sleeping [rehearsal]; I'm only sleeping [take one]; Rock and roll music; She's a woman; Strawberry Fields forever [demo sequence]; Strawberry Fields forever [take 1]; Strawberry Fields forever [take 7 and edit]; Penny Lane; A day in the life; Good morning good morning; Only a northern song; Being for the benefit of Mr Kite [takes 1 and 2]; Being for the benefit of Mr Kite [take 7]; Lucy in the sky with diamonds; Within you without you [instrumental]; Sgt Pepper's lonely hearts club band (reprise); You know my name (Look up the number); I am the walrus; The fool on the hill [demo]; Your mother should know; The fool on the hill [take 4]; Hello, goodbye; Lady Madonna; Across the universe

Apple CDP 8 34448 2 (CD)

The Beatles Anthology 3: A beginning [George Martin instrumental]; Happiness is a warm gun; Helter skelter; Mean Mr Mustard; Polythene Pam; Glass onion [demo]; Junk; Piggies; Honey pie; Don't pass me by; Ob-la-di, Ob-la-da; Good night; Cry baby cry; Blackbird; Sexy Sadie; While my guitar gently weeps; Hey Jude; Not guilty; Mother Nature's son; Glass onion; Rocky raccoon; What's the new Mary Jane; Step inside love/Los Paranoias; I'm so tired; I will; Why don't we do it in the road; Julia; I've got a feeling; She came in through the bathroom window; Dig a pony; Two of us; For you blue; Teddy boy; Rip it up/Shake, rattle and roll/Blue suede shoes; The long and winding road; Oh! darling; All things must pass; Mailman; Bring me no more blues; Get back; Old brown shoe; Octopus's garden; Maxwell's silver hammer; Something; Come together; Come and get it; Ain't she sweet; Because; Let it be; I me mine; The end

Apple CDP 8 34451 2 (CD)

Lennon solo

1968

Unfinished Music No. 1 – Two Virgins: Two virgins 1; Together; Two virgins 2; Two virgins 3; Two virgins 4; Two virgins 5; Two virgins 6; Hushabye, hushabye; Two virgins 7; Two virgins 8; Two virgins 9; Two virgins 10

Apple SAPCOR 2 (Track 613012)
Apple T 5001
Rykodisc RCD 10411 (CD)

1969

Unfinished Music No. 2 – Life with the Lions: Cambridge 1969; No bed for Beatle John; Baby's heartbeat; Two minutes silence; Radio play

Zapple ZAPPLE 01
Zapple ST 3357
Rykodisc RCD 10412 (CD)

The Wedding Album: John and Yoko; Amsterdam

Apple SAPCOR 11
Apple SMAX 3361
Rykodisc RCD 10413 (CD)

The Plastic Ono Band – Live Peace in Toronto 1969: Blue Suede shoes; Money; Dizzy Miss Lizzy; Yer blues; Cold turkey; Give peace a chance; Don't worry Kyoko (Mummy's only looking for a hand in the snow); John John (Let's hope for peace)

Apple CORE 2001
Apple SW 3362
CDP 790 428 2 (CD)

1970

John Lennon/Plastic Ono Band: Mother; Hold on; I found out; Working class hero; Isolation; Remember; Love; Well well well; Look at me; God; My mummy's dead

Apple PCS 7124
Apple SW 3372
FA 4131021
CDP 746 770 2 (CD)
528 7402 (CD)

1971

'God save us'/'Do the Oz' (with Ono) for The Elastic Oz Band [single]

Apple APPLE 36
Apple 1835

Imagine: Imagine; Crippled inside; Jealous guy; It's so hard; I don't want to be a soldier; Give me some truth; Oh my love; How do you sleep; How?; Oh Yoko!

Apple PAS 10004

Apple SW 3379
CDP 746 641 2 (CD)
524 8582 (CD)

1972

Sometime in New York City: Woman is the nigger of the world; Sisters, oh sisters; Attica State; Born in a prison; New York City; Sunday Bloody Sunday; The luck of the Irish; John Sinclair; Angela; We're all water; Cold turkey; Don't worry Kyoko; Well (Baby please don't go); Jam Rag; Scumbag; Au

Apple PCSP 716
Apple SVBB 3392
CDS 746 782 8 (CD)

1973

'I'm the greatest' for Ringo Starr on *Ringo*

Apple PCTC 252
Apple SWAL 3413
EMI MFP 50508
Capitol SN–16114
EMI CDP 795 884 2 (CD)

Mind Games: Mind games; Tight a$; Aisumasen; I'm sorry; One day (at a time); Bring on the Lucie (Freda People); Nutopian international anthem; Intuition; Out the blue; Only people; I know (I know); You are here; Meat city

Apple PCS 7165
Apple SW 3414
EMI MFP 50509
Capitol SN–16068
CDP 746 769 2 (CD)
542 4252 (CD)

1974

'Mucho Mungo'/'Mt Elga' (with Nilsson) for Harry Nilsson on *Pussycats*

RCA APL 1–0570
RCA CPL 1–0570
7863 505 702 (CD)
74321 950 252 (CD)

Walls and Bridges: Going down on love; Whatever gets you thru the night; Old dirt road; What you got; Bless you; Scared; #9 dream; Surprise, surprise (Sweet bird of paradox); Steel and glass; Beef jerky; Nobody loves you (when you're down and out); Ya ya
Apple PCTC 253
Apple SW 3416
CDP 746 768 2 (CD)

'(It's all da-da-down to) Goodnight Vienna' for Ringo Starr on *Goodnight Vienna*
Apple PCS 7168
Apple SW 3417
CDP 780 378 2 (CD)

'Rock and roll people' for Johnny Winter on *John Dawson Winter III*
Blue Sky 80586
Blue Sky PZ 33292

1975
Rock 'n' Roll: Be-bop-a-lula; Stand by me; Rip it up/Ready Teddy; You can't catch me; Ain't that a shame; Do you want to dance; Sweet little sixteen; Slippin' and slidin' ; Peggy Sue; Bring it on home to me/Send me some lovin'; Bony moronie; Ya ya; Just because
Apple PCS 7169
Apple SK 3419
EMI MFP 50522
Capitol SN–16069
CDP 746 707 2 (CD)

'Fame' (with Bowie and Alomar) for David Bowie on *Young Americans*
RCA RS 1006

RCA APL 1–0998
RCA PD 80998 (CD)
EMI CDP 796 4362 (CD)

'Stand by me' (King and Glick)/ 'Move over Ms L' [single]
Apple R 6005
Apple 1881

'Move over Ms L' for Keith Moon on *Two Sides of the Moon*
Polydor 2442–134
Track 2136
Pet Rock 71278 60038 2 (CD)

Shaved Fish: Give peace a chance; Cold turkey; Instant karma; Power to the people; Mother; Woman is the nigger of the world; Imagine; Whatever gets you thru the night; Mind games; #9 dream; Happy Xmas (War is over); Give peace a chance
Apple PCS 7173
Apple SW 3421
CDP 746 642 2 (CD)

1976
'Cookin' (in the kitchen of love)' for Ringo Starr on *Ringo's Rotogravure*
Polydor 2302–040
Atlantic SD 18193
Atlantic 82417 2 (CD)

1980
Double Fantasy: (Just like) Starting over; Kiss, kiss, kiss; Clean up time; Give me something; I'm losing you; I'm moving on; Beautiful boy (Darling boy); Watching the wheels; I'm your angel; Woman; Beautiful boys; Dear Yoko; Every man has a woman who loves him; Hard times are over
Geffen K 99131
Geffen GHS–2001
Geffen 299 131 2001–2 (CD)
EMI CDP 791 425 2 (CD)
528 7392 (CD)

1982

The John Lennon Collection: Give peace a chance; Instant karma; Power to the people; Whatever gets you thru the night; #9 dream; Mind games; Love; Happy Xmas (War is over)*; Imagine; Jealous guy; Stand by me*; (Just like) Starting over; Woman; I'm losing you; Beautiful boy (Darling boy); Watching the wheels; Dear Yoko

Not included on US version

Parlophone EMTV 37
Geffen GHSP 2023
Parlophone CDP 791516 2 (CD)

1984

Milk and Honey: I'm stepping out; Sleepless night; I don't wanna face it; Don't be scared; Nobody told me; O sanity; Borrowed time; Your hands; (Forgive me) My little flower princess; Let me count the ways; Grow old with me; You're the one

Polydor POLH 5
Polydor 817 160 1
Polydor 817 160 2 (CD)
EMI 535 9592 (CD)

1986

John Lennon Live in New York City: New York City; It's so hard; Woman is the nigger of the world; Well well well; Instant karma; Mother; Come together; Imagine; Cold turkey; Hound dog; Give peace a chance

Parlophone PCS 7301
EMI CDP 746 196 2 (CD)

Menlove Ave: Here we go again; Rock 'n' roll; Angel baby; Since my baby left me; To know her is to love her; Steel and glass; Scared; Old dirt road; Nobody loves you (when you're down and out); Bless you

Parlophone PCS 7308
CDP 746 576 2 (CD)

1998

John Lennon Anthology: Working class hero; God; I found out; Hold on; Isolation; Love; Mother; Remember; Imagine [take 1]; Fortunately; Baby please don't go; Oh my love; Jealous guy; Maggie Mae; How do you sleep; God save Oz; Do the Oz; I don't want to be a soldier; Give peace a chance; Look at me; Long lost John; New York City; Attica State [live]; Imagine [live]; Bring on the Lucie; Woman is the nigger of the world; Geraldo Rivera—One to One concert; Woman is the nigger of the world [live]; It's so hard [live]; Come together [live]; Happy Xmas; The luck of the Irish [live]; John Sinclair [live]; The David Frost Show; Mind games (I promise); Mind games (Make love, not war); One day (at a time); I know; I'm the greatest; Goodnight Vienna; Jerry Lewis Telethon; A kiss is just a kiss (As time goes by); Real love; You are here; What you got; Nobody loves you (when you're down and out); Whatever gets you thru the night [home]; Whatever gets you thru the night [studio]; Yesterday [parody]; Be-bop-a-lula; Rip it up/Ready Teddy; Scared; Steel and glass; Surprise, surprise (Sweet bird of paradox); Bless you; Going down on love; Move over Ms L; Ain't she sweet; Slippin' and slidin'; Peggy Sue; Bring it on home to me/Send me some lovin'; Phil and John 1; Phil and John 2; Phil and John 3; When in doubt, fuck it; Be my baby; Stranger's room; Old dirt road; I'm losing you; Sean's 'little help'; Serve yourself; My life; Nobody told me; Life begins at 40; I don't wanna face it; Woman; Dear Yoko; Watching the wheels; I'm stepping out; Borrowed time; The Rishi Kesh song; Sean's 'loud'; Beautiful boy; Mr Hyde's gone (Don't be afraid); Only you (and you alone); Grow old with me; Dear John; The great wok; Mucho Mungo; Satire 1; Satire 2; Satire 3; Sean's 'in the sky'; It's real

Capitol CDP 830 6142 (CD)

Index